HAVERGAL BRIAN ON MUSIC
Volume One: British Music

HAVERGAL
BRIAN
ON
MUSIC

Selections from his Journalism
edited by
Malcolm MacDonald

VOLUME ONE
British Music

Musicians on Music
No. 3

TOCCATA
PRESS

Music examples prepared by Barry Peter Ould.

Toccata Press and the Havergal Brian Society gratefully acknowledge a generous grant towards the cost of publishing this book from the Rex Foundation of San Francisco.

British Library Cataloguing in Publication Data
Brian, Havergal
    Havergal Brian on music : selections from his
    journalism. – (Musicians on music,
    ISSN 0264-6889; no. 3)
    Vol. 1 : British music
    1. Music – History and criticism
    I. Title II. MacDonald, Malcolm, 1948–
    III. Series
    780'.9   ML160

    ISBN 0-907689-19-1
    ISBN 0-907689-20-5 Pbk

Set in 11 on 12 point Baskerville
by TJB Photosetting Ltd., South Witham, Lincolnshire.
Printed and bound in Great Britain
by Short Run Press Ltd., Exeter.

Contents

Four: DELIUS

Five: BANTOCK

Six: BRITISH MUSIC IN PERFORMANCE

Seven: NATIONALISM, LEAGUES AND COMPETITIONS

Eight: NEAR-CONTEMPORARIES

Nine: YOUNGER COMPOSERS

Contents 9

Introduction

HAVERGAL BRIAN, JOURNALIST

Few British composers of music have shown a parallel aptitude for the written word. Hubert Parry, among his other achievements, was a distinguished historian; the writings of Tovey and Cecil Gray have effectively overshadowed their own compositions; Ivor Gurney typifies the rare breed of composer-poet; John Foulds, Lambert, Sorabji, Tippett, van Dieren and Vaughan Williams have each penned a stimulating book or collection of essays; while among contemporary symphonists Robert Simpson and the late Edmund Rubbra have demonstrated genuine and trenchant critical gifts. But these are the main exceptions to the rule. Elgar, though a splendid writer of letters, left little else apart from a couple of brief prefaces and one series of lectures that cost him considerable pains and was not published until long after his death. And though many composers have been prevailed upon to contribute an article or two, or have served brief periods as concert reviewers, few indeed have chosen, or allowed themselves to be drawn into, a situation where the economic basis of their lives depended largely upon a career in the lowly profession of music journalism. A major exception here is Philip Heseltine, who packed a staggering amount of journalistic and editorial work into a brief period in the early 1920s – including eight of the first nine issues of *The Sackbut* after he had taken over, in 1920, what was then *The Organist* and broadened its scope immensely.[1]

Yet even Heseltine's critical activities pale beside the virtual half-century in which Havergal Brian (1876–1972) devoted much of his time and energy to the profession of musical journalist. Brian turns out to have been as dauntingly prolific in prose as he was eventually to be in his purely musical output. His literary legacy (sometimes

---

[1] See note 18 on p. 354

11

pseudonymous, often unsigned), culled from the pages of the dozen or so publications with which he was associated, is so large and various as to be in the strict sense of the term unquantifiable – but it certainly runs to thousands of items. Never at a loss for the written word, he could write with easy fluency (although his productions often bear the marks of haste) and was clearly in some ways ideally fitted for the journalist's life. When we consider that Brian is popularly portrayed as a lone, shy, unworldly, eccentric and uncommunicative figure in British music, it may come as a surprise to find him situated so near the centre of musical events, coping equably and even enthusiastically with the business of deadlines and the latest news from all quarters.

The nature and scope of Brian's literary activities are important for our understanding of him as a composer, for they completely subvert the still-current view of him as an 'amateur' musician, isolated and out of touch with the musical life of his own time, ploughing his dogged furrow in blissful ignorance of what his contemporaries were doing, both in this country and abroad. The precise opposite turns out to be the case. Brian was an active participant in and witness to the musical events of the first half of the century. He was in an ideal position to study a vast range of scores and the musical literature of several languages, and he made the most of his opportunities – as he did to attend a multitude of concerts and, perhaps even more important, rehearsals. He was personally acquainted with many of the leading musicians of his age; and as an accredited 'gentleman of the press' he was excellently placed to observe many more of them at close range. Glazunov, Josef Hoffmann, Emmanuel Móor, Rachmaninov, Paul Robeson and Sousa are only a random sample of the artists he interviewed in pursuance of his duties.

Throughout the years that he wrote about other people's music and music-making, Brian was writing works of his own – among them his early choral and orchestral pieces, his opera *The Tigers*, and the first seven of his Symphonies (most notably the enormous First Symphony, *The Gothic*). Although very little of his music was played after the Great War, Brian continued to regard himself as a composer first and foremost, and this attitude colours his journalism, in which he often writes as if speaking on behalf of composers in general. In the past thirty years there has been a significant revival of interest in Brian's music, and much of it has now been performed; yet opinion remains strongly divided on its worth, and on Brian's ultimate position in the pantheon of English music. But that question need not detain us in this and succeeding volumes of selections from his musical journalism. All we should bear in mind – not that he lets us forget it for very long – is that he *was* a composer. No other British composer was such a consistently interested, and tirelessly inquisitive, reporter of the musical life of the first half of the 20th century.

*   *   *

Brian's journalistic – as distinct from his compositional – career can be divided into four well-demarcated periods. The first begins in the winter of 1904–5, when he was invited at short notice to fill the post of principal Manchester correspondent of *The Musical World*. This magazine – a revival of a Victorian journal which had ceased publication in the 1890s – had been launched as a weekly paper on 15 October 1904; but its first Manchester critic, whose most important function was to review all the Hallé Concerts at the Free Trade Hall, was a naturalised German who quickly proved to have an insufficient command of English. Although there is no documentary evidence to show exactly when Brian assumed these duties (the Manchester reports were always unsigned), there is a quite dramatic change of style and outlook with the Hallé critique in the issue of 26 November 1904, and this sets the tone for the remaining three years of the journal's existence. I have no doubt that the concert in question was the first that Brian reviewed.[2] It is true that a report in *The Staffordshire Sentinel* of 30

---

[2] The programme is hardly without interest: Beethoven's *Coriolan* Overture, Henselt's Piano Concerto (the soloist was Ferruccio Busoni), Frederic Cowen's *Rhapsodie Indienne* and Brahms' Third Symphony, all conducted by Hans Richter. The period 1904–8 did not encompass Richter's

December 1904 says that *The Musical World* 'has invited Mr.
Brian to write the criticisms of the Hallé Concerts....Mr.
Brian undertakes the responsible duties with the New Year',
but the reviews for the end of 1904 seem to me self-
evidently the work of the same hand as those of 1905. I
assume that Brian was originally 'tried out' on an *ad hoc*
basis, receiving the post officially only from 1 January 1905.

Originally published in Manchester itself, after the first
year of publication *The Musical World* was re-organised as a
monthly and moved its offices to London; but it continued
to reflect the very wide range of musical activities which
characterised the North and West of England during the
first decade of the 20th century. Until the demise of *The
Musical World* in February 1908 Brian remained its principal
Manchester correspondent and a regular contributor of
other matter. His activities centred on the Hallé Concerts,
which he reviewed every week during the season (the conversion of the magazine to a monthly did not allow him any
more space per issue, so that his coverage of each concert
was reduced to a quarter of what it had been at the beginning of his tenure); but he also wrote up other Manchester
musical events and sometimes reviewed concerts in the Potteries, in Liverpool, Birmingham, and (possibly) Leeds,
although he was not the regular critic for those areas. In
addition he covered some of the major festivals, provided
reviews of books and newly-published music, and wrote
occasional articles and columns on a wide range of subjects.
Some of these can be identified with certainty, either
because Brian himself referred to them in letters or in later
writings, or (in a smaller number of cases) because the
authorship can confidently be inferred on the grounds of
style and the opinions expressed. But at this time he hardly
ever signed his contributions, and it is likely that the pages
of *The Musical World* contain much more of him than I
have considered for inclusion in these volumes. (I have

---

finest seasons – *The Musical World* came on the scene too late to allow
Brian the chance of reviewing the premiere of Bartók's *Kossuth* and left
it before he could review that of Elgar's First Symphony, although he certainly attended both events.

occasionally referred to such 'doubtful' items in my anno-
tations.) During the same period, and for several years
afterwards, Brian found a sporadic outlet for his pen in
newspaper work, particularly for his local paper, *The
Staffordshire Sentinel*. These included articles, some very
detailed concert reviews, and in the winter of 1909–10 a
signed weekly column entitled 'Music and Musicians'. He
also wrote short local reports for *The Musical Times*.

The second period begins in 1914, with Brian's own
removal to London after the break-up of his first marriage,
and it extends to the beginning of his association with *Musical Opinion* thirteen years later. This was a very unsettled
time in which journalism was only one of the ways by which
he attempted to support himself and a growing second family, and at first it bore little fruit. As with his music, he wrote
far more than was actually published, and we would not
have known about much of it had he not reported his
activities – on an almost daily basis at some points – in letters
to his close friend Granville Bantock. Even so, the chrono-
logy is complicated and the facts often difficult to ascertain,
but the following outline is probably accurate.

In 1914 and again in 1916 Brian attempted to write a semi-
autobiographical novel, some chapters of which he sent to
Bantock – but all trace of this has been lost. In the former
year he offered articles to *The English Review*, but it was the
publication in *The Daily Mail* of 25 November 1915 of a letter
castigating British attitudes to German music in wartime
that marked the resumption of Brian's journalistic
activities; and after he moved to Birmingham in early 1916
he worked, from October to mid-1917, on the staff of an
automobile magazine, *The Motor Trader*, writing material of
strictly non-musical significance. But he also started (in late
1916) another book, on musical topics (the chapters that
were written included 'The Orchestra' and 'Conducting');
and in parallel with this effort he began to pile up a series of
about a dozen articles on contemporary musicians (he
names Beecham, Henry Wood, James Whewall, Holbrooke,
and Bantock himself among the subjects; the Bantock article was apparently very substantial) which he offered to a
variety of journals – including *The English Review, The New*

Age, and *The Saturday Review*, as well as several magazines in
the USA.

As far as I can determine, none of these items was actually
published (although some of the articles were accepted by
Alfred Orage of *The New Age*), and no manuscripts survive.
But they did presumably help Brian to form some useful
contacts with editors, and laid the groundwork for his
gradual break back into print in the early 1920s, when articles and reviews began to appear over his name in *The British
Bandsman* (for whom, between June and November 1923,
he also contributed a more-or-less-weekly and sometimes
satirical column, once again called 'Music and Musicians',
under the pseudonym 'Wassail'), *The Chesterian, The Monthly
Musical Record, Musical Opinion, The Sackbut*, and – from a
slightly later date – the organ magazine *The Rotunda*. (Between May and November 1924 he was also writing a 'survey
of contemporary British music' for a German publication;
but this has not been traced, if indeed it ever saw print.)
Aside from music-copying and a little teaching, such journalism was his main means of sustenance during the lean
years in Sussex while he was writing his gigantic *Gothic* Symphony.

The death in May 1927 of Samuel Langford, the influential and much-respected critic of the *Manchester Guardian*,
prompted Brian, still in Sussex, to apply for the post – for
which his experience on *The Musical World* would naturally
stand him in good stead. He was acknowledged to be a
strong contender, but Langford's understudy Neville Cardus was preferred for the job (a fact which did not affect
their cordial relations over the years). Brian was offered a
position as the paper's 'second string' critic, but instead he
decided to move back to London, where the following
month he was hired as Assistant to the Editor of *Musical
Opinion*, the monthly journal with which he had been cultivating contacts over the past decade.

Brian's thirteen years with *Musical Opinion* – from June
1927 to May 1940 – constitute the third, and incomparably
the most productive, period of his journalistic career. The
vast part of his literary output at this time was written for
Musical Opinion, although he did a little work for *Radio Times*

and, towards the end of the period, for the journals *Modern Mystic* and *Tomorrow*.[3]

Although founded in 1877 and still in publication today, *Musical Opinion* enjoyed its real hey-day in the inter-war period, and especially during Brian's deputy editorship. With each issue comprising over 100 large-format pages, and an astonishing range of subject-matter being covered by some of the leading musical writers of the time (regular contributors included Gerald Abraham, Eric Blom, Dmitri Calvocoressi, Eaglefield Hull, Alfred Kalmus and Percy Scholes), it was then a very lively journal, somewhat more 'popular' in style but with a similar intellectual weight to, and rather more flair than, the contemporary *Musical Times*. By the early 1930s it had also developed a marked propensity (uncommon among British publications since the demise of *The Sackbut*) for sympathetic and understanding treatment of an unusually wide gamut of contemporary music. I think it is fair to ascribe this in large part to Brian's influence. The magazine's proprietor and editor, Arthur W. Fitzsimmons (who died in 1948), was a fair-minded writer of averagely conservative tastes, whereas Brian – as we shall see in this and subsequent volumes – found qualities to relish in composers as diverse as Schoenberg, Schütz, and Billy Mayerl. Fitzsimmons seems to have preferred to remain in the background and let his deputy guide the magazine from day to day; so Brian's large-hearted enthusiasm was expressed throughout each issue in a wide variety of guises. As well as editing other writers' work, Brian wrote substantial articles under his own name, and many small ones over his initials 'H.B.'. He also contributed a stream of unsigned material: news items, profiles of musical personalities, stray thoughts on current topics, interviews, and reviews of concerts, books and printed music. In addition, when *Musical Opinion* began to dispense with

---

[3] Between 1934 and 1936 he also wrote – and, this time, completed – a book on 20th-century composers which had apparently been requested by a publisher in Australia; but the typescript was neither acknowledged nor returned and the mysterious publisher did not answer Brian's letters. Brian eventually concluded he had been the victim of a hoax. .

engraved music examples, he supplied the examples for all contributors' articles in his clear and characteristic hand.

A feature of *Musical Opinion* – as of many musical magazines of the period – was its array of regular monthly columns from writers who often sheltered their identities beneath whimsical pseudonyms. Dmitri Calvocoressi and Basil Maine contributed columns under their own names, but there was also the monthly 'Thoughts from my Tub' by 'Diogenes the Younger', 'The World of Opera' by 'Factus', and similar items in the 'Organ World' and 'Trade' sections (by 'Octavius' and 'Autolycus' respectively). Who these gentlemen may really have been is now impossible to determine ('Factus' might have been Fitzsimmons); but it is at least known that 'Schaunard' – who, at the time Brian joined the staff, was contributing the opening editorial column ('Musings') at the beginning of each issue – was A. J. Sheldon, a Midlands writer whose background was not dissimilar to Brian's. Brian (who had already written as 'Wassail' for *The British Bandsman*) did not at first have a column of his own; but in September 1927 a new unsigned section entitled 'Personal and Otherwise', mainly character-sketches of musicians currently in the public eye, began to make its appearance; and so too did a section called 'The Musician's Diary', at first little more than a series of short paragraphs on coming musical events. Both were largely Brian's work. By October 1929 the 'Diary' had developed into a distinct sequence (without overall title) of brief articles, each separately headed and a few paragraphs long, dealing with topics of the day; while 'Personal and Otherwise' had already metamorphosed into an occasional feature, 'Personalia', featuring usually only one or two musicians per month, and at more length than before, based on interviews with the subjects.

Then in July 1931 A. J. Sheldon died. 'Schaunard' disappeared after the August issue; in his place, in September, there arose a new editorial column, 'On the Other Hand' signed by 'La Main Gauche'. Simultaneously the untitled sequence, which for some time had been developing into something like this new column, was dropped; 'Personalia' continued, but was now contributed by a number of different writers, Brian being only one of them.

Presumably Brian invented his own *nom de guerre*; presumably, too, its 'leftward' tendency had not so much a political significance as an echo of the old injunction that the right hand should not know what the left hand is doing. Certainly he relished his anonymity as 'La Main Gauche' and the opportunity it provided to cultivate a separate literary persona. This effect can be seen most clearly when LMG (as I shall call him for the sake of brevity) ventured a second bite at the cherry by discussing topics which 'H.B.' had dealt with elsewhere in the same issue. A good example will be found in this first volume of his writings: Brian's short, formal book review of Eric Fenby's *Delius as I Knew Him*, juxtaposed with LMG's far more outspoken horror at the revelation of the declining years of the man he had known and admired three decades before. LMG was always one of the liveliest parts of the magazine: plain-spoken, combative, full of likes and dislikes, a respecter of (some) persons but no respecter of institutions.[4]

Brian did not write every word of every LMG column. His estimate in later life was that he had produced about 90 per cent of it; and after a close study of all the columns involved I think this is an accurate figure. As Paul Rapoport has commented:[5]

> As first-person writing was prevalent in these articles, many sections of them can easily be identified as Brian's. Familiarity with the style and content of other articles, written by Brian and others, also helps to suggest Brian's authorship. [...] Some can plausibly be identified as Brian's by their close connection with, if not duplication of, contemporaneous

[4] For the past few years a selection of items from the LMG column have been reprinted, on a regular basis, in the *Newsletter* of the Havergal Brian Society, selected and annotated by me. A few of these are duplicated in the present selection, but the majority have not been reprinted before.

[5] *Havergal Brian and his Symphony 'The Gothic'*, Master's Thesis for the University of Illinois at Urbana-Champaign (University Microfilms, Ann Arbor, 1972), pp. 18–19. This thesis contains the only previous consideration of Brian's LMG articles.

material appearing in *Musical Opinion* with Brian's name signed to it.

Brian's writing style is in fact a very distinctive, even idiosyncratic one, readily identifiable once one has cultivated some familiarity with it; and the bulk of the LMG column is clearly the work of a single individual – a composer who has had works performed by Wood and Godfrey and who possesses a vast fund of reminiscence of musical life in the Midlands (and especially the Potteries) in the early 1900s. But there are a few sections where this strong sense of personality disappears and the style and opinions change radically. I have excluded all such passages from consideration in these volumes.

A similar problem of identification arises with the multitudinous unsigned writings, but Brian provided two useful guides to their selection a couple of years before his death. Presented with photocopied pages of *Musical Opinion* by Graham Hatton, he was able to authenticate many anonymous pieces as his – although the exercise does not seem to have been conducted on a systematic basis. He also vouchsafed the information that the majority of all book reviews were his work, whereas record reviews were done by Fitzsimmons, and that they had shared the reviews of new scores and sheet music between them. Since Fitzsimmons' rather bland style is in striking contrast to Brian's, this helps considerably to sort out the music reviews. Inevitably, in such a large mass of material, there are a number of cases where it is nevertheless impossible to be certain about authorship, and I have accordingly passed these items by. For this reason, an absolutely complete concordance of Brian's journalism could never be compiled.

Towards the end of his time at *Musical Opinion* Brian contributed a couple of items (one a very important autobiographical article, 'How the *Gothic* Symphony Came to be Written') to *Modern Mystic and Monthly Science Review*, an 'occult' and arts publication founded and edited by Norman V. Dagg, an amateur musician and freelance journalist who admired Brian's music enormously and had worked with him for a time on *Musical Opinion*. With the outbreak of World War II *Modern Mystic* was terminated and Dagg founded a new magazine with broadly similar contents but slanted more towards economics and questions of the post-War world order: *Tomorrow (A Journal for the World Citizen of the New Age)*. It began as a weekly but in 1940 became a monthly and ceased publication altogether between June 1940 and April 1941. To its earliest numbers Brian contributed a regular series of articles on composers, but vacated its pages after January 1940 and supplied only very occasional musical news items of no real interest to its later incarnation (which lasted until 1946 and called itself 'An Independent Non-party Non-sectarian Monthly').[6]

Brian departed the offices of *Musical Opinion* in June 1940 as the magazine shed staff and pages, to devote his time to war work with the Ministry of Supply; but he maintained some contact with it and continued to contribute articles and reviews on an occasional basis throughout the 1940s – although more and more infrequently. This fourth and last phase, of much diminished journalistic activity, sounds a faintly valedictory note – not least because some of the most substantial items are either frankly autobiographical or obituaries for his old associates, such as Henry Wood, John Coates, and Granville Bantock. With a set of reminiscences entitled 'The Faraway Years', published in January 1949, the month in which he celebrated his 73rd birthday, Brian finally laid down his journalistic pen. Yet as a *composer* he was just on the point of entering his 'third period', with four operas, 25 symphonies, and several other works to be written in the next 20 years.

* * *

I have already said that a complete listing of all Brian's journalism is an impossibility; and a 'collected edition' of all

---

[6] It would be pleasant to think that this lapse of activity was due to *Tomorrow*'s increasingly crypto-fascist political stance. Norman Dagg is believed to have ended his days as a member of the British National Party, which perhaps explains the curious fact that the B.N.P. appears on the list of subscribers to the Fund that helped finance the world premiere of *The Gothic* in 1961.

the identified writings would serve no useful purpose, for a large proportion of his work was, of necessity, perfunctory and ephemeral. Indeed, with the possible exception of a few of his larger articles, none of his writings was directed at posterity – he was a campaigner seeking to arouse the interests and passions of his own day. Yet a substantial amount of his work retains interest, even fascination, both in its own right and as a historical source; and the problems of selection are daunting, for the sheer volume of writings is immense. Their number is no less astonishing than their range: *everything* musical was grist to Brian's mill, and there is no chance of conveying, within a single volume, the breadth of his concerns.

Considering his journalistic output as a whole, I have decided to divide it into six broad categories, each of which will eventually be represented by a volume of selections. These are: the British music of his own time (both its composers and the evolution of its national spirit and institutions); contemporary music in Europe and the USA (which will include his writings on Strauss, Schoenberg, Busoni, Bartók, Berg, Varèse and many other figures); conductors, performers, and other contemporaries (such as Beecham, Wood, Richter, Toscanini, Furtwängler, John Coates); the great composers of the past (Bach, Handel, Berlioz and Bruckner among them); more general musical topics; and the more frankly autobiographical of his writings.

These are of course somewhat artificial divisions, for Brian did not have a compartmentalised mind: he would always discuss general principles with reference to specific cases, draw a parallel from a past century to illuminate a present situation, or in discussion of a certain composer be led to an anecdote about a conductor who had been involved with the composer's music. Many of the LMG articles display almost a 'stream of consciousness', one subject sparking off the next from paragraph to paragraph until it is well-nigh impossible to say what the true point of the column *is* – save to provide a thoroughly entertaining discourse. Many of the composers, works and events mentioned in this volume will inevitably crop up in others, although in different contexts.

This volume – which is concerned with the music and musical issues that lay closest to his heart (though not necessarily highest in his esteem) – will probably prove to be the bulkiest of the series. My selection represents roughly a third of the articles, reviews and other features whose subject-matter rendered them eligible for inclusion. All the items reprinted here seem to me to possess some intrinsic interest – stylistic, historical, critical, or anecdotal – although I freely acknowledge that these virtues are not all equally present in every one. The alternative would have been a much, much slimmer volume containing only the most polished articles; but this, I felt, would misrepresent Brian – the kind of writer he was, the sort of journalism he was engaged in, and the scope of his musical world-view. But I venture to hope that the natural readership of these selections is much wider than the circle of people who have already become interested in Brian as a composer. It seems to me that, as volume is added to volume, they may build into an important historical source for the musical life of the first half of the 20th century.

*   *   *

Music journalism – for excellent reasons – has never been considered one of the major literary forms, and few of its practitioners have produced a legacy that we can read for itself alone: the two outstanding exceptions, significantly, were not primarily musicians but professional literary men – Bérnard Shaw and Ezra Pound. Brian is not in their league, nor even – considered as a writer pure and simple – in that of the three critics he most admired, namely Tovey, Newman and Cardus. He was well-read in three languages (English, French and German) and had some knowledge of a fourth (Italian), but he would never have considered himself a literary figure. He was a composer who happened to exercise a fluent pen – both to give vent to matters which concerned him and, by no means incidentally, to help to earn his daily bread. In his blacker moments he described himself as a 'hack', and the conditions under which he worked were hardly conducive to the birth of deathless prose.[7]

Certainly you will not have to look far in Brian's writings to find all the blemishes of journalism produced in a hurry: slack repetitions, unconsidered hyperboles, casual sentence-structure, occasional turgidities, and the passing inaccuracies of a writer relying on his memory rather than a reference book. But against that we must set the astonishing range of his interests and sympathies, the general rectitude of his critical judgement (sometimes far ahead of his time), his eye for character, his passionate sense of personal involvement with his subject, his sly and sometimes wicked sense of humour, and a point of view whose idiosyncracy nevertheless encompasses a massive common sense.

Moreover, as the surviving tapes of interviews with him prove, Brian was a considerable raconteur; he loved a good story, and like most raconteurs he tended to recycle his best ones. Even in a selection of this nature some of his favourites keep surfacing: Frederick Corder in tears when the Hanley Cauldon Choir sang Cornelius' *O Tod, du bist die kühle Nacht*; Willy Hess as orchestra leader 'saving' the first performance of *King Olaf* when Elgar's conducting came adrift; Bantock at New Brighton, rehearsing *Tristan* when he should have been using the time for a programme of light music; Delius' apoplectic rage at the Hallé librarian over the lack of extra players for *Appalachia* – but also Delius, standing with bowed head on the wharves of the Mersey, lost in the reverie of creation. Brian treasured such memories, yet for him they were clearly more than that – rather they were symbols showing how a true musical life might be lived, in the real world, with a passion for excellence.

So we should not discount the literary *persona* for its lack of gloss: Brian's mature prose style – slang, quaintnesses and all – has an inimitable flavour. One feels oneself in the presence of a strong and definite character. On occasion, let

---

[7] He was paid 'a penny a line', he remembered, and was usually at the mercy of the compositors, with few chances to see a proof.

it be said, a difficult character. Not for nothing did Robert Simpson once label Brian 'the awkward cuss'. When talking of composers and performers whose efforts he admired, no writer could be warmer in his praise or firmer in his friendship. But his deep-seated distrust of established arbiters of public taste, of merely commercial criteria for artistic value, of the motives ruling the organisations on which British music depended for its existence, and his horror of academicism, frequently provoked him to a bluntness of utterance that a more diplomatic man, or one with a thicker skin, might have avoided. This spontaneity of feeling sometimes adds a dash of vinegar to Brian's words, but is also one of his treasurable qualities. He can be tactful, he can be restrained; but he is never merely polite for politeness' sake.

Although he seldom bothers to essay large-scale literary effects, he could do so perfectly well when the mood was on him (the long introductory section to 'The Art of Eugene Goossens' is perhaps the most striking instance in this volume, and in its obliquity to its main subject illustrates a feature of Brian's writing which is equally characteristic of his music). Smaller felicities abound: the gift for epigram ('a country that neglects Parry deserves never to have known him'); the passionate gardener's delight in enunciating a catalogue of flower-names suggested by a piece of Cyril Scott; the ironic downrightness (in the same article) of the plain trencherman who can say of Scott's *Rainbow Trout*: 'I have never seen a trout which suggested fine music. I always felt they would be nicer on the grill'; or the way he can irradiate a prosaic piece of description with a sudden shaft of pure poetry – as, here, in talking of Vaughan Williams' *Pastoral Symphony*:

> Occasionally there is a sudden flare, as though dry brushwood had been thrown onto an expiring flame, lighting up the countryside. Then it expires and we are again amongst the silent night shadows and the stars.

But the purely literary reasons for re-issuing some of Brian's journalism will never be the predominating ones. To admirers of Brian the composer, his writings will have intrinsic appeal because they are *his*; and even non-admirers should find much interest in the fact that a composer of his period and background heard, studied, and commented upon so much music. As Trevor Bray (no uncritical champion of Brian's works) wrote after I published substantial extracts from the journalism in Volume 3 of my study of Brian's Symphonies,[8] the writings prove him to have possessed 'one of the most forward-looking and catholic musical minds of his time'.[9]

Yet it seems to me that there are two further, pressing reasons for resurrecting Brian the writer. The period of the so-called 'English Musical Renaissance', from the 1890s to the 1930s, is still an imperfectly-studied and thus imperfectly-understood one (and I include in this not only the activities of British composers but the growth and decline of the institutions and conventions within which they worked, and the dissemination in this country of contemporary music from other parts of the world). Brian's omnivorous interests made him a natural chronicler, and as a result his writings should still prove a vital primary source for the period. But more: as composer and critic in one, as listener and campaigner, and as a true 'provincial' who knew that the heart of England was somewhere other than London, his writings retain an immediacy lacking from more sober and considered studies of those years. In responding to topics of the day and causes of the hour (always viewed against his admirable conviction that British music was *neither* the most important thing in the world, *nor* the least: a state of balance at which few British writers have ever managed to arrive), he gives us a vivid sense of what it was like to be alive in those times, of how it all felt to one who considered himself personally involved.

---

[8] *The Symphonies of Havergal Brian*, Vol. 3, Kahn and Averill, London, 1983.
[9] *Music & Letters*, Vol. 64, No. 3, May–August 1983, p.297.

ACKNOWLEDGEMENTS

A debt of gratitude is due to Bryan Hesford, the then editor of *Musical Opinion*, for his encouragement at the beginning of this project and his permission to reprint any material which appeared in the magazine. In tracing Brian's writings through many old or defunct publications I have been much assisted by the staffs of the Barbican Library, London (with special thanks to Robert Tucker), the British Library in Bloomsbury and its Newspaper Division at Colindale, and the University Library, Cambridge. Many other people helped with the provision of copies and the elucidation of queries, among them Martin Anderson, the staff of the BBC Written Archives Centre at Caversham, Gwydion Brooke, David Brown, Paul Chipchase, Lewis Foreman, Graham Hatton (who laid important groundwork for this project while Brian was still alive, questioning him about his journalism and getting him to identify unsigned articles), Raymond Head, the staff of the National Sound Archive, Paul Rapoport, Brian Rust, Mike Smith, Robert Threlfall, and Roger Wright of the British Music Information Centre. Proof-reading help, much appreciated, was provided by David Brown, Lewis Foreman and Guy Rickards; and the Herculean labour of compiling the index was undertaken by John Grimshaw.

Musical examples from Delius' *Appalachia* and *Mass of Life*, copyright of Hawkes & Son (London) Ltd., 1951 and 1952, are reproduced by permission of Boosey & Hawkes Music Publishers Ltd.,; from Bax's Symphony No. 1 and Walford Davies' *This ae Nighte* by kind permission of Chappell Group Publishers; from Cyril Scott's *Egypt, Danse Orientale, Danse Languoreuse* and *Rainbow Trout* by permission of Schott & Co. Ltd; from Arnold Cooke's *Holderneth* by kind permission of Oxford University Press; and from Goossens' *Nature Poems* and *Hommage à Debussy* by permission of J.W. Chester Ltd.

Not least, thanks are due to the Rex Foundation of San Francisco for a generous grant to the Havergal Brian Society which allowed me finally to embark on this long-planned series.

EDITORIAL NOTE

The titles of the individual items are generally Brian's. In a few instances I have supplied titles of my own: these are in cases where the original was untitled (for example, sections taken from LMC columns written before October 1934) or where Brian's original title, divorced from its contemporary context, does little to convey the nature of his subject-matter.

Obvious printing errors, and mis-spellings of proper names – which are as likely to have been the typographer's fault as Brian's – have been corrected without comment (but not 'period' spellings – e.g., Glazounow, Borodine, Scriabine – which have been retained where they occur). I have also corrected redundancies of punctuation, such as Brian's occasional habit of using a comma in conjunction with a dash (,–), and punctuation before rather than after the close of a quotation; although in all other essentials his punctuation has been allowed to stand. The house-style of *Musical Opinion*, and some of the other journals he wrote for, demanded that titles of books and musical works appear in Roman type within double quotation-marks; but to avoid the archaic and cluttered appearance this convention causes on the page, such titles have been converted to Italic type, without quotes.

Some items have been slightly abbreviated. Excisions (marked by [...]) are generally of matter repeated and better developed elsewhere. A few items of exceptional length are represented by extracts and prefaced by a note explaining the omissions. In one case ('The Songs of Granville Bantock', pp. 153–159) two broadly similar and almost exactly contemporaneous articles have been conflated to produce a single compound text.

All the music examples in this volume have been ably re-copied by Barry Ould, while retaining exactly the substance and layout of Brian's original quotations. For ease of reference they have been renumbered in a single sequence extending throughout the book. In the original publications the examples were all engraved, with the exception of Ex. 29 from Arnold Cooke's *Holderneth*, which appeared in a facsimile of Brian's manuscript.

I have tried not to over-burden the pages with footnotes. Nevertheless a fair number have had to be employed, to explain (where it has proved possible) contemporary references; to identify persons or literary quotations unlikely to be familiar to present-day readers; and to amplify or cross-reference Brian's text where necessary. The numbering of the footnotes starts afresh at each of the main divisions of the volume.

M.M.

PART ONE

THE SPIRIT
OF ENGLAND

────────── ◦ ──────────

This opening selection has been chosen because, unlike
much of Brian's writing on music of the so-called 'English
Musical Renaissance', these items take the longer historical
view and establish some sort of context for it. None of them,
however, was conceived as a formal article, being selections
from his regular monthly column 'On the Other Hand' from
Musical Opinion. The first comes from the issue of October
1932 (p. 16), and like the next item was originally untitled.

CORDER, WARLOCK, DOWLAND
AND ENGLISH MUSIC

The letter of Arnold Bax to *The Times* was a distinguished
salute at the passing of Frederick Corder:[1] and at the same
time it revealed his position as a teacher of composition.
Corder's methods were unorthodox: and yet, as the teacher
of a famous and brilliant phalanx of English composers, his
methods were justified by results. I remember, years ago,
discussing Corder's method of teaching composition with a
well-known man who had studied under him.[2] I was told
that it was Corder's habit to place his advanced pupils direct

---

[1] Corder, born in 1852 and Professor of Composition at the Royal
Academy of Music since 1888, died on 21 August 1932. Bax had been one
of his many distinguished pupils.
[2] Probably Bantock.

on such works as *Tristan* or *The Ring* and encourage them to
emulate the ways of Wagner. At one time it seemed that Corder was to have a full life as an opera composer. Carl Rosa
had produced his *Nordisa*, and it was having an excellent
reception. But Rosa died suddenly in the noontide of a brilliant career, and with him were buried the hopes of Corder
and others of whom he seemed destined to be the leader.[3]
He found his way to the Royal Academy, where his work did
much to enhance its prestige. Corder continued to write
music, but it does not appear to have been known to many
save his friends.

Thus in some respects I regard Corder's deflection from
opera as a tragedy for English music of that type; indeed, in
my more moody periods I see tragedy stalking our own
national art through all the ages. English music sustained a
loss through the death of Peter Warlock, whose name will
for long be associated with the revival of interest in songs of
the sixteenth century. If we could catch again the spirit of
those days, English music would stand at the dawn of a new
era. Warlock had the germ of that spirit within him, and
often have I seen him at the British Museum[4] engrossed in
the study of songs of the Elizabethan and Jacobean periods.
That was the time of triumph for English music, and the
sweetest singer of them all was John Dowland. The fruits of
his life are now enshrined in the sumptuous book just published by the Oxford University Press under the title of
English Ayres, transcribed by Peter Warlock and Philip Wilson.[5] [...]

---

[3] *Nordisa* was produced in Liverpool in 1887, but Rosa died in 1889.
[4] During the late 1920s and early 1930s Brian spent much time at the
British Museum studying obscure scores and composers' manuscripts,
partly out of insatiable curiosity and partly researching for future articles. See also pp. 353–354 for Brian's obituary of Warlock.
[5] Vols. IV to VI of *English Ayres* were published by Oxford University
Press in 1931, as three separate volumes, which does not fit Brian's
description of a single 'sumptuous book just published' in 1932. But Fred
Tomlinson, in *A Peter Warlock Handbook*, Volume 2 (Triad Press,
Rickmansworth, 1976), notes that the British Museum received a composite bound copy of all six volumes in 1932; quite possibly it is this that
Brian means.

In the same book as the Dowland songs will be found songs and airs by other men of the period, the majority of whom were provincials who had drifted to London.[6] This suggests to me that the spirit of English music will be found again by the countryside, and not in cosmopolitan London. There by the hedgerows, as Rupert Brooke sang, is that which is 'for ever England'; and some day English music may give back to Englishmen the thoughts by England given.

I am aware of the many efforts to bring back appreciation of the indigenous spirit of English music and dancing; perhaps the efforts are too obvious for a people like the English, who cannot be driven, but who will tumble over one another to follow. The fault is that the spirit of English music should ever have been allowed to die. It is only an idle thought, but at times I wish that we could somehow turn our fairs gradually to carnivals of old English music. We have got as far as the school teacher and the younger children, but there it all seems to end. If we could have a travelling booth for English songs and dances, joining up with the various sloe fairs and goose fairs, we might find a response that would lead farther than we are hoping at present.

THE CONTINUITY OF BRITISH MUSIC

This is a rare example of a whole 'On the Other Hand' column (February 1934, pp. 397–399) in which the various topics of the day are woven into a discourse with a single over-riding theme.

The six concerts of British music organised and broadcast by the B.B.C. were a splendid gesture on the part of Adrian

[6] The other composers include Thomas Campian, Michael Cavendish, John Danyel, Alfonso Ferrabosco the Younger, Robert Jones, and Philip Rosseter; see Tomlinson, *op. cit.*, pp. 76–77, for a complete listing.

Boult and those in association with him.[7] The concerts were heralded by many notices of varied fervour, followed by others telling of small audiences at Queen's Hall, but of course without knowledge of the numbers listening in. The effect was to convey an impression that the good ship British Music lay in the Doldrums. Then came Friday, January 12th, and the last concert, when we had reproduced all the clamorous features of an end-of-the-season Promenade Concert. After my own experience inside the hall, joined to assurances from friends who listened, I have no further interest in what the other man says or writes. The effort had, so far as public response is concerned, fully justified itself, though I do not conceal from myself the fact that now as ever British music will still have to fight for a position, not with the average quality of what is written abroad, but with a selection of the best, which is, generally speaking, what is performed here.

The festival has certainly demonstrated that our best native composers are in no way inferior to Continental composers of the present decade; indeed, excepting Sibelius, nowhere abroad among writers of symphonic works do I see a man fully comparable to Bax. But Bax does not glean his art from English influences, seeking it rather in the Western Isle: it is steeped in Celtic mythology. The composer remaining faithful to English influences is Vaughan Williams, whose equal for musical structure among present-day Continental symphonists I have yet to find. He builds solidly, and his work is unassailable. The most promising of the other thirty men given a show is Patrick Hadley, who previously was but little known. His orchestral and choral symphony, *The Trees so High*, has moments that are stirring and even magnificent. The writing is concentrated, close and sure: urged by the old traditional story, the mind of the composer sprang upward and forward, bringing back to us a very beautiful, if somewhat unequal, work. Hadley needs only opportunity and encouragement. I first heard a work of his three years ago, at a chamber concert given by Gordon Bryan at Æolian Hall. The programme included music

[7] See pp. 191–193 for Brian's short review of this important concert series.

by Lambert, Walton and Hadley, and I then formed the impression that the work of the man unknown to me had the greater staying power.[8] His last work confirms my first impression. The conductor, Adrian Boult, came through the festival with flying colours: he had undertaken a great task, conducting four concerts of works which must have been more or less unfamiliar to him. Landon Ronald conducted one concert, and the Ethel Smyth concert had the great advantage of Thomas Beecham's direction.

For forty years we have heard clamour for a better or more persistent presentation of British music, and now, under the changed circumstances of the B.B.C. being the dominant force in music presentation in this country, we may hope for an equitable choice between what is brought from abroad and what is home grown. The B.B.C., more than any individual *entrepreneur,* does stand fast against gusts of public opinion. It has ever persisted in turning the British mind to British music, as all other nationals do by instinct, except, of course, the Americans, who are in leading strings. In France, foreign music is little heard: in Italy, Russia and Germany similar exclusiveness is practised, though in successively less degrees. It might be worth while, for a few moments, to seek the beginnings of this openmindedness of the British, which has re-acted so harshly on our art-music.

If we go back four hundred years to the late Tudor period, when under Elizabeth the feudal heritage was thrown off, we find that the dominating influence in all but material things was Italian. It was with us in gardens, in literature and in music. Elizabeth spoke Italian fluently, and until the middle nineteenth century Italian script was used by all ladies having any claims to refinement. Peter Phillips, the sixteenth century English composer who settled in the

---

[8] The concert was on 30 October 1929 and Brian reviewed it on p. 230 of the December *Musical Opinion*: the programme consisted of Lambert's Piano Sonata and *Eight Poems of Li-Po* (receiving their world premieres), unspecified songs by Hadley and Walton's Piano Quartet. Although Brian praised the Hadley items for their 'sinewy independent strength', he seems in fact to have been most impressed by the Walton. The pianist Gordon Bryan was the soloist in this and the Lambert Sonata.

Netherlands, was complimented on his Italian style. Handel also, though a German, was a carrier of the Italian tradition. Later, we have fallen successively under the influence of Mendelssohn, Brahms, Wagner, and Strauss, with Debussy running alongside. Thus there is plenty of precedent for Englishmen to be foreign-minded as regards music: in some cases foreign music stimulates the mind as a foreign menu stimulates the palate. But mostly we turn to foreign music by habit, and we have been doing so for a long time.

Of course, during and after the six concerts there were the usual complaints from the friends and acquaintances of composers not included in the honoured thirty-one. The restriction to works written during the past twenty-five years, whether wise or necessary, consequently cut out music by men who have had something to say. Again, the insidious influence of clamour is apparent in the choice and quantity. Mr. J. A. Forsyth says, in effect, that kissing goes by favour.[9] Perhaps so; but the fear of further complaint that this or that person is being unwarrantably passed over is a stronger influence. Music is not unlike politics: ministers say that they will do a certain thing if and when they are supported by public opinion. This is only an invitation to make sufficient noise to enable them to push aside colleagues carrying bantlings not so lusty. A group of M.P.'s coming from one shire or representing particular interests can often get things done that otherwise would be left undone or forgotten. I agree that some composers are fortunate in having representatives who can command the ears of ministers in charge of music. Of the thirty-one composers represented at the festival, sixteen were trained at the Royal College of Music, eight at the Royal Academy, and the other seven – Elgar, Delius, Scott, Smyth, Berners, Quilter and Fogg[10] – were either self-taught or received training abroad.

Compulsory retirement at a fixed age must be a great

---

[9] Unidentified.

[10] Eric Fogg (1903–1939) was a pupil of Bantock and equally noted as both composer and conductor (mainly for the B.B.C.). Brian, for one, thought very highly of his music.

adventure in any man's life: it may only take him back to a seat in the garden, or perhaps forward to a seat in the Cabinet – or maybe leading an English Orchestra to the Antipodes or to India, after the manner of Jardine.[11] One of these alternatives will shortly confront Sir Granville Bantock when he vacates the Chair of Music at Birmingham University. He has energy enough to conduct two orchestras, and I hope that he will decide to fire a trail for English music through all the Seven Seas.[12] Many of us look upon the years spent at Birmingham as a loss to English music: doubtless, the students have increased in numbers, and certainly good teaching must have good results. But I feel that the glamour that one time accompanied Sir Granville's conducting would have been a great asset to English music during recent years when the public has begun to doubt the alleged invincibility of foreign musicians.[...]

His approaching retirement reminds me of the excitement that ran through the Midlands when Richard Peyton put down the money to found the Chair: but it was on condition that Edward Elgar occupied it. Of course, Elgar was everything in our eyes, of greater stature than the most notable foreigners, and at least the equal of Richard Strauss. There was a lot of civic pride about: and had not Elgar disclosed his vision of Birmingham as an art-centre for music, rivalling Leipzig both in its Conservatorium and its Gewandhaus concerts? A permanent orchestra of a hundred and a resident conductor whose name should be known throughout the land. Elgar doubtless wished these things, and their realisation even in part would have done much to enlarge the horizon of musicians in Birmingham.

I can recall nothing being done directly to realise the dream; but Elgar did give a number of lectures that startled

[11] The precise point of the allusion escapes me – but it apparently involves John Jardine (1844–1919), first Baronet of Godalming, who attained considerable eminence in the Indian Civil Service, becoming Chief Secretary of the Bombay Government, Vice-Chancellor of Bombay University, and President of Bombay Royal Asiatic Society.
[12] On his retirement from Birmingham Bantock became Chairman of the Corporation of Trinity College of Music in London. As an examiner for the College, he made a world tour in 1938–39, at the age of 70.

the tender-hearts and worried the academicians.[13] They were remarkably unconventional but full of undeniable truths. No other Professor would have stopped in the middle of a lecture to applaud the work of young contemporary composers and to plead for its recognition. In one of his early lectures he spoke of the then extraordinary activity in music: Brahms, Cornelius, Hegar and the Elizabethans were being revealed to us through the activities of the Morecambe Festival. Elgar declared that similar high-pressure work was being done in England, and instanced the music of Bantock, Walford Davies, and Holbrooke.[14]

Then the lectures ceased, and Elgar was seldom seen or heard in Birmingham. Neither the Conservatoire nor the Gewandhaus was there when finally he resigned from the Professorship. Granville Bantock and Ernest Newman were freely mentioned as men suitable for the position: and though the former was chosen, I still think that English music would have fared better had Bantock been left free to lead and direct our newly awakening art before the great public. Besides, Bantock was at opposite ends to Elgar in religious thought, though both were, so to speak, anti-academic. He was a silent man, and consequently the belief

[13]   Richard Peyton, a wealthy Birmingham patron of the arts, offered the city's University £10,000 to endow a Chair of Music, on condition that Elgar was asked, and agreed, to become the first incumbent. Elgar's only 'teaching' during his brief tenure was his series of six lectures, formulated and delivered with difficulty, which aroused intense controversy. But they remained a touchstone for Brian throughout his life – the intellectual justification of what he and his contemporaries were doing. They have been published under the title *A Future for English Music and other Lectures*, ed. Percy Young, Dobson, 1968.

[14]   The prepared text of Elgar's first lecture (*op.cit.*, p.43), given on 16 March 1905, contained no specific references other than a generous tribute to the quality of music being produced by 'the younger generation'; but Elgar had made a marginal note to refer particularly to Bantock's *Time-Spirit*, Walford Davies' *Everyman*, and Holbrooke's *Queen Mab*. In his second lecture ('English Composers', not given till 1 November), the names of these composers were again linked (*ibid.*, pp. 92–93). It should be noted that *The Musical World* for 25 March 1905 carried a detailed report of the first lecture ('Sir Edward Elgar in Birmingham', p.208) and an article ('Elgar's Ideals', p.204), exploring the salient points on which Elgar had touched. Both these items are unsigned; both are quite possibly by Brian.

went unchecked that he had sown all his musical wild oats and would settle down like that Second Son to the end of his days. But he built far better than many thought he would: he framed a complete system of musical education at the university, on modern lines. He gave no public lectures, but poured the wealth of his great musical experience and knowledge into the ears of the students at the University.

A remarkable thing about Bantock is his perfect good humour: he has neither pride nor prejudice to protect, and maintains a constant friendship with all around him. After he left the Royal Academy he went for some months conducting musical comedy for George Edwardes, and now he travels extensively in the interests of musical competitive festivals and examinations. This ceaseless movement suggests the genesis of Bantock's musical inspiration: it may be in Bagdad or in Samarkand, but it is not by the English countryside, where Delius and Vaughan Williams love to linger. All his important choral and orchestral works have that sensuous oriental colouring which Mr. H.J. Foss thinks is absent from the palette of the English composer.[15] Actually, the charge used to be made that Bantock's music was too theatrical, which being interpreted means that it is rhapsodical, highly coloured and tuneful. The spontaneity of his invention frequently suggests improvisation. At one time I thought of Bantock as a possible successor to Sullivan.

My estimate of Bantock as a conductor is based on his work with the Liverpool Orchestral Society, with which he gave many early performances of Strauss and Debussy. He had succeeded Alfred Rodewald, who was a most accomplished amateur in music and incidentally a cotton broker of some wealth.[16] Though the scheme passed away with his early death, Rodewald was considering the possibility

---

[15] Hubert Foss (1899–1953), founder of the Music Department of Oxford University Press, was a copious writer on music; I have not traced the comment to which Brian refers.

[16] Alfred E. Rodewald (1860–1903), Liverpool textile magnate and conductor, was a close friend of Elgar. He gave the world premiere of the first *Pomp and Circumstance* March, which is dedicated to him and the Liverpool Orchestral Society, and probably subsidised Bantock's concerts at New Brighton. It was at his cottage in Bettws-y-coed that Elgar scored part of *The Apostles*, as recounted on p.89.

of a Festspielhaus on the lines of that at Bayreuth, to be
situated somewhere between Liverpool and Manchester. I
still revel in the vision of Birmingham as an English Leipzig
and of Lancashire as a British Bayreuth.

I wonder how many English musicians trouble to
remember the birthdays of Queen Elizabeth, and yet to the
musicians of her reign and to one minister at least (Thomas
Gresham), music owes more than can be told in any article.
Gresham was the Queen's plenipotentiary abroad during
troublous times, and seemingly was often in fear for his own
safety. Addressing Elizabeth in 1560, he wrote: 'I would
most humbly beseech your Highness to be a comfort unto
my pore wife in this my absens'. Gresham by his will dated
July 5th, 1575, left property to the 'maior and corporation',
to spend on the provision of lectures on music and other
arts. So let us now praise this famous man.

Writers on music mention the 'great Elizabethan period',
but would have been hard set to support the phrase with
much detail before the Rev. Canon Fellowes's work was
revealed to us through the munificence of the Carnegie
Trust.[17] The music of the great composers of Tudor times
has thus been made known. Doubtless Queen Elizabeth saw
that wonderful collection of madrigals made in her honour,
The Triumphs of Oriana, and approved its publication; but
probably she never saw a printed copy, for it was not issued
in that form until the year 1603, when she died, having been
in a bad state of mental and bodily health for some time previous.

My present interest in Elizabeth and her composers arose
from reading in an American paper a report of a concert
given by the Elizabethan Club of Yale. It was to mark the
four hundredth birthday of the Queen: and I think it just
sweet of those Americans to say, 'The centuries may have
rolled by, but the music presented on this occasion made the
Tudor period seem just a short time ago'. Dowland, Byrd,
Farnaby, Wilbye, Morley and Bennet were represented at
this festival, held on November 16th, though the history
books say that Elizabeth Tudor was born at Greenwich on

[17] *Cf.* note 3 on p.203.

September 7th, 1533. Strange it is that no Englishman or woman though of celebrating the quadracentenary. The Oriana Madrigal Society missed an opportunity, for under Kennedy Scott it would have made the welkin ring.

Fashion alone is responsible for the neglect that awaited the music of Elizabeth's time. It was derived from the ancient modes: and what we presume to call modern music began when her reign was ending. Musicians ought to know this music, which was written before the definite establishment of key: it is neither quaint nor archaic, as those know who have listened to the madrigals at northern competition festivals, or to the masses of Byrd sung by the Oriana Madrigal Society. We certainly ought to be made familiar with the instrumental music of the 'spacious days'.

In this laudable work of popularising Elizabethan music in England, the various teaching and examining bodies have a wonderful opportunity of advancing their position before men. Instrumental works by Farnaby, Bull, Byrd, and the others might be included in the syllabuses, with explanatory notes. These Elizabethan composers of instrumental keyboard music were exceedingly skilful and their resources and contrapuntal ingenuity were extraordinary. Their fugues were called ricercare, fantasias or fancies. Constructed on the old modes, their habits were free. After definite key was established, and the name Fugue given to this type of composition, its habits during the two hundred years following became sadly cut and dried.

What should put backbone into any movement to follow our Elizabethan composers is the fact that all the quaint contrapuntal conceits beloved of Sebastian Bach, and practised more recently by Arnold Schönberg, were very well known in Tudor times. I could wish that present-day teaching looked at home more frequently for inspiration, for what is found abroad is often nothing more than a flower from a plant carried out of England in those days when Thomas Gresham was visiting the capitals of Europe in pursuance of the policy of Elizabeth, and when men fled to avoid the rigours of religious reprisals.

Dowland, Bull and Peter Phillips certainly travelled abroad. Phillips was born in England of Roman Catholic parents, and migrated to the Netherlands where after service with the Archduke Albert he entered the Church and gained preferment. He was a remarkable player of the organ, and many of his madrigals and masses were published in Brussels: a few are to be found in famous English collections. He wrote a series of keyboard pieces, several of which are included in the *Fitzwilliam Virginal Book*, and a volume of eight-part madrigals was issued at Antwerp. Morley published two English madrigals by Phillips in 1598, and a pavan and galliard in 1599. Peacham, in the *Compleat Gentleman* (London, 1627), referred to him as one of the greatest masters of music in Europe. Dr. Burney, a century later, was attracted by an organ fugue on a subject by Phillips.

It would be a good 'sales promotion' scheme for English music to push the Elizabethans, and mostly because they are 'good goods', ranking with the best of any age or clime. Why not honour their memory with a festival at which their works should have pride of place, supported by music of English character written in more recent years?

THE SPIRIT OF ENGLAND

From 'On the Other Hand', in *Musical Opinion* for April 1935, pp. 587–588. The title, like that of the next item, is Brian's.

The desire for the expression of the spirit of England in English music programmes is again becoming vocal: but its consummation is always for to-morrow, or if anything is done it remains an incident in the past. Let us take the activities of the B.B.C. as typical, and we find occasional hours devoted to English music in a spirit of benevolent patronage. I wonder what would be the state of public opinion in Berlin, Vienna or Paris if the programmes of the principal concerts were mainly foreign, and if native works were relegated to the end of the concert.[18] There would be risings

[18] The modern practice is to relegate them to the beginning.

throughout all Austria if any conductor offered the deadly insult of an evening or hour with Austrian composers in a manner similar to what is done regularly in England. The spirit of English music is a minus quantity among those who should have it ever before their eyes.

For this spirit of England our programme makers think only of Elgar, and there is some fear they will not do so for long now that the force of his personality is gone. His idiomatic phrases, clear and distinct in everything he wrote, breathe the spirit of England. One may be more sympathetic and reach more quickly to certain composers by reason of temperamental affinity: but in looking round or amongst European composers of to-day, I see none so easily recognisable as Elgar. Here then is what we need: English character without nationalism, and that can be found widespread in our literature. It is not that Elgar repeats himself: we may pass quickly from the pages of the slow movements of his Symphonies – with their subtly woven close texture – to the slow variations in the *Enigma*, the Angel's Song in *Gerontius*, through the secular cantatas and the oratorios, and include 'Dreaming' from the last orchestral work he wrote (*Nursery Suite*), and note how his personality persists through his phrases and deceptive cadences. 'That music had a dying fall' more clearly expressed the elusive character of his cadences, yet he is as purely English in his thinking as Tennyson.

Without contriving to reach posterity, Thomas Arne did so when he wrote that immortal tune, *Rule, Britannia*. It came as an accident, and something similar happened when Elgar wrote his military march, *Pomp and Circumstance* No. 1. It is a superbly fine tune, and as 'Land of Hope and Glory' breathes much of the spirit of England, at least as that spirit comes to most of us sometimes and to others at all times.

Parry, one of the sanest, most acute and imaginative writers English music has produced, is quoted by Vaughan Williams as saying, 'True style comes not from the individual but from the products of crowds of fellow workers who sift and try and try again till they have found the thing that suits their native taste....style is ultimately national'. Elgar's native genius gave expression to this spirit of England without having to pass through the process and conditions which Parry had in his mind when he addressed the Folk Song Society. For this reason many folksong enthusiasts suspect that Elgar was influenced by folk songs. On the contrary, Elgar had the spirit of England in his bones: he could express it in no other way. The affinity between him and the mass of English people was natural: and consequently it is as futile to turn a deaf ear to his national music as it is to try to stifle the voice of England.

THE FIRE
AT THE CRYSTAL PALACE

From 'On the Other Hand', January 1937, p.297.

The burning down of the Crystal Palace[19] has destroyed the building in which British orchestral music was cradled: but it has not obliterated its history or the tradition there begun. We may regret that never again shall we see the building where Berlioz stood in 1855, when Manns began his great career as conductor of the Crystal Palace Orchestra. In the spring of that year Richard Wagner was conductor of the Philharmonic Society: he was staying at Portland Terrace, and apparently divided his time between conducting and working on the score of *The Ring*. But surely Richard took some sort of a holiday and visited the 'great noise' of the times, which owed something of its initiation to a German prince and its already growing fame for music to a Prussian ex-bandmaster. Anton Bruckner, the man who cannot be suppressed,[20] certainly went there, for we have records of a series of organ recitals he gave at the Palace.

[19] The Crystal Palace, built for the Great Exhibition in 1851 (when it was erected in Hyde Park), was transferred to Sydenham in 1854, where it remained until it was burnt down in December 1936.
[20] A reference to Brian's own frequent campaigning, at this time, for performances of Bruckner's music.

Manns' concerts grew in fame, until they took a hold on the imagination of all England as strong as that of the Handel Festivals. That musicians flocked regularly to Sydenham we all know: and I remember keenly Elgar's grumblings to me about the cost and the discomforts of the journeys, for he had to come up from Worcester to go down to Sydenham, though I believe there was compensation in time to study the scores *en route*. It is not too much to say that the Palace, and with it Grove and Manns, had much to do with the musical upbringing of England's greatest composer, Elgar. Not that he was shown any great favour, for it was only after a successful performance of *Caractacus* at Leeds that he was given a show at the Palace. Manns included the 'Severn' Music and the Triumphal March from *Caractacus* in the programme of a Saturday afternoon concert.

As it happened, on the night of the disaster, I stood only a few hundred yards from the Palace looking out of my window:[21] and then, what seemed only a beautiful glow in autumn, burst into flames and I realised that the Palace was burning. In what seemed a few moments the centre transept crashed and in my dismay I thought that all Manns had done was vanquished. Of course, it is not so, for music in England and English music have long since been removed to places of greater safety, that is, where it is not in the keeping of one man in one place. Our music has survived the passing of the Hanover Square Rooms and St. James's Hall: and, truth to tell, the Palace as a Temple of Music remained only to remind us of a great beginning. There had come the music of Spohr, Raff, Meyerbeer, Gade, Marschner and others, men who had their day and have almost ceased to be: and there also came the music of Beethoven, Schubert, Schumann, Berlioz and Brahms, which will last while music endures.

But Manns, after all, was only playing opposite to Grove,

[21] At the time of the conflagration Brian was living at 10a Lunham Road, Upper Norwood, London SE19. The distance from here to the Crystal Palace was a little more than half a mile. His previous residence, 1 Jasper Road, SE19, had been closer still, near enough for Brian to feel the vibration caused by the pedals of the Crystal Palace organ.

the one being the necessary complement to the other. Grove was a man typical of the Victorian age, he created an Empire of Music in England. Great in other ways, he was greatest when he fostered orchestral music at the Crystal Palace: later he helped the Prince of Wales to establish the Royal College of Music, and was its first director. It is a duty almost to point out that the fortunes of the Palace began to dim when the influence of Grove passed: who knows but that his genius would have found means to hold the attention of the public, which never completely abandoned Sydenham? The brass band movement is dearly attached to the Palace, and the leaders of the Church Music Festivals will be hard pressed to find a home so suitable.

PART TWO

THE OLDER GENERATION

This section brings together Brian's thoughts on a few senior composers, though omitting his most-admired British 'elders', Elgar, Delius, and Bantock, each of whom receives a section to himself in this volume. As in Part One, they are all drawn from the *Musical Opinion* column, 'On the Other Hand'. The opening item, on Cowen, is made up from two short passages, the first from *Musical Opinion*, June 1934, p. 765 and the second (occasioned by Cowen's death) from November 1935, p.108.

SIR FREDERIC COWEN

I was reminded how deeply sentiment enters into our lives by seeing Frederic H. Cowen's new song, *One Morning on the Seashore* (published by Broadhurst). Longfellow's lyric is slender and fragrant, indeed, almost too tender for musical treatment; but Cowen's delicate hand has the necessary deftness, which is remarkable in a composer of eighty-three. Here it is, for voice and piano, or arranged for a small orchestra of flute, oboe, clarinet, bassoon, horn and strings. It is hardly credible that a man should be writing now with such grace who fifty years ago gave us *The Promised Land* and *The Children's Home*, two songs which enjoyed great popularity.

My association with Cowen's music began, ever so many years ago, when as a chorister of eleven, I sang in a performance of his early cantata, *The Rose Maiden*.[1] Time for the rehearsal of the trebles was filched from other sessions by an assistant master who knew how to impart his enthusiasm to his pupils. A few years later I was studying Schumann's music, particularly the scores of the Overtures and the *Rhenish* Symphony. The Overture to *Manfred* fascinated me, and hear it I must. Cowen, then conducting the Hallé Orchestra, the Liverpool Philharmonic and the Royal Philharmonic, was to give a concert in the town near where my father was living: so I wrote to him at Manchester, saying how much I should like to hear the *Manfred* Overture when he came our way with the Manchester band. The story is disappointing, for nothing so modern was included in the programme; but readers will be less disappointed than I was. I consoled myself by thinking that my letter had never reached him, but now I think that my calligraphy and diction disclosed my age and unimportance. However, I still recall the pleasure I had in listening to the performance of his own delightful orchestral pictures, *The Language of Flowers*.

The last time I saw Cowen was at Leeds, at a concert of the Leeds Philharmonic Society and the Hallé Orchestra, some thirty years ago.[2] Cowen conducted his choral work, *The Seasons*, and Stanford conducted a complete performance of Berlioz's great *Requiem Mass*. Sad to relate, of my attendance at that concert I remember only two things – the flash from the ring that Cowen was wearing, and the fact that Stanford remained seated whilst conducting Berlioz! The last time I met Sir Frederic, he was on the point of departure for a long journey abroad. He was then nearing eighty, and they tell me he chooses at times to travel in a tramp steamer, with all the seeming discomfort going to a passenger aboard. 'He just sleeps on a deal board.' This rejection of the artifices of much modern life suggests the source

---

[1] The only performance of this work in the Potteries that I can trace occurred at the North Staffordshire Triennial Festival in 1891 – by which time Brian would have been 15. But he could be referring to a school performance. At age 11 (1887) Brian was a treble in the choir of St. James's School, Longton.
[2] At the Leeds Festival in March 1907.

and natural beauty of Cowen's music: he seeks and finds inspiration in the garden and in viewing the landscape. Why should we wonder at the appeal of his songs?

*   *   *

Certain broadcast lectures suggest that, even with the average listener, curiosity exists about mass mentality. Shall we ever know why a musician is extolled in one age execrated in the next? (Well, neglected if not execrated, which is a worse fate!) We have had recently an instance in the case of Frederic Cowen, whose ballads alone for some years reminded us that a musician of that name ever existed. Before his death some of his works broke again into life, following some brightly written articles and pert letters appearing in the papers. Cowen was evidently an intellectual, capable to his last days of expressing himself neatly and with decision. But where in those letters[3] was the musician whom we in our own youth had known as the composer of *Thorgrim*, the *Scandinavian* Symphony, and the orchestral suite known as *The Language of Flowers?* The portraits published recently show him very much as I knew him first, forty years ago, when conductor of the Hallé Orchestra – smartly dressed, alert and keen-eyed. I saw him last at his flat near Lord's, at the moment of his departure for a cruise, not on a luxury liner, but probably on a tramp!

I have told before that as a boy I sang in his *Rose Maiden*, and later saw him conduct *The Language of Flowers* and the *Scandinavian* Symphony: but how was I to reconcile the mentality of the composer of those works with one who could bring himself to adopt the standard of Hemans and Weatherly?[4] In his better self he was a fine figure, perhaps

---

[3] A few months before his death Cowen became embroiled in a newspaper controversy by alleging that ultra-modern composers did not know how to write melody. Brian, in his LMG column for June 1935, paid tribute to the old man's spirit, but averred that there was plenty of melody even in Schoenberg's *Five Orchestral Pieces*.

[4] Felicia Dorothea Hemans (*née* Browne; 1793–1835), English poetess, best known for *Casabianca* ('The boy stood on the burning deck'); and Frederic Weatherly (1848–1919), prolific composer of popular songs.

the biggest in the company after Elgar; in addition, he was the first English orchestral conductor of any importance, holding appointments simultaneously in London, Manchester, Liverpool, Bradford, Crystal Palace, Cardiff and the Scottish Orchestra. What were the gifts that enabled him to sway for so long the musical mind of England? Nobody stops to enquire: but they put in the headlines – Death of the Composer of Three Hundred Ballads! Did that sapient newspaper suspect that it was traducing a great English composer, even though it were out of his own records? But there, Englishmen always have been bad supporters of English music, cheering the wrong men at the right time or the right men at the wrong time. Just when English music was rising out of the darkness, the Birmingham people slipped again under the tutelage of Germany, passing over Sullivan, Cowen and others in favour of Richter.[5]

This neglect or derogation is doubtless one cause for the turning aside of Cowen from the fight: thumbs would always go down when an Englishman was within an ace of victory. I was keenly interested, only the other day, in some remarks made by Dr. Palmer, the organist of Canterbury Cathedral. He was protesting against the severe criticism often levelled against John Stainer, and said: 'With the consent of the Precentor, I always have a Stainer service in the Cathedral, not because I like it, but rather as a protest against such criticism'. Well might we say to certain conductors, thinking of their attitude to certain composers, 'Go thou and do likewise!'

---

[5] Although Richter is best remembered as director of the Hallé Orchestra (from 1897 to 1911), he had first appeared before British audiences at the Royal Albert Hall in 1877 (when he shared the podium with Wagner). He became principal conductor of the Birmingham Triennial Festival in 1885.

EDWARD GERMAN

From December 1936, p. 203. German had died
on 11 November.

Though Edward German was only a casual acquaintance
of mine,[6] I, being of the generation succeeding his, watched
his career very closely, and came to the conclusion that he
well deserved all the success that was his, both for his personal charm and for his clever musicianship. The only luck
that came his way was the coming and going of Arthur Sullivan. For twenty years before his death, Sullivan had been
creating a new stage and a new audience, and when he died
the public, managers and publishers wanted another such
as he had been. German's music was as tuneful as that of
other men of the time writing light operas or musical com-
edies, and moreover it was better woven. That German
never occupied the position Sullivan had done in the
number of successes is doubtless due to his lack of a col-
laborator of the intellectual standard of Gilbert. Such men
are only occasionally found associated with the stage and
rarely allow themselves to run in double harness. The libret-
tists who ventured after Gilbert could not see the sword for
the diamonds on the hilt.

It has fallen to my lot to give a brief sketch of the career
of Edward German Jones, for such was his real name, a fact
I have not seen mentioned in the papers for forty years.
When I first saw the statement it was accompanied apologet-
ically by an explanation that George Alexander Macfarren
had advised dropping the Jones. German was born at
Whitchurch, in Shropshire, in 1862, and his first teacher
was the organist of the Parish Church. This teaching seems
to have inclined him towards the organ, for later we find
him entered as an organ student of Dr. Steggall at the Royal
Academy of Music, though while still at home he had taught
himself to play the violin. This instrument he continued to

---

[6] A short article by Brian on 'Henry Irving and Music' in the February
1931 *Musical Opinion* drew an appreciative letter from Edward German in
the following issue, and this possibly initiated the 'casual acquaintance'.

study at the Academy under Weist Hill and Alfred Burnett. But clearly his musical mind was broadening, for in 1885 we find that he won the Charles Lucas prize with a *Te Deum* for chorus and organ. Then for a time he was teaching the violin at the Academy, and incidentally playing anywhere as a professional violinist. Now were the years of the Gilbert and Sullivan successes, and small wonder that Richard Mansfield, who was then in possession of the Globe Theatre should appoint a young musician of twenty-six, but full of promise, as his musical director. Here was German's lucky opportunity, and for Mansfield's production of *Richard III* German wrote the incidental music. The all-observing Henry Irving must have noted the worth of German's association with the stage, for in 1892 he was asked to write the incidental music to *Henry VIII*. This was another red-capped milestone in German's career, for an Irving production at that time surpassed all other similar things in London. German rose to the occasion, and produced what is probably the most brilliant achievement in modern British theatrical music. Anyhow I can recall no success surpassing that of the *Henry VIII Dances*. Everybody was after him for similar work for similar productions, but equal success was never obtained, though the music to *Nell Gwyn* had and still has considerable popularity.

Whilst a student at the R.A.M. he had tried his 'prentice hand at light opera, but his aptness for such work was first fully realised and acclaimed in the production of *Merry England* at the Savoy in 1902. German doubtless maintained his position with other operas, but he never surpassed *Merry England* as all will agree who witnessed its revival a few years ago. (How much a composer's work is dependent on astute management!)

Like Sullivan also, German had aspirations towards more ambitious music. His Symphony in E minor was produced at the Crystal Palace in 1890, and his Second Symphony at Norwich in 1893. His most widely known works in this direction are the *Welsh Rhapsody* and the *Theme and Six Diversions*, both of unusually fine quality of workmanship and orchestration. German's music was distinguished by a gracefulness and spontaneity entirely his own, qualities which caused his songs and part-songs to remain popular for many years.

SIR JOHN MCEWEN

From August 1936, p. 911, on the occasion of McEwen's
retirement from the R.A.M.

I sincerely hope that reasons of health are only a contribut-
ory cause of the retirement of Sir John McEwen from the
position of Principal of the Royal Academy of Music. Health
is doubtless one true reason, for I have noticed that, on the
few occasions when I have lunched with him during the past
ten years, our more robust food has been passed in favour
of a light diet. These intimate details may be excused when
I say that I also hope that another reason may be a desire to
return to composition untrammelled by the cares of office.
It is a curious fact that, with the coming of Sterndale Bennett and after, each principal of the R.A.M. had acquired
fame as a composer before appointment to office; also,
after appointment, there has been a marked falling off in
musical composition. Evidently creative work and administrative work are an ill-matched pair. Sterndale Bennett had
a reputation in Germany very near to that of Schumann and
Mendelssohn, and we know that his German friends regret-
ted the appointment. It was to a visitor at the Academy that
Bennett said, 'How can I compose when I have one leg
chained to a piano all day?'
     The two facts may have neither association nor signifi-
cance, but it is true that during the régime of Sterndale Bennett the fortunes of the R.A.M. fell very low; but evidently
not so low as not to revive under the tonic of a grant of five
hundred pounds a year from the Treasury (Mr. Gladstone
being at the time Chancellor). Later, affairs still being
regarded as unsatisfactory, Disraeli refused the grant. The
committee was in a quandary, and even sought to resign the
charter to the Queen, though for legal reasons that could
not be done. So a new committee was formed: and then

followed a return of the Academy to general favour, a return of Mr. Gladstone to office, and a return of the grant. Since that time the Royal Academy of Music has never looked back, and now has a reputation and influence extending throughout the British Empire and is in addition regarded as one of the foremost music schools in the world.

Whatever else may have happened, the modern Royal Academy is the work of a succession of capable principals. I do not, like some, argue that the administration of a great school of music is worth the sacrifice of a composer; but I go on regretting the fact that most composers disappear as composers when they take up administrative work. I have mentioned Sterndale Bennett as one instance: Macfarren and Mackenzie are others. As for Sir John McEwen, he may have resigned early enough to save himself. During his years as student and professor at the R.A.M. (1891–1924), he slowly and gradually built up a reputation as a composer of distinct originality and of very serious aims. I know of no composer in this country who holds greater respect from his contemporaries than John McEwen. He has never been a 'top liner' at a triennial music festival, but not one who has had that distinction has yet produced a work more striking or more original than his *Border Ballads* (of which *Grey Galloway* is an especial favourite of mine), and the *Solway* Symphony in C# minor. These big orchestral works may have been written as a challenge, for it is known that McEwen's heart lies in chamber music, of which he is a meticulously fastidious composer. He once said to me, 'Composing music can only be taken as a hobby, if it is to be done seriously'. In this way, all McEwen's works have been written to satisfy his inner self, and not for the glare of publicity. His string quartets are well known to lovers of chamber music, the one called *Biscay* being a great favourite: Dr. Colles of *The Times*, when writing of the concert of McEwen's chamber music given at the R.A.M. centenary celebrations (1922), referred to the rare opportunity of hearing these works together, and said their total impression might be described as music 'for those who are ready to forego excitement and take measured delight in fine quality'.

But I must say that since Sir John McEwen became

principal of the R.A.M. in 1924, I have not heard of a single work emanating from his pen.[7] Neither did he talk of having written any when I last saw him a few weeks ago at the Performing Right Society luncheon. By retiring now, he may again surprise us by another masterpiece like *Grey Galloway* or *Solway,* for such works have added rare lustre to the modern school of English music.

PARRY AND THE R.C.M.

From June 1933, pp. 763–764.

Much of the success of the Royal College is due to the activity and personality of its directors, of whom so far there have been only three – Grove, Parry and Allen. To these men may be added Stanford who, though not a director, did a giant's work for the college he loved. Of these men, it is my loss that I have met only Sir Hugh Allen, whose success at the college is linked with capacity for work and a genius for organisation. However, I knew much of Parry's music, and in *The Musical World* – published at Manchester, thirty years ago – I drew attention to his neglected choral works. The article was read by some members of the Hallé Orchestra. A few weeks later, whilst with a group of them, the late Simon Spielmann approached and rated me soundly for the suggestion.[8] Parry, to him and his friends, was much too

---

[7] McEwen was a very prolific composer, but seems to have written very little in the years 1924–1936: only his Thirteenth String Quartet and Sixth Violin Sonata fall into the period, with two small orchestral suites at the very end of it. After his retirement his productivity increased once more throughout the last 12 years of his life.

[8] Simon Spielmann (or Speelmann – both spellings are found, not only in Brian's writings) was a prominent Manchester musician who frequently acted as Leader of the Hallé, and sometimes conducted it when Richter was indisposed. This incident is also recounted by Reginald Nettel (*Havergal Brian: The Man and his Music*, Dobson, London, 1976, p. 48), who mis-identifies the player concerned as the violist Maurice (or Moritz)

dull for Manchester. 'Well', I said very meekly, 'will you have Bantock and Holbrooke?' This passed unheeded, so I left them saying in my most benign manner: 'But the Inter-mezzo in Parry's *Judith* ("God breaketh the battle") is a very good piece of work and a striking aria for tenor'.

Some years later I was asked to suggest a programme and a composer to a society that had won fame through its per-formances of Elgar, Bantock and Delius works.[9] I suggested Parry's *Job*, *Blest Pair of Sirens*, and the orchestral *Variations*. The Hallé Orchestra was engaged, and Parry agreed to con-duct his own works and some miscellaneous items. Among the latter was the Overture, *Raymond* (Ambroise Thomas), which probably he had never conducted before. It came on last, and the applause was deafening, during which the lib-rarian hastily gathered in the band parts. But the audience still cried Encore! so Parry bowed again, seized the parts, and then tossed them from the conductor's desk to the var-ious players. All present were highly amused, and the con-ductor no less.

Well, as I say, I never met Parry, doubtless to my great loss: but he knew enough of me, and was kind enough, to send me a copy of his book on Bach. This year of the R.C.M.[10] happens to coincide with the Brahms celebrations, and that is one reason why Parry's music is not so much in evidence in current programmes. But for many a long year he will live in the works of those whom he taught.

Spielmann, presumably a close relative. There does not appear to be any article devoted to Parry in *The Musical World* during the period in ques-tion – Brian perhaps means 'Looking Backwards: the Hallé Concerts 1904–5' (issue of 1 April 1905, p.224), a retrospective piece which includes programme suggestions, Parry among them, for future seasons.

[9] The North Staffordshire District Choral Society. The ensuing concert took place in November 1905, and was reviewed in the December number of *The Musical World* by a critic so hostile that he cannot have been Brian. A slip of the pen – or the memory – has caused Brian to separate these two incidents by 'some years' instead of a few months.

[10] The Royal College of Music was celebrating its Jubilee.

STANFORD
AND THE 'LONDONDERRY AIR'

The bulk of this item is drawn from 'On the Other Hand',
February 1935, pp. 395–396. As often happened in Brian's
column, one thing led to another, and the narrow topic of the
'Londonderry Air' broadened out into a general appraisal of
Stanford's music. Continued thoughts on the subject promp-
ted Brian to contribute a formal article, 'Charles Villiers
Stanford', to *Musical Opinion* (April 1935, p.602) – part of
which is appended here.

To appease certain non-musical friends, I propose here to
set down all I know or can deduce about the Londonderry
Air. I first heard the air in Stanford's *Irish Rhapsody* in D
minor, included in the programme of a Hallé Concert at
Manchester in 1904 or 1905, conducted by Hans Richter.[11]
Some years later I heard the *Rhapsody* again at Queen's Hall.
Although the beauty of the melody was remarked at the
time, nobody seemed inquisitive, and I for a little while
accepted a leg-pulling suggestion of an Irish friend that it
was by Stanford out of Parry. The popularity of the Londonderry Air is undoubtedly concurrent with the musical
activities of the B.B.C., whose artists have played it times
without number: until now it takes an equally prominent
place in the repertoire of that superb artist John McCor-
mack and of the most lowly street singer.

Yet the origin of the Air still eludes us. My own opinion is
that it is of no great age, and this because the leading note,
the seventh, is sharp and not flat, as is found in most traditional airs. I have not noticed this reasoning expressed
elsewhere, though the most interesting article on the history of the air, so far as it is known, appears in the last issue
of the *Journal* of the English Folk Dance and Song Society.
In the article Miss Anne G. Gilchrist tells us that the air was
first printed in a volume of Irish airs collected by George

---

[11] Probably early 1904; it was not in the 1904–5 season, the first covered
by *The Musical World*. The work in question is the first of Stanford's six
Irish Rhapsodies.

Petrie and published in Dublin in 1855.[12] It is inscribed
'name unknown', but Petrie in his notes says that the melody
reached him from a Miss Jane Ross, of New Town,
Limavady, co. Derry, who had collected others and for-
warded them to Petrie. The strange thing is that she made
no comment about this Londonderry Air other than it was
'very old'. But is it, in fact, very old? What makes me and
others doubt the alleged old age is that the melody comes
before us full grown and developed: it has not, and to our
knowledge never has had, any variants. Of equal significance is the fact that the melody first appeared unattended
by the usual story in verse; moreover, it is seen not to fit any
Irish metre. Ballad writers have since endeavoured, with
varying success, to set the melody to words.

The only conclusion I reach is that some person of name
unknown did write the lovely and immortal melody called
The Londonderry Air. Such single inspirations are not
unknown in music: and in this case I venture to suggest that
the inspiration came to Jane Ross, and that shyness alone
robbed her of fame.

The use of the Londonderry Air in the *Irish Rhapsody* set
me thinking of Stanford's other works, of the comic opera,
Shamus O'Brien, and of his choral works, *The Revenge* and
The Battle of the Baltic, also of his *Songs of the Sea*.[...]

The comic opera, *Shamus O'Brien*, is often mentioned,
and there is no reason why its first success should not be repeated and maintained. The *Irish Rhapsodies* are popular
wherever produced. His *Songs of the Sea* and *Songs of the Fleet*
are wonderful, for though Stanford was a landsman he
could give his music a true nautical touch. Of course, a man
so gifted and fortunate could and did secure publication
and performance of much large-scale music; but what was
successful at the great provincial festivals has no great
appeal after fifty years. His case is that of Sullivan, only
more so. But there is in the Stanford collection much that

---

[12] *The Petrie Collection of the Ancient Music of Ireland.* Stanford himself
edited a second edition of this monumental work in 1900. The so-called
'Londonderry Air' was, of course, set by several other composers, notably
Hamilton Harty and Percy Grainger.

will reward seekers after popular music, some of which is already in fairly frequent performance. [...] He found it comparatively easy to secure first performances in England, and was not unused to performances in Germany, following his Leipzig training and consequent friendships. *The Veiled Prophet of Khorassan* was given at Hanover in 1881. I as a youth knew a Cambridge friend of Stanford who had been present at that performance in Hanover, and he told me of the wonderful enthusiasm of the audience. The news spread to London, and off went William Boosey as emissary of the great John Boosey to offer £500 for the English rights of the opera. Yet only one performance was ever given in London – at Covent Garden. A recent perusal of the score of that opera convinced me that the enthusiasm of that German audience was well founded and the rights (from an artistic angle) well worth the publisher's offer. Stanford was twenty-nine at the time.[...]

The score discloses an Irishman's natural fondness for minor tonality. The workmanship is expert, with impetuous invention; there is a rattling good overture and a delightful ballet.[...] His second serious opera, *Savonarola*, was heard at Hamburg. His next opera, *Canterbury Pilgrims*, was produced by the Carl Rosa Company at Drury Lane, and *Much Ado About Nothing* at Covent Garden. It is not too much to say that in the scores of these operas is music far better in quality and tunefulness than has yet been found in the shreds and tatters of much we have recently heard broadcast.[...]

Stanford seems all his life to have worked on the national tunes and airs from Ireland, and consequently could have had no compunction when incorporating them into his major works. The Irish idiom persists throughout his *Irish Symphony* (Op.28), though he only made use of actual airs in the finale of that work: these tunes were 'Remember the glories of Brian the Brave' and 'Let Erin remember the days of old'.[13]

I can remember no other Irish composer who had such a wide knowledge of Irish tunes and melodies as Stanford

---

[13] There are also Irish airs in the scherzo and slow movement.

had, nor could any other musician appreciate better the quality of a tune. So when he wrote the first *Irish Rhapsody* (dedicated, by the way, to Hans Richter), he made use of a fast Irish trotting tune and the slow Londonderry Air. Richter always enjoyed a performance of this work, and from the entry of the Air with the 'cellos put an ineffable tenderness into his conducting.

I think that of all first class British composers, Stanford has been the most injured. There is enough bright music of his composition to relieve us for years from the drawing-room nothings presented with deadening reiteration in B.B.C. programmes. He had a popular success with his comic opera, *Shamus O'Brien*, which gave Granville Bantock an early chance as a conductor on tour with the company playing it. Stanford certainly got all his large scale works launched, but for reasons not to be attributed to the lack of any special quality, they did not remain long in commission. I have interested myself lately browsing over scores written by Stanford when in his twenties and thirties, and I turn from them with the conviction that they still have a bright future. His work is certainly less enterprising than that of Elgar, but he is no less sure of himself: his music does not 'date' any more than does the music of Brahms, whom Stanford is said to have set up before him as a musical idol. This idea is preposterous, for Stanford is only minutely German but mightily Irish. I do not think that nautical prejudice will explain his partial eclipse, for the mass of English people have always been markedly sympathetic to Irish music and musicians; indeed, to this sympathy I attribute in part the great popularity of the Londonderry Air. It may be that in certain exclusive circles he was not always well received. As the composer of seven operas, seven symphonies, a large number of choral, orchestral works and songs, his name should be seen frequently in concert programmes.

*   *   *

I had no idea, when recently I began to renew my interest in the music of Charles Villiers Stanford, that a biography

was being written by Plunket Greene.[14] Something must
have come to me on the air, directing my footsteps to Great
Russell Street, there to be happy on various occasions perus-
ing the scores of a musician who somehow, but quite unde-
servedly, has been elbowed aside. The new book should do
much to put these things right. Another interesting coinci-
dence is that in this present number Lieut. Colonel Dixon
should tell us how, when he was at Cambridge in the early
'nineties, he heard Plunket Greene singing Stanford's
music.[15] I also remember Plunket Greene singing well nigh
forty years ago: the thrill of Schubert's *Erl König* comes back
to me now as I then first heard it from an artist.

The book is well timed, for it will help forward what I
regard as a spontaneous revival of interest in our national
music: all seem to have sickened of the moanings and dis-
ruptions of American music which willy-nilly intrudes itself
upon us as we search for a station not distinguished by
timorous tenors lacking every spark of virility. Compare
them to the men who sang 'Father O'Flynn' in the old days,
and then wonder at the assurance of those who dare to
ridicule the ballad singers of the 'eighties. If they did sing
ballads, they could also sing Handel, which is what many of
the pets of Broadcasting House cannot do. What the old singers had was imaginative spontaneity of interpretation, and
none more so than Plunket Greene.

Plunket Greene knew Stanford intimately – at Cambridge, the Royal College of Music, and as conductor of the
Leeds Festival. At each of these places Stanford found sufficient opposition to keep his combative strength in order:
but in the end, I fear, he went down before the hosts. I cannot help thinking that Stanford lacked the diplomacy – or is
it tact? – of his contemporaries, Elgar and Bantock. A certain amount of plausibility should have replaced the excess
of pugnacity: but Stanford was all or nothing. The regrettable circumstances in Stanford's life, as in Elgar's, is that

---

[14] Harry Plunket Greene's *Charles Villiers Stanford* (Arnold, London,
1935).
[15] In a letter to the Editor on p.618 from a Lt. Col. George Dixon, a frequent correspondent on a wide range of subjects.

the fighting took place over the recumbent body of our national music, when all leaders should have done nothing that would hinder it rising. But that seems to be our fate in matters of music: nationally we never can be brought to the full belief that music by an Englishman can be quite as good as that by a foreigner. This artistic abasement extends even to dance band leaders and their supporters.

ARTHUR SULLIVAN

Brian twice devoted parts of 'On the Other Hand' to the subject of Sullivan's posthumous reputation, in May 1933 (p.683) and June 1939 (p.778). I give below the 1939 version, slightly expanded with material from 1933.

There are those frankly attached to Sullivan who consider that he merely amused himself in Savoy Opera, after he had found that it brought him the ease denied to most composers who pursue the higher but harder path. His serious works have certainly declined in popularity: but Sullivan enjoys that distinction with many other composers, English and foreign. Sullivan was great in other ways, unsupported by William Schwenk Gilbert. His anthems will be sung while the Church endures. We meet his genius in full flight in song and part-song; and among the fifty-seven hymn-tunes he wrote I signal out the setting of *Onward, Christian Soldiers* as music that will inspire when all opera lies in the dust.

His birth was humble enough, and I do not propose to explain his genius or why he became so enormously successful against his own nature. There is no doubt that Sullivan set his heart on winning a place amongst the great masters of serious music, and his achievements in this direction had established his fame in England and Germany before he turned to the composition of an art then considered frivolous, now established as a classic. Those of us who, in our youth, sang in anthems by Sullivan, or his processional hymn, or the oratorios *Light of the World* and *Martyr of Antioch*, were conscious of uplifting and stimulating music.

We were unconscious then of the transitory nature of things or that in a few years all would pass away, save for *Onward, Christian Soldiers.* The distance of time in the number of years is but a puff of smoke since the evenings when the newest excitement in choral music was the opening of Sullivan's *The Golden Legend,* depicting a storm with Lucifer and his devils on the tower of Strassburg Cathedral.[16] It is not Sullivan's fault that all this now strikes us as being as pantomimic as the performance of the water sprites in Smart's *Bride of Dunkerron,*[17] and it is impossible to believe that a future revival can replace that work where it stood without the return of the Victorian era and its atmosphere of glorious serenity. Some of Sullivan's finest work is contained in his opera *Ivanhoe,* the Symphony in E, the Violoncello Concerto, his two overtures, and some very beautiful suites of Incidental Music written to Shakespeare and other plays. His great reputation may save these works from oblivion, though it has not saved them from a gradual decline.

A few years ago Sullivan's Overture, *In Memoriam,* was one of the most popular works in the orchestral repertoire; to-day it is rarely heard. On the other hand, Sullivan had an instinctive genius for catching the public ear. He appeared to do it easily. Such songs as *The Lost Chord, Sailor's Grave* and a host of others served their purpose in cementing social cordiality, and were vehicles on which an army of contraltos and tenors attempted to ride to success. Elgar tried hard, as other serious composers have done, to win success by writing popular ballad songs and published many, but he never won half Sullivan's popularity.

From the fatal decline which habitually attacks 'period' music in every country in every age, Sullivan would have but an insignificant reputation with the present generation but for the accident which brought together himself and

[16] Brian contributed a long and lively review of a local performance of *The Golden Legend* to *The Staffordshire Sentinel* of 15 March 1910.

[17] The reference is to the Victorian oratorio by Henry Thomas Smart (1813–1879); Brian heard it at the North Staffordshire Triennial Festival of 1893.

William Schwenk Gilbert. The history of that association permanently maintains in the series of comic masterpieces which we cherish under the name of 'Savoy Opera'. Here is something indubitably English and having all the national characteristics of *savoir faire* and subtlety; something which no other nation possesses: superior to Johann Strauss or Offenbach.

Composer and librettist are inseparable: as to whether in Savoy opera the prize should go to Sullivan or to Gilbert, I do not care to discuss, save to say that Gilbert stands in increasing need of annotation, while Sullivan sails along smoothly, unaffected by eddying currents of fashion and folly. Gilbert was no Sheridan. Those who in England run after the Savoy operas are certainly attracted for the greater part by Sullivan's music, which 'dates' very slowly. His music is a facile blend, showing Irish ancestry and his absorption in English life. No English composer was ever more cosmopolitan in his outlook, nor had any other such a gift of sparkling melody. In this respect he rivals the composer on whom he set his heart, Franz Schubert.

I would like to recall Sullivan's geniality and kindness to his fellows. I have no fortunate recollections of him at the Leeds Festival which he conducted for fifteen years, or of the National School of Music (now the Royal College of Music) which he helped establish and was its first principal. All this was before my time.

So many instances of Sullivan's unselfishness and his regard for others are known: I will add one of which John Coates told me, that is not so well known.[18] During the excitement of the South African War *The Daily Mail* induced Kipling to write a patriotic poem which he called *The Absent-minded Beggar*. It was immediately set to music by Sullivan; then a singer was wanted. *The Daily Mail* recommended John Coates who had already made a reputation as a baritone; but during a world tour of *The Geisha*[19] his

[18] The famous tenor John Coates (1865–1941) was a lifelong friend of Brian's and one of the artists he admired most. We will hear more of him in subsequent volumes.
[19] Once popular operetta (first staged 1896) by Sidney Jones (1861–1946).

voice developed upwards – like Jean de Reszke's – and he finished the tour as a tenor robusto. On his arrival at Sir Arthur's flat, Coates met the composer who, with a twinkle in his eye, explained that his setting was for a tenor, and patted the singer on the back saying 'You are a baritone'. Coates persuaded Sullivan to hear him, and the composer played the piano accompaniment. Delighted and surprised, Sir Arthur said he was just the man he wanted. Hence in a few nights John Coates was travelling the halls of London enthusing audiences with his singing of *The Absent-minded Beggar*. Such was a famous singer's odd introduction to his career *via* Sir Arthur Sullivan.

PART THREE
ELGAR

━━━━━━━━━━━━━━━◆▬▬▬▬━━━━━━━━━━━━

Brian probably wrote more often about Elgar than about any other composer, and I have thought it appropriate to give a generous selection. The first performance of *King Olaf*, at the 1896 Staffordshire Triennial Festival, was the crucial experience which quickened his resolve to become a composer. The encouragement he received from Elgar over the next decade was immensely important to him, and his personal involvement in bringing about the second (and first truly successful) English performances of *The Dream of Gerontius*, in Manchester and the Potteries in 1903, increased his sense of a bond between them. By recommending Brian's partsong *Shall I compare thee to a Summer's day?* to the committee of the Morecambe Festival Elgar secured Brian his first prestigious performance and his first publication; and Brian was his guest at the Worcester Three Choirs Festival of 1905, another event which left an indelible memory.

'Elgar at that time meant far more to me than any *other* man dead or alive', Brian recalled in 1937, writing to his friend Walter Allum. But after the 1909 Musical League Festival they did not meet again, and Elgar ceased to answer Brian's letters when he was trying to scrape a living in London in 1914. In subsequent years they corresponded a little, but Elgar remained distant, although he gave Brian some arranging work in the early 1920s. As we now know from Michael Kennedy's *Portrait of Elgar*, Brian was not the only one to experience a seeming rejection, and not to understand – at the time – that Elgar felt his friends had deserted *him*. As a result his writings, while full of love for the music (his admiration was nevertheless not wholly uncritical, as we see from 'The Elgar Manifesto'), sometimes display an ambivalence about the man – which is perhaps especially and painfully acute in the remarkable obituary essay. In the following years, however, prompted by the appearance of several books on Elgar, Brian became increasingly fascinated by,

and sympathetic to, the complexities of his character. The letter to Allum quoted above continues: 'If we drifted & relations became less cordial, well, it was my fault...'.

Enigma at the Hallé

This is one of Brian's earliest concert reviews, for *The Musical
World* (11 February 1905, p.101).

The *Enigma Variations* by Elgar must always be regarded by
the English musical public as a novelty on account of their
historical importance. They have served the purpose of
drawing attention to the great genius of the composer and
the fact that there has arisen in England a school of composition quite independent in thought from any of its contemporaries, at the head of which stands Sir Edward Elgar.
Surely no one present at their first production at a London
Richter Concert a few years ago would have predicted that
in so short a time from their first hearing they would have
found their way into almost every musical centre in Europe
and America where there exists an orchestra capable of
playing them! Dr. Richter's faith in the genius of Elgar (as
seen in his persistence at the outset of the career of the *Variations*) has since become the faith of all serious musicians
who can independently and discriminately appreciate the
highest in art.

Elgar with his *Variations* score might have repeated Beethoven who said of a particular work 'It will wash', for it
improves each time of hearing. There is something unique
in these *Variations*. No matter whether it be in form or colouring, they are all intensely original, while the whole work
is saturated with the Elgarian expression. And what a
gamut of expression *is* Elgar's! Sentimentality, humour,
satire – indeed, everything from a gossamer-like weaving to
brusqueness follow on the top of each other, and in what a
remarkable manner Elgar handles the orchestra! In his
hands the orchestra becomes a new instrument, giving
forth an entirely new rainbow of orchestral colouring – the
Elgarian. The *Variations* were superbly played: none calls for

special remark, except perhaps for the solemn impressive-
ness of the 'Nimrod', and the fine singing tone of the 'cellos
in the Twelfth Variation; also the silvery tone of the brass in
the Eleventh Variation and Finale.

The Apostles in Hanley

Another early *Musical World* review (8 April 1905, pp. 247–
248). The performance in question was one of the many
important concerts given by the North Staffordshire District
Choral Society as trained by James Whewall, of whom more
is said in Part Ten.

Elgar's oratorio *The Apostles* was given in the Victoria Hall,
Hanley, on the 30th ult. by the North Staffs. District Choral
Society. It was its first representation in the district, and
expectancy ran high for some time prior to the event as to
the impression the work would make in performance. Criticism had been passed by the neophytes, suggesting that the
work was devoid of melody. Expressions had been used
which are not infrequently heard when Richard Strauss is
under discussion. Of melody in *The Apostles* there is a rich
abundance; indeed, so thickly is it strewn with melody that
one is hardly conscious of it at all – giving rise to the suggestion that 'an influence which can be forgotten becomes
omnipotent'. We are living in an age when definite expression in sound is becoming realised. The days of pretty
melodies for melody's sake, and oratorios with set airs and
choruses, are passing away; henceforth they must sink into
a whole scheme of expression to convey impression. Elgar
has done this in an unmistakable manner in his oratorio *The
Apostles*. Melodies cannot be picked out here and there with
the usual 'This is nice!' or 'That is pretty!' – they must be
judged as they lie in the whole mass. As to the performance,
it can only be described in glowing terms. The whole district
rose to the occasion, the large hall being packed, and many
unable to obtain admission.

The choir, which was responsible for the choral portion,
has had a brilliant career. Originally coming into existence

for competitive purposes, it has on three occasions won the
Blue Ribbon at the Welsh National Eisteddfodau, and, several years ago, made a deep impression with performances
of *The Dream of Gerontius* in Hanley and London. The vocal
tone-colour is of a rich hue, not met with elsewhere. For several months this choir worked hard with a view to obtaining
perfection on the day of performance. That has been
realised, it having gone forth from composer and principals
that the performance was the finest yet experienced.
Undoubtedly this rests upon the remarkable manner in
which the chorus had been trained. Undoubtedly this is the
secret of their success. The chorus director, Mr. James
Whewall, is one of the few conductors who can infuse inspiration into his vocalists, thereby drawing out all the poetical
content of whatever they may be singing. This unique body
of vocalists sings with that beautiful polish only to be found
in the best orchestras, while by their facial expression they
show that they are completely under the influence of the
composer. Taking this into account, it is not surprising that
the rendering of *The Apostles* made a deep impression. A
perfect choir, the Hallé Orchestra, and principals selected
by the composer could but have one fine result.

Perhaps never before has Sir Edward Elgar drawn so well
on an audience: it was a remarkable sight to look over it and
observe the solemn expression on every face throughout
the performance. Each succeeding scene was well portrayed. Points made by the composer in 'The Tower of Magdala' and the character of Judas Iscariot became clearer
than ever before. Mrs. Henry J. Wood as the Angel and the
Virgin sang with all the necessary emotional touches and
purest vocal art. Her representation of the broken-hearted
Mary 'at the foot of the Cross' was most affecting and real.
Miss Muriel Foster as Mary Magdalene brought out the
character in full by her *abandon*, helplessness, and remorse.
Her full conception of the idea in the 'Fantasy' was made
more perfect by the way in which the fleeting vision was
suggested by choir and orchestra. It was one of many thrilling moments. The recitation of the 'Beatitudes' by Mr.
Ffrançon Davies was most impressive and solemn, being
listened to in breathless silence, the choir as 'Apostles'

intensifying the rendering by their interpolations and reflections. Mr. W. J. Ineson as Peter sang in a manner which clearly suggested that fearless disciple, his indication of Peter 'walking on the sea' and the denial of Christ in the house of the High Priest was well drawn, while the suggestion of Christ rebuking Peter, given to divided soprani and contralti, was sung in a manner which can never be effaced from the memory of those who listened to it. The rendering of 'Turn you to the Stronghold' was a triumph in expression for choir, principals, and orchestra alike. Mr. Gervase Elwes made his first appearance in this work at this performance, and as the Apostle John fully realised all the importance of that character. Perhaps his best work was done in the scene with Mary at the foot of the Cross. One of the most remarkable displays of Elgar's original genius is to be found in his delineation of the character of Judas in *The Apostles*. To fully realise it, it is possible only with such an artist as Mr. Andrew Black, and a choir who can alternately give the haunting suggestions of the scenes outside and within the Temple. The expression was finely brought out at this performance; never before has a chorus risen to such a height of realisation of this scene, while Mr. Andrew Black's description of the cunning and dejected Judas, ever driven as before his inner thoughts – with its bitter orchestral undercurrent – was impressively worked out. In the scene at the Sepulchre the 'Alleluias' of the Angels (given to divided soprani and contralti) were most delicately given and sounded as though suspended from above. The scenes in the Finale, which are suggested as proceeding simultaneously, 'On Earth' and 'In Heaven', were well portrayed, the glow of orchestral and vocal tone-colour, which moves into a long *crescendo*, ending in one of the finest climaxes ever written, was powerful indeed: the stupendous mass of glistening sound at the climax will never be forgotten by those who were privileged to hear it.

An outburst of enthusiasm from the audience followed its close, the composer receiving a long-continued ovation, which was also extended to Mr. James Whewall, whose artistic work with the choir was the outstanding feature in this perfect performance. It was a great event, and the honour remains with the spirit which dominates this young and brilliant society. If they continue to maintain the present high level, they will before long secure a world-wide reputation. There must be no falling away from such a high artistic standing.

'The Elgar Manifesto'

Most of p.504 of the March 1931 edition of *Musical Opinion* was occupied by a declaration which appeared under the headline 'Sir Edward Elgar: MUSICIANS' PROTEST AGAINST PROFESSOR E.J. DENT'S ALLEGED INJUSTICE'. The 'Protest' had been distributed by the Press Association to the editors of leading English and German newspapers. Its authors declared that they wished 'to record an emphatic protest against the unjust and inadequate treatment of Sir Edward Elgar by Professor Dent in his article on "Modern English Music" in Adler's monumental *Handbuch der Musikgeschichte* (second enlarged edition, 1930). [...] the learned professor devotes 66 lines to Parry, 41 to Stanford and only 16 to Elgar. [...] the statement that "for English ears, Elgar's music is much too emotional and not free from vulgarity", the summary dismissal of all his orchestral works as "lively in colour but pompous in style and of a too deliberate nobility of expression", [...] cannot go unchallenged. [...] the works of Elgar [...] are held in the highest honour by the majority of English musicians and the musical public. [...] Professor Dent's failure to appreciate Elgar's music [...] does not justify him in grossly misrepresenting [...] the esteem in which he is held by his countrymen'. There followed a list of signatories – among them Leslie Heward, Beatrice Harrison, Hamilton Harty, John Ireland, Augustus John, E. J. Moeran, Landon Ronald, Albert Sammons, George Bernard Shaw, William Walton and Peter Warlock; a postscript from Shaw likening Elgar to Beethoven and ridiculing Parry and Stanford; and a translation of the offending 16 lines.

On the facing page, placed there no doubt for maximum effect, there appeared a dissenting voice of commonsense from *Musical Opinion*'s frequent correspondent 'H.B.', couched in the form of a Letter to the Editor:

SIR, — I should be obliged if you would allow me to comment on what I think is a blunder in issuing the public protest, no matter by whom it may be signed. Elgar needs no such defence. The question of space is trite. Surely those who would measure mind by inches are not worthy of our consideration: so it matters little what can be found or not found in a German History of Music. After all, Professor Dent has done as much for English music and musicians as any one of the gentlemen who have signed the protest.

However, what the signatories have done is to open an old grievance. Many of those of the Schools have never really liked Elgar: and that because he had succeeded without their benison. Elgar certainly had no intention of slighting them: he, like most of us, was a creature of circumstances. At the time when his little work, *Lux Christi*, appeared, the Schools had the field of public performance almost entirely to themselves and yet here was a man, unheralded and unknown, succeeding with a new idiom in British music, and with something that was adjudged better than anything hitherto prevailing. But it was no fault of Elgar that the music of his older contemporaries should soon be regarded as dull and faded, and fit company only for piles of *Kapellmeister* music.

The highly strung and luminous quality of Elgar's music, which obscured much of that by contemporary writers, led also to depreciative and unreasonable criticism. But Elgar cannot justly be held responsible for that. Certainly injustice was done to the work of Mackenzie, Parry and Stanford by those who flocked to the new banner that had been unfurled. It had a portent of greater daring and more enterprise: the idiom seemed more popular: and the older men came to be looked upon as at least uninspired.

After all, there was nothing unusual in this movement: such things have taken place after the birth of many artistic and social impulses. History abounds in such incidents: and consequently I am surprised that George Bernard Shaw, who at least knows something of music, should be concerned about Professor Dent's criticism. Musical criticism, even of the very best, seems to attract little public attention and has practically no influence. It was not by favourable and friendly criticism that Elgar came to be regarded as the greatest English composer of his time: he attained his high position through the workings of his own genius and the happy chance of being able to secure performances of his works as he wrote them. Perhaps the happy chance does not today recur so frequently: but the light of his genius is as bright as ever.

Some days ago I was reading a letter in which it was suggested that Richter's attitude towards Elgar was ironical. I do not agree, for Richter was an honourable man. At the conclusion of the first performance of Elgar's *Gerontius* at the Birmingham Festival, which Richter conducted, an out-cry arose against the alleged extravagant orchestral demands and the novelty of the choral technique, which somewhat dismayed the festival chorus. Richter was quick to respond, writing in Elgar's full score: 'Let drop the chorus: let drop everything: but never let drop your own original genius!' Richter's attitude in the years that followed was consistent with his modest, restrained hero worship. I have seen him rehearse *Gerontius* with the score before him: but he only used it for reference, and for long intervals not at all. Richter was supported in his attitude towards Elgar by a public that was world wide. This support of Richter does not destroy the criticism of Professor Dent. Not all Elgar's music was valued by Richter. Dent is not the first to allude to the bombastic tone pervading some of his popular works.

H.B.

February 15, 1931.

Sheldon's *Elgar*

Brian's Introduction to A. J. Sheldon's *Edward Elgar*, published in book form by *Musical Opinion* (London, 1932) as a memorial to its late contributor.

The chapters making this book originally appeared, some six years ago, as articles in *Musical Opinion*. Reference to them has since been made in other articles dealing with Elgar and his music, and consequently it has been thought that some service would be given to the subject by present-ing them in the present form. The writer was the late A. J. Sheldon, at one time music critic of *The Birmingham Daily*

Post and for many years a writer under the pseudonym of 'Schaunard' in *Musical Opinion*. He evidently had no intention of treating his subject in the form of a book: and thus there is no intention that the present re-issue of the articles shall be considered as something in competition with the works of Buckley and Ernest Newman,[1] both of which are excellent in different ways. Sheldon's work is doubtless discursive: but it covers very completely all Elgar's important works. It is unquestionably an excellent supplement to the books mentioned. Sheldon writes of Elgar as his musical hero: but while he is often overpowering in his enthusiasm, he never shows less than real love for his hero's music. This zeal or earnestness occasionally led him astray. Many will disagree with the statement in the first chapter, 'But who will allege that in the transfiguration section of Strauss's poem, we get any sense of transfiguration at all'. Sheldon did not know that Strauss's Transfiguration was akin to that of Elgar. In point of fact, one was born of the other. The late A. J. Jaeger told the present writer many years ago that the Passage to the Presence did not exist in the early manuscript of *Gerontius*. Jaeger suggested the episode to Elgar, who only agreed when shown that Strauss had already done it.[2]

Sheldon conceived his first love for Elgar during a performance of *The Dream of Gerontius* when he was a singer in the Hallé Choir. Though he did not quite understand what it was that thrilled him, his mental perception and musical understanding of the work developed simultaneously. In a little while Sheldon could from analysis discover what it was that had moved him: but more, he could write on his subject with a fine grasp of its true meaning and significance.

[1] R. J. Buckley, *Sir Edward Elgar*, John Lane, London, 1912; Ernest Newman, *Edward Elgar*, John Lane, London 1905.
[2] Michael Kennedy, in *Portrait of Elgar* (Oxford University Press, 1968, revised edn. 1982, pp.108–112), chronicles Elgar's and Jaeger's exchanges by letter over this passage. He makes the point that, in acceding to Jaeger's suggestion, Elgar was in fact reverting to his original conception of the work. Jaeger seems to have made only the most passing reference to Strauss; but the correspondence was not yet published at the time Brian was writing, and Jaeger may of course have remembered – and told – things differently.

It was just that attention should be drawn to Elgar's kinship with César Franck. There is also another composer, the
late Philipp Wolfrum (almost unknown in this country),
who for some years, doubtless unconsciously, held a
charmed sway over the mind of Elgar. I refer to those years
that preceded the production of *Gerontius*. It is impossible to
avoid this suggestion when we have before us certain organ
works by Wolfrum, or the very beautiful choral and orchestral work known as *Ein Weihnachtsmysterium*. The 'dreaming'
of Elgar that so fascinated Sheldon belongs to that same
dream-world in which Wolfrum's mind dwelt. We see it in all
its fulness in the song of the Virgin watching over her sleeping newborn babe, which is the centrepiece of that work.
The spirit that was Wolfrum's had come to Elgar, and we see
him conducting Wolfrum's oratorio at Worcester in the late
'nineties.[3]

Though there may be disagreement over several of Sheldon's comparisons of Strauss and Elgar, few will dissent
from his summing up of Elgar. Elgar is the fulfilment of the
dawn promised by Parry, Stanford, Mackenzie, Smart, and
even Barnby.[4] Elgar also, as is shown, must have felt the
influence of certain German composers: but his own pre-
cious individuality was too strong to be overborne by any of
them. This may be due to the fact of Elgar's ancestry: the
distinctive clarity of his texture, the peculiar cast of his
dream, neither has any kinship with that of his English contemporaries. Elgar has always been insistent on his remote
Scandinavian origin. The name Elgar will be recognised in
the form of Oelgar, Algar, and Helgar. Its interpretation is
the heroic Faery Spear. There are many who dispute the
influence of racial persistence through the centuries; but,

[3] Philipp Wolfrum (1854–1919) was chiefly noted for his choral music.
There is an anomaly here, as his *Weihnachtsmysterium* is generally listed as
having been completed only in 1899 and introduced into England at the
1903 Hereford Festival. But Wolfrum and Elgar certainly knew each
other; Brian may be thinking of an earlier work. He himself much
admired the *Weihnachtsmysterium*, and possessed a copy of it.
[4] Sir Joseph Barnby (1838–1896), prolific composer of glees – including
the once phenomenally popular *Sweet and Low* – and hymns, Principal of
the Guildhall School of Music.

not wholly without reason, there are our admittedly ancient
families who hang their pride in ancestral portrait galleries.
Compare the portrait by Velasquez of Philip II of Spain at
the National Gallery with the portraits current of King
Alphonso, or that of Frederick the Great with pictures of
the Emperor William II. If such resemblances are to be
traced during two or three centuries, why not for a
thousand or even two thousand years? Facial and other
characteristics persist and have their influence. Who can say
how many centuries are needed for the chrysalis of a great
composer to develop before it emerges complete and ripe
with the fascinating wonder and individuality found in the
few men of genius who have lived during the past few centuries? Each has an imprint that is easily recognisable, even
though it be only in a thing as simple as a modest cadence.
Elgar has this distinct and personal quality. It may be the
Scandinavian languor of the part song, *My love dwelt in a
Northern land*, or the hauntingly beautiful introduction to
King Olaf. Neither of these can be regarded as 'typically
English'; and this fascinating strain, so highly charged with
Scandinavian wistfulness, ebbs and flows through all Elgar's
music. When opportunity offers it never fails to scale the
heroic heights attained by exceptional masters.

This distinctive quality is the hall-mark of Elgar's genius.
One may take any part song by any English composer, and
by placing it beside almost any part song by Elgar, perceive
how, even in the way of simple chordal expression, Elgar's
touch is fresher and brighter than that of his contemporaries. This is a quality that cannot be taught in the class
room or captured by admirers: it persists, sometimes stead-
ily, as in the slow movements of the two symphonies, or with
a frenzied, almost uncontrollable impulse, as in the more
excitable moments of the choral works, the first movements
of the symphonies, and particularly in the early masterpiece, the *Enigma Variations*, which contains all the finest
characteristics of the composer's genius.

In his idiom and orchestral sensing, Elgar is indisputably
his own master. His ensembles are not like those of any
other composer. In his instrumentation, he treats each
instrument as his own familiar friend. Writing for brass and

strings, he is most daring and expert. The clarity of the harmonic tissue of his simple part songs is a characteristic of his orchestral writing. His finest efforts are amazing masterpieces – the revelation of an aptitude and relish for pursuing what is his greatest pleasure, composition.

When *The Dream of Gerontius* was becoming known, in the early years of its career, extraordinary tributes were paid to the originality of the work. Its inspiration was referred to as being transcendental and at white heat, equalled only by such works as Tchaïkovsky's *Francesca da Rimini*, Wagner's *Parsifal*, &c.

There are many qualities in Elgar's music. If only England had been a country of opera houses instead of concert rooms and choral societies, which are the conditions that have definitely and permanently influenced Elgar's music, he might have left a permanent impression on opera. There are two instances – the Death of Ironbeard in *King Olaf*, and the Angel of the Agony in *Gerontius* – which show Elgar as skilful in the art of characterisation, and equal to similar supreme moments in the operas of Richard Wagner.

We have to be thankful for what Elgar has been and is: the finest and most original English composer since the Elizabethans. Indeed, he has been more, for he was the means of reviving the quest of musical composition among his contemporaries, and he is for ever an inspiration to younger men.

'Land of Hope and Glory'

From 'On the Other Hand' in *Musical Opinion*, October 1932, p.16, and November 1932, p.116.

I should like to hear Elgar thinking aloud about his brilliant Military Marches and the wonderful success of the Trio of the first, in D. The first two were first played by the Liverpool Orchestral Society in October, 1901. Later the trio was adjusted to some verses by A.C. Benson, a Cambridge don and son of the Archbishop of that name. Under the title of 'Land of Hope and Glory', away went the trio round the world, being sung with fervour wherever the English language is spoken. It may be that the sentiment is merely symbolical, but as sung and applied to England, the words are sinister in the extreme: they would amply justify any charge of hypocrisy made against us. How can the Mother of the Free, made mighty by God, extend her bounds except at the pain of those who have not the benign blessing of might? 'Britannia, rule the waves' is a mild boast beside these dreadful words, and has the excuse of being an exhortation to Britons to repel those who would enslave them.

*　　　*　　　*

My disparagement of the words of the patriotic song, 'Land of Hope and Glory', appears to have upset the complacency of some readers. That does not trouble me, for some researches suggest to me that Benson himself had a very poor opinion of the verses by which he seems destined only to be known to the man in the street.[...]It is curious that a mind like Benson's, unusually placid and the quintessence of fastidiousness, could have produced the lines used for the song. For reasons best known to himself, they do not appear in any printed collection of his poems.[...]

An Elgar Biography

The first of several important books on Elgar to appear in the 1930s was the study by the Rev. Basil Maine (1894– 1972) – who, as a monthly contributor to *Musical Opinion*, was Brian's colleague and friend. They remained in contact until the mid-1950s: Maine, himself a composer of songs and choral pieces, sometimes consulted Brian on points of technique, and Brian is known to have orchestrated a *Te Deum* of Maine's, although the manuscript has not been found. Brian reviewed Maine's Elgar book in the June 1933 issue of *Musical Opinion* (pp. 777 – 778), and also used it as the point of departure for his 'On the Other Hand' column in the same issue (pp. 763–764). It is this latter treatment I give here.

Basil Maine's two-volume Life of Elgar[5] is a distinguished and brilliant offering in acknowledgment of a great career,

[5] *Elgar: His Life and Works*, Vols. I and II, Bell's Musical Publications, London, 1933 – the first 'official' biography of Elgar.

and I hope an earnest of what the author will do for music in the years to come. His other literary work has shown promise and fulfilment. As it happens, my own years of musical appreciation seem to begin with the first performance of *King Olaf* at Hanley: I remember it well, for some crossgrained fellow behind admonished me severely for persisting in a demonstration of approval at the end. My imagination had been fired. I had previously borrowed from a chorus singer his copy of the music: and here I was far more thrilled than I had been when I heard for the first time Berlioz's *Faust*, Schumann's *Paradise and the Peri*, Verdi's *Requiem*, and Wagner's *Lohengrin*.

King Olaf, by the then unknown composer Elgar, was and is a wonderful inspiration, and unblushingly emotional. Mr. Maine tells us that it was written and produced when Elgar was in indifferent health. I can confirm this, for as he walked to the conductor's desk he looked too frail for the task and seemed at times as though he did not know the score. The audience was small, and on that cold foggy morning could be said to reflect the general atmosphere. The orchestra had been drawn from London, Manchester and Birmingham, and was led by Willy Hess. The principals were Medora Henson (soprano), Edward Lloyd (tenor), and Ffrangçon Davies (bass). But Lloyd, owing to a train mishap, had missed the final rehearsal, an omission that nearly wrecked the performance at 'And King Olaf saw the light' (sung by Lloyd). Disaster was saved by Willy Hess, for whose grasp and intuition Elgar always expressed himself as very grateful. At the close, however, the small audience, chorus and orchestra rose and acclaimed the composer, for they knew in their hearts that they had assisted in making history.

It was Swinnerton Heap's enthusiastic pleading before the committee of the North Staffordshire Festival that led to the production of *King Olaf*, and the faith that was in him came from his having heard Elgar's first orchestral piece, *Intermezzo*, played at one of Stockley's concerts at Birmingham.[6] Elgar had no such champion in Leeds: and I do not

---

[6] The *Intermezzo* (originally *Intermezzo Mauresque*), second movement of

accept the suggestion that, had *King Olaf* been produced there, recognition would have come to Elgar two years earlier.

Recognition of Elgar was rapid when his genius was supported by Hans Richter, the conductor, and by August J. Jaeger, who was a tower of strength at Novello's. Mr. Maine quotes letters showing how deep was the affection between composer and conductor. I did not know Richter well; but with Jaeger, after I had been introduced to him by Lady Elgar at a Three Choirs Festival, I continued on friendly terms until his death. He pleased me greatly by his frank opinions, his ebullient enthusiasm for music, and his perfect sincerity. Jaeger was one of the best friends the British composer ever had.

Jaeger became Elgar's friend at a time that was critical for the composer. There is no doubt that it was he who took the manuscript score of the *Enigma Variations* to Richter, who did not wait to produce them. It was due to Jaeger that Germany's salutation to Elgar was so generous and warmhearted. Many speak of the happy state of Elgar in having had so many fine singers and instrumentalists to interpret his works; but he has been no less happy in his friendships.

---

the Suite in D of 1882–3, was neither Elgar's 'first orchestral piece' nor the first to be performed, but this was certainly Elgar's earliest orchestral performance of any consequence. W. C. Stockley, conductor of the Birmingham Festival, introduced the *Intermezzo* on 13 December 1883, and also premiered the entire suite in 1888.

The March 1934 issue of *Musical Opinion* led with Brian's obituary of Elgar (pp. 493–494).

Edward Elgar
1857–1934

It was with deep regret that the world learned on the morning of Friday, February 23rd, that Edward William Elgar, after a long and painful illness, had passed away. He leaves us full of honour, and the world of music will feel the loss intensely. None more than he has carried the standard of musicianship higher or borne the dual role of man and musician with greater dignity.

Many are come to speak well of Elgar, for that is easy now that he lies in death: but I come to speak only of him as I knew him in early years and as I saw him in more recent times walking with the great. Not that he had changed more than his age would warrant: he carried always a sense of imperturbable dignity that varied little whether he was bored by the importunities of a young composer or was stung by the rebuffs of those who while they lived could not concede the position that his genius demanded. They are gone, and as musicians are well-nigh forgotten; Elgar also is gone, but the sound of his music and his influence on the art goes echoing throughout the land, in a great sweep, forever onward.

Nature was doubly kind to Elgar, for while endowing him with a rich genius, she had also girded him about with the stout armour of defence, or it may be only a keen sense of self-preservation; but, whatever it was, he never found himself, like so many equally able creative musicians, alone or in want.

Doubtless, much of what Elgar has written will pass away and the first to go should be that which Dent looked at with so cold an eye, and which led to the undignified protest. Yet Dent was right. A difficulty I have never solved remains. The music in question came at a time when a great political apostasy was sweeping over the Midlands: all Elgar's thoughts and bearing were in sympathy with the party that changed over, and need we wonder that he gave something of his best to further the cause he had deeply at heart.[7] Instinctively also he chose well for his personal position, for afterwards neither sling nor arrow could reach him. The composer of the new and fervid national anthem was favoured by the highest in the land, and from that fact came to the man-in-the-street the invincible conviction that Elgar was a great genius. But the music that was to carry him to the Pantheon and to place him in the brotherhood of Purcell was not of this type. I first found it in *King Olaf*.

There is good reason to believe that Edward Elgar would not follow any movement farther than he himself wished or thought it wise to go. He was first and always a musician, but with a wide vision that could take in other arts and sciences. He could not be bound body and soul to any party or section. In Manchester, in 1908, a persistent rumour went the rounds that the First Symphony was to be dedicated to General Gordon. Perhaps the rumour was the work of injudicious friends, or maybe it was only an unintelligent appreciation of events coming from the known fact that the

[7] For the 'undignified protest' see 'The Elgar Manifesto', pp.70–72. As for the 'great political apostasy', Brian is presumably referring to the traumatic schism in the Liberal Party in the 1880s and '90s, although Elgar is generally reckoned to have been a Conservative. The rebellion of the Liberal right wing, led by Joseph Chamberlain, was occasioned by the issue of Home Rule for Ireland. These 'Liberal Unionists' voted with the Conservatives and put up electoral candidates against the official Liberal ones. Whatever Elgar's views may have been on the Irish Question, he was doubtless more in sympathy with the strain of Liberal Imperialism which eventually, almost as a by-product, came to dominate the Party.

symphony was cast in a heroic mould. Elgar, however, had no intention to fall for an idea that would have pinned him to a party; so in an article in *The Daily Telegraph*, which paper at the time published all that was authentic about Elgar, we find the rumour described as ridiculous, followed by the statement that the dedication was to Hans Richter. Had Elgar at the time heard of the reward that came to Brahms for his child-like faith in Bismarck?

Elgar's attitude to the critics is difficult to reconcile: it was at one time, in the case of the London men, tinged with a certain provincial despite, and with reason, for much better men were then writing in the counties than in the capital. In a Birmingham lecture Elgar described London music critics as sleepy, woolly-headed, devoid of imagination, and totally lacking in any ability that would enable them to 'spot a winner'. It is useless trying to smooth away anything Elgar said: he always meant to be taken seriously, and spoke strongly for that reason. He probably thought better of London music critics when the best men of the north migrated south. Kalisch[8] and Elgar must have collaborated to produce a whole newspaper page of thematic quotations and verbal analysis to herald the production of *The Apostles*. A London editor of to-day would gasp at any such suggestion from his music critic. They might favourably consider or even demand a couple of columns about the very last farewell appearance of a popular singer.

Thus we see Elgar as no simple-minded musician: he was never the dupe of any flatterer. On the contrary, he was always strong enough to make his own way. He was mostly judiciously silent, speaking only through the medium of one journalist at a time. I can recall a succession of at least five such men, and I invariably knew where to look for knowledge of what Elgar was doing and what he was thinking.

Despite this instinctive shrewdness, Elgar was essentially a kind man. Another rumour, based on this fact, was that

---

[8] Alfred Kalisch (1863–1933), critic, translator, and musicologist; one of the first champions of Richard Strauss' music in England. Brian's recollections of him will appear in a future volume of selections.

he, in the case of William Wolstenholme, the blind organist and composer, had acted as his amanuensis at a certain examination. Elgar at length denied the kind impeachment, but added that he would gladly have done so had the opportunity been his. This is true, for it accords with the help he gave during many years to young composers who had the temerity to forward their manuscripts to him. Lady Elgar told me that Sir Edward and herself would devote hours to a consideration of these works, she playing and he listening attentively. But, unfortunately, only occasionally was he roused, when he would exclaim: 'Ah, here is real music. Who is he?'[9]

Perhaps I am wrong when I look on Elgar as a man fighting for himself. 'The composer' may well have been all composers. When he did speak, he spoke with a purpose. Addressing 'My Lord Mayor' at Liverpool, on the occasion of the festival of the Musical League,[10] he deplored the fact of the lack of recognition of English composers in this country. 'Too often', he said, 'had that recognition come first from abroad. It was almost impossible for a composer to get any commercial return for a serious orchestral work which would keep him in bread and cheese; and it was imperative from the composer's point of view that people should be educated up to the point of appreciating their own composers.' Well, twenty-five years have passed since that memorable festival took place. Fortuitous circumstances came to the aid of Elgar, but in the main the English composer remains in the position he occupied in 1908.

One other aspect of Elgar's activities shows how he was at once encouraging and discouraging. During the short time he held the Peyton Professorship of Music at Birmingham University he was in rebellion against himself and the fate that took him to the class-room. He might have done more for English music had he stuck to his guns: but he went.

---

[9] Lady Elgar had in fact told Brian that these were the words which Elgar used when she first played over to him an early anthem of Brian's.
[10] At luncheon in the Town Hall on 25 September 1909. Elgar was President of the League, although his own works were not represented in the Festival.

Still, he did give a series of lectures that were original, fearless and open-minded. They reflected what could be seen in *King Olaf*, and that was not composition as then taught in the schools. His indictment was scathing: and he demanded that music should be considered and treated from its only possible angle, as an art of sound: not as something to be written on paper according to rules laid down. The result might be quite beautiful to look upon, but it was not music. The lectures may have borne fruit: but more likely the changes we now see in the teaching of composition are the result of study of Elgar's own remarkable works. In any case, Elgar broke down the barrier that encircled artificial music and reduced it to nothingness. The academician as we knew him in all his power and glory is gone: and we now see men like Vaughan Williams and Holst and Bax, whom the old methods of teaching never could have produced. The award for this change goes without dissent to Edward Elgar, who as a modern Sir Galahad cleared and showed the way.

Elgar and the British Public

The following month Brian was still thinking in melancholy, indeed bitter, terms of Elgar's struggle for recognition, as this portion of the April 1934 'On the Other Hand' (pp. 589–590) shows.

None of the sketches and articles written about Elgar seems to have disclosed new facts; indeed, for the most part, they show a closer acquaintance with R. J. Buckley and George Grove than with Edward Elgar. This is what I should have expected, for never did Elgar, even over wine and walnuts and in seeming confidence, say anything he did not wish to be made public. He was a wise man. There was, however, one original view put forward in a letter, to the effect that a performance of an Elgar work at Graz showed German appreciation of the English composer. Then those performances at Oxford in 1931 showed how keenly English musicians welcomed all that was put forward at the ninth annual

estival of the International Society of Contemporary
Music!

What I don't like about most of the writings is the com-
forting suggestion to the English people that they did not
neglect Elgar. I know that numbers of people sing *Land of
Hope and Glory*, but that is not enough to acquit them of neglect. I wish, for the sake of truth, to mention a few facts
about Elgar dating prior to the war and long before the
B.B.C. put him on the map of popular projection. I do so
with some confidence, for Elgar was my musical idol from
my youth up, and long before Gerald Cumberland, in these
columns twenty-five years ago, said of me, 'He comes to
us...with the love of Elgar in his heart'.[11]

I say very definitely that English appreciation of Elgar is
due mainly to two small groups of men, who spent their
money freely in fostering and promoting the works of a
composer whom they rightly regarded as an extraordinary
genius. I make no attempt to order the relative importance
of these men. In the English group were Archibald
Ramsden, Percy Harrison, and H.C. Embleton;[12] and in the
German group, Hans Richter, August J. Jaeger, Leo Schus-
ter, and Richard Strauss. I should need a volume to record
all their efforts, so here I can only refer to the few incidents
that come to my mind whilst writing. Immediately after
Elgar's death Strauss spoke of his many years' friendship,
and of the pride he had felt in being associated with the
early successes in Germany at Düsseldorf, when *The Dream
of Gerontius* was performed at the Lower Rhine Festival of
1902.

Thirty odd years ago English music subsisted almost entirely on the efforts of provincial amateur choral societies, and
the present generation can have little appreciation of the

---

[11] 'Pen-Portraits of Musicians. No. VII – Havergal Brian' by Gerald
Cumberland (C.F. Kenyon), in *Musical Opinion*, October 1909, p. 385.
[12] Archibald Ramsden (1835–1916) was a Leeds piano-dealer and co-
founder with Elgar of the 'You be Quiet' Club; Percy Harrison was a Birmingham impresario who promoted some of Elgar's earliest concerts;
Henry Embleton (1854–1930) was a shipping magnate, and the patron of
the Leeds Choral Union, who encouraged Elgar over the years to complete his trilogy of oratorios.

bloodless, unimaginative quality of the performances of English music. The first big choral work of Elgar shone out like a Neon light amidst a cluster of old-time gas jets. It was not that he came with a new and revolutionary idiom. Elgar only breathed new life into a body that was faint and well-nigh spent. Conductors of English choral societies were not slow to learn that here was a composer whose works provided a new and glorious adventure and consequently at long last no English composer ever had such popularity with his cantatas, oratorios and part songs. But I say very positively that in the early years Elgar's music had to be stuffed into the ears of the British public by a body of friends such as composers of his quality have rarely had.

The success of Elgar's orchestral works is another story. Before their popularity could be secured, great sacrifices in money and effort had to be made, and it is to those who helped in this way that credit must be recorded before it is too late. The English public is not to be credited, as the journalists suggest, with the early discovery and acclamation of a genius. Elgar was also well served by his singers, artists such as Muriel Foster, John Coates and Ffrangçon Davies.

It is said, if not printed, that Elgar was not a little exclusive, and could not suffer all who approached him gladly. This is true; and so was Beethoven, whom I can in fancy see snorting at the impudence of those who in these times venture to criticise him. My own experience of and association with Elgar, extending over many years, was that he was always a good friend; and, when his works were concerned, not only accessible but a willing helper. In the days when *The Dream of Gerontius* was unknown, I secured a performance of the masterpiece, but I had first to play the work through from the piano score to various members of a choral society committee. I was given a Yes on the condition that the composer would conduct, and this Elgar agreed to do. But the committee had not counted the cost of an orchestra of seventy-five to a hundred professional players, which, with the principals, would come to more than would be realised by the sale of all the tickets. This is where Elgar was always helpful: he agreed to an orchestra consisting half of amateurs, who were given their parts early for practice at home. Elgar also decreed that the chorus-master should share the conducting, but wonderful as this man[13] was with his choir, he was, well! not quite so successful with an orchestra. His share was to conduct the chorus, 'It comes from the misty ages' (*The Banner of St. George*), which also was in the programme. Elgar stood in the wings, listening. Then something went wrong; and I shall never forget Elgar's face when, chuckling with laughter, he rushed to the artists' room saying, 'Just listen to this extraordinary mix-up: the orchestra is a bar ahead of the choir'. Yet that same choir, a few months later, sang at the first London performance of *Gerontius*, at Westminster Cathedral, with the London Symphony Orchestra, Sir Edward conducting.[14]

I don't think the British public should be flattered into the belief that it willingly did anything to advance the cause of Elgar or his music. It needed all the goodwill of the friends I have mentioned, added to the persistent entreaties of many conductors, to overcome the steady determination not to change. There was a time, before the war, when it seemed that the music of Elgar would go into the repertoires of some Continental and American organisations: but, as Elgar had apparently no friends in Russia, France or Italy, his music had no performances in those countries. The idea that Elgar is or should be on the musical map of other countries arises from a mistaken notion that musicians of other countries are counterparts of English musicians: they are not. For the greater part, excluding the few who travel, they are narrowly national, and to excuse this attitude they complacently assume that England has no music of her own creation. So *en revanche* I say, let them get on with it. We have the advantage in hearing the best music of all countries, English as well.

I have one other point to elaborate, and that concerns the monetary reward coming to composers. We know that Elgar's position improved of late years, mainly, I believe,

---

[13] James Whewall.
[14] The Hanley performance was on 13 March and the London premiere on 6 June 1903.

through the fees coming to him from the Performing Righ
Society, and also from the B.B.C.; but up to 1922, h
deplored the poor reward coming to composers of larg
scale works. About that time I had occasion to bare my ow
position to the late Charles Volkert of Schott's,[15] and he, a
we all know, was as good a friend within his means as an
composer ever had. I wanted work, and asked for i
whether in England or Germany. But the war had laid it
heavy hand on all, and Mr. Volkert had perforce to poin
out that the reward to musicians in Germany was at the bes
of times meagre and precarious, and always less than wha
was current in England. Musicians, he said, were actuall
starving in Germany. I could do no more than thank him fo
his kindness in listening to me: he was visibly affected; an
as I was about to leave, he bent forward and said, 'Do yo
know, your friend Elgar sat in that very chair yesterday an
said his career as a composer had not been worth while
Doubtless Elgar was a braver man than I: he bore his so
rows with dignity and in silence. But this talk of the recogn
tion of the British public galls me. It is just journalist
blather.

The Elgar Manuscripts

This article appeared in *Musical Opinion* for September 1934
(p. 1029), and gives a rare glimpse of Brian the bibliophile,
taking a connoisseur's delight in the score as physical object,
scanning it with a practised eye for detail.

The British Museum has recently been enriched by th
temporary deposit of some Elgar manuscripts, amon
them being that of the full score of *The Apostles*. I was prob
ably in the first flight of those to descend on Great Russe
Street and for a little while I had in my own hands thi
now interesting and famous piece of music-writing. I
confirmed all my earliest impressions of the genius o
Elgar: here one may visualise him working with wondrou

[15] Charles (or Karl) Volkert was head of the London office of Schott
from 1881 until his death in 1922.

apidity, and rarely showing any sign of hesitancy or cor-
ected blunder.

Coming after the orchestral exhilaration which Elgar had
hown us in *King Olaf,* in *Caractacus,* and in *The Dream of
erontius, the orchestral score of *The Apostles* appears unusu-
lly modest. It occupies nearly four hundred pages, which
re bound in grey boards. In the year 1903 Elgar was, if I
ay say so, on top of his form: no other English composer
ad ever before been so much applauded by the finest
usical minds in England and Germany. Yet it was no neces-
ary stimulation, for the works which drew the plaudits
nte-dated the applause. For some years Elgar worked at
igh pressure. It began during the composition of his early
ratorio, *Light of Life,* and continued until the completion of
erontius. As a psychological and physiological speculation,
his may be important: but really Elgar was not unlike the
reatest composers, in whom the fever-heat of genius
lways ebbs and flows. Here and there – as in the surging
usic descriptive of the storm, and in the passage where the
horus sings 'Let us fill ourselves with costly wine' – the
agic hand of the old Elgar stands out, which could raise
verwhelming storms at will, baffling in the quickness of
heir coming and going.

In *The Apostles* Elgar portrayed men of simple pious mien,
nd he characterised them accordingly. This reverence for
is subject – for he was his own librettist – was no deterrent
o the rapidity of his thinking or invention. Work was begun
n the score on June 29th, 1903, and continued during two
nonths, being completed on August 17th. A portion of the
irst part seems to have been scored in Wales, for page 233
s signed, EDWARD ELGAR, *Bettws-y-coed, July, 1903,* followed
y the name of his wife (C.A.E.) and of his only daughter
Carice): then came the names of Rodewald and other
riends who were guests at the time. This tells us how neces-
ary a highly cultivated social life was to Elgar: he was stimu-
ated by the presence of friends, and as his fame became
reater, the size of his intimate circle of friends went on
xpanding.

The score was finished at the composer's home, Craeg
Lea, Malvern. The name of the house was an anagram of his

own name and his wife's initials. Elgar's wonderful and
helpful wife assisted him with the score. He wrote the
names of the instruments on the first page only and his wife
continued. It may be surmised that she did the bar-ruling
and may have written in the chorus and vocal solo music, for
the notation and writing are certainly not that of Elgar. That
which he did – the scoring – was thrown off rapidly, swiftly
and with unerring accuracy. In all the four hundred pages
I found not more than half-a-dozen cross-outs. Certain
pages suggest to me the rapture of Beethoven, for both
composers seem to have written under similar mental pressure.

All the instruments are given with Italian names. I note
that the size of the orchestra is as modest as the manner of
writing. In the first seventy pages or so, the cor anglais is
written at the top of the score, though afterwards it takes its
place under the oboe. Elgar used a thirty-four stave paper
and the two extra staves at the bottom of each page are
rarely written in. We feel his musical sensitiveness frequently, and I see that he was especially concerned with performances where the wind would be doubled. He has written very distinctly that the woodwind and horns must only
be doubled at the places marked.

The Apostles is a singularly light-weighted score, and is
strong testimony to Elgar's contention, once expressed to
me, that much contemporary English music suffers from
being over-weighted, showing that our composers are too
apt to put in all they know and leaving nothing to the
greater art of suggestion.

We are all now speaking of Elgar's enigmatical nature: it
is rightly expressed, and being so, it can never be solved to
the satisfaction of all who approach. It is intriguing to me
how he managed to steer his course as a great composer
with such success, carrying the burthen of many varied
interests. He was always prepared to consider others, and
was most generous in giving his time when genuinely
interested. Though, whilst scoring *The Apostles* he was stimulated by much social intercourse, it is quite obvious from the
last page of the manuscript that he was carrying something
in the recesses of his mind. At the end, beside the final

hord, he wrote:

> To what a heaven the earth might grow
> If fear beneath the earth were laid,
> If hope failed not, nor love decayed.

These pregnant lines are from *The Earthly Paradise*.[16] They must have rung in Elgar's ears in accord with some concious or subconscious thought. I have spoken with Elgar often, but recall nothing that could associate him with fear or failing hope: the explanation may be that there still lingered within him and was borne along memories of what had happened to him or to his kindred in the invisible past.[17] Elgar the Mystic will go with us into the invisible future.

The Apostles was first performed at the Birmingham Triennial Festival, under Hans Richter, in the October of 1903, two months after its completion. I can still recall the excitement of the occasion, for the Press had been at its best as a herald. Elgar had given us the best that was in him, though some among us hoped that a new era was beginning. After the performance, those who had been most prominently concerned added their names on the score: officers, conductor and principal artists on the front page, and the members of the orchestra and chorus on four pages at the end of the book. In a clear bold hand, Hans Richter wrote his name, saying that he was 'a true friend and an earnest admirer of the genius who had invented and scored this really original masterpiece'. The smallest and neatest handwriting of them all is that of Elgar's friend, A. J. Jaeger, who had written the analytical notes of the performance. Thirty-one years have passed, and now I count but few living of those who made up the orchestra and chorus on that memorable day.

It has been said that it would be an easy task to construct the personality of Elgar out of his compositions. I doubt it: for then each would have only a man after his own heart,

---

[16] By William Morris.
[17] This idea of atavistic 'racial memory' appears also on pp. 74–75; and see p. 104 for a similar notion about Delius.

coming from his own reactions. I would say that it is possible
to get a better impression of his genius from a slow study o
his scores. The first glimpse I had of an Elgar manuscrip
score was in Jaeger's office at Novello's. The American mai
was in, and with it had come the first instalment of the ful
score of *The Kingdom*, on which Elgar was working during
his visit to the States.[18] We both pored over those first page
with the deepest interest, admiring the unerring rapidity o
the work and the extraordinary skill shown in scoring and
the bold handwriting.

Elgar and the Third Symphony

This comes from 'On the Other Hand' in the October 1935
Musical Opinion (p. 13).

Elgar's dealings with the Press were always enigmatical, bu
at the same time remarkably successful: he seemed to shur
the fourth estate, and then with favour bestowed on a par
ticular writer, he would secure publicity for himself and his

[18] In April 1906. Writing to Bantock in a very jaundiced mood on 2:
December 1916, Brian remembered the incident in less restrained terms
'Do you know I was once at Novello's with Jaeger when Elgar had sent the
first instalment of his "Kingdom" from America. Jaeger had been talking
about Elgar and swelled head. As Jaeger turned the pages over he said -
"he's got it bad this time, growing pains all over". Elgar had written – "
am the chosen of the Lord". Jaeger cut it out'. Given the fallibility o
memory and Brian's emotional state at the time, it is difficult to know
what weight to accord this reminiscence; but perhaps something of the
kind is at the root of Brian's comparatively cool response to the work a
its premiere (see pp. 180–181). Brian's statements notwithstanding. Elga
had already sent Part I of *The Kingdom* to Jaeger from Wales by mid
January 1906; anything he sent from America must have been a later sec
tion. But although the words 'I am the chosen of the Lord' do not appea
anywhere in the final version of the work, it is certainly Part I which con
tains the closest verbal resemblance – 'The Lord hath chosen you to stanc
before Him and serve him: you shall be named the Priest of the Lord'
and it is known that Jaeger criticised this passage to Elgar. Perhaps Briar
was present on two separate occasions – in January, when Elgar sent in
Part I, and in April, when a further portion arrived from the USA – and
had conflated the two in his mind.

work beyond the dreams of the most versatile press-agent. Witness the stroke which came when Kalisch published in a London morning paper[19] the astonishing article on *The Apostles*, illustrated with many music examples, which could only have been printed with the assistance or co-operation of the composer. Similar successful publicity is following Elgar even after he has left us, for the article on theThird Symphony, by W. H. Reed, in *The Listener* is of absorbing interest. It is published as a 16pp. supplement, thirteen of which are made up with photographic music examples of fragments of material written and laid aside. It is thus in a form to be preserved and treasured by many.[20]

Few ever knew how Elgar worked, but privileged among those few was W. H. Reed, his friend during thirty years, who doubtless had no intention of writing what he knew until asked to tell the story of what we must call the Third Symphony, that work which, though never in being, will stand to the enduring credit of the British Broadcasting Corporation. Elgar accepted the commission in 1933: he must have done so with some trepidation, for twenty years and more had passed since the completion of his Second Symphony. Whatever his feelings, we must remember his inborn nervous organisation and the fact that he was no longer a symphonist in practice. With these fragments of a projected third symphony before us, we shall continue to wonder whether the two previous symphonies and the cantatas were also born of similar casual inspiration. That we may never know: but some of these fragments were in existence before the coming of the commission, after which there was some attempt at assembling.

Did anyone ever know the real Elgar? – a question we all raise when a man in person is not what we think he really ought to be. I was always seeking to reconcile Elgar's impulsive, erratic, nervous and shy temperament with the brave, martial character of his fast music and the marvellous calm

---

[19] *The World*, 15 October 1903.
[20] This supplement, with the facsimiles of Elgar's autograph sketches, appeared in *The Listener* of 28 August 1935; it was reprinted in Reed's *Elgar as I Knew Him* the following year.

serenity of his slow movements. In these fragments we see
Elgar at work: ill at ease, unsettled, starting again and again
at varied segments of the four movements: none of them
ever complete: fleeing from an episode in the fourth movement to the development section of the first.

Though the sketches give us no clue to the complete
work, we can readily believe that it had taken definite form
of Elgar's mind. In construction it was to be more simple
than the previous two symphonies, and there was a remarkable throw-back in a revival in the first movement of the old
repeat, not by marking a double-bar repeat, but by indicating *prima volta*. How ill-starred the picture appears of Reed
playing bits of the manuscript sketches on his violin, accompanied by Elgar at the piano, in order to get an impression
of the ideas committed to paper; but Reed never knew his
whereabouts, whether at the beginning, in the middle or at
the end.

The manuscripts of the Elgar orchestral scores I have
seen are remarkable for vivid, impulsive handwriting, and
for the few cross-outs. Probably no one could pass him in
speed at composition and scoring. Elgar kept a flag flying
over the tent in the garden of his cottage at Malvern, in
which he wrote the orchestral score of *King Olaf*: it was a
sign that he was composing and did not wish to be dis-
turbed. An old friend once gained entrance, and found the
floor strewn with hastily written pages. Jaeger of Novello's
remarked on Elgar's mercurial sensitiveness, which was
part of an organism that once started seemed destined to go
on for ever. The story of the slowing down is told quite vividly by Mr. Reed: and in the writing of the composer's own
hand we see in the final example the approach to the inevitable end. It were better perhaps that one had never seen
this last fruitless effort at composition: only those without
understanding can miss the poignancy of it all. The spirit
was passing: and as it sped its way onwards it beckoned one
and wished there should be no tinkering with what was left
undone. Burn it rather than that! Fortunately, it would
seem to be impossible for anyone, however wicked or
wrongminded, to make an Unfinished Symphony of what is
left to us: it is not even broken, for it never was in existence.

The Enigma of Elgar

W.H. Reed's *Listener* article was in fact a foretaste of his volume of reminiscences, *Elgar as I Knew Him*. Brian's review of this Elgarian classic appeared in the October 1936 issue of *Musical Opinion*, pp. 28–29.

'ELGAR AS I KNEW HIM.' By William H. Reed.
(Victor Gollancz, Ltd.) 15s. net.

This book is frank from the beginning, for the enlargement of the title, 'As I Knew Him', disarms those who are for ever hoping that some day Elgar may be revealed through his own letters and not through the pen of another. We should wish for nothing so false as the Confessions of Rousseau or of De Quincey, but we should like to know what Elgar thought of those who after the turn of the century, when his greatest work was done, fêted and flattered him to the end. Elgar stood up to them so well that one suspects he was almost persuaded of his own greatness, but was determined that no such ignoble feeling should deter him from doing a kindly act to peer or peasant. Elgar was so much on his guard! Even when Reed ran after him, following a rehearsal at Queen's Hall, to ask if he taught harmony and counterpoint, Elgar unblushingly exclaimed, 'My dear boy, I don't know anything about those things'. But is it discreet to repeat answers which, while intended only to be oblique, are in fact not true? What power was it in Elgar that brought stiff-necked men before him as humble dragomen?

Notwithstanding this abrupt beginning, Elgar and Reed became great friends, and if a reviewer may have an opinion on friendships, the patient violinist paid for that friendship a thousandfold. In the endless transmutation of the violin works from sketch to completion, Reed was there and was repaid by marks of friendship shown to few others: but there is no elucidation of Elgar's mind. He remains the enigma of which Sheldon and Maine sought the solution in his music! Of course, the man had dogs, a flat in town, lived in various country cottages, and all that. Also he seems to have taken the advice of Tennyson's Northern Farmer, for

he went where money was.[21] He was fond of half explana-
tions: soon after the first performance of the *Enigma Vari-*
ations, when asked who were the friends depicted in the
work he said enigmatically that they were gentlemen.

Though Mr. Reed is no Boswell, he gives us excellent pictures of things that happened, down to the time when the
light failed before the completion of the third symphony.
One of the first things Mr. Reed was invited to do was to
share with the composer the first playing of the lovely Violin
Concerto, which was first produced by Kreisler. Reed also
saw Elgar's interest in his choral trilogy diminish to zero; for
though the composer had a cupboard filled with sketches
and the plan of the work complete in his mind, he would
neither play any of the music nor talk about it. Thus Elgar
died with the third oratorio and the third symphony only in
the process of composition. With the incomplete trilogy, he
appears to have lost all faith in his work.

Mr. Reed's description of Elgar's personality is the best
yet written: it needed the intimacy of a friend who not only
was his companion in country rambles but who also played
in orchestras under Elgar. Reed is right in saying that no
conductor ever got as much out of his own works when conducting them as the composer. He gives numerous examples of Elgar's fastidiousness at rehearsals with his innumerable nuance marks. We also remember a remarkable performance of *Gerontius*, when fifty percent of the orchestra consisted of amateurs who had studied their parts at home.[22]

Elgar, both at rehearsal and at performance, allowed the
music to speak for itself, and appeared thoroughly to enjoy
it. In conducting his own works he never failed to inspire his
forces and to get the most from them by sheer force of personality. His remarks at rehearsals were unconventional
and curt, and probably saved much time and fuss by their
directness. 'Don't starve the quaver' must have saved the
turning over of many pages by the players to whom it was

---

[21]   Half-quotation from Tennyson's dialect poem *Northern Farmer. Old*
Style: 'But I knawed a Quaäker feller as often 'as towd me this:/ "Doänt
thou marry for munny, but goä wheer munny is!" '
[22]   Another reference to the Hanley performance of 13 March 1903.

addressed. Outside his music, Elgar was a man of innumerable hobbies and interests, varying from architecture to
horse-racing: he loved to recount stories of his early strug-
gles, and revisit scenes which had impressed themselves
upon him. Nothing can be more pathetic than the composer, at the time when inspiration was becoming rare –
though he was then a world personality – visiting the tiny
cottage where he wrote the great *Dream of Gerontius.*

To us the principal feature of the book lies in the style of
writing. All the incidents are given at first hand, for they
actually happened between Elgar and the author.
Moreover, the discussion of Elgar's music and the much
debated question of his personal style reveal more than has
hitherto been written. But of that mysterious gift for character delineation in the orchestra, in which Elgar was unique
and yet so different from Strauss, even Elgar when asked by
the author could offer no solution. In this respect some of
his finest work is contained in the full score of *The Apostles*;
yet there is hardly a 'cross out' or an alteration in the whole
score: a tribute to Elgar's infallibility and invincibility in
scoring. In the far away years, when Elgar lectured at Birmingham, he gave the impression of being a modernist.
Apparently he remained such, evincing an equal sympathy
for something striking in a piece of jazz music, a Schumann
symphony or a work of Stravinsky.

Nothing more dramatic ever happened to him than during the last few days of his life when a record was being
made of his *Caractacus.* The band was 'laid on' from the
recording studio in London to the chamber where Elgar lay
dying. But, oh! the thoughtlessness of it all: sucking up the
last flicker of the composer's life that a commercial enterprise should not fail. Do those who were present now walk
in peace? How Elgar must have thought of those far-off
days when he penned the mighty 'Britons, alert', or the
'Triumphal March' in Rome: or was there running in his
mind the lovely music of 'By the Banks of the Severn', which
we imagine to be within the circle of shadows cast by the
Cathedral.

Accompanying the book are numerous photographs, all
but one new to us. Mr Reed has doubtless got nearer to a

revelation of Elgar than any previous writer: but we cannot say that Elgar's personality has yet been solved. Perhaps, when others of the inner circle of friends have paid their tribute, we may feel that we know the man more completely – a circle which preceding Mr. Reed's first acquaintance with Elgar in 1902, included Rodewald, Vasco Ackroyd, Ernest Newman, Granville Bantock, and their wives: and among them doubtless Elgar spoke freely, without that constraint which at Shenley led to the avoidance of all that concerned music.[23]

[23] The village of Shenley in Hertfordshire was where Elgar's friend Edward Speyer had his home, 'Ridgehurst'; Elgar was a frequent guest there, and Reed (pp. 51–52) relates how he spent a weekend there with Elgar and Suggia during which Elgar insisted on devoting his entire time to playing a new form of snooker. The only additional information I can provide about Vasco Ackroyd is gleaned from passing mentions in several of Brian's other writings, which make clear that he was an orchestral violinist, an enthusiast for British music and had some connection with the Liverpool Orchestral Society.

PART FOUR
DELIUS

———————————●———————————

Although, as we shall see below (p.138), Brian later dated his first meeting with Delius to January 1908, there is some evidence that they must have met before then, probably in the latter half of 1907. They were certainly in correspondence in October of that year, and although Brian was unable to attend the first British performance of *Appalachia* in November (at the Queen's Hall under Fritz Cassirer), Granville Bantock wrote to Delius in December praising Brian warmly and assuring Delius that he would shortly meet him 'again'. Whether for the first time or not, the two composers certainly became acquainted at Beecham's performance of *Paris* in Liverpool in January 1908; and a week later they sat together at the Liverpool concert in which Bantock gave Brian's *English Suite* No. 1 and the world premiere of Delius' *Brigg Fair* on the same programme. Brian was already an enthusiastic convert to Delius' music and, through his contacts with the Staffordshire choirs, was instrumental in arranging the performance of *Appalachia* which Delius himself conducted at Hanley the following April. The Potteries heard *Sea Drift* under Beecham in December, and again Brian was a guiding spirit in this enterprise. Meanwhile Delius had been one of the judges of the 1908 Norwich Festival competition in which Brian's cantata *The Vision of Cleopatra* gained second prize. The entries were pseudonymous, and Delius later wrote to Bantock that had he known 'The Holy Pabrun'[1] was Brian he would have insisted on the score being awarded a joint first prize. They continued to meet and correspond throughout the pre-War period, partly because of Delius' involvement, as Vice-President, with the Musical League (both of whose Festivals

---

[1] One of Brian's favourite humorous *noms de plume*. He often signed himself thus (or just 'Pabrun') in his letters to Bantock.

99

included works by Brian).

Brian's writings on Delius are less numerous than those on
Elgar, but owing to the remarkable size of the essay entitled
The Art of Frederick Delius, with which this selection begins,
they almost equal them in bulk. Indeed, in the absence of his
various books, finished or unfinished (for which see Introduction, p.15 and note 3 on p.17), this essay stands as Havergal Brian's most substantial prose work. Although clearly
conceived in series with *The Art of Cyril Scott* and *The Art of
Eugene Goossens*, both represented elsewhere in this volume,
it far outgrew them in scope and size, and had to be serialised
through no less than eight successive issues of *Musical Opinion*. It not only surveys practically every work in Delius' output then available, but also contains some of Brian's most
interesting writing on the development of the art of music in
general, and Delius' place within that development.

Yet to reproduce the essay in full would seriously un-
balance this book. I have therefore decided to reserve the
passages of more general significance for a later volume,
while giving here those parts that deal directly with Delius, in
a somewhat abbreviated form. Those who wish to read the
article as it first appeared should consult the following issues
of *Musical Opinion* for 1924: March (p.598), April (pp. 700–
701), May (pp. 799–800), June (pp. 906–907), July (pp.
1002–1003), August (p. 1098), September (pp. 1194–1195),
and October (pp. 49–50). In the following condensed version, the major passages omitted are summarised in smaller
type.

The Art of Frederick Delius

After a substantial prologue dwelling on the previous century
of musical development, which has ended with Delius 'quite
unconsciously [...] saying the last word' upon the Romantic
period, the main part of the article begins as follows:

The music of Delius has a wistful charm and dreamy melancholy which comes from the heart of one who has recoiled
in sadness and retreated in horror from the coarse brutality
of modern life. In its style the music has an elusiveness akin
to that of his predecessor, Chopin. Just as there are not
more than half-a-dozen pianists who possess the secret to
the charm of Chopin, so there are probably not more than
the same number of orchestral conductors who can reveal

the charm of Delius. He is essentially the composer's composer. It is the greatest honour to the genius of Delius that
his greatest admirers have always been his contemporaries.
No higher tribute can be paid to original genius than this. It
is invidious at this stage to mention by name those whom
one remembers to have fought for the recognition of this
composer, but the one who stands out most clearly, who
could and did give practical sympathy, was Sir Thomas
Beecham, and it is due to his persistence that we have been
brought into a full understanding of this composer. It is also
curious that whilst London remained in a state of expectancy awaiting performance of his larger works an out of
the way district like the Staffordshire Potteries was giving
full homage to the largest works of Delius.[2]

*   *   *

If Delius has unconsciously gathered the threads from
those romantics whose epoch his own work closes it cannot
be said that his own work has been greatly influenced by
theirs. Sometimes one feels a tinge of Grieg, and though
Schumann and Chopin are not usually mentioned in the art
of Delius, it is with those two composers that he has real
spiritual kinship. Apart from this resemblance, which is
purely a spiritual one, there is no influence in the art of
Delius. He broke away from conventionality much in the
same way as did Whistler, the painter. In this music we miss
that death-trap of the great majority, the two-bar phrase,
the half and full close and those rounded periods of the
'tired Tims'. This music lives by its greater vitality of imagination and endless continuity. The conductor who finds it
not difficult to lop off fifty bars or so from a work to bring
it to a speedier conclusion will find it difficult to do this
with a Delius work, for his sense of design is so exquisitely balanced that the elision of one bar would wreck the
whole. In this way his art resembles a highly polished art of
improvisation – with this difference, that what appears as

---

[2] A reference to the performances of *Appalachia* and *Sea Drift* mentioned
above.

improvisation in the art of Delius is the outcome of long brooding. His finest inspirations are lavished upon the orchestra, and he usually writes for a very large one. At no time has the wood-wind been so delicately treated as in the Delius works. He has a penchant for lingering and brooding over the flower garden of the orchestra, as the wood-wind has most appropriately been called.[3] He has a mannerism, to be found in most of his works, of leaping a ninth, in the melodic contour – a mannerism curious to Strauss and Bantock – and will descend by a seventh. When the melodic contour is complete he will round it off by falling a fifth. Like all artists of original genius, the music of Delius has aroused hostile criticism. So long as the art lasts will this state of things continue. There can be no standard rule of criticism any more than there can be standard piano-playing or conducting.

We know that it is possible for a pianist to be a very wonderful Brahms or Beethoven player, yet the same player may not get within a hundred miles of a complete understanding of Chopin or Delius. Consequently this type of artist has no sympathy for the latter, just as the few fine players of Chopin usually give the classics a miss because they are out of sympathy with them. The same applies to orchestral conductors. No conductor can be equally fine in all schools – he must fail somewhere. The conductor whose mind is superb with the romantics will be superb in the works of Delius.

*   *   *

The cause of frequent misunderstandings of an artist of original genius, often arises through his violent departures from preconceived opinions. It has always been the case that the original artist leads, whilst others follow. In some cases the originality of an artist does not show itself until years of incubation have elapsed, during which time his

[3] Brian – the keen gardener – always relished this phrase, which he had heard used by Henry J. Wood in a lecture about the orchestra given at Kendal, Westmoreland, in about 1903; *cf.* p.390.

mind has been busy maturing and possibly absorbing influences from predecessors and contemporaries. The early works of Beethoven, Brahms, Wagner and Strauss, are a proof of this contention, for though those works may be finished products *as* works, they do not contain the real ego or personality of those composers. As a rule we do not seek the composer in his early works, we only look in them for indications of the finished artist which is revealed in his later works.

In the case of Delius we have a phenomenon towards whose art neither his predecessors nor contemporaries will serve as guide. Those who wish to understand Delius must put aside preconceived opinions – for the patterns of the classics or the contemporary romantics will not help. There is no figure like him in musical history either in outlook or personality. His development has been of slow growth. His thoughts reach him through a mesh of chromaticism and, although he works easily and leisurely, through a complex web – his works contain a miracle of loveliest melody. Many of his melodies approximate to the folk song type, of which he is very fond, and several of these have been used by him as a *motif* to carry a long and well developed and equally well designed structure, as in several works like *Brigg Fair* or *Appalachia*, written in symphonic variation form.

One uses the expression 'symphonic variations' very guardedly – for in one instance Delius calls such a work a rhapsody – lest it should be confounded with other things bearing the same name, but which are no more than the exploitation of a cold, frigid theme in the style of academical exercises. The Delius manner of handling a theme is indicative of everything else this poet and painter does.

His initial theme often commences insignificant enough like the tiny rivulet, which, beginning as something almost contemptible, moves forward not hindered by any obstacles, continuously moving in sunshine or rain, day or night. The great thing is that it does move, ever growing bigger and bigger until it finally passes into the immensity of all things. A thousand composers can invent themes – but it is only the highest type of genius who can manipulate them into a great living whole. If Wagner's speculation upon the

symphony of the future was that its course would be shaped
very much after the manner of the *Tristan* Prelude, upon
bigger lines, in one continuous movement, then some of the
Delius works are almost inside the promised land. For there
is nothing redundant in them, no passage work or padding.
Some of his finest efforts are done in ancient time measures,
$\frac{3}{2}$, $\frac{6}{4}$, $\frac{4}{2}$. His remote ancestor must have been some Norse
god, who sang and lulled his people to comfort with runes
of sadness, holding up to them the mirror of man's destiny,
showing its helplessness against the hand of fate.[4] It is with
some such ancient sagas that Delius has fullest kinship. His
two great choral works, *Sea Drift*, the *Mass of Life*, the orchestral poems, *Paris*, the *Song of the High Hills*, indicate plainly
enough the soul of one who sits brooding and speculating
upon the tragic hand of fate, in far away silent places. Like
all great artists he is no slave to a thought. If his tragic verse
is sung with such magnificent eloquence, his pastorals and
songs of passions are no less so. There are wonderful nature
paintings in Wagner and Debussy. In the Delius, there are
also magnificent things; but the idea is caught and fixed
quite differently.

Some years ago a famous orchestral conductor once
'pulled' at my imagination by suggesting that an orchestral
work would be a great novelty, which embraced all the
wood-wind in completed families, making use of the bass
flute, oboe d'amore, bass oboe, basset horn, &c.[5] Original in
all things and not less so in his orchestral scoring, Delius had
almost anticipated this suggestion. Though he does not
employ the bass flute, oboe d'amore or the corno di bassetto, he almost always writes for an enormous orchestra –
with the wood-wind in 'fours' – including bass oboe, E flat
clarinet and always six horns. A typical Delius score, such as
is used in the *Mass of Life*, *Paris*, or the *Song of the High Hills*,

[4] Brian was fond of intimating such 'Norse' racial connections – *cf.* his
comments about Elgar, pp. 74–75 and 91.
[5] This was Henry Wood, on his way to Queen's Hall to conduct the London premiere of Brian's *English Suite* No. 1 at the 1907 Proms. By the time
Brian wrote this passage, he was already at work on the composition
which would (in passing) embody Wood's suggestion – the *Gothic* Symphony.

consists of 3 flutes, piccolo, 3 oboes, cor anglais, bass oboe, 3 clarinets and bass clarinet, 3 bassoons, double bassoon or sarrusophone, 6 horns, 3 trumpets, 3 tenor trombones, bass tuba, 2 harps, celesta, tympani and percussion, and a 'demand' for seventy strings. In the *Song of the High Hills*, he writes for 4 tympani with two players. So far as I know he is the first composer to use voices as an integral part of the orchestra, and he does this with great effect in the *Appalachia* Variations, and yet with greater effect in the *Song of the High Hills*. Here the voices are used with the orchestra and afterwards alone in eight parts with a soprano and tenor soloist to continue without pause or interruption the development of the orchestral tissue.

In the majority of the works there is much divisional writing in the strings. In the two pastorals, *On Hearing the First Cuckoo in Spring* and *Summer Night* (published by Tischer & Jagenberg), the scoring is for small orchestra – i.e., strings, wood-wind (in twos) with two horns. The first pastoral is fairly well known in this country and is a wondrous piece of nature painting. It reveals Delius's fondness for the use of a slow $\frac{6}{4}$ measure with the harmonies spread across divisional strings – upon which a haunting melody moves, with quiet cuckoo calls in the wood-wind.

Summer Night on the River, though quite as exquisite a miniature as the *Cuckoo*, is expressed very differently. Here the quiet modulations of moving water are suggested by wood-wind moving over the pedal in the string basses ($\frac{12}{8}$ measure) which lead to a short episode of close sustained harmonies in the strings ($\frac{9}{8}$ measure). This is succeeded by a section in $\frac{6}{8}$ measure – wherein atmospheric painting prevails – which moves to the main theme heard upon solo 'cello. Around this, light arabesques play in wood-wind. The main theme passes to solo violin and solo viola. The music makes for a large *crescendo* and then dies away. Such is a brief analysis of two orchestral miniatures by a composer who loves to 'spread' himself upon huge canvasses, and where a greater choice of hues is obtained by using a very large orchestra.

*   *   *

I once asked the late A. J. Jaeger what was the most extraordinary thing he had experienced in modern music. He replied that it was at Düsseldorf, where he called upon Professor Julius Buths, who was then conductor of the Lower Rhine Festival. Buths met Jaeger with 'Come along, I have a piece of remarkable music!' He took Jaeger along to the music room and played from full score a piece of music. It was *Paris, or the Song of a Great City*, by Delius. Jaeger seemed to think that Professor Buths's skill in playing from full score so complicated a work was phenomenal. I have heard something similar from an English conductor, who could play whole stretches of the Delius *Mass of Life* at the piano from memory, and who must have memorised it from the orchestral score, for at that time the vocal score of the mass was not published.[6] *Paris* is published by Universal Edition and was written twenty-five years ago. It is not a familiar work in this country. I have heard one very fine performance of it under Beecham when he took the New Symphony Orchestra to Liverpool in 1908. Beecham, always keen and alert, was on his mettle and gave a thrilling performance of the work.

Charpentier, poet and composer, has written an opera in which he symbolises the soul of 'Paris'; he takes several hours to unfold the drama.[7] Delius, feeling the subject in another way, symbolises it in the orchestra in a few minutes. With Delius, his *Paris* appears to be the incantation of one who has known the snares and allurements of the city no less than its charms. Through his dreams these impressions return, and their remembrance becomes spiritualised through the music.

The work commences *ppp* in the key of D major, $\frac{6}{8}$ measure, *Adagio*, with a long pedal in basses and drums. Upon this the bass clarinet enters in its lowest register with a *motif* which is passed to 'celli; the solo oboe steals in with a theme

[6] Presumably Beecham – see p.145 for him playing of the *Mass of Life* to Brian, impromptu.
[7] In *Louise* – which Brian saw (and much admired) during the Beecham Opera Season in 1914. It made him feel, he wrote to Bantock, 'as though I would like to burn every note I had written – and start all over again'.

of great tenderness, horns and violas follow, a fragment breaks out from the high clarinet and a haunting night cry is heard upon bassoons. The oboe theme returns, the night cry persists, afterwards descending to the basses. A second theme appears on bass clarinet, evidently a variant of the original *motif* and repeated by cor anglais. So far the drama has moved slowly over a drone bass suggestive of figures moving in darkness. Here the context changes from $\frac{6}{8}$ to $\frac{4}{4}$, at the same time the second theme descends to the basses. The character of the music at once alters. Harps and string arpeggios enter, the second theme commences to move with great breadth in the basses, imitated by trombones and tuba, and again by horns. The night cry is heard upon trumpets, whilst the first oboe theme wails overheard doubled by a clarinet. There is a swish and turmoil suggestive of something trying to free itself, the basses swell out their theme, the imitation in the brass becomes closer, the night cry grows louder, then, making for a hurly-burly crash it suddenly dies away. It is the soul of Paris freeing itself. So it begins with a palpitating dance measure (*Vivace*, $\frac{6}{8}$ measure) in a new section.

It is said that every great city has an earth boom – a distinctive sound or acoustical phenomenon which can sometimes be heard miles away. This *Vivace* section rushes away as though seeking a resting place, everything is alive and awake. Admist the expectancy suggested by the innumerable notes in a glockenspiel, wood-wind and strings, a figure is hurled out *fortissimo* in the basses. This is surely the earth boom of Paris.

Like the preceding section, this *Vivace* heads for a climax and dies away, resolving in an *Adagio* section ($\frac{4}{4}$ measure) which begins upon solo flute. The violas take it over, passing it to solo oboe, the melody moves in true Delius fashion like an endless chain with fine eloquence and passion. Gaiety again returns and the continuation of the work is carried on in the same reflective style as the preceding sections. Later we meet a March which enters upon a pair of melodies in glockenspiel, harps, violas and 'cellos: these jostle very comically side by side. The palpitating dance measure again returns, and making one supreme effort from the whole orchestra it exhausts itself and immediately dies away. The drama is over and we once again return to the darkness where fragments from the mysterious themes which opened the work are heard, the conclusion haunted by the ominous night cry.

It will thus be seen that the structure of *Paris* has no relationship to any predecessor or contemporary amongst symphonic poems. However chaotic such a structure may appear to those who have not met such a design before, one can only draw upon the remembrance of a wonderful performance plus a close acquaintance with the orchestral score, which leaves one mightily impressed and dazzled by its originality and high poetical values.

*   *   *

It has been remarked that Delius receives his impressions through a mesh of chromaticism. He has two methods of using his impressions. On the one hand he is fond of treating his melodic matter with slow descending chromatic harmony; on the other hand his method is contrapuntal in a manner entirely his own which combines the greatest freedom in part-writing; very often he will seize on a *motif* from one of his themes and pass it through a striking series of imitations, chiefly canonical. His manners are always subservient to his picture. Like John Constable he has been spurred to some of his finest efforts by beautiful English scenery and nature musings. His recently published orchestral works consist of *A Song before Sunrise* for small orchestra and inscribed to Philip Heseltine; *Eventyr* ('Once upon a time') founded on Norwegian folk-lore, and *North Country Sketches* are for large orchestra. The latter is inscribed to Albert Coates. These works are published by Augener Ltd., and reveal Delius in his happiest moods. *Brigg Fair*, an English Rhapsody for large orchestra, is inscribed to Percy Grainger and published by Leuckart of Leipzig. This work is inspired by English scenes and Lincolnshire romance and is based upon a Lincolnshire folksong. It was first introduced into England by Professor Granville Bantock. It remains a fine example of Delius's manner of handling a simple theme and passing it through a procession of ever changing dreams suffused in chromatic harmonies continuously developing and rounded off by the attainment of a fine climax. The personal note of the quaint folk legend is never absent.

The *Song of the High Hills* (Universal Edition) is scored for a large orchestra with chorus. This work, different in style and manner, bears similar features to *Brigg Fair*, in that it is an inspiration derived from nature musings, and with that work makes a pair of this composer's finest pastorals. A great deal of this pastoral music is built upon the ancient dance rhythms favoured by the Elizabethan composers. An instance of a Delius work built upon a more modern dance rhythm is *A Dance Rhapsody* (Leuckart, Leipzig) for large orchestra, and greatly in favour with the Queen's Hall Orchestra. The idiom is Scotch. Though it moves with rare freedom and gusto as befits a lilt born of kilts and bare legs, it is controlled by fine delicacy of imagination. The *Dance Rhapsody* is by no means the finest Delius work; it does contain the element of popularity.[8] As the work has been gramophoned by Sir Henry Wood and the Queen's Hall Orchestra it is probably well known. The character of the music lends itself to gramophone treatment, and a striking instance of the composer's originality may have been noticed in the record, where the first violins continue with the dance *motif* alone over moving harmonies in six horns, bassoon, bass clarinet and English horn. The writing for the horns sounds as beautiful and novel as it appears in the score.

A more striking instance of the composer's fondness for exploiting dance rhythm is the *Lebenstanz* or *Life's Dance* published by Tischer & Jagenberg of Cologne. It is scored for a large orchestra. Here we get one of those rare

---

[8] Brian heard the *Dance Rhapsody*, apparently for the first time, on 14 February 1914 at Queen's Hall (in a Henry Wood concert which also included Stravinsky's *Fireworks* and music from Strauss's *Ariadne auf Naxos*) and wrote enthusiastically about it to Bantock the following day. But on 20 August, writing after a second hearing, his attitude was much less favourable. Curiously, in the present article he nowhere mentions the existence of the *Dance Rhapsody* No. 2 of 1916.

instances where consummate mastery of technique moves with an excited imagination glowing at white heat. The work palpitates with daring and audacity – a strange instance in this composer's art where the tenderest mixes with the most grotesque. It would be highly interesting to quote examples from all these orchestral works, showing his genius for dissolving a melody in novel chromaticism and again using a portion of it as a *motif* for novel kinds of imitation. More important still is his freedom of style in orchestration, for there is no branch of the orchestra which he does not adorn with originality.

These works make different appeals in different quarters. Some people prefer the Pastorals, others the *Dance Rhapsody*. In my opinion the two finest works are *Paris* and *Appalachia*. These works are practically unknown in England. I have heard two performances of *Appalachia* – one in London under Sir Thomas Beecham when the chorus singing was really atrocious and the orchestral playing really brilliant. The other performance was under the composer: the chorus singing was beautiful and as perfect as it ever will be, and the orchestra was decidely not sympathetic. So a really fine performance of this work is still due.[9]

*   *   *

> There follows an extended discussion of artists and composers who have given expression in their work to humanity's desire for liberty and brotherhood. Shelley's *Prometheus Unbound* and Beethoven's Symphonies, especially the Ninth, are cited as examples.

[...] Frederick Delius [...] went to America early in life to manage an orange farm in Florida. He was in a State where negro slavery had been rife, must have walked over ground famous for the vile overseer's whip and click of the revolver in days of black slavery. Delius, prone to dreaming and speculating upon the mystery of life, saw a picture in his mind of an ancient race, the original race of America, being

---

[9] The performance under the composer was at Hanley, 2 April 1908; I do not know which Beecham performance Brian means.

snuffed out before a merciless conqueror. The conqueror
not satisfied with having the country imported another
race, the Africans, and chained them up as slaves. Their
horrible history in the plantations and eventual emanci-
pation is well known. Delius felt all this: hence we have
Appalachia, which is the Red Indian name for America. This
work has a message, which is, that you cannot kill a race by
slavery. *Appalachia* stands in the same position in the Delius
orchestral works as the Ninth Symphony does in the symphonies of Beethoven.

It is Delius's finest and ripest orchestral effort. The whole
thing is an inspiration and a shining light from end to end.
The work opens with a call on the horns (Ex.1).

Ex. 1

This fragment is used as a *motif* upon which to set the seal of
the work; it passes through various instrumental groups
and leads to a magnificent outburst where an army of banjos seems to twang away. This gradually fades away over
fragments of the melody which anticipate its real entry. This
appears upon the cor anglais supported by bass clarinet and
bassoons. Its poignancy deserves quotation, for it is an
ancient slave melody (Ex.2).

Ex. 2

If you turn it over, so to speak, and look at it you will find
that the first phrase is twice repeated, so that the real length
of the theme is modified somewhat. Knowing this, the score
of *Appalachia* becomes all the greater miracle, for it is upon

this slender thing that this mighty work has been built. It is inscribed to Professor Julius Buths, and is published by Harmonie of Berlin. Its form is that of continuous variations, and a chorus is used. The voices are used with original effect – in places they seem to rise and fall as from distant parts of the plantation where the slaves were working. It would have been an easy matter for a work of this kind to have caught a wild, fanatical corybanticism. The meaning is unmistakable as Shelley's *Prometheus*; to the yells and shouts for freedom which this downtrodden race voices through this composer, comes a childish humour as a laughter through tears. It seems born of that extraordinary pæan which the American poet, Vachell Lindsay, depicted at the reception of General William Booth as he entered heaven with a 'Grand chorus of all instruments: Tambourines in the foreground'.[10]

> The hosts were sandalled and their wings were fire!
>   (Are you washed in the Blood of the Lamb?)
> But their noise played havoc with the angel choir.
>   (Are you washed in the Blood of the Lamb?)
> O, shout Salvation! It was good to see
> Kings and Princes by the Lamb set free.
> The banjos rattled and the tambourines
> Jing, jing, jingled in the hands of Queens.

Some such spirit courses its way through this work, sweeping everything aside like a vast river, though the composer keeps it within bounds from downright sensationalism. It is a work in which the singing, the strumming of banjos from an innocent, harmless race echo and re-echo amidst the crack of merciless whips and cries of pain – a profound sorrow struggling for expression and freedom – with an

---

[10] This – typical of Brian's sometimes unusual but clearly intensely-felt cross-connections between music and literature – is the only time, as far as I know, that he refers to the poetry of Vachell Lindsay. *General William Booth's Entrance into Heaven* was only published in 1914; and Charles Ives' now-famous setting of it, composed in the same year, was not published at the time Brian was writing.

ending that fate has something better in store for the black races.

*   *   *

> I omit the ensuing discussion – little more than a list of titles, poets, and publishers – of Delius's songs. There follows a synopsis of the action of *Fennimore and Gerda*, almost without musical comment, and a similar synopsis of *A Village Romeo and Juliet* – after which Brian continues as below.

This opera belongs to Delius's finest inspirations and takes rank with *Sea Drift* and *The Mass of Life*. It has the sure grip of the finest Greek tragedy. Fate is cruel and remorseless.[...]

This work had several presentations by the Beecham Opera Company. The music is written in that compact continuous symphonic manner which distinguishes the finest work by this composer. It is music of the greatest purity and as romantically pathetic as the story itself.

When living in Birmingham during the war – in the midst of war horrors and the riotous whirl of machinery making munitions[11] – I got wound up and had a sudden impulse to do something. I did. I caught the next train to London and made my way to a Royal Philharmonic Concert. I doubt if there is a finer orchestra in Europe than the Philharmonic. The programme contained the wonderful stretch of music which follows the close of the fifth tableau, where the children wend their way to seek rest in the Paradise Gardens in the closing scene of the opera. Some composers would have had these two lovers declaiming their love in frenetic duets. Not so Delius. At this fine climax in the drama he dismisses the children and pours out, in the orchestra alone, all the feeling and love which lie in their hearts in one of the most eloquent and soulful symphonic movements ever written. It is the epitome of *A Village Romeo and Juliet*.

This music transfixed my mind and I was only awakened

---

[11] Brian worked at the munitions factory of The Electric and Ordnance Accessories Company, a branch of Vickers Limited, from January to September 1916.

from my deep reverie by what appeared to me at that moment the soulless strains of the Tchaïkovsky Fifth Symphony. I fled from the hall. This overpowering sense is rare and to me it is the only gauge by which we can assess a great composer. One meets with it at rare intervals in a lifetime.

Yet this opera is little known, and I know of no other performances of it in England apart from the Beecham ones. As the Black Fiddler significantly remarks in the opera: 'None knows when Father Time will make odd things even'.

*   *   *

> Brian now inveighs against 'academic' attitudes in general, and in particular the academic insistence that large-scale instrumental composition must conform to the classical forms. This excursus forms an introduction to a rapid survey of Delius' four concertos. Each is briefly characterised, with music examples; Brian praises them all, but his favourite appears to be the early (and to our ears rather uncharacteristic) Piano Concerto. He follows this with a similarly hurried discussion of the chamber music – we rejoin his text towards the end of this section.

The Sonata for Violin and Piano (published by Forsyth Bros.)[12] is distinguished by an aloofness found only in the choicest works of Delius. This work moves with exquisite grace, a commingling of bright with sad moments, and the construction is quite an original design, yet brimful of melody and harmonies of ever rich and changing hues and lusciousness. The *Legend* for Violin and Piano (also published by Forsyth), a bagatelle in stature by comparison, has the same melodic interest and charm.

In all the Delius instrumental works, one is conscious of a powerful mind searching, concentrating and striving to render articulate thoughts which remain unresolved in language but which resolve themselves into music. The expressions of a soul, intimate, introspective and passionate, struggling against a remorseless fate. If one could imagine

[12] This is the so-called Violin Sonata No. 1 (actually Delius' second) of 1914. No. 2, although composed by the time of writing, had not yet been published.

Goethe (with his philosophy), Shelley, Wilde and Pater (with their almost tropical luxuriance in language) thinking and expressing their thoughts in music, we get somewhere near to the working mind of Delius.

Like his prototypes, Delius marvels at the chromaticism of his art, and his mind becomes immersed in its endless beauty. Nowhere in the instrumental works do we meet a coarse, ugly thought. If we become stimulated into admiration akin to awe, the thoughts reach us through a purified mind, even if it glows at furnace heat; and though such a mind glows by its vast introspection and concentration, it never once carries us away by childish laughter or childish spirits. If Delius sees life whole, he gazes to the middle and stands aghast, and becomes obsessed by the tragedy of it. From such a deep well does all this music spring. Nowhere has Delius attained finer distinction than in his choral writing.

Songs of Sunset

These are published by Leuckart of Leipzig, are inscribed to the Musical Union of Elberfeld, and consist of settings of a number of poems by Ernest Dowson – for solo voices, choir and orchestra. Those who know Dowson's essays and poetry will have noticed how his mind constantly throws itself back, analysing its own experiences and speculating upon life and the things which happen naturally in the evolution of time and cannot happen again. The music dates from a little later than the *Sea Drift* music and has the same finished quality of that work – though the separate poems prevent the central connecting link of continuous thinking such as the central idea of *Sea Drift* gives. The fine solo for baritone in the *Songs of Sunset* gives the key to the complete work:[13]

> By the sad waters of separation
>   Where we have wandered divers ways,
> I have but the shadow and imitation
>   Of the old memorial days.

[13] In the latter part of the article Brian quotes very extensively indeed from Delius' texts. This, and most subsequent quotations have been shortened.

In music I have no consolation,
  No roses are pale enough for me:
The sound of the waters of separation
  Surpasseth roses and melody.

Sea Drift

It is in the record of every great artist that some particular work stands out with greater lustre from the rest. We have drawn attention to this in the art of Delius, in the orchestral works, *Paris*, *Appalachia*, the Piano Concerto, the opera, *A Village Romeo and Juliet*.

In *Sea Drift* and the *Mass of Life*, Delius gave us two of the finest pieces of continuous concentrated thinking in the realm of choral and orchestral music. Both works appear to have been forged in one piece. The inspiration remains at a high altitude throughout and never droops. Of the two works, *Sea Drift* is of exquisite beauty. It is as beautiful as a spotless saintly woman.

I don't know if a hand was ever held up against this delicate thing, for it remains a mystery to me why its performances are so infrequent. It was first produced in this country by Sir Henry J. Wood at the Sheffield Festival in 1908, and performances by Sir Thomas Beecham followed closely after the Sheffield one.

Sea Drift is a setting for baritone solo, chorus, and orchestra, of a poem by Walt Whitman. It is inscribed to Max Schillings and published by Harmonie of Berlin and Universal of Vienna. Its note is personal and tragic. In the poem, the poet sings of how, when he was a boy, he watched two birds build their nest by the shore near the sea and of the continuous joy and rapture in their daily home life. How the poet watched the she-bird sitting on her nest whilst the he-bird sang his song of love and companionship. Then the tragedy happens. The rest of the story consists of a rhapsodising upon the tragedy and the ghostly solitariness of the he-bird, who remains singing alone by the seashore, crying to his mate who was to return no more.

The composer's setting is as original in conception as Whitman's handling of the little tragedy. Delius sets his work out like a painter. With fine, delicate orchestration, we

have the sea pictured with its continuous restlessness and
with the boom of distant breakers. Into this the chorus
enters, with voices massed, singing in close, thick harmonies; these dissolve, leaving the baritone solo to carry on
the story of the tragedy. Sweeping in and out of and sometimes around the narrative is a vivid, descriptive orchestration, which with the voices rises like fountains of sound, tier
upon tier, and then gently subsides, leaving the baritone
soloist expressing the more personal and human note; the
music moving without interruption until it reaches a climax
in a dramatic cry, as the uselessness of waiting and watching
is revealed to the he-bird.

The concluding lines of the he-bird, given to the baritone
soloist, contain the most poignant music to be found in the
art of Delius:

> O I am very sick and sorrowful.
> O brown halo in the sky near the moon
>   drooping upon the sea!
> O troubled reflection in the sea!
> O throat! O throbbing heart!
> And I singing uselessly all the night!
> O past! O happy life!
> O songs of joy! in the air, in the woods:
> Over fields, loved, loved!
> By my mate, no more with me!
> We two together no more!

Such a setting, even in 1924, would be sufficient to excite
general comment and admiration. But this work was written twenty years ago, when Wagner, Strauss, and Debussy
were spreading their influence universal. Yet this composer's note is his own; he remained firm to his own ideals
and unshaken by any other; so the originality of this work is
all the more striking because it is a part in a perfect sequence
of fine works which make up the art of Delius.

Things have changed somewhat since its first production.
Twenty years ago there were only one or two conductors
capable of adequately handling a performance of such a
work. In these days we have a number of conductors who
might give a performance of it, even if they missed attaining
the ideal. Perhaps some of our young men, on the look out

for novelty, as beautiful as it is original, will give their attention to one of the most distinguished works in recent European music.

The Mass of Life

Since civilisation began, each successive epoch has produced wise men in the order of poets or philosophers,
whose mission on earth is to record by inspiration those
flashes of wit, irony, passion and all the various emotions
which are united in the pages of the finest literature in every
country. Stretching from the remote East to ourselves is an
unbroken line of books, each expressive of its author's
genius or inspiration. From these we get the teachings
and sayings of the Hebrew prophets, of Confucius,
Buddha, and Mahomet. More recently, Marcus Aurelius,
Jesus Christ and his Apostles, St. Francis of Assisi, Jacob
Boehm, Paracelsus, &c.[14] The sayings and writings of
these philosophers and divinities, now enshrined, are the
heritage of every country. To this order belongs the German
philosopher, Frederick Nietzsche, whose philosophy and
thoughts upon life found expression in his work, *Also sprach
Zarathustra*.

Also, Richard Strauss drew inspiration from its pages for
one of his finest symphonic poems. The libretto for *The
Mass of Life* was selected from *Also sprach Zarathustra* by
Delius's friend, Fritz Cassirer, to whom the work is
inscribed. There is a sub-dedication to another friend of
Delius, Arthur Kronig, in the concluding portion of the
mass. The work is divided into two parts and is written for
eight part chorus, four solo voices and large orchestra. It is
published by Harmonie of Berlin. The more rapturous and
thrilling moments are given to the chorus, the more personal ones to solo voices. The use of the voices is, as usual
with Delius, often close packed harmonies for creating
great powerful effects; or, as an integral part of the orchestral machine, and sometimes so, as in *Appalachia* or *From the
High Hills*, without words.

---

[14] In a letter to Bantock of 20 February 1942, Brian recalled having
owned works of Boehm, Swedenborg, and Paracelsus 'many years ago'.

Zarathustra, who embodies the work, is a dual personality; many of us have met him before, but not as Nietzsche presents him. Most artists have this dual personality, which is the reason why so few of them understand themselves and make it impossible to understand others too. In the case of Zarathustra, the inner voice is in control, leading him to all that is noble and healthy and shunning all that is foul and mean. It is an effort to develop a human being stripped of the small and petty things of life – a being in which hate and selfishness have no part. Hence I regard *Zarathustra* as among the inspired books, for it is another attempt to create minds in which base poisons of every-day life have no part. Hence Delius calls his selection from these inspired utterances *The Mass of Life*. His method embraces the oratorio plan of separate choruses and solos, largely complete in themselves, yet part of an endless chain of theme which makes up the whole work.

PART I

The work opens with eight-part chorus and orchestra – the thing pelts away with a maddening joy and fervour – in F major.

> O thou my will,
> Dispeller thou of care,
> Thou mine essential in life,
> Preserve me from all petty conquests.

This slowly climbs to a rapturous outburst thrown out by chorus and orchestra (Ex.3), which runs in and out of the texture right to the end of the movement.

Ex. 3

A recitativo for baritone follows:

> Now lift your heads, all:
> Lift them, brothers,
> High! higher!
> Nor forget the light fantastic toe.

This invitation to laughter and cheerfulness is followed by a
solo for tenor, which begins with quiet mysticism in
orchestra supported by alto voice amidst delicately tinted
orchestration.

> In thine eye I gazed of late,
>   O wondrous life!
> Gold saw I in thy night eye gleaming.
> My heart stood still,
> Seized with a voluptuous longing.

This solo is passed to contralto, who returns to the meditation upon the dance – the music losing its vague dreamy
aspect and growing more assertive as the tenor soloist sings:

> Toward thee I bounded.
> Alas! ah my bound thou swiftly fledest!

At this point chorus enters (wordless). Solo soprano and
contralto take up the theme: the movement swings with fine
splendour as the meditation continues:

> I suffer,
> Yet all would I suffer
> For these right gladly.

> Thou, whose coldness kindles,
> Whose hate beguiles,
> Whose flight bindeth,
> Whose scoff charms—

right into a palpitating dance movement, which swings with
fine vigour and develops into a real frenzy (Ex.4):

> That is a dance
> Over hill and dale.
> I am the huntsman,
> Wilt thou be my hound
> Or wilt thou be my chamois?

Ex. 4

Like many of Delius's fine inspirations, this movement is built upon slender material – such as the pair of soprano themes. The second soprano theme had previously first appeared among the horns in the baritone recit., where Zarathustra exclaims:

Nor forget the light fantastic toe.

It is the development of these dual themes which captivates our admiration, for they continually flit about either in orchestra or in voices and at moments grow overpowering and audacious. The music eventually fades away and the baritone enters upon a new soliloquy (Ex.5):

O, ye my new companions,
Ye strange minded ones,
Ye higher born mortals,
How well ye please me to-day,
Since ye waxed light hearted!

Ex. 5

Then follows one of the most exquisite moments in the work (Ex.6).

> O Zarathustra!
> Far off, from good and evil,
> We discovered our island.
> Our ever verdant meadow,
> We twain alone.
> Reason 'tis that we should
> Love one another.

Ex. 6

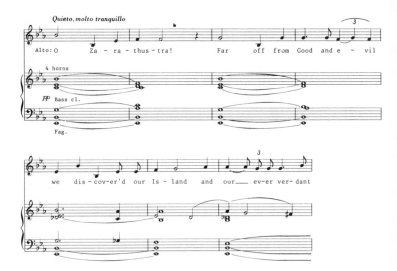

From this point of subdued eloquence, the music grows darker: the deep solemn notes of a midnight bell are heard amidst the silence of the night.

Delius, always inspired by solemnities and deep silences, pours out the loveliest utterances. The music begins to droop and become almost stationary. A chorus is heard chanting:

> O, solitude of all giving ones.
> O silence deep of all light shedders.
> Night reigneth.

Baritone solo chorus and orchestra continue amidst hushed silence:

> Woe is me! How is the time fled?
> Sank I not beneath deep fountains? [...]
> Oh man, thou higher born man,
> Mark well!
> This my speech is meant for subtile senses.
> Attend and hearken:
> What saith the solemn midnight hour?

The reply to this opens out very beautifully in slow sinking chromatic harmonies in horns and woodwind over a pedal in string basses.

> Night reigneth!
> Now louder murmur the leaping
> Crystalline fountains.
> And is not my soul like a high
> Leaping fountain?

The music spreads and envelops the whole orchestra, breaking into a pæan of joy as the soloist continues declaring:

> The unrequited, ne'er to be requited,
> Dwells in me.
>
> That for utterance clamours.
> A deep longing for love
> Rages within me.
> That speaks itself nought
> But love's sweetest language.

passing to the dreamy melting harmonies of the opening and closing of Part I in a solemn stillness in chorus and orchestra.

> Softly now awaken
> All the songs of fond lovers:
> And my own soul
> Is the song of a lover.

It is love music, certainly very beautiful and highly sprititualised. There is no dross here.

PART II

The first half of the Mass, concluding amidst solemnities, is
recalled by the Prelude of Part II, opening in a similar
atmosphere. In the short prelude, where muted strings sustain, we hear horn calls and their echoes. Then, without any
preparation, we are suddenly pitched into blazing sunlight;
for chorus and orchestra break into joyous praise mindful
of an exultant procession, much resembling the opening of
Part I. Here the manner and context is quite different. In
the bright key of A major, the work opens out, voices and
orchestra clanging away,

> Arise! now thou glorious midday!
> The sea storms!
> Away! ye ancient ocean farers!
> Steer our bark to yon regions

making for a dramatic climax in the orchestral and choral
basses (Ex.7) at

> That way fare
> Wilder far than storm wracked sea.

Ex. 7

Another change of mood follows the last climax. Some
delicate melodic work in woodwind appears as soli voices
break in with

> 'Tis gone, the lingering sorrow
> Of my Springtide.

> Summer am I become,
> Yea summer's midday!

Once again the chorus breaks in triumphantly:

> Like a tempest comes my bliss
> And brings me freedom!

with a portion of the strenuous opening repeated.

A meditation for baritone solo follows. Opening with low sustained chords in muted strings, on which fragments flit in wood-wind, solo voice enters with

> Lyre, my solace,
> Come enchant me!
> I love thine undulating,
> Inebriating, quivering tone!

It will have been observed in the brief analysis of Part I how extraordinary are the moods of the various meditations as they follow each other. This solo for baritone, a thing of exquisite purity and beauty, droops down as Zarathustra contemplates the deeper thought which night inspires. This movement passes amidst a delicate tracery of quiet arabesques in woodwind and sustained strings. The succeeding movement enters amidst similar mysterious tones in much divided muted strings and woodwind. From out of this nebula, a figure rises in the basses: trombones are heard. The bass figure reappears, but broken and agitated, over which woodwind sing away *in alt*. It is a sudden vision, which vanishes quickly, leaving a palpitating dance movement in full flight in female chorus and orchestra. Zarathustra appears on the scene. As he enters, amidst the revellers, he sings:

> Stop not dancing I pray
> Ye beautiful maidens!
> I came not hither to spoil
> Your sport with angry look.

The dance is resumed with more passion and zest. Its mad prancing makes one sit up, quite hot. For brilliance in virtuoso orchestral technique, this dance has no rival in the art of Delius.

The dance concluded, Zarathustra is once again alone. He sings a new soliloquy of wonderful eloquence and tenderness (Ex.8). Subdued figures in female voices heighten its solemnity.

Ex. 8

A pastoral melody for solo oboe commences the following movement, whilst low harmonies in divided strings follow; the oboe melody is echoed by English horn. Its meaning is significant when chorus enter with

> Glorious Midday sleeps on the meadows.
> Thou liest in the heather.
> Hush!

So, apparently in the meadow with nature's sounds around him, Zarathustra lies and listens and is lulled by them. He continues

> This is the coveted hour of solemn silence,
> When no shepherd sounds his reed.

and the chorus sing

> Sweet solitude of purpling heather—
> O bliss! O bliss!

The music grows more mysterious. Over agitated tremolos in strings, Zarathustra exclaims:

> What befell me?
> Hark! was it time hence that fled?
> Am I not falling?
> Fell I not?
> Hark! neath the fountain of endless day.

He becomes more vehement. In close harmonies in divided strings and chorus, Zarathustra continues:

> O now break, now break, heart!
> Hast known life's rapture.
> Hush! would'st thou now carol?
> O my fond spirit.

Contralto and soprano soloists carry along the meditation, which gradually expands to a broad climax for orchestra, soloists and chorus in an outburst:

> Fair fortune smiles—
> Thus smiles a god?

A change to quieter atmosphere follows. Chorus sings,

> Rise! thou sleeper!
> Zarathustra
> Thou midday sleeper!

to which he replies in a baritone solo of remarkable eloquence, punctuated with chorus exclamations.

Midnight again approaches: this atmosphere is wonderfully depicted in a short prelude which begins in a long drawn melody in the string basses, amidst sustained woodwind and the constant plucking of the low strings in two harps. At the close of this the baritone solo leads direct to one of the supremest moments in this work, so remarkable for fine solos given to the baritone. Zarathustra sings:

> Ye higher born mortals—
> The midnight hour is nigh:
> Now into your ears
> I something fain would whisper—
> What yonder ancient toller
> Into mine ear tells—

As secret, as dreadful as heartfelt
As yonder midnight bell
Into mine ear revealeth.

This tolling of the midnight bells, which begins in the lower strings of the harp, is a strain which slowly grows and becomes more dreadful and overpowering and has even a comic aspect for Zarathustra.

Although Zarathustra is so solemn – almost always so – there are moments when (in the middle of his solemnities) he breaks out into a naive utterance, as he realises that there may be another aspect to his thoughts. This will be observed in his rhapsody upon the midnight bell:

Oh! how she sighs!
How in her dreams, she laughs!
That ancient, solemn tolling
Midnight Bell!
Hush! Hush!
Much then is told us
Which in daytime must not be heard.

The tolling continues, though at this point the music changes in aspect. Chorus enter and accentuate the solemnities of the scene. Zarathustra continues:

O man mark well;
What tolls the solemn Midnight Bell!

Then, admist a magnificent movement, in which myriads of lights and censers swing, the music slowly expands to a full throated pæan from solo voices, chorus and orchestra as the work concludes:

Joy for all things craves eternity.
Who craves not joy?
She is lustier, heartier, hungrier,
Than all our woe.

Making one more final effort, it rises to a thrilling climax from chorus, soloists and orchestra and breaks upon:

O bliss! O pain!
O break heart—
Joy craves endless day.

EPILOGUE

In closing the pages of *The Mass of Life*, there is a consciousness that in climbing the peaks which make up the art of
Delius the summit of the last and greatest has been reached.
Here, in this work, we find all those things which stir him to
great moments – pastoral scenery, vastnesses, silences,
human life; everything on a big scale. The elemental and
dramatic spur him as they once did Weber, Berlioz and
Wagner. In Delius, it is all so different and not less eloquent.
With such a chain of soliloquies and meditations, which
make up *The Mass of Life*, it may be argued that there is no
central plot or plan. Of course, plot is always with us;
neither is there a central plot in *Tristram Shandy* or in the
great B minor Mass of Bach, which this work of Delius's
resembles by reason of its long sustained inspiration and
grandeur. The music is the thing, and it must stand or fall
on its merits as a continuous series of soliloquies. It is a chain
of wonderful thoughts, like the words of the B minor Mass.
In the Delius work, the whole thing is fragrant with wisdom
and commonsense, *plus* a philosophy equally naïve and
humorous.

The question has been asked: Why did I write upon
Delius, since his friend Philip Heseltine had already written
upon him?[15] My reply is that I did not know of Heseltine's
book until long after its appearance, and this appreciation
was well on its way. Considering the great originality of
Delius, he has had very little publicity. He is of a retiring, shy
disposition and loathes the world and limelight. His
greatest satisfaction is obtained by burying himself in a far
away cottage and getting on with his work. Unlike many of
his contemporaries, he wastes no time in the *rôle* of amateur
policeman. [...] Neither is he ever caught playing the part of
Mephistopheles disguised as Orpheus.

It is to Sir Thomas Beecham that we owe the early performances of this work, and they were certainly not cor-
dially received. We have a stereotyped manner of receiving
all new work – if it is off the beaten track. After all that has

[15] Philip Heseltine's *Frederick Delius* (John Lane, London, 1923) had
been published just before Brian's article began to appear.

been performed in the intervening years, we are now better prepared for another performance of this remarkable work; and it is to be hoped that a generous feeling of fairness and rightness will go out to this composer, and we shall soon have another opportunity of hearing it.

Sir Thomas Beecham's enthusiasm for *The Mass of Life* was right, for he had found a *rara avis*. If other people could but feel it too, this work would soon be established. Still, one must not despair, seeing that it took a couple of centuries to establish the Bach B minor Mass.

It may be argued that this appreciation is more enthusiastic than critical. What I endeavoured to do was to see things from the Delius point of view. Also, in a life spent mostly (for thirty years) among full scores, I have not found any which draw forth greater interest and admiration than those of Delius. He treats the orchestra with greatest friendship and affection. All his work is so exquisitely finished and so wonderfully well balanced. He seems to take meticulous care, and everything seems to happen so naturally, even if he uses three piccolos, as in *Appalachia*. There are extremes for the bassoons in *Paris* and for the horns in *Appalachia*. But it doesn't seem to matter much whether it is woodwind, brass, percussion or strings: he uses plenty of them, with greatest finish, and gets the best out of them.

Perhaps we may reach another period when the Delius works will again be enthustiastically taken up. I am greatly indebted to Messrs. Curwen for lending all the scores published by Universal, Harmonie and Leuckart. Also to Tischer & Jagenberg, Augener Ltd., and Winthrop Rogers. Without this generosity the appreciation would have been impossible. Delius's attitude and intent may be summed up from one of his letters written from Italy:

> I am here, ill, hoping that sunny skies will improve my health. You do and say what you like, – you know and understand my mind completely. But I want to be left alone, and get on with my work.

After the appearance of the analysis of *Appalachia* in an earlier number, he sent me five of his finest songs by way of

appreciation for what I had written.[16] One can best conclude an appreciation of Delius with an extract from the
work of another great mind which so much resembles his
own in scope and vastness:

> In the tides of life
> In the storm of deeds—
> I throw the shuttle hither and thither—
> And to and fro:
> An eternal ocean,
> A restless weaving
> A glowing life.
> Thus at the roaring loom of time
> I sit and weave
> The Godhead's living robe.[17]

The Delius Festival

These two short articles were prompted by the first-ever
Delius Festival, which was held in London from 12 October
to 1 November 1929 under the direction of Sir Thomas
Beecham. Both appeared in *Musical Opinion*, the first in the
November issue (pp. 130–131), the second in December
(pp. 240–241).

I.

Delius is one of the few world's geniuses whose ways and
means defy analysis. In the opinion of the academics, music
should conform to the laws of academical analysis. The
great works of Delius, Wagner, Palestrina, Byrd, &c., pro-
ceed from intuition and defy analysis. Allied with the
marvellous intution of Delius is his introspective brooding
on fatality and chance of circumstance – the shadowy

---

[16]   Probably the 5 *Lieder (aus dem Norwegischen)*, published as a set in 1890.
This copy, which was inscribed to Brian not only by Delius but by his wife
Jelka, was eventually given by Brian to an acquaintance in 1967, when he
disposed of most of his books and music before moving house for the last
time.
[17]   Lines spoken by the Earth-Spirit in Act I of Goethe's *Faust*. The quotation does not match any of the published translations I have been able to
consult, and may well be Brian's own.

substance of life and its disillusionment. This philosophical outlook is tinged with a vast yearning and love for humanity, and saturates his music, which takes the form of an endless spinning of the most delicately shaded chromaticism, moving uninterruptedly like the sea. Just as the art of Wagner is a natural development of the later spiritual tendencies of Beethoven, so is the art of Delius a natural development of Wagner from the spiritual qualities of *Tristan* and *Parsifal*. Here and there, as in *Sea Drift* and in the closing scene of *The Village Romeo and Juliet*, where the ruthless laws of fate rise with storm-like anger, fretting and tossing, the despairing and crying tragedy within is painted with extraordinary realism. Otherwise, the art of Delius remains elusive and subjective.

The first day of the Delius Festival was a great rally – a reminder of one of those pre-war audiences when everyone from London and the provinces packed the Queen's Hall. What this music would mean without Sir Thomas Beecham no one may prophesy. He has had the substance of it in his heart for many years, and has been a convinced pleader for Delius for over a quarter of a century. The first concert was made memorable by the singing of Dennis Noble in the solo part of *Sea Drift*; by Heddle Nash and Pauline Maunder as the two children in *A Village Romeo and Juliet*; and by the sublime dignity of Sir Thomas Beecham, who conducted the entire concert from memory. At the close there was an outburst of approval from the audience, which rendered spontaneous homage to the composer. Delius, a broken and pathetic figure in the balcony, quietly acknowledged his victory. This concert was given under the auspices of the Columbia Graphophone Co., with the London Select Choir, conducted by T. Arnold Fulton, and a specially selected orchestra.

The continuation of the concerts of the Delius Festival at Queen's Hall on October 18th indicated the inexhaustible variety of the composer's invention and inspiration. *Eventyr*, drawn from that ghostly realm which was wont to inspire Michael Drayton,[18] has also inflamed Delius into a

[18] Drayton (1563–1631) is best remembered for his *Poly-Olbion* and *Nymphidia*, pastoral and 'Faery' epics respectively. Brian's partsong *The Fairy*

finely sustained effort in ghostly pictorial writing. *Cynara*, a setting for orchestra and baritone of a poem by Ernest Dowson, and sung by John Goss, is a work of highly coloured orchestral weaving, expressive of the excesses of passion and its subsequent reproaches. *Arabesk*, a setting for baritone solo, chorus and orchestra, of a poem by the Danish poet, J.P. Jacobsen, ought not to have waited so long for a London performance. If the poem does not grip with the extraordinary power of *Sea Drift* and *Appalachia*, it is in its way, hardly less beautiful: the expression of the doubts and fears of living are something quite new in the *métier* of Delius, though not less poignant than the expression of the two works mentioned.

Of the familiar Delius works, Evelyn Howard Jones played the solo part of the Piano Concerto with unusual warmth, though there are a few real opportunities for the solo instrument, for the pianoforte is conceived as an integral part of the orchestral score. We had an instance of the composer's extraordinary psychological insight in his use of the chorus in *Appalachia*. Many Delius admirers are inclined to place this foremost amongst his work. As a series of orchestral variations, *Appalachia* is unique, there is not a page of the orchestral score that is without the element of surprise – not that of the Berlioz order – but in the newness of Delius's harmonic and polyphonic tissue. It has a style and colour scheme which eludes cold analysis: but the steady gaze of its fascinating beauty never sags and it is an extraordinary moment when the chorus makes its first entry. Its subsequent employment in the finale makes one of the most thrilling climaxes in the realm of music.

As in *Arabesk*, we had in *Appalachia* very imaginative work from John Goss and the London Select Choir – the latter made the most of their golden opportunities in the Finale. As is now customary, Sir Thomas Beecham conducted from memory. The orchestral interpretation was a memorable experience. This concert was given by the B.B.C., and included the London Select Choir, augmented by members of the Royal College Choral Class and the B.B.C. National Chorus, with the B.B.C. Orchestra.

Palace (1914) is a setting of lines from *Nymphidia*.

II.

The extraordinary enthusiasm which attended the recent
Delius Festival and drew over-crowded audiences at the
Æolian Hall and Queen's Hall on each occasion is less a matter for congratulation than for reflection. No amount of
argument can offer a genuine solution to the sudden popularity of a composer who not long ago was supposed to have
but a few faithful friends. It may be chagrin to those few to
know that Delius is now worshipped by many others, for
some ten thousand attended the festival. Many, no doubt,
heard each concert. The miracle lies in the sumptuous and
exquisitely sustained interpretation.

During the festival, efforts were made to show how
English all this wondrous music is. We confess, however,
that our patriotism does not lead us so far as to recognise
the genuine English character in the music of Delius,
neither are we anxious to discover it. The art of Delius does
not work in circumscribed limits: if we reflect on his life and
the influences which have inspired his finest works –
Appalachia, Sea Drift, Mass of Life – we cannot discover which
is supposed to approximate to English character. During
the festival, these three works stood out conspicuously as
peaks in a mountain chain. The *Mass of Life*, in particular,
overtowered like Mount Everest.[19]

Now that the festival is past, we are sure than no pen will
successfully explain what it is that fascinates us in this
hothouse music, which has all the alluring enchantment of
tropical flowers and plants, over which hangs a thick vapour
saturated with a thousand perfumes. Such is the
background of his finest work: the danger in performance
lies in missing the correct perspective. From this point of
view the festival has been a triumph in delicately shaded
interpretation. Without the supersensitised mind of
Beecham, which responds so wonderfully to Delius, the festival would have meant little.

Who is to estimate the position of Delius? His individuality and originality of outlook are not denied: the exciting

[19] Brian briefly reviewed the performance in the 'London Concerts' section of the same issue of *Musical Opinion*.

scenes at the close of each performance suggest that most people were affected by it. Herein lies the secret of the interpretation. It is not necessary to labour the point that during the performance of the *Mass of Life*, which continued for two hours, we cannot recollect an occasion when such enormous forces appeared so completely magnetised to the will of the conductor. We remember other occasions (particularly with Nikisch) when such a state of high tension in the orchestra produced memorable results. This magnetic power sealed the final triumph of the festival.

Two composers – Chopin and Wagner – remind us of Delius. Both were given to long-sustained flights of continuous and highly involved chromatic writing of haunting beauty. As to how it all happens, constructively, we have no wish to know, or the fascination would dissolve, as the mystery of the rainbow dissolved before Keats. There are long stretches of continuous writing in *Tristan* and *Parsifal* coloured with a spiritual essence of remarkable beauty. It is on this same rarely attained plane of thought that some of the finest music of Delius is written. Having admitted its rare exotic qualities, many now seek to explain it. To some, Delius is the end of the great Romantic period. Neither Byrd nor Palestrina knew that they were closing a period: Monteverdi did not know he was beginning one: Bach was too much occupied with his multifarious domestic and artistic duties even to realise what he was really doing.

In recent years we have made acquaintance with much ugliness: yet, if such marvellously sustained and wonderfully beautiful music can flow from Delius after all we had received from a previously supposed closed romantic period, there is no reason why some future composer should not write something to excel it.

Delius' Personality

The November 1929 *Musical Opinion* also contained (p.144)
this short article, in the untitled sequence which marks an
intermediate stage between Brian's original 'The Musician's
Diary' and his later 'On the Other Hand' columns. I have
supplemented it with a paragraph in similar vein from 'On
the Other Hand' for May 1939 (p.686).

In days gone by it was interesting to listen to Delius discussing music and his contemporaries when he felt in the mood
to let himself go. His remarks were always original and
interspersed with a great deal of wit. In his retirement his
own sickness and slowly creeping incapacity for creative
work and absence of intercourse with his former colleagues,
have silenced those impromptu discussions which were
such a joy to those who were privileged to join in them. On
the eve of his departure for London to take part in the
Delius Festival, he expressed himself quite strongly on the
tendencies of the 'atonal' school, which he regards as the
'wrong note school', and whose adherents he regards as
sensationalists. He is more severe on those who cry 'Go back
to –', for it is his opinion that music cannot 'go back' to anything, it must 'go on'. His sensitiveness is shown in the matter of inspiration, which he finds almost entirely from contemporary music. It is always a rare quality, and Delius
thinks that since the death of Bach the world has only produced a dozen composers of genius. The craze for sensationalism has affected young composers who ache to
become celebrities before they even know themselves.
Delius suggests that if they cannot search inwardly and find
the genuine article they will be better employed digging in
the garden or in some other useful work. These are the
reflections of a genius whose career has been one of slow
development and who also had to wait until he was seventy
years old before his life's work received universal homage.
    Two of the greatest influences in his life were derived
from listening to negroes singing in the plantations of
Florida in his youth, and later when he went to live in

Leipzig he met Grieg, whose friend he became. This friendship continued until Grieg's death.

*   *   *

I must protest against the exhibition of drawings of Delius made by Augustus John and James Gunn. However excellent the pictures may be as works of art, they do not represent Delius. I wonder if anywhere can be found a portrait of the composer of thirty years ago, just when he had completed the music which made him famous and when he lost no opportunity of defying convention.[20] Delius was then no figure of complacency – a man of forty-five, tall and erect, sparsely built, and with piercing greyish-blue eyes when talking of music. His attire was at least out of the ordinary, for he affected a Sammy hat and an Inverness cape, the right end of the latter being thrown back, so exposing his right hand on the knob of his walking stick. He looked ready to meet the world in arms: and this is how, I think, other generations should know him.

The Passing of Delius

This is from 'On the Other Hand' of July 1934, p. 861, and immediately follows the notice of Holst's death given on pp.285–288.

The death of Delius did not come to us with the tragic suddenness as that of Holst: he was seventy-two, but at the age when Holst died he had written all that has made him famous. My last glimpse of Delius was at the festival organised for his honour by Sir Thomas Beecham at Queen's Hall a few years ago. He was then indeed a pathetic figure, reclining on a long chair placed in the balcony – blind, thin and fragile. A quarter of a century earlier I often saw him, thin

---

[20] As we now know (e.g., from the Robert Threlfall/Lionel Carley *Delius: a Life in Pictures*, O.U.P., 1977), the Delius iconography is quite extensive. In particular, the 1903 and 1912 portraits by Ida Gerhardi seem to have something of the quality Brian remembers here.

and pale even then, and made more so by his black garb of a wide-brimmed felt hat and cloak thrown partially back over his left shoulder. One occasion was in the foyer at Queen's Hall, when he was in a circle of friends comprising Norman O'Neill, Balfour Gardiner, Frederick Austin, and Thomas Beecham. My introduction to Delius came in 1908, at the Philharmonic Hall, Liverpool, where, in his championship of Delius's works, Beecham had brought the New Symphony Orchestra.[21] Enthusiasm was great, for we were all anxious to hear the nocturne, *Paris*. Delius was present, with well known musicians, among whom I remember seeing Bantock, Harry Evans, W. G. McNaught, Harry Cooper,[22] &c. Beecham conducted the Delius work from memory, amidst extraordinary enthusiasm. *Paris*, an orchestral nocturne, suggested clearly a personality as interesting as that of Elgar or of Strauss, but different from either. Thus began the Delius cult, which grows and grows in ever-expanding waves, fully justifying Sir Thomas Beecham's early prescience.

During the morning following the concert I travelled with Delius by the overhead railway to the mouth of the Mersey, just to satisfy his craving to gaze at the sea, which he did with his head uncovered. My next meeting with him was at a concert in the Midlands, at which Beecham conducted *Appalachia*, with the Hallé Orchestra, the other work in the programme being Elgar's *Gerontius*.[23] Now, the *Appalachia* orchestra needed more players than that for *Gerontius*, and

[21] See p.99 for evidence that this may *not* have been their first meeting. The performance of *Paris* took place on 11 January 1908.

[22] Harry Evans (1873–1914), the great Welsh choral conductor, who premiered many English works and gave the second performance of Brian's *By the Waters of Babylon*; William Gray McNaught (1849–1918), choral conductor, adjudicator, and educationist, editor of the *Musical Times* 1909–1918. 'Harry Cooper' I cannot identify, unless he is the tenor Henry Cooper listed in several issues of *The Year's Music* (J.C. Virtue and Co., London) for the 1890s, with a London address.

[23] Brian's memory appears to have confused two different occasions: the *Appalachia* performance is the one referred to in footnote 9 (p.110), which Delius himself conducted; whereas Beecham conducted *Sea Drift* in Hanley on 3 December of the same year. The facts are correct again at p.144 below.

in fact the 'extras' had been engaged, but the main body arrived without them. The incident reflects the indifference with which the composer was then regarded in certain circles: Delius resented it and spoke very bitterly to Jennings, the Hallé librarian. Beecham did the best possible under the circumstances by 'cuing in' the missing orchestral 'extras' from memory. Later I met Delius in the company of his wife at various performances of his works, notably of *Sea Drift* and of the *Mass of Life*, and I found him in her presence brightening in conversation, his greyish blue eyes lighting up freely. The lady herself was quite distinguished in bearing and appearance, and I can well believe that she abandoned the prospect of a distinguished career as a painter to serve her husband.

Many Delius enthusiasts think to discover a similarity between Elgar and Delius: this, except in a spiritual sense, is not clear to me. Delius, in the far-away days, could neither understand nor appreciate Elgar. When tributes to the genius shown in *Gerontius* were thick in the air, I was with Delius present at a performance of it: probably it was the only one he ever heard, and he was obviously disappointed: it was, he said, 'too Mendelssohnian', and not very original. For my part, I find it difficult to speak freely about Delius's music, which can only be fully understood in the hearing, and then remains a great memory. I say this even though I wrote, years ago, columns of descriptive analyses of his works for this journal, and received the commendation of the composer and a present of an inscribed copy of his songs. His music is a mixture of the most exotic poetry and painting, and I see him as an impressionist after the manner of Blake: his finest music is of nocturnal quality; but Delius is unlike any other composer in manner and outlook. But, like other composers, we find in his early music the stimulus of other men, notably of Wagner, Grieg and Debussy.

Delius in Decline

This is a book-review from *Musical Opinion*, December 1936, p.216.

'DELIUS AS I KNEW HIM.' By Eric Fenby.
(Bell & Sons.) Price 8s 6d.

This is a remarkable book, though the author himself might say its value lay rather in its subject than in its writing. But the book is, in its way, as revealing, poignant and gruesome as a tale by Edgar Allan Poe. However, those who make the acquaintance of Delius first through these descriptive pages telling of his last years, can at most realise the spectre of a once great man: and those who knew him in his prime will scarcely enjoy the reading of the book. Moreover, the ghastly picture of Delius, drawn by James Gunn, is reproduced again to accompany the book. He was egotistical, indulgent to himself, interested above all only in himself: but still with a redeeming tinge of originality that never seems to have left him. Thirty years ago, to see him enter the foyer of Queen's Hall was to feel oneself in the presence of a man of distinct personality, and that apart from the cut of the clothes he wore. He spoke in short staccato sentences, which thrust themselves into our most cherished beliefs and at the time seemed quite unanswerable: indeed, it seemed safer, for the sake of peace, to agree with what he said than to have the point thrust home.

This distinct personality, combined with his fascinating music, drew around Delius a circle of English and German friends, who rightly regarded him as a wonderful composer. Here was a man producing the most sensitively written romantic music since Chopin. Like Chopin, too, Delius was prone to profound introspection, which is not the same thing as melancholia. There is no cheerfulness in the music of Delius: he exults and sings finely and fiercely when overcome by tragedy. But in spite of his derision of all current religious beliefs, composers found themselves drawn towards his music. His attitude was much the same before classical music, which he ridiculed as so many square-cut patterns, stuffed: it was tailor's music!

When Delius fell by the way and became blind and partially paralysed, the writer of this book, Eric Fenby, wrote offering his services as amanuensis. Considering the years that Delius had spent at Grez-sur-Loing, alone with his wife and his music, it was a great adventure. Fenby arrived when the sands were running out: the patient, blind and a shadow of his former self, was given over to two nurses. But the spectre talked and anathematised, as in those days when he carried himself so proudly. Fenby seems to have stood up well to his self-sacrificing task, and with unusual courage: he must have been wonderfully helpful, persevering until Delius was subdued into loving him. All were pressed into keeping him interested when the absence of gnawing pain made such a task possible. Fenby read to him for hours on end; then he would ask for gramophone records with Beecham conducting, or for concert broadcasts of his own works, but always with Beecham.

We admit to a prejudice against all writings purporting to tell of the private life of an artist. In this case, however well it is done or sympathetically written, one cannot quite escape the atmosphere of a charnel house. Some day, let us hope, we shall all realise that the only worthy way of remembering a composer is to perform or listen to his music. Then will cease also the corpse-raising business. They carry the bodies of dead composers from one end of Europe to the other, and from France into England,[24] to the vast satisfaction of the morbid and to the profit of the picture papers.

Delius: The Last Phase

In the same issue of *Musical Opinion* (pp. 201–202), 'La Main Gauche' took Fenby's book as the text for more outspoken comments and reminiscences, as the leading matter of 'On the Other Hand'.

To those who knew Delius at the height of his amazing vitality, Eric Fenby's book comes as a sad revelation. *As I Knew*

[24] Delius was given temporary burial at Grez, but in May 1935 his body was brought to England and reinterred at Limpsfield, Surrey.

Him shows us the man bedridden and blind: and one may
again, in this case of Delius, question the propriety of telling
the story of the depth of human suffering. I do not deny the
right of anyone to do so: I would only choose to pass by on
the other side. The career of Delius as a composer was over
long before Mr. Fenby went out to act as his amanuensis,
and the disclosure of the futile efforts at further composition haunt me with terror. However, setting aside the record
of the tragedy of departing physical life, we realise the mental effort to live. In the village home at Grez-sur-Loing, we
still hear the voice of the man who feared nothing and
defied everything, the Delius whom I knew thirty years ago.
He never ceased to aver that culture, art and the mind had
been rooted out by Christianity. There was, in his
philosophy, no such thing as English music: only music written by men who happened to have their abode in England.
And more, music in England had only thrived, and could
only thrive, within the orbit of fashion set by the party
strongest in power. We have had the fashion of Handel, succeeded by that of Mendelssohn: and then the waxing and
waning of Tchaïkovsky, Wagner, Strauss, Brahms and their
satellites. When Delius arrived Elgar was in the ascendant.
All these and similar acid reasonings bear the similitude of
truth: but they do nothing to change the meanderings of
intellectual life, which cannot take a straight course: so all
our regrets are futile.

I deplore the absence of any book about Delius that
would re-create the sense of life in and around him when
his masterpieces were written. Mr. Fenby felt the sinister
aspect of much that confronted him at Grez-sur-Loing: and
well he might, for it was the approach to death through
unresigned suffering. We are told that Delius might have
been a better man had he been Christianised. That to me
only means that he would have been different at the end
had he been different at the beginning. The point for us is,
would Delius under different circumstances have written
better music? Knowing Delius as I did in the hey-day of his
powers, I prefer not to recognise him in the stricken figure
of Grez. And yet I am pursued by the thought that the other
man was already in him when he asked me to go with him

from a crowd of personages. We went away and stood by the sea: he silent and bareheaded. I, with this experience, should have been prepared for the voluntary exile in a village in France, which to other men would seem something worse than a penal establishment. Certainly, Beecham came breathing the breath of life; but Philip Heseltine was ill received. Balfour Gardiner was a visitor: still the spirit of Lazarus was consuming the mind, and this was revealed in the spasmodic action and phrase rather than in the polite epistle. Delius was revealed to Delius early in life and in his young days in Florida had divined a mission. Was it a flight from cruelty and suffering, from which he himself was not to escape? How strongly both are portrayed in his slave-work, *Appalachia*. Delius, by our Christian standards, could not be accounted a saint: and yet no saintly book can ever be more heart-searching than *Sea-Drift* or the 'Walk to the Paradise Garden'. Though I dislike this book as much as I dislike the Grand Guignol, I will not fail in my recognition of the courage and devotion of Mr. Eric Fenby who sat by the composer until the end came and brought peace.

The music of Delius, heard for the first time, had on listeners an effect not unlike that caused by his tilts at religion, at women, or at academic musical composition. Had Delius never found a Beecham, his music would have remained where it was thirty years ago. Every man of genius is forbidden by routine, for his work provokes opposition. Nothing more provocative and irritating resembles the common attitude to Delius as the case of Hugo Wolf. We do not need to-day to be told that the man who wrote *Penthesilea* or the *Italian Serenade* was a genius. Probably had not Hugo Wolf wielded such a fiery sword in the *Salonblatt*, opposition to his art would have been less effective and would not have delayed so long the recognition of his genius. When Hans Richter put *Penthesilea* in the trial rehearsals of the Vienna Philharmonic Orchestra (in 1886), the object was to reveal its suitability for concert performance. Wolf managed to gain admission, and accused Richter of making nonsense of the work and of stirring the players to ridicule. Richter had said that he had not intended to play the work through, but he did wish to have 'a glimpse of the man who had

presumed to say such things about the master Brahms'. I
take the facts and the quoted phrase from Ernest Newman's
Hugo Wolf.[25]

From this we must conclude that the better way for a
genius is to bury his talents, and thus avoid irritation to
those less gifted. Wolf did not do so, and Delius could not.
When Richter was conductor of the Hallé Orchestra, his
programmes gave complete satisfaction to the majority. A
minority[26] clamoured for the works of other modern composers than Elgar and Strauss, and from among them arose
a body determined that the reign of Richter over Manchester should cease. About this time Fritz Cassirer had given a
first performance in London of Delius's *Appalachia*, and
Manchester demanded that and more. Bantock came forward at Liverpool with *Brigg Fair*, which was the work, I
believe, with which Richter was to stifle criticism. The procedure at Vienna seems to have been repeated in Manchester.
Richter, neither knowing nor caring for the Delius score,
read through part of it with the orchestra, and then, stop-
ping the rehearsal, had the parts collected and the score
retrieved from where he had thrown it. Right or not in
detail, the story illustrates the mentality of Richter. However, the fight for Delius had begun, and no petulance on
the part of Richter could stop it. I was then writing for a
paper in the North, and a person known in London sent a
letter, after the *Appalachia* performance at Queen's Hall,
asking me to do 'nothing to help forward such music'. But
Bantock had told me that *Appalachia* was a masterpiece.

At that time I had neither seen nor heard a note of Delius.
Then came a letter from the secretary of a famous Northern
choral society, and he asked me what I thought of Bantock's
advocacy of *Appalachia*. If it were to be done, it would be
given at a *Gerontius* concert, and Delius must conduct. Now,
nobody in that society knew the name of Delius: they might
be aware of the orchestral specification of *Gerontius*, but
little they recked of that of *Appalachia*. Eventually a contract was made with the Hallé Orchestra, and a subsidiary

[25] Published by Methuen, London, 1907.
[26] Brian among them: *cf.* pp. 200 and 367.

contract for the extras for *Appalachia*. Now Delius comes on the scene, on tenter-hooks about those 'extras', for unintentionally the responsibility for them had become mine: and imagine my position and consternation when later, at the rehearsal, I had to explain to Delius that Jennings (the Hallé librarian) knew nothing at all about the extras contracted to be supplied. Small wonder that Delius turned in his wrath and abused Jennings roundly, likening the orchestra to a village band.

After performances in London and the provinces, Delius began to secure recognition: but we may doubt that full recognition would have been his had not the genius of Beecham been linked with his own. Beecham has much to his credit for things done in concert hall and opera house, but his greatest achievement is the establishment of Delius. Thirty years ago, for no other reason than missing a train, Beecham called upon me, and immediately on entering the room began to enthuse about the *Mass of Life*. He seated himself at the piano, and from memory continued to play almost without ceasing for two hours, calling out the orchestration as he went on. For me it was an extraordinary experience, and I suppose only possible with a phenomenon like Beecham, who absorbs and memorises an orchestral score without regard to length or complexity.

By this time (that is, 1908), all that makes for the reputation of Delius had been written. It turned out impossible for him to surpass *Sea Drift*, the *Mass of Life*, the *Village Romeo and Juliet*, *Appalachia* or *Paris*, which are five unique and very different concepts. Nothing written later has the same flair or sense of immensity. We say that every great composer bears the impress of one who has gone before: but there is little of that influence heard in the works of Delius. Even when listening to Strauss's *Till Eulenspiegel*, we become conscious of Liszt's *Mephisto Waltz* or of his Rhapsodies. But with *Paris* we are alone, for Delius brought nothing with him to the conception of that work. His strangely fascinating system of composition was individual: yet his striving for flowing continuity was precisely that for which Wagner fought and won. Though Delius scoffed at Wagner, he stands nearest to him in his ideals.

PART FIVE

BANTOCK

———————•———————

Brian was writing glowing reviews of Granville Bantock's music some time before the two men met in 1906 (*cf.* his note on the premiere of *Omar Khayyam*, Part I, on pp.183–185); but once they became personally acquainted they were firm friends until Bantock's death 40 years later. Although the relationship had its ups and downs there is no doubt that it was marked by strong mutual affection and esteem; one of Brian's principal reasons for moving to Birmingham at the end of 1915 was simply to be nearer his friend. It comes as no surprise, therefore, that Brian's writings on Bantock are numerous, and evince an admiration for his works which later generations of critics have not found themselves able to share. It seems likely that (especially in the period before the 1914–18 War) Bantock's works assumed an importance, by virtue of their epic scope and anti-Victorian, hedonistic out-look, that they were not subsequently able to sustain on purely musical grounds. Nevertheless, with interest in Ban-tock currently undergoing a modest revival, Brian's verdicts are hardly without interest.

We begin with a profile written for *The Staffordshire Sentinel* of 18 November 1909, not long after Bantock succeeded Elgar as Professor of Music at Birmingham University. Note the progressively more creative use Brian makes of news-paper 'sub-heads'! No later writing of Brian's shows him so enthusiastically in thrall to his friend's personality.

Prof. Granville Bantock: a Sketch

Granville Bantock, the Peyton Professor of Music at the University of Birmingham, and the Principal of the School of Music, Midland Institute, Birmingham, is the son of the eminent surgeon, Dr. George Granville Bantock, and was

born in London some forty years ago. He was privately educated, and a career in the Indian Civil Service was originally
intended for him. Music, which had not strongly asserted
itself in his boyhood, became an absorbing passion in his
teens, and eventually thrust out all desire for a career in the
Indian Service. In his early days and up to his late teens he
was self-taught. At the age of 20 he placed himself in the
hands of a professional teacher, and at the age of 21 he won
the Macfarren Scholarship for composition at the Royal
Academy of Music, London.

It will thus be seen that Bantock's genius, like that of
Elgar, Berlioz, Wagner, and Delius, was latent. Professor
Corder, who was one of the examiners when Bantock
entered the competition for the Macfarren Scholarship,
and who became Bantock's professor in composition on
entering the academy, has recently stated that the scholarship was not awarded to him for what he had accomplished
or what he could do – but for the great promise his work
gave. Professor Corder must now feel a happy man. After
the usual course at the Royal Academy Bantock, full of
enthusiasm and bubbling over with great schemes, found
himself in an unsympathetic world. During many ups and
downs he ever retained his enthusiasm and continued to
turn out a long stream of compositions, which, of course –
as in the case of all young composers – nobody wanted.

It is always interesting to observe the influences in a
young composer's work, and those which may be found in
Bantock's early works and which have helped to shape his
idiom are the influences of three most modern composers,
Wagner, Berlioz, Strauss. Three giants, each of whom in
turn has nipped conventional tradition and put the tables
and rules of the academies in the fire. Before Bantock came
into his own, however, he had to do much spade work. Left
to his own resources after leaving the Royal Academy, he
became the conductor of pantomime and musical comedy
touring companies.

TRAVELS

He travelled round the world with a musical comedy company several times, and the last occasion proved memorable.

He has told me that on this last occasion he was standing outside a second-hand bookshop in New York, when his eye alighted on a copy of Fitzgerald's translation of the *Ruba'iyat* of the Persian poet, Omar Khayyam. Bantock bought it, read it, and made up his mind to set the whole of it to music, if ever he had the opportunity. Thus, as in the case of Elgar with *The Dream of Gerontius*, the poem lay soaking in Bantock's mind many years before he commenced the composition of his great secular cantata. At the end of this second tour around the world Bantock was again stranded – and for many months he tried hard to obtain work in his profession, but without success. After much waiting and application, he accepted a post as musical director at New Brighton Tower. Here the genius of Bantock as an organiser had its chance.

HIS CAREER

The history of Bantock as musical director of New Brighton Tower is an absorbing one: indeed, it is the history of the fulfilment of all that promise made earlier in his career. When he arrived at the tower[1] he found himself appointed conductor of a brass band. It wasn't likely that Bantock would content himself with such an organisation. By sheer personal effort he in a short time had the brass band replaced by a magnificent orchestra. Here his genius as a conductor had full scope, and it was used unselfishly. Bantock, having a fine orchestra at his command, invited others to share his joy. He invited young composers, who couldn't get a hearing elsewhere, to send in their works, and he rehearsed and produced them. I know four English composers who admit that but for the help Bantock gave to them whilst conductor of the Tower orchestra their careers must have remained stationary. He also introduced the practice of giving a whole programme to one composer, and invited Parry, Stanford, Mackenzie, Elgar, William Wallace, and other English composers to conduct programmes of their works. This was a very happy period in Bantock's life, and in additions, as conductor to the Tower orchestra, he was much sought after

---

[1] In 1897.

elsewhere – his excursions including the conducting of concerts in Brussels and Antwerp.[2]

PROFESSOR AT BIRMINGHAM UNIVERSITY
After some years at the Tower, he was appointed Principal
of the School of Music, Midland Institute, Birmingham,
and last year, on the resignation of Sir Edward Elgar, he was
appointed Peyton Professor of Music in the University of
Birmingham. The restlessness and force of character which
marked his work at New Brighton has shown itself since his
appointment to the Chair of Music. Soon after the appointment he issued the syllabus for the degree of Bachelor of
Music. It is a staggering document and makes short work of
the academic syllabuses found at other English Universities.
Candidates presenting themselves for the degree must first
prove themselves to be artists possessing what is usually not
found amongst academics – imagination. Candidates must
know opera from Mozart to Debussy, symphonies from
Beethoven to Elgar, to stand a *viva voce* examination upon
Richard Strauss's *Ein Heldenleben*. Ye gods – it is enough to
give the dons of other universities mental paralysis!

The latest scheme of Bantock's is the formation of a permanent orchestra for Birmingham and, judging from the
large number of notable persons who attended the initial
meeting at the University the other day, the scheme seems
destined to be successful. And what of Bantock and his
music? He lives at Broad Meadow, a beautiful old-fashioned
and large country mansion a few miles out of Birmingham,
in the direction of Worcester. In manner and habit there is
nothing to indicate the restless revolutionary burning
beneath the surface. His life passes in a quiet but ideal
atmosphere.

HE IS A POLYGLOT IN LANGUAGES,
has the reputation of knowing some dozen languages as
familiarly as English, and a voracious reader. He is frequently seen carrying parcels of second-hand books, and

---

[2] In 1900 and 1901. Of Brian's 'English' composers, incidentally, Stanford was Irish and Mackenzie and Wallace were Scots.

never travels without some. Some time ago I was staying as his guest in a well-known hotel in the north. We chatted until very late, both going to bed apparently tired. At three o'clock in the morning, I went to Bantock's bedroom to get some mineral water: expecting to find him asleep I was surprised to find him in bed, but with his bed covered with books. Bantock himself was sitting propped up in bed, smoking a large cigar – he's never without one – quietly enjoying the original Persian edition of the poems of Hafiz. His large library at Broad Meadow contains a rare and choice selection of the finest in literature, and in addition he has a large room devoted to Napoleonic literature and relics. His wife shares his artistic life for she has written the words of many of his finest works, and has in every sense the same big, broad-minded outlook which characterises her husband. Bantock has been called 'The British Wagner'. I don't like the title or believe it. I prefer

'THE BRITISH BERLIOZ'.

Wagner was a snob; his treatment of Hugo Wolf proves it – Bantock is big and always accessible and ever ready to help or advise – where possible. Like Berlioz, he is the son of a surgeon, and like the great French composer his mind has a vast and restless outlook. His works are significant of their composer. He has assaulted every department in musical composition, church music, several operas, chamber music, pianoforte, 'cello, 20 orchestral works, besides 10 volumes of songs, oratorios, and cantatas. The songs of China, Japan, Persia, and India have had a phenomenal career in America, and his *Sappho* songs, which an eminent German critic describes as the finest in existence, along with the Comedy Overture – *The Pierrot of the Minute* – seem to have entered upon an excursion round the continent of Europe.[3] Leaving out of consideration the fine works *The Time Spirit* and the *Sea Wanderers* – both of them fully

---

[3] As Trevor Bray points out in his *Bantock: Music in the Midlands before the First World War* (Triad Press, Rickmansworth, 1973, p. 19), *The Pierrot of the Minute* was the most popular English work – after Elgar's First Symphony – to be played abroad in 1908–9.

representative of the mastery which distinguishes Bantock's finest works – to say nothing of the large number of beautiful partsongs which are familiar with northern part-singing choirs, there remains his great masterpiece, the secular cantata

'OMAR KHAYYAM'.

When the first part of the cantata *Omar* was issued to the musical world, there was some bewilderment and much rubbing of eyes. In spite of all that Bantock had previously done – and it must be taken into consideration that his development had been slow – it was not expected that the composer had, in such a marked degree, the 'big fist'. Wonder centered upon what he would do with the remaining portions of *Omar* – would he sustain the intensity of the first part? Part II followed at the Cardiff Triennial Festival of 1907, and the conclusion of this stupendous creation had its first production at the recent Birmingham Triennial Music Festival. The whole work is a rare marvel of sustaining power, and as Elgar's *Gerontius* remains the greatest religious work of modern times, so is Bantock's *Omar* the greatest secular work. One may turn to Strauss, Max Reger, Sibelius, Debussy, or any contemporary of Bantock's, but there is nothing to be found to equal it in magnitude and intensity. Perhaps the finest peroration of *Omar Khayyam* has been made by Ernest Newman – the only musical critic for whom I entertain any admiration – he says: 'The value of *Omar Khayyam* is that it brings into English secular music, for the first time, the thoughts and feelings of men brought up in the full tide of modern culture and modern humanism'.

The Songs of Granville Bantock

Brian wrote two quite different articles with this title within a few months of each other. Naturally they overlap in many respects. What follows is a compound text: the earlier, shorter essay (for *The Chesterian*, No. 30, March 1923, pp.167–169) is reproduced almost in full, but – as it was naturally confined to Chester publications – supplemented and expanded with material from the second, longer one for *Musical Opinion*, September 1923, pp. 1121–1123.

A poet whose work created endless discussion during the past forty years, is said to have remarked when contemplating certain paintings by Velasquez in Madrid, that he felt a sensation as though he was squeezing grapes and pomegranates and the juice was oozing through his fingers.[4]

Some such mental process appears to course through the mind of Bantock when attracted by a fine poem. No contemporary composer has shown greater *finesse* in his selection of poetry and Bantock rarely if ever fails to 'get there' with the poet whose verse he sets and which becomes finer and richer when elevated to the dignity of song. Germany gave us four great *lieder* writers in a century: Schumann, Schubert, Hugo Wolf and Richard Strauss. England produced another in Granville Bantock. His mind works easiest when revelling in the seductiveness of an exotic love poem, if it is artfully and subtly woven. Then Bantock's imagination is the more readily quickened and concentrated. He has been tremendously sustained by the poetry of Robert Browning, of his wife Mrs. Helen F. Bantock, and of his friend Alfred Hayes.[5] He has adorned every type of poetry and covered the whole gamut of emotion from the grand orchestral symphonic manner, to that of the plain simple ballad. The only thing he has not published is the

---

[4] The allusion has proved too circumspect for identification (we are looking for a well-known poet, but not in his works, only in a remark he is 'said to have' made). Velasquez was certainly an enthusiasm of several writers of the 1880s and 1890s, and the culprit might be Rossetti, W.E. Henley, even R.L. Stevenson or (possibly) Oscar Wilde.
[5] Hayes was the Secretary of the Midland Institute, and one of Bantock's favourite chess partners.

comic song. He loves to dream of slender fauns and dryads, slim Arab maidens, but he settles down just as readily amongst the purple robed Emperors of China as in the exotic clamour of the East. One of his many friends confided in me that (theosophically) he thought Bantock might have been, in a previous life, Sultan of Turkey or Emperor of China. I believe that Bantock has been greatly attracted to the East by his own love of colour and keen dramatic instinct. There is nothing neurotic about him. He sees life blazing fiercely and cannot escape the influence which drives him to exaltation, though he is no less human when influenced by the passage of death.

Years ago when I was writing up the weekly *critique* of the Hallé concerts in Manchester for the defunct *Musical World*, the editor handed me some volumes of modern music for review, amongst which was a volume of songs by Granville Bantock called *Lyrics from Ferishtah's Fancies*. Later I received another volume of songs entitled *Sappho*.[6] The association of artist and wife, as in the case of Bantock and his wife, has had the most remarkable results. She has seen eye to eye with her husband in his love for the Orient, and they jointly produced six volumes of songs of the East, *Six Jester Songs*, and a very fine dramatic scena, *The Song of the Genie*. These oriental songs, not made so by any artificial means, embrace every emotional feeling from grave to gay, combined with the most exquisite workmanship and fertile genius. They eventually became more ornate and decorative as the number of songs increased, and reached a climax in a series of Symphonic songs known as *Ferishtah's Fancies* (Browning), *Sappho*, and *Ghazals of Hafiz*, which placed Bantock in the forefront of contemporary songwriters. In the *Ferishtah*, Bantock drew his inspiration from Browning, whilst in the *Sappho*, his wife selected the poems from the Greek poetess. In these two volumes Bantock attained to power and greatness which was the culminating point of a long road he had travelled ever striving for and seeking and

[6] Brian's brief but laudatory review of *Ferishtah's Fancies* (and of the *Ghazals of Hafiz*) appeared on p.54 of *The Musical World* for 15 July 1905. I have not traced a review of *Sappho*.

gradually finding personal expression.

These songs are absolute Bantock; no other composer could have written them. At one bound they lifted him to a plane occupied by a few solitary great ones — mostly hailing from Germany. Each song is perfectly chiselled, the inspiration glows and remains at white heat. If you take the thirteen philiosophical speculations of Browning which make the *Ferishtah* right through from 'The Eagle' to the epilogue — 'O love, no love!' – or the magnificent orchestral Prelude and nine songs which follow and complete the *Sappho*, you feel as though each of the two books was conceived as a whole inspiration and each volume makes one vast song of a great singer.

Thus, before the recent detestable war, Bantock had won for himself a place in the sun, where he will assuredly remain in company with all those great ones, who, in the past hundred years, have etherealised fine poetry into fine music.

As befits so fine an artist as Bantock, his manner varies with the mood or *spirituel* of the poem: he can write as simple and effective as Blake, or, if necessary, he can alter his style and develop in the grand symphonic manner.

Looking back over the past ten years, I am always perplexed why it was considered necessary to close down the English branches of German publishing houses in London during the recent war – whilst the German branches of London firms were allowed to continue in Germany. A large number of English composers suffered great losses by the shutting down of Breitkopf & Härtel, and no composer suffered more than Bantock – as all his finest songs and other works had been taken up by B. & H. before the outbreak of war.[7]

Recently Bantock has taken up his Browning again, and Messrs. Swan & Co. have published a large number of his settings from the *Dramatic Lyrics* and other poems. In each

[7] Brian suffered too – Breitkopf had just completed the publication of six of his orchestral works when the Great War broke out: the overture *For Valour* was, indeed, still being printed, which may account for the comparative rarity of the score.

of them is found Bantock's keen insight into poetic values, and if none of the poems calls for any great or dramatic excitement, there is amongst all of these late settings the composer's superior craftsmanship, and several like 'The Guardian Angel', 'Wanting is – what?', 'A Woman's Last Word' linger long in the memory when the sounds have died away. 'The Moon Maiden's Song', from *The Pierrot of the Minute* (Dowson), has a gossamer-like charm and delicacy; and there is a setting of a lyric by Raymond Bantock (his son) in the form of an unanswered question, 'When you sang to me'; and 'The Shulamite's Song', from the *Song of Songs* conceived in Bantock's sustained and elevated oriental manner.

There were murmurs during the war that Bantock was at work on a symphony for solo voices and orchestra. This proved to be incorrect. What was true was that he had taken up four long poems (*Pagan Chants*) by a new poet named Wilfrid Thorley, entitled 'The Dead Dryad', 'The Crippled Faun', 'The Hind in Ambush', 'The Faun Despondent'. So far Messrs. Swan & Co. have only issued the first two, whilst the others are at present being engraved. We do not know Mr. Thorley, but we do like his work. It has the real *flair* and vibrates with colour and dramatic surprises. He lingers on words and phrases, we should imagine as did Oscar Wilde. These songs are the most important things that Bantock has done since the *Sappho* and *Ferishtah's Fancies* in the large manner. In the epilogue of 'The Dead Dryad' there is fine picturesque tenderness [...].

There is a graphic picture of the hunted, panting faun, after he has hunted the dryad's queen, at the close of 'The Crippled Faun'. [...]

It is quite natural for Bantock to be in perfect ease in setting Mr. Thorley to music, and it might be remarked that his finest moments are often expressed in two and three part writing. Messrs. Swan also publish further Bantock nature or pagan music in *Three Songs from the Greek Anthology* for flute and voice, 'Pan's Piping', 'Wood Music', 'The Garden of Pan', a very tender and sad setting of 'A widow bird sate mourning' (Shelley) and a very dramatic setting of Shelley's 'Hymn of Pan'. Amongst the finest things Bantock has ever done must be mentioned his *Seven Songs for Children* (Swan & Co.). The lyrics are by his wife, with delicate suggestive drawings by his daughter Myrrha. Perhaps Bantock does not set a very high value on these things; we don't know, we prize them greatly.

The war seems to have had a chastening effect upon many composers! Pre-war ornate and decorative luxuriance have given way nowadays to a much simpler style.

Nowhere can this change to a simpler style be seen to greater effect than amongst the *Chinese Songs* of Bantock. The hot glare and elaborate decoration of the earlier *Ferishtah* give way to a more contracted style. The same enthusiasm and finished workmanship remain.

As in all Bantock's songs, the sentiment of life, love and death, spurs him to his finest efforts.[8] The two books of *Chinese Songs* (Chester) contain much of Bantock's finest and ripest work.

In the first book there is a song 'The Old Fisherman', a song sung under the old Moon, in which there is a strange, vague picture of faraway solitariness obtained by the simplest means. 'The Ghost Road' covers the ghastly emptiness of all things, which the passage of time and years brings along: in his manner of singing this strange legend, Bantock has achieved a wonderful 'Death Procession', yet full of sorrow. 'The Celestial Weaver', a fine companion song to 'The Ghost Road', spiritualises the face of a stone figure which for centuries has stood gazing quietly across the waters of Lake Konenning:

> Immovable she stands
> Before the shining mirror of her charms,
> And, gazing on their beauty, lets the years
> Slip into centuries past her, gazing on their beauty!

Whilst the music of 'The Ghost Road' is free and outspoken, that of the 'Celestial Weaver' is quiet in its sadness and has a rare spiritual fervour. By way of contrast to the

---

[8] By contrast, Brian named *his* 'three great themes' as 'love, hate & death' in a letter to Bantock of 20 June 1919; he was currently finding them in the setting of Elizabethan lyrics.

preceding, 'The Return of Spring' is joyously light and gay, and ripples along in very happy fashion.

In the second set of *Chinese Songs* we have 'The Tomb of Chao-Chun', the legend of a strange woman whose haunting beauty carried with it misfortune and death: the music moves quietly along giving the impression of a silent procession. There is much of Bantock's lightest grace and charm in 'A Dream of Spring': often written in two parts, and containing several of the choicest examples of the composer's fondness for lengthening a two-bar phrase to a three-bar phrase. Bantock's fondness for this sort of thing does not conceal any of the quiet beauty which apparently shone through the lattice window:

> Last night within my chamber's gloom some vague light
>   breath of Spring
> Came wandering and whispering, and bade my soul take
>   wing.

'Desolation' is an impression of the past 'pomp and circumstance' of a King of Liang. Balzac could not, in six lines, have better suggested 'how little remains, of the much that was', and Bantock is quite happy with this Chinese dream – which seems to foreshadow that equally wonderful English poem:

> The glories of our blood and state,
> Are shadows, not substantial things.[9]

'The Pavilion of Abounding Joy' winds up the second series of *Chinese Songs*. Although its title would presume so much, the joy is really veiled in tears – like April rain in sunshine: only at the end do we leave the bewitching sadness and emerge into real bright sunlight.

Messrs. Elkin also publish two sets of five each of Chinese songs, the poems by E. Powys Mathers. In the first set the song, 'The Emperor', stands out conspicuously by the subtle characterisation of the heavy pomp and circumstance of

---

[9] Funeral Ode from *The Contention of Ajax and Ulysses* by the Royalist poet and dramatist James Shirley (set as a cantata by Parry).

the emperor contrasted with the delicacy of the limning of the empress. The air is heavy with exotic scents, the emperor is away from the empress; he thinks of her, and she longs for him. Their thoughts appear to float and pass from one to the other, depicted in quiet two part and three part writing which Bantock knows and loves so well, and which reaches a breathless climax where the emperor thinks:

> My beloved moves her fan and
> Sends me a perfume from her lips.

Another *rara avis* is 'The Peach Flower', a picture of wonder and quiet charm set to a slow waltz rhythm in fitful minor harmonies, through which pass the fretful story of a red peach blossom and a black swallow.

In the second set there is 'A Feast of Lanterns', deftly drawn in a scene of animation. 'Yung Yang' is a dream picture or a soliloquy on days long past and the sadness which their remembrance brings. There is a similar doleful, wistful longing in 'The Golden Nenuphar', and perhaps the finest of the Elkin songs is 'Adrift', a big song, with close sustained expression in Bantock's concentrated manner and appropriately inscribed to Frank Mullings.

These Chinese songs of Bantock differ from his earlier oriental settings by their reticence and quietude. In depicting these strange Chinese legends with so much shyness and reserve, Bantock proves how wonderfully accurate his instincts are as regards this strange and silent intellectual Eastern race, whose art and literature is so wonderful and distinguished, yet, over it all hovers a strange sadness, falling silently like April rain.

Bantock, the Viola,
the Atom, and *Macbeth*

This is excerpted from the *Musical Opinion* column 'The Musician's Diary' from the issue of September 1927 (pp. 1194–1195).

Our explorers are penetrating too far. On the one hand, we have Professor Bantock addressing an audience in great solemnity, and issuing a decree – that of banishment from the orchestra of the viola. Now we are not told what happened to Professor Bantock upon the day in question which caused him to roll his thunder. It may be that he suddenly awoke with a new inspiration for 2–2 music, and, seeking an exit for the viola by way of excuse, he alighted upon the amazing idea that there was no need for its use. In times gone by we have listened to Professor Bantock's thunder on other things and men, always prefaced with a 'perhaps', or 'if', or 'it might be', and so on. Perfectly harmless, all of it – not intended, perhaps, to be amusing – yet sometimes we have wondered if he were not just 'trying it on', or indulging in a little fooling. There is far too little merriment in the world of music, especially just now. We have got into the habit of going about things in a doleful, sad manner; indeed, we are getting back to the seriousness of a decade or more ago, when we carried Tschaïkovsky's Sixth Symphony in our button-holes. It may be that, like ourselves, Professor Bantock has realised and felt this, so what else could he do than say, 'Now I'll take the first opportunity of waking everybody up!' He did. But it is all so much like many other things he has said in the past, that we apply only a little humour to it, which convinces us that Professor Bantock is just pulling the proverbial leg. For in telling us that the viola must go, he has left out the most important point, and that is 'where must the viola go?' Also, more important still, if the viola goes what is to happen in all the performances of orchestral music which has been written for two centuries, when it is performed? The viola has a sad face – all its own. Some of the young bloods have even taken pity upon it – pitying it so

much as to try and lift it out of its perpetual sorrow by allowing it to sing above the violins.[10] The sorrow of the viola is
unmistakable; quite individual, and unlike anything else in
the orchestra: and what on earth has it done to hurt Professor Bantock that he should wish to oust it from its permanent position? If the viola must go, other instruments may
have to go too, and what with the going and coming, composers and conductors may anticipate an exciting time.

Then there is Professor Buck, who is also Professor Bantock's friend.[11] He, no doubt, feeling very roguish, smoking
a 'Colorado Claro', and addressing an audience the other
day in place of Sir Hugh Allen, indulged in little quips about
good cigars and bad ones, and expressed the opinion that if
we could only split the atom, we might enter upon a new era
with new hearts, and with new imaginations. All very
speculative, of course. If we could but split the atom, we
might find a way out of many troubles; not only an escape
from bad cigars and damp matches, but also from bad
music and so many repetitions of excellent music which
would perhaps meet us again with a fresh face if it had a
short rest occasionally. The main thing, and that in which we
must indeed rejoice so exceedingly, is that the two professors have said something. Even if we cannot banish the
viola, or split the atom, we must thank Professors Bantock
and Buck for drawing our attention to these matters.

The incidental music to *Macbeth*, which Granville Bantock the *composer* has arranged for the piano (Swan & Co.),
was originally written for Sybil Thorndike and Lewis Casson. Professor Bantock has a natural *penchant* for the
theatre, but perhaps not a great number of people know
this , or that he has also a big vein of the comic in his make-
up. He can sing like a nightingale, drawl like a hooded crow,

---

[10] Presumably a reference to Lionel Tertis' advocacy of the instrument
and perhaps also to Hindemith's *Kammermusik* concerto of the previous
year (Brian had already written admiringly of Hindemith in the early
1920s). I am not familiar with any orchestral score in which Bantock dispensed with the violas to create what Brian terms a '2–2' disposition of
strings, but it would be quite characteristic of his zest for instrumental
experiment.

[11] Percy C. Buck was then Professor at the University of London.

and even oblige with a little tune *à la* Tom Costello or Charles Coborn.[12] Remembering this, we turn to the incidental music, which consists of eight numbers: (1) Fanfare, (2) Lament, (3) March, (4) Pibroch, (5) Procession, (6) Dance of Witches, (6A) Witches' Chant, (7) Quickstep. The flavour is decidedly Scotch throughout, and its musical construction is simple and easily assimilated. The Lament is quietly beautiful and sad – eloquently expressive of

> Methought I heard a voice cry
>   'Sleep no more!
> Macbeth does murder sleep'.

The Procession impresses us most by the deft manner in which a long movement is spun out of the chord of A minor, yet never failing to keep the attention alert. The Dance of Witches is a rondo and is really good. In its original dress for the theatre, it is written for three bassoons. We can quite well imagine Sybil Thorndike listening to this and remarking to Lewis Casson, 'Why, it is too terrible to believe!' Of course, what is grotesque upon three bassoons is not necessarily so upon the blacks and whites of the piano; yet it is always 'bubbly' music, and ripples in a rare way. Not the least interesting feature about this music is the *facsimile* of a rare print of the 'penny plain and twopence coloured' order, showing in colours a quaint picture of Mr. Anderson[13] as Macbeth.

---

[12] Both were famous music-hall artists. Costello (1863–1943) was noted as singer of the ballads *Comrades*, *The Ship I Love*, and *At Trinity Church I Met My Doom*. Coborn (1852–1945) was especially celebrated for his singing of *The Man who Broke the Bank at Monte Carlo* and for composing the song *Two Lovely Black Eyes*. Brian relished a good music-hall number as much as the next man, as is demonstrated by the set of *Symphonic Variations on 'Has Anybody Here Seen Kelly?'*, which formed part of the Prologue to *The Tigers*.

[13] Lawrence Anderson was a member of Casson's touring company for this production – although Diana Devlin's biography of Casson (*A Speaking Part*, Hodder & Stoughton, London, 1982) suggests that he himself played Macbeth.

Bantock's *Pilgrim's Progress*

This is a concert review from *Musical Opinion*, January 1929,
p. 343.

This work is rather a surprise, as coming from Bantock. Let
us say at once that it is in many ways a fine artistic present-
ment of the matter. It was produced under the composer at
the B.B.C. Symphony Concert of November 23rd at
Queen's Hall, with the New National Choir and the B.B.C.
Orchestra. The choir is a very fine one, with beautiful tone,
balance and precision, and showed intelligent appreciation
of the work. The soloists were Megan Tellini, Gladys Palmer
and Enid Cruickshank (the Three Shining Ones); Trefor
Jones (Christian); Keith Falkner (Bunyan; in place of Norman Allin, indisposed); and Harold Williams (Apollyon).
The book is effectively laid out by Bowker Andrews.

The work opens with a Narrative by Bunyan, whose part
was finely rendered by Mr. Falkner: and this is followed by
an orchestral representation of Bunyan's Dream. The Hill
of Ascent, which also is portrayed in the orchestra, is succeeded by the Loosing of the Burden; after which we get a
fresh tone-colour, with harps, and the Greeting of the
Three Shining Ones. Christian at the Cross follows, with an
antiphonal treatment of solo and semi-chorus: and then a
chorale, treated not in Bach's way but simpler, more massive
and again with antiphonal phrases. This is broad and effective, and Mr. Trefor Jones filled the part of Christian, both
here and throughout with real feeling. The Valley of the
Shadow of Death, again, receives orchestral treatment: and
this is a subject which appeals to Bantock's imagination, as
to everyone else's. It is genuinely touching.

The next section, 'The Fight with Apollyon', with a
chorus of devils is highly pictorial, and shows Bantock's
strong imaginative control of orchestral effect, and choral
writing, in striking colours. The orchestra is lurid and
the scene is given with diabolic realism. It is one of the
things that Bantock can do with fine dramatic effect. Mr.
Harold Williams, as Apollyon, was excellent and very realistic.

'Vanity Fair', too, an orchestral piece, is just suited to Bantock's genius, and, as might be expected by all who know his *Fifine at the Fair*, is highly pictorial. Here, and throughout, the superb handling of the orchestra is noticeable. Upon this, after a few words from Bunyan, follows 'Christian's Song of Deliverance', after which comes 'The End of the Journey' (Bunyan); and then 'The River of Death', which is very impressive: Bantock, like all of us, can enter into the feelings engendered by this prospect. 'Through the Golden Gate' opens with the golden tones of trumpets, 'The Three Shining Ones', and a chorus of angels, with simple broad harmonies, and, as is fitting, free from 'musicalities'. After this, comes a big and effective chorus, 'Let us now praise famous men', which, although the words are biblical, makes one wonder whether it is really congruous with Bunyan's very personal view of salvation. A short orchestral Epilogue, and Bunyan's words, 'So I awoke, and behold it was a dream', close the work. We all know that Bantock makes no pretence of sharing Bunyan's views of personal religion; but that does not prevent this being a truly fine work in its way. He has a great power of throwing himself into sympathetic relations with a man whose work he is setting. Much of his work on Browning deals with ideas, with which, intellectually, he would not agree; but the greater, subliminal self emerges and takes command at certain crises; (it is so, even in *Omar*); and in the present case, Bantock, with his great musical powers, has given us a fine artistic rendering of the work, and a genuine homage to the man, Bunyan, whose tercentenary is being celebrated. We sincerely hope that the work will soon be given again, and so enable us to make its closer acquaintance.

Atalanta in America

This is from 'On the Other Hand' in the March 1935 *Musical Opinion*, p. 491.

I am pleased to see that Eugene Goossens is preparing Bantock's choral symphony, *Atalanta in Calydon*, for performance at the Cincinnati Festival next May. As it happens, I remember its first performance, given at a Hallé Concert in Manchester.[14] At the time we had had a surfeit of unknown Russian music, out of which Tchaïkovsky's symphonies came into the light; the symphonic poems of Strauss excited orchestral players and audience alike; and Elgar had come into his own. The chance for the English explorer had come, for the general practitioner in music was submerged in the new sea of colour and expression. Bantock struck out and survived, though he was drenched with the waters of the Neva and the Rhine. He might have been caught up in the flood carrying Elgar to success, but he struck out for himself and wrote *Omar Khayyam*, a large-scale orchestral and choral symphonic cantata. He was applauded for a beautiful and original choral work, which many still regard as his best achievement.

Atalanta is something quite different, and is doubtless Bantock's answer to the inevitable 'What next?' after a composer has produced a successful work. For some years unaccompanied choral music had been cultivated at the competition festivals, particularly at Morecambe, and there the masterpieces of the Elizabethan madrigalist came again into being. We also heard original works by Brahms and Cornelius, which stirred choralists as much as the symphonic poems had excited orchestral players. I remember Peter Cornelius's part-song for eight mixed voices, *O Death, thou art the tranquil night* (Canon Gorton's translation). Its performance was a sensation: for the first time voices were heard exploring a musical range of expression previously

[14] *Atalanta in Calydon* was first performed on 25 January 1912 at the Free Trade Hall, Manchester, by the Hallé Choir under Bantock.

known only to the orchestra. We were in a land all new. It was the finest piece of unaccompanied choral writing introduced from abroad; but Cornelius never again ventured along those paths. He had really 'scored' for voices, a task more difficult than writing for voices.

The art of 'scoring' for voices unaccompanied lay dormant until Bantock arrived with his choral symphony, *Atalanta*. This was a long stride forward from the ten minutes' work of Cornelius: nothing less than the dimensions of a four-movement symphony was sufficient for Bantock. Of course, he was solemnly arraigned for transferring orchestral methods of scoring to voices: well, if he was to break away from old-fashioned methods of unaccompanied vocal writing, he must perforce score for voices. At the performance, the one question was, Would it come off? Could we endure the lengthy duration of continuous unaccompanied vocal tone, and could the choir keep to pitch? The risk was there, and Bantock took it, giving to the choirmaster (R.H. Wilson) a great opportunity. The Hallé choir won through, bringing laurels for themselves and all associated with the work.

In the press forward for the presentation of other familiar and new works, *Atalanta* has been pushed aside, despite its position as a choral masterpiece: so I am glad to learn that Eugene Goossens has the work in rehearsal in America, where a popular and artistic success might turn the thoughts of composers to fresh fields.

Bantock and his *Pagan Symphony*

This article appeared in the December 1936 *Musical Opinion*, pp. 212–213.

Among the unrecorded events of the period 1914–1918 none recurs more persistently than the break or cessation in the production of our creative artists. Only now we see these things clearly. Delius broke with the world just before that time: but the urge to write remained with him until the end, so we might well have had another masterpiece instead of complete cessation. The case of Granville Bantock is similar: but recent events tend to show that the period in question was nothing more than an interregnum. His setting of Fitzgerald's *Omar Khayyam*, written some thirty years ago, was a brilliant example in a brilliant period of English musical composition. He had begun to write while a student at the Academy, but years elapsed before he acquired that bold, flowing habit that is the aim of so many composers of serious intent. More than that, he singled out for performance, when the opportunity was his, works that showed evidence of real and lasting purpose and were not slave-bound to cold curriculum. Bantock was the ardent advocate for Debussy, Delius, Elgar and Sibelius, and has been for long an ardent admirer of Richard Strauss, whom he regards as the greatest of the line since Wagner. Two of his Strauss performances are remarkable, both with the Liverpool Orchestral Society. When Rodewald died, the question of a new conductor arose – Emil Kreuz or Granville Bantock! and the decision was influenced by the programmes of each. Bantock selected *Ein Heldenleben* and *L'Après-midi d'un Faune*, and the appointment was his! On another occasion, the same society announced a two-part programme with *Ein Heldenleben* and Beethoven's Symphony in C minor. After the interval following the performance of the Strauss work, and the audience reassembled, the secretary, to the astonishment of all, stepped forward and said that the committee had decided to repeat *Ein Heldenleben*, so enthusiastically had it been received.

Bantock's predilection for *Ein Heldenleben* is not without significance. He heard Delius's condemnation of the classical model, but remained silent. However, by the processes of condensation and amplification, those who attached themselves to Strauss saw that the structure of the four-movement classical symphony was visible in *Ein Heldenleben*, a work which plays continuously from end to end, and is polyphonic while the classical symphony is homophonic. Similarly continuous are the two symphonies of Bantock, *The Hebridean* and that recently published called *The Pagan*. Also like *Heldenleben*, both the Bantock works portray stirring battle music. Of the two, *The Pagan* will probably be far more popular than the first symphony. If here Bantock avoids the classical pattern, he occasionally uses musical figurations that have been the common property of composers since Buxtehude; whilst his sense of balance of structure is unfailing. His methods are his own and are of importance in that they are more a contribution to contemporary music than would be anything written in the manner of the late eighteenth century.

Bantock is a secularist and a greater colourist – the Augustus John of British music – and what he writes bubbles over with geniality and sweetness. This *Pagan Symphony* is more accessible to orchestras than the composer's other orchestral works, and that by reason of the avoidance of difficulties and by a specification which is available to stock orchestras without engaging extra players. A new departure in the publication of the score is that it is a photographic reproduction of the original manuscript.

Bantock, tremendously influenced by the new movements in pre-war days, has remained uninfluenced and unimpressed by post-war tendencies. But there is the old Bantock enthusiasm and warmth of expression, the passion for tonality, for clarity of texture and faultless workmanship, which together have made him a great master of the orchestra. His sense of mimicry and the desire to be rude will be found in the opening of the Scherzo marked 'Dance of Satyrs', and are of plainly discernible pagan intent. Here the bassoons begin with a canter in two parts and carry on, producing the sort of foggy quirks that Rabelais might have written had he been a composer. When this passes to the other wind and brass, it loses none of its humour, but is not quite so deliberately pagan. This movement is interrupted by the battle scene, the clash of drums and brass, succeeded by another Scherzo, which is very happy and artless, and certainly not rude like the first one. A short monologue introduces the gay, bustling Finale in C major, though it continues as a palpitating dance, and freely modulates through the usual key corridors, returning quite faithfully to the spot where it set out, in C major.

For those who may wish to study or perform the *Pagan Symphony*, it may be added that the work takes thirty-two minutes in performance. The score is published at 10s. net; and the complete set of parts, with extra strings, 8 gs.; or the full score and parts can be hired for 5 gs. (Joseph Williams, Ltd.)

The Fire Worshippers

This item appeared – under the title 'At Long Last' – as part of the 'On the Other Hand' column for June 1939, p. 776.

I was pleased to see in a recent issue of *Musical Courier* a photograph of Sir Granville Bantock at the piano taking a young American conductor through the full score of his early dramatic cantata, *The Fire Worshippers*. We in England are a strange people, deluding ourselves with the belief that no work is worthy unless sanctified by performance at a festival, though we sometimes remember that the great masterpieces of Continental origin have lacked that initial advantage. America has no festival tradition, and consequently performances of a work may take place free from the prejudices, good or bad, that obtain here. Hence the performance of Bantock's work at Helston, Cornwall, on March 27th and an American performance in April.

I do not introduce the subject in order to protest against the neglect of a masterpiece. *The Fire Worshippers* is not that, neither is it so regarded by its composer. I once asked Bantock why it did not 'go': he replied that it was too Wagnerian and that it had never been sanctified by festival performance. Bantock was a student at the Royal Academy of Music when he wrote the work, at the time Frederick Corder was encouraging his advanced pupils to 'compose like Wagner'. Actually, the influence of Liszt is more marked. The opening storm theme undergoes many transformations, but the manner of the metamorphosis is that of Liszt, and not that of Wagner. Bantock to this day regards Liszt as the greatest revolutionary in the history of music.

The words of *The Fire Worshippers* are adapted from Thomas Moore's *Lalla Rookh*, an oriental epic, showing Bantock's early fascination by eastern lore. He entered the

Royal Academy of Music at the age of twenty-one, and three
years later could have been regarded as a seasoned composer, having on the stocks, complete or incomplete, *The
Fire Worshippers* and the oratorio *Christus*; and in addition
was editor and proprietor of *The New Quarterly Musical
Review*, an excellent magazine, which he is said to have
started with a capital of ten pounds and made to pay its way.
At any rate, through it was introduced to English musicians
writers who after became famous, including Ernest Newman; and by the time Bantock was twenty-five he had added
to his work by conducting.

The Overture to *The Fire Worshippers*, played by Manns at
the Crystal Palace in 1892, introduced Bantock to the concert room. A complete performance of the work did not
take place until seventeen years later, when it was given at
Streatham.

From the beginning of his career, Bantock's outlook has
been avowedly secular and unconventional. As an instance
of this, there is an episode in his early oratorio, *Christus*,
which was never completed, though parts have been published and performed: a setting of 'The wilderness and solitary places shall be made glad', which curiously enough,
had its performance at a Three Choirs Festival. Bantock's
music is no traditional cathedral setting, with the minim as
the unit note. He turns 'The wilderness' into a bright and
piquant dance for soprano solo, accompanied by harp, flute
and cymbal, because Bantock argued, the Jewish maiden
would be breaking her heart with joy and singing like a
nightingale inspired by the promise of spring. I find in *The
Fire Worshippers* a germ or generator – viz., the dissolution of
the continuous four-part chorus into a quasi solo treatment
of each choral unit, a necessity coming out of Bantock's
treatment of voices, which makes an actual choral ensemble
highly novel and effective. There is dramatic instinct and
spontaneous lyrical melody, all of which reached their
maturity fifteen years after in the composer's setting of
Fitzgerald's *Omar Khayyam*.

The Fire Worshippers is an early example of a concert opera:
though it contains so much that rarely fails to inspire performers and impress audiences, it has not become a popular

work. However, it may succeed in the United States.

Granville Bantock

This essay – in effect, Brian's obituary for his friend – appeared in the December 1946 issue of *Musical Opinion* (pp. 79–80); Bantock had died on 16 October. I have supplemented it with two paragraphs from the contemporaneous Foreword which he contributed to the Bantock Memorial Concert programme at the Midland Institute, Birmingham, on 12 November 1946, just under three months before his 71st birthday.

One Sunday afternoon, when a boy of nineteen, I sat in a country rectory in Cheshire listening to a conversation about the wonderful things produced at a recent Chester Triennial Music Festival. Amongst the new works were the first performance in an English cathedral of a selection from *Parsifal* and a symphonic poem called *Saul* for orchestra by a young English composer named Granville Bantock, a name unknown to me; yet I was destined to know the name and its owner very intimately. *Saul* seemed to me a curious subject for a symphonic poem by an English composer, and it disclosed Bantock's early approach to that oriental transcendentalism, through the Hebrew Bible, which was later to loom so magnificently in his noblest and largest works.

Christus, a large scale oratorio written shortly after *Saul*, is an unorthodox treatment of a familiar subject. Bantock selected the words from the Bible and they are subjected to a Bantock style of processing. The well known 'The Wilderness and Solitary Places' is set for soprano solo, harp, flute and cymbal, and the result is an original depiction by very economical means. *Christus* also reveals a remarkable capacity at an early age for invention, and his stream of thought was so copious that he was not inconvenienced by simultaneously having half-a-dozen large-scale works on hand. Such an unusual gift suggests a finely organised mind allied with determination and thirst for adventure.

Bantock got his great chance, or, at least, made it, at New

Brighton on the Mersey, as orchestral conductor and highly efficient organiser. At that time the Eiffel Tower of Paris was the latest world sensation. An English syndicate erected a replica of this tower at New Brighton. Bantock was engaged as conductor of a brass band intended for amusement and dancing. Within a few months he transformed or replaced the brass band by an orchestra. His Sunday symphony concerts, with an orchestra of a hundred performers became a newspaper sensation in the North. Long before the New Brighton Tower was finished I paid it a visit, my curiosity aroused by Bantock and his orchestra. I found the large ball room where the concerts took place in a state of chaos; heaps of timber lying in confusion and pandemonium from the hammers of an army of carpenters. On the pillars were large bills announcing next Sunday's symphony concert and its symphony, *The Ocean*, by Anton Rubinstein. Through the noise I heard the sound of an orchestra, and on looking above me, I saw a bay surrounded by tarpaulin sheets, behind which the orchestra was rehearsing the Prelude to *Tristan*. I mention this as indicative of Bantock's grit and grim determination.[15]

His heart was as expansive as his mind, and many composers, including Elgar, Holbrooke, Wallace, Stanford, Parry, Mackenzie and Cowen pilgrimaged to the Merseyside town to hear or conduct their works. Bantock was a busy man, yet he found time to continue composition. After he moved to Birmingham as Director of the Midland Institute School of Music, the orchestra and its music at New Brighton gradually disappeared and the famous tower was pulled down.

Sterndale Bennett and Alexander Mackenzie found their responsibilities as directors of the R.A.M. incompatible with musical inspiration. Their official duties neutralised in-

---

[15]   Brian seems rather to have mislaid the point of the anecdote here. In a slightly earlier article on Bantock for *Tomorrow* (issue of 25 November 1939, pp.106–7), he explains that he and Bantock did not actually meet on this occasion; but when they were introduced in 1906 Brian alluded to it and Bantock was highly amused, saying he had had no business to be rehearsing *Tristan* because he had been expected to prepare the orchestra for a concert of light music!

spiration; yet it is from the time of Bantock's taking up his official work in Birmingham that his career as composer really began. After the success of the first part of his *Omar Khayyam* at the Birmingham Triennial Music Festival, Bantock quickly became a national figure. The succeeding parts of *Omar* produced at the Cardiff and Leeds Festivals completed a masterpiece, essentially secular, of extraordinary geniality and an amazing sense for orchestral graphic painting. *Omar* bears no analogy to any contemporary work; to find its counterpart we must seek the large group canvasses by Augustus John in the sister art of painting. As a master of the orchestra, Bantock has no superior. Not only in *Omar* but in the song cycle *Ferishtah's Fancies* and *The Great God Pan*, Bantock's orchestral *métier* has a seductive sensual quality, with an effortless improvisatory style of melodic invention, unusual in English music and unlike that of any other composer.

It was soon after the production of *Omar* that I first met Bantock. We seemed to meet through the natural laws of gravitation – for I remember we sat up until the early hours of the morning talking as though we were brothers meeting once again after having been long separated. Then his chief concern was the welfare of modern British music.

Elgar had recently accepted the chair of music at Birmingham University and there was an expectancy in the air as to what was to happen next. Elgar talked of making Birmingham an English Leipzig with a magnificent Conservatoire of Music, staffed by professors of modern outlook and to establish a permanent symphony orchestra of 100 players. Bantock was the moving spirit behind Elgar's talks – Bantock was the prompter!

Bantock was apparently too big a man to allow his official duties in Birmingham to absorb him. He was a born pluralist. He succeeded Henry J. Wood as conductor of the Wolverhampton Festival Choral Society. On the death of Alfred Rodewald, founder and conductor of the Liverpool Orchestral Society, Bantock conducted a performance of Strauss's *Ein Heldenleben* in Liverpool; Dr. Hans Richter, who heard that performance, recommended the Liverpool Orchestral Society to engage Bantock as their conductor.

He maintained this appointment for eight years. As adjudicator at Competition Music Festivals, Bantock was in constant request and for such occasions he composed numerous finely wrought *a cappella* works. He also founded the Midland Competition Music Festival in Birmingham and for some years this festival was the largest of its kind in the country.

His faith in the choral movement which, begun in Westmoreland, spread through various Lancashire coast towns to the Midlands, inspired Bantock to compose symphonies for voices *unaccompanied*. The first of these symphonies, *Atalanta in Calydon*, had its initial performance at a Hallé Concert in the Free Trade Hall, Manchester. During its performance, Bantock was surprised by a telegram of congratulation from Dr. Hans Richter.

The foregoing account is but an incomplete history of the work of a composer whose works and personality were in constant demand. Then came the Great War and wreckage, for wars are destructive quite apart from combatants on the battlefield. Bantock was not the only composer wrecked by the Great War. Yet he did not lose his enthusiasms. An ardent admirer of the music by Richard Strauss, Bantock attended the festival of Strauss operas given at Frankfurt soon after the close of the Great War.

As conductor of the Liverpool Orchestral Society, Bantock introduced the work of Sibelius for the first time in England. He succeeded Elgar as Professor of Music at Birmingham University and when he retired under the age limit (sixty-five) Bantock went to live in London in order to extend the work of Trinity College of Music. Here he commenced a new life, that of a wandering examiner, visiting all parts of Ireland and the British Isles, besides making trips round the world. At the age of seventy he flew from New York to Barbadoes to conduct examinations. On his return from his first trip to South America he expressed some concern at the extraordinary musical activity he had found in that part of the world – a state of affairs which was entirely unknown to us in this hemisphere.

When the recent war broke out Bantock felt that all music would perish: later, as the war continued into its fifth and sixth year he expressed the opinion that the public might seek relief from its harrowing experiences in music. It would seem that in this prophecy Bantock was correct, for there has never at any time, certainly not in London, been such interest in orchestral music or so many orchestras concertising at the same time.

If his culture is to be mentioned here, it may be said that Bantock was polyglot in languages, an omnivorous reader, a diligent student who never neglected his studies. He was an extraordinary man and musician and we shall not see his like again. The neglect of his works is not his fault.

PART SIX

BRITISH MUSIC IN PERFORMANCE

━━━━━━━━━━━━●━━━━━━━━━━━━

Only in the earliest part of his journalistic career was Brian free to write extensive concert reviews. The publications he worked for in the inter-war years favoured brief reports with a minimum of critical comment. By their nature these are hardly worth reproducing, although they do provide a useful register of the enormous amount of music that Brian heard in live performance. (Most of his writing on, for instance, Frank Bridge, Herbert Howells, Constant Lambert and Ethel Smyth – to name composers not notably well represented in this volume – is confined to this medium, or to equally exiguous reviews of printed music.)

I include here a selection from the fairly limited number of long reviews – which tend to be of festivals or concert series rather than single events. Such reviews – even of the historic Birmingham Triennial Festival of 1906 – were not usually devoted exclusively to British music; I have retained Brian's comments on the non-British parts of the programmes, both for their intrinsic interest and to indicate the context in which the British works were heard.

THE BIRMINGHAM TRIENNIAL FESTIVAL

This review comes from *The Musical World*, 16 October 1906, pp.111–112.

The gods who rule the weather must surely have a special grudge against musicians – for the Hereford Festival was held during the only wet week of a long, dry summer, and the beginning of the Festival at Birmingham was the signal for the breaking of another spell of fine weather. But it would take more than torrential rain to damp the ardent spirits of those who met together on the 2nd, 3rd, 4th and 5th inst., in the Birmingham Town Hall, the interior aspect of which conveyed no idea of the dirty weather outside. The weather may have been reponsible for a certain thin, dry tone emitted occasionally by the sopranos, but the tone of the chorus generally would be hard indeed to surpass. The outstanding feature of the chorus was its wonderful balance of tone; the tenors were exceptionally good, and for once a chorus was to be heard in which the middle parts were every whit as resonant and strong as those on the outside. There were times when one could have wished them gifted with a little more elasticity of phrasing and a larger fund of emotion, but even in these particulars they achieved now and again some capital effects.

The orchestra was drawn mainly from the Hallé combination, with additions from Birmingham and London. On the whole, Dr. Richter had at his command a magnificent orchestra. Sometimes, particularly in the works of Elgar, a little more sensitiveness would have been an advantage, but in the Brahms Symphony and the Beethoven Mass they drew a rugged tone that was in character with the works. The leaders were Messrs. Schiever and Rawdon Briggs.

The Birmingham Festival of 1906 will long be remembered because of the intrepidity of the committee in giving three new and important works by British composers; and accordingly we propose, owing to the exigencies of space, merely to record the performances of *Elijah* and *The Messiah*, and devote our columns to the consideration of works of more consequence to the present day and generation. For once in a while there was some justification for the inclusion of *Elijah* in the Festival programme, it being sixty years since it was first performed at a Birmingham Festival. The next date that suggests itself as suitable is 1946 (except that the Festival will not, in the ordinary course, fall to that year), when it would celebrate its centenary; but the probabilities are that the oratorio will appear in 1909, and every other

Festival still to come.[1]

The principals at this Festival were Mme. Albani, Miss Gleeson-White, Mme. Ada Crossley, Mr. John Harrison, and Mr. William Higley.

In *The Messiah* the principal soloists were Mmes. Albani and Ada Crossley, Messrs. John Harrison (in place of Mr. William Green), and Ffrangçon Davies.

The Apostles

On Tuesday evening, the 2nd inst., Sir Edward Elgar secured what is perhaps one of the finest performances of his oratorio *The Apostles* that has ever been given.[2] A composer is not invariably the best interpreter of his own work, but no other conductor can bring out the themes of this oratorio with such poignancy and deep effect as the composer of *The Apostles*. Under his direction the *motiven* are fitted into the work with unerring certainty of purpose. To quote but one instance: the variety of tones with which the *motif* symbolising Christ as the Man of Sorrows was introduced, must have proved a revelation to many conductors present. Again, under Sir Edward Elgar's conducting, the themes assume a character, a boldness and clearness of outline that others seem powerless to impart; while the tone-colours of the orchestra, always beautiful, always bright, take on a certain translucent quality that other conductors not seldom miss. There were many surprises in Sir Edward's reading of the work for those who were familiar with their *Apostles* even as conducted on previous occasions by the composer. The chorus 'The Lord hath chosen them' was taken at a greater speed than usual, while some of the dramatic dialogue was unnecessarily dragged.

---

[1] Brian did not underestimate *Elijah*, but he resented its hold upon the programming priorities of festivals, orchestras, and choral societies. In *The Musical World* for 15 February 1907 he acidly reviewed a Hallé performance with the complaint that 'this work was first heard at these concerts 41 years ago; it has been performed here 44 times since. It is time it was given a rest for a season or two at least'.

[2] Although it had been premiered only in 1903, *The Apostles* was already very popular; see pp.67–70 for Brian's review of a 1905 performance in Hanley.

Miss Agnes Nicholls sang the soprano solo music with consummate ease and vocal finish, and her interpretation of the sentences given to the Angel Gabriel was exceedingly telling, her voice having an effect of distance that she does not always achieve with such conspicuous success. Miss Muriel Foster gave another fine rendering of the Tower of Magdala scene, singing with a confidence that was altogether admirable. Mr. John Coates again sang the tenor part with his accustomed skill.

The event of the evening was undoubtedly the singing of Mr. Charles Clark in the part of Judas. The power into which he infused his opening phrase betokened a Judas the like of which we had not before known and his singing of the passage 'Let him make speed' insisted upon a phase of the character of the betrayer not usually brought out – his self-deception as to the motive actuating him. Mr. Clark's singing was always dramatic, and at the same time always with purely vocal tone. He proved himself an acquisition to the oratorio platform.[...]

Elgar's *The Kingdom*

On Wednesday morning the Town Hall was packed to its utmost capacity to hear Sir Edward Elgar's new work *The Kingdom*, conducted by the composer himself. It is hardly possible upon a first performance to give an authoritative statement as to the total significance of a work, particularly when as in this case, the score is withheld until the eleventh hour. History goes to prove how foolish all such prognostications become. Further hearings are always bound to modify one way or another one's first impression of a work, and it is therefore more satisfactory to all concerned to speak of the first performance in general terms.

Sir Edward Elgar has not been fortunate in his selection of a subject for Part III of *The Apostles*. Howsoever historically interesting may be the foundation of the early Church, it does not make for musical enthusiasm. The work gives the impression of being too much upon one level; there is no Judas in it, no sinning Magdalene to point a contrast to the repentant Peter and the Holy Women; and for this reason the work becomes monotonous. Again, it was inevitable that *The Kingdom* should in a large measure be reminiscent of the previous work, and the Prelude and scene in the Upper Room are largely concerned with picking up the threads of what has gone before; the themes therefore have a tendency to become wearisome before the end is reached.

Apart from this, the work contains abundant evidence of the composer's skill in orchestration, his blending of the colours being beautiful as ever; but we miss those frequent mystical touches of *The Apostles* that raise one to a higher plane; there is no place in *The Kingdom* that stirs the blood like that one phrase in *The Apostles* – 'And the Lord turned and looked upon Peter'. It may be that subsequent hearings of the work may qualify these impressions, and may at the same time discover the links that bind it into a composite whole, which a first hearing did not do.[...]

At the close Sir Edward received quite an ovation, being recalled to the platform again and again. *The Kingdom* was followed by a spirited rendering of the Bach Cantata *Sing ye to the Lord*,[3] in which the chorus demonstrated the mettle of which they were made. They came through the ordeal triumphantly, Dr. Richter obtaining a performance of supreme dignity and reverence. At the end of it Dr. Richter brought forward the chorus-master, Mr. R.H. Wilson, to receive acknowledgment of his services. Brahms's Symphony in C minor gave us the orchestra at its very best, and brought the concert to a close.

The Bells, by Joseph Holbrooke

Five important compositions, two of them novelties, and two vocal solos were too much for the programme of one evening – and that the evening after the first performance of a long work like *The Kingdom*.

Mr. Holbrooke's choral work *The Bells* was the item of chief importance. Much had been heralded up and down the country about the extraordinary instruments demanded by the composer for the performance of this work, and though all his requirements could not be supplied, many of those that were proved inaudible to many

---

[3] Brian must mean the motet, BWV. 225.

of the audience. Poe's jingles have, curiously, never been set
to music before, and it will be quite unnecessary for any
other composer to attempt to set them in the future, Mr.
Holbrooke having plumbed their depths and given the
musical representation of them. The opening Prelude,
which is practically an epitome of the whole work, might
very well be played apart from the rest of the work. Into the
rendering of this Dr. Richter and the orchestra entered with
a just appreciation of all the colour effects to be obtained
from the score, the imitative bell passages, with their
resounding overtones, being very faithfully performed.
The chorus sang wonderfully well, considering the trying
nature of their task; and if they did not always bring out the
dramatic contents of their words, and if they let a few pianissimo passages escape their notice, much will be forgiven
them for the horror they put into their tones in the passage
'They are Ghouls'. In the 'Alarm Bells' section Mr. Holbrooke has shown himself a master of vocal part writing,
while into the 'Iron Bells' he has poured all his power of
characterisation. The 'Wedding Bells' might easily degener-
ate into common-place with a less noble and dignified conductor than Dr. Richter, but upon this occasion it was safe.
There is much striving for effect for its own sake; the whole
work is exceedingly cleverly scored, and it amazes by its skilful and daring orchestration, but the pulse never quickens,
the breath never catches, throughout the work.

Mr. Percy Pitt's *Sinfonietta* is really symphonic in length,
taking from forty to forty-five minutes in performance.
Here again is a work that is cleverly and skilfully orchestrated, but that leaves one cold. It presents a great many
effects of which the causes are, to say the least, not obvious,
but further hearings may dispel much of its vagueness.[4]

Mischa Elman is gaining in power of tone, and in refinement of his phrasing.[5] He played the Beethoven Concerto

---

[4] Percy Pitt (1870–1932) became better known as a conductor – he spent
several years as an assistant to Beecham – and later as Musical Director of
the B.B.C. Brian reviewed a few of his other compositions over the years,
never very enthusiastically, but wrote a sympathetic profile of him for the
'Personal and Otherwise' column of *Musical Opinion* for March 1928.

[5] Elman was 17 in 1906, and had another 50 years before him as an

with an almost careless ease, so little effort did he display in tackling even the most difficult passages. He was loudly cheered, and recalled again and again at the end of his solo.

Miss Agnes Nicholls displayed the beautiful qualities of her voice in an aria from Mozart's *Il Seraglio*, and Mr. Ffrangçon Davies sang with much feeling 'King Saul's Dream' from Parry's oratorio. Under Dr. Richter the orchestra gave renderings of Strauss's *Don Juan* and Berlioz's *Carnaval Romain* with a finish that spoke volumes for their extraordinary powers of endurance and staying qualities, their work on that one day having been nothing short of titanic proportions.

Omar Khayyam, by Granville Bantock

On Thursday evening Mr. Granville Bantock's new work, founded upon Omar Khayyam's 'Rubaiyat', was presented for the first time.[6] There was a feeling of expectancy in the atmosphere, Mr. Bantock being well known in Birmingham as the Principal of the Midland Institute. It has been urged that the Persian poem is not as a whole a fitting one for musical setting, that while certain quatrains lend themselves to musical treatment others are too philosophical to adapt themselves readily to musical requirements. The justification of Mr. Bantock's choice lies in the score; of the fifty-four quatrains already set it would be difficult to remove one without jeopardising the whole structure, so closely is it knit together. Moreover in the composer's treatment of the words, dividing them among the Beloved, the Poet, the Philosopher, and giving those of general import to the chorus, they fall so naturally into place that the mind is unconsciously drawn from one to another, with no sense of the discontinuity that may occasionally be felt in reading the poem. Mr. Bantock has, indeed, by his music, supplied the links that unite the whole poem.

This work must be acknowledged the triumph of the Festival. Mr. Bantock has sounded a new note in music. After

---

internationally renowned virtuoso.

[6] This was only Part I of what eventually became a vast three-part setting.

our bending the knee to Apollo for many years he has brought us face to face with Dionysos in Persian garb; he has not only given us the spirit of the East as we had not previously experienced it, he has sounded the note of healthy Paganism that dares all and fears none, which before had not been heard. Musically, the work is full of contrasts many of which were not realised at this performance. The chorus, unfortunately, sang their opening phrase 'Open then the door' in much the same way as they might have sung 'Sing me then to sleep', so that the impressive phrase that follows immediately and changes the colour of the whole chorus, changes the *mise en scène* indeed at one stroke from the finite to the infinite, lost its effect. This was but one such lapse of many, but a knowledge of the score[7] enables one to see that the work only suffers temporarily by reason of defective rendering. Mr. Bantock's plan of dividing his string orchestra into two proved to be more than a sensational fad, many delicate effects being obtained such as had not been heard in any previous work during the Festival. The scene of the Caravan in the Desert was a piece of colour-painting that will not be forgotten readily by any who heard it played by the Festival orchestra.

Anxiety to do their best was plainly written upon the faces of principals, chorus, and orchestra, and some of the effects were undoubtedly marred by the lack of ease that this entailed. The principals did not sing with the confidence that future performances of the work will ensure, but Mme. Ada Crossley and Mr. John Coates entered thoroughly into the spirit of the work as was evident in their singing of the duet 'A Book of Verses', and again in 'When you and I behind the veil are past'. Mr. Baker has yet to learn something of Persian philosophy before he can make a thorough success of the part.

At the end of the work Mr. Bantock received a furore of applause; chorus and orchestra, moved by an irresistable impulse, stood up and applauded, while 'bravos' resounded through the hall. It was indeed a five minutes of intense

---

[7]   Brian had reviewed the scores of *Omar* and Holbrooke's *The Bells* in *The Musical World*, 15 September 1906, pp. 87–88.

excitement, and Birmingham has reason to be proud that
Mr. Bantock's work has emanated from that city.

Dr. Richter took the orchestra in hand and gave a deeply
impressive rendering of Strauss's Symphonic Poem *Tod und
Verklärung* and Wagner's *Tannhäuser* Overture. Mme. Ada
Crossley sang Gluck's 'Divinités du Styx' in her fullest, rich-
est voice.

Beethoven's Mass in D

After singing in the works of Mendelssohn, Elgar, Bach,
Holbrooke, Handel, and Bantock, and singing in the bet-
ter-known works with conspicuous ability and power, it
would not have been suprising had the energies of the
chorus flagged before Beethoven's monumental Mass in D.
But their voices seemed incapable of fatigue, and the opening Kyrie was as full-blooded as had been their tone in the
Bach cantata on Wednesday. The occasional leanness of
tone of the sopranos must be laid to the account of Beethoven, who made his demands with a god-like indifference
as to whether human voices could meet them. Once more
the perfect balance of the parts produced the utmost effect,
sounding at times like blocks of solid tone. Here we had a
chorus able and willing to enter into the vast conception of
the work held by Dr. Richter and the result was one of the
greatest performances we are likely to hear. The 'Gloria in
Excelsis' was taken at a terrific speed, yet so perfectly was
the rhythm maintained that never at any moment did there
seem to be undue haste. The conductor, principals, chorus,
and orchestra were fused into unity while interpreting one
mighty conception. The same sense of ease was apparent
also in the fugue 'Et vitam venturi', and the feeling of awe
and mystery with which they sang 'Et incarnatus est' is one
of the unforgettable things of the Festival.[...]

The violin solo of the 'Benedictus' was played by Mischa
Elman with unerring insight into the lofty nature of the
work. He afterwards played the Concerto of Tchaikovsky,
with which music he is always manifestly in complete sympathy, and on this occasion he gave evidence of his power to
enter into every mood and phase of thought of the Russian
composer.

Miss Muriel Foster made her last appearance on a Festival platform (her farewell is to take place in Manchester next month) in singing an old cantata *O amantissime sponse Jesu* by Christian Ritter, a contemporary of Bach, but about whom very little is known.[8] To Herr Richard Buchmayer we owe its present edition and arrangement. Miss Foster sang it in tones of ecstasy, and the perfect phrasing that has always been an essential part of her rendering.

The *Parsifal* Prelude concluded the morning performance. In the evening the Festival came to an end with Mendelssohn's *Hymn of Praise*, Stanford's *Revenge*, and Wagner's *Flying Dutchman* Overture.

TWO ENGLISH NOVELTIES

A Hallé Concert review from *The Musical World*, 16 December 1907, p. 147.

Miss Agnes Nicholls, at the concert on the 5th inst., brought to Manchester two new works from the autumn Festivals. Her husband's setting of Keats's *Ode to a Nightingale* has been produced at Cardiff;[9] and Mr. Granville Bantock's *Christ in the Wilderness*, from which she took the soprano aria – 'The Wilderness and the Solitary Place' – made its appearance at Gloucester. Miss Nicholls was, herself, unfortunately suffering from the effects of a severe cold, which

[8] Modern scholarship has added little to our knowledge of Ritter, although it is known that he spent part of his career at the Swedish court; and he is now considered an interesting forerunner rather than exact contemporary of Bach. *O amantissime sponsa Jesu* was his first work to reach modern publication, and this must have been one of its earliest performances.
[9] Agnes Nicholls (1877–1959) had married Hamilton Harty in 1904, and he had written the *Ode to a Nightingale* specifically for her. *The Musical World* of 16 September 1907 carried a long review of the Cardiff Festival which also included the premiere of Part II of Bantock's *Omar Khayyam*: this could well be by Brian, but there is insufficient evidence to be sure.

occasioned a little restraint in the use of her voice: but the spirit with which she presented both works was entirely artistic and admirable. Mr. Hamilton Harty's *Ode* was not so well performed as at Cardiff; Dr. Richter's reading lacked much of the tenderness that characterised the composer's conception, while the mystical atmosphere of the opening prelude was almost entirely lost in a fog of sound, in which the voice of the nightingale was all but inaudible. The orchestra played tentatively and timidly; this was probably due to lack of rehearsal and to their playing from MS parts. In spite of all this second hearing of the *Ode* deepens the impression, and makes us desirous of hearing it again when it will be well performed and, at the same time, free from the nervous anxiety of a Festival performance. It has moments of such arresting beauty and fidelity of expression that it seems a pity the composer should have been in such haste to give it to the world. Could it but have had a few years in the alembic of the composer's mind, it would probably have emerged as a setting worthy in all points of the superb poetry that inspired it. The work was well received.

Spontaneous and spirited was the applause that followed the singing of 'The Wilderness and the Solitary Place'. Manchester has lately had many opportunities of becoming acquainted with the dramatic works of Mr. G.B. Shaw, and a better preparation for the music of Mr. Bantock could hardly be chosen. There is one feature of Mr. Bantock's music that is strangely allied to the methods of Mr. Shaw: he has a way of shocking all preconceptions that would stultify the imagination, and thus it is that the audience at the end of 'The Wilderness' was not so much horrified at the unconventional setting of familiar words, as astonished at its truth! It is surely significant of the increasing hold this composer is taking upon the public, that of the three novelties produced at these concerts, two have been by Mr. Bantock. We trust we shall not have to wait long before hearing the whole of *Christ in the Wilderness* in Manchester.

THE PROMENADES

Part article, part review, this appeared in *Musical Opinion* of
September 1927, pp. 1172–1173.

When the vague announcement was made to the press some
months ago that there *might* not be either Queen's Hall
Orchestra Symphony Concerts or Promenades in the
future, many of us did not become panic-stricken. Interviews with public men were sought by the press, and their
views solemnly recorded. No one offered a practical solution, or even suggested the name of someone who would
shoulder the financial responsbility. On the other hand, a
few who had watched the ascendancy of Sir Henry J. Wood
from the days when he commenced his career as a conductor had also known previous occasions when he stood face
to face with unusual difficulties. Sir Henry, having solved
his own troubles by working in conjunction with the British
Broadcasting Corporation, the arrangement appears to us
as having far-reaching consequences owing to its greater
scope.[10] The Proms are national concerts in fact now; for by
broadcasting they will pass into thousands of households
where formerly they were only a name. The Proms, having
died, have risen covered with a greater glory. The festive
gaiety and excitement which distinguished the opening
may be accepted as a tribute of congratulation to Sir Henry
Wood's undaunted courage and fearlessness in having got
round the difficulties which threatened to submerge the
concerts altogether.[...]

The fifth concert, on Thursday, August 18th, was our
first participation in this annual festivity. Having been
absent for some years, it was interesting to meet again so

[10]   In March 1927 Messrs. Chappell, the lessees of Queen's Hall, who had
provided the financial underpinning for Henry Wood's Promenade Concerts since 1915, withdrew their patronage; after a period of uncertainty
the BBC took over the concerts and engaged Wood to continue conducting them. The 1927 season, the first week of which Brian reviews here,
was therefore the first under the dispensation that has continued until
the present day.

many familiar faces.[11] Sir Henry Wood has a charmed life, and looks younger than ever. The question arose on this as on many former occasions: whether we should just sit down and enjoy the concert, throwing aside critical scrutiny, or have a smoke and listen critically to the weaving and the spinning.[12] We chose to do the latter.

In a very fine essay written upon *rubato* many years ago, M. Paderewski offers – with qualifications from his point of view – the opinion that Berlioz was quite devoid of emotion. He admits that Berlioz appreciated and understood the unusual fantasies which thronged his imagination, but that he did not conceive his music emotionally—like Chopin, for instance.

If we accept this, what then forms the background of such a wonderful painting as the overture *Le Carnaval romain*, quite graphically thrown upon the mind's screen by Sir Henry J. Wood? Surely, if Berlioz conveys to our minds the same vision which he felt and saw, then he assuredly caught it emotionally. Elgar's *Wand of Youth*, a most charming box of delicacies, revealed how delicately he can shoot colours through his texture and express quaint ideas.

Dorothy Howell[13] has a mind full of real poetical thoughts. Her Piano Concerto – of which she herself was the soloist – contains charming flights lit up with deft harmonic touches – a natural gift for mixing her colours and downright earnestness for spinning and weaving. There was a fine understanding between the orchestra and herself, but the construction of the concerto necessitates endless episodes; and we fear that if we heard the work often, it would suggest that it would gain by shortening. We say this in spite of the fact that we enjoyed a work which appeared as having been cast in one piece and finely moulded. It was a great surprise for us – a surprise that she is so distinguished a composer and equally so a pianist.

The wind got a chance to show its qualities, in the

---

[11] Brian had only recently returned to London after more than a decade living in Birmingham and on the South Coast.
[12] 'No Smoking' regulations were a thing of the far future.
[13] For more on Dorothy Howell, see pp.355–356.

Beethoven Rondino in E flat, inside this very old-world atmosphere. The two horns particularly distinguished themselves by every kind of *nuance*: especially arresting were some quaint *arpeggii* passages, lying very low, but distinctly well played.

In the *Scheherazade* (of Rimsky-Korsakoff), we have an orchestral suite which astonishes in many ways. Its foundation is so well-known that if it has been once seen as a ballet it is comparatively easy to reconstruct mentally when the work proceeds as an orchestral piece. Here again we detect the hand of Berlioz. The spinning and the weaving is pushed away into a comparatively subordinate position that the orchestral tissue shall be suffused again and again in every possible colour scheme. How ravishing the final moments are, how intimate the antiphonal matter between the solo violin and orchestra: but were strings and brass ever more gloriously written for? True, there are moments when the hero seems to nod and the light looks like going out; but in such a rare basket of fruit, we can well dispense with the trimmings.

Berners' *Fantaisie Espagnole* was conducted by Mr. Charles Woodhouse – quite brilliantly too – with a complete grasp of the composer's score, though somewhat shy and reserved. We felt that if Lord Berners had conducted the work himself, he would have made ever so much more noise and made it hotter. The instrumentation undoubtedly reaches us *via* Russia. It is a brilliant crimson: think of the exciting things 'said' by the horns! In spite of the Spanish designation, we experienced a feeling during its performance that the work had its origin far east of the Alhambra.

The fairy music of *Hansel and Gretel* contains some of the most charming and innocent music ever written, prefaced by a beautiful Overture. The Proms had a very sumptuous version of the Overture, delightfully unfolded in its performance as though conceived in one uninterrupted piece.

We mention Bach (the greatest man) last because in the Sinfonia for organ and orchestra to the Cantata 29, *Wir danken dir*, he provided us with the rarest feast. Those who left the hall before the piece began will never realise how much pleasure they missed. This work, modernised by Sir

Henry Wood, impressed us as one of the most completely satisfying things yet experienced. It is a long stretch of finely sustained breadth, grandeur and healthy joyousness. Written in the broadest ancient German style, it needs neither French nor Italian influence for its interpretation. The apparent concern of Sir Henry Wood was to give the work a free hand and to let the music tell its own story. Its performance was thoroughly German in character, and a reincarnation of Hans Richter at his best. The surprise given us by this music will not fade away. Of course, it was made so by the magnificent organ playing of Mr. Fred Kiddle and the broad, intense playing of the orchestra.

Miss Clara Serena sang the aria 'O love, from thy power' (Saint-Saëns), whilst Mr. William Anderson sang 'My power is absolute', from *Boris Godounov*. Both artists received sympathetic applause from the audience. Later, to piano accompaniment, they contributed songs by Byrd, Vaughan Williams, Lully, Bullard and Lane Wilson.[...]

THE B.B.C. CONCERTS OF BRITISH MUSIC

A review from *Musical Opinion*, February 1934, p. 431.

The six concerts of British contemporary music given by the B.B.C. at Queen's Hall[14] should be taken as an earnest rather than as a fulfilment of good intentions. It was obvious that all the names of composers which stood for definite accomplishment in British music during the past thirty years could not possibly be included. For this reason the names of Parry, Stanford, Cowen, and German do not appear. Amongst contemporary British composers missing

[14] This important concert series – for which Elgar had been commissioned to write his ill-fated Third Symphony – took place in January 1934.

from the programmes are Foulds, Sorabji, Dyson and Van Dieren.

The first concert, on January 1st, was conspicuous for one novelty, a Symphony by R.O. Morris (a distinguished professor at the R.C.M.), whose work was at least remarkable for its musical erudition. At the same concert Lambert's *Rio Grande* re-appeared with undiminished freshness and buoyancy. A surprise was the splendid performance of Delius's *Song of the High Hills.*

The second concert was given over entirely to the works of Ethel Smyth.[15] The other concerts of the series contained important works by Benjamin, Bliss, Fogg, Bainton, Goossens, Boughton, Vaughan Williams, Bax, Dale, Bocquet[16] and Berners. The question may well have been asked why larger orchestral works were not chosen to represent Bantock and Holbrooke? The same might be asked regarding McEwen, who at the fifth concert was represented by the torso, *Prelude.* Why not his *Grey Galloway* Poem, or the *Solway* Symphony? At this concert two new works were heard: a Rhapsody for pianoforte and orchestra entitled *Phantasm*, by Frank Bridge, with Kathleen Long as soloist; and *The Love Talker*, by Armstrong Gibbs, with Muriel Brunskill as soloist. Scholarship combined with imaginative invention distinguished each work, though Bridge is doubtless the more distinguished orchestral writer.

Villon, by William Wallace, a one-time much discussed novelty, was really fortunate to be included: whilst Elgar's Symphony in A flat, conducted by Landon Ronald, overshadowed other works in the programme.

The last concert was the most conspicuous because it contained a series of important novelties. A large audience with real Promenade enthusiasm was attracted; and the B.B.C. orchestra, choir and Adrian Boult certainly gave of their

---

[15] This one concert received a separate review from another writer, so Brian barely mentioned it here.

[16] See Arnold Bax's *Farewell My Youth* (Longman, Green & Co., London, 1936), pp. 36–38, for amusing vignettes of his friend Roland Bocquet (1878–?), a prolific song-writer who had made his home in Germany since before the First World War.

best. There was, perhaps, too much that was contemporaneous. Why not have included Cowen's overture, *The Butterflies' Ball*, or Stanford's *Irish Rhapsody* in D minor? In such a programme they would have lessened the pressure of Holst, Delius, Ireland, Hadley, Moeran, and Walton. Holst's *Hymn of Jesus* appropriately led the procession: it is unyielding, forceful, powerful. A *Fantastic Dance* by Delius, played for the first time, indicated its source clearly. John Ireland's *Prelude* for piano and orchestra[17] (also played for the first time), with Helen Perkin as soloist, was much too brief to be placed in such a programme. The work which made the deepest impression of all the new works heard at the festival was Hadley's *The Trees so High*, for orchestra, baritone solo and chorus. It has three instrumental movements and an orchestral and choral finale. The weakest writing is in the orchestral sections, particularly in the Scherzo, which moves in spasmodic circles and never seems really to 'go'. The complexion of the work changed immediately the chorus entered, and from this movement to the close, the composer displays an original and unusual gift for polyphonic writing, orchestral colour, and a sense of climax. Walton's *Belshazzar's Feast* was a most appropriate postlude for this Festival of British Music.

LEITH HILL MUSICAL FESTIVAL

A review from *Musical Opinion*, May 1937, pp. 722–723.

The four days' competitions of the twenty-eighth Leith Hill Musical Festival concluded on April 9th with a choral and orchestral concert in the Dorking Halls, conducted by R. Vaughan Williams. The chorus was made up of choral societies from Banstead, Epsom, Fetcham and Leatherhead, and the Dorking Madrigal and Dorking Oriana societies. Isidore Schwiller led the orchestra and Arnold

---

[17] Brian must mean the *Legend*.

Goldsborough was the accompanist. The exceptional qualities of the large chorus allowed it to be successfully used in
a performance of the madrigal, *As Vesta was from Latmos Hill
descending* (Weelkes), sung with the refinement of a selected
choir of fifty voices. *Since thou, O fondest*, an unaccompanied
part-song by O'Connor Morris, was also interpreted with
sensitive delicacy. At the final concert a shortened version of
Parry's *Judith*, beginning with the finale of the first act of the
original, received a magnificent performance. When this
work was first produced, at the Birmingham Festival of
1888, it was rightly regarded as a stroke of genius; and this
performance, under Vaughan Williams, may go far to
restore the work to the position it held for many years. If
Parry's technique in *Judith* lacks modern virtuosity, it does
not fail by comparison in depth of expression or continuous
thinking. Occasionally he 'catches fire' in his choral movements: in 'The God of our Fathers' and in the finely conceived finale beginning with Judith's joyous outburst 'I will
sing unto the Lord'. The grandeur and nobility of Parry's
music was portrayed through the masterly conducting of
Vaughan Williams and the excellent singing of Renée Flynn
(Judith), Edward Reach (Manasseh), and George Hancock
(Holofernes). Parry, his own librettist, styles his work
'Scenes from Judith'. From its layout, the work lends itself to
dramatic stage performances, if ever such a project should
be contemplated. In no way does *Judith* resemble the typical
oratorio. The big tenor solo, sung by Manasseh, 'God
breaketh the battle', just before the conclusion, remains to
my mind the biggest and finest thing of its kind since
Handel. In days gone by, well-known tenors added to their
reputation by their singing of it, and the performance on
this occasion by Edward Reach was memorable for its magnificent vocal quality and dramatic fervour.

Debussy's setting of Rossetti's *The Blessed Damozel* was
also performed, with Renée Flynn (Blessed Damozel) and
Millicent Russell (Narrator). The festival concluded with
Vaughan Williams's *Flourish for a Coronation*,[18] followed

[18] Which had been premiered at Queen's Hall under Beecham only a
few days before.

immediately by Parry's national hymn, *Jerusalem*. The *Flourish* is music which instantly suggests a spectacular ceremony. The first part is a frenzied and emotional Handelian hurly-burly – grandiose and diatonic, sharpened by clashes, syncopated rhythms and big bold tunes. This is followed by a short movement of eloquent dignity and gradually expanding power, and the return of the riotous opening. It is likely that the *Flourish* will be heard many times long after the Coronation is over. As an occasional piece, it is an inspiration.

The orchestra got a chance to display its expressive qualities in the Pavane from Edward German's *Romeo and Juliet*.[19] In a tersely written note of this work, Vaughan Williams drew attention to German's unique genius, and made the prophecy that in fifty years his name will be honoured when other more ambitious composers are forgotten. The note concluded:

> Shall we ever cure ourselves of the snobbery which raves over some perfunctory little dance by Mozart or Schubert – probably dashed off in a hurry to satisfy an importunate customer – and refuses entry into the Pantheon to such a charming little tune as this Pavane?

Such is the spirit animating the festival which brought forth the revivals of the works by Parry, German and Debussy.

MODERN MUSIC

This is taken from the 'On the Other Hand' column in the July 1938 *Musical Opinion*, p. 857.

The two concerts of modern music given at the Boosey & Hawkes music studio proved to be an annex to the concerts

---

[19] German had died a few months earlier, in November 1936. For more on his incidental music to Shakespeare plays, see p.50.

of the ISCM Festival.[20] Many of the composers represented
at the festival were present at the first concert: so the audience was both international and enthusiastic. Four items in
a programme lasting nearly two hours forced on me the
limited colour range of the piano, which to me is mono-
chromic and expressionless. Even one song would have
made a diversion.

Bartók played eleven pieces from his encyclopaedic piano
work with the all-embracing title of *Mikrokosmos*. I do not
know if he has yet completed this cycle of one hundred
pieces. I had not seen Bartók for ten years, and that last
occasion was the B.B.C. rehearsal of his Piano Concerto,[21]
when in his shirt sleeves he wrestled at the piano, and
Edward Clark similarly deshabillé fought with the lions of
the orchestra. Bartók is tremendously sure of himself, and
his pieces have seemingly inexhaustible variety. Yet he can,
when he likes, write very fancifully in an idiom which he
regards as out-moded.

Nor was the young British composer, Benjamin Britten,
less adventurous, and of him I would like to prophesy that,
when he has sowed his (musical) wild oats, he will return like
other straying sheep to the fold. Britten is talented, and
being a really accomplished pianist, was able, with Frederick Grinke, to interpret his *Suite* for violin and piano
exactly as he felt it. This short panoramic suite of inventions
and moods contained a Lullaby of rare imaginative fantasy.
Here are the indications of great things by the composer in
maturity.

The young Russian, Nikolai Lopatnikoff, played his
Sonatina in a robust, dashing style, suggesting a Transeuropic

---

[20] The 1938 International Society for Contemporary Music (ISCM)
Festival was held in London. During it, two chamber concerts were given
at the Boosey & Hawkes Music Studio by composers featured in the
Festival.
[21] That was on 10 October 1927, for an all-Bartók concert which Brian
covered for *Musical Opinion* (his review will appear in a later volume of
selections). According to issue No. 1 (January 1939) of *Tempo*, Bartók
played a further 15 numbers from *Mikrokosmos* in the second of these recitals. *Mikrokosmos* eventually ran to 150 pieces, not 100, but that may have
been the quoted figure at the time Brian was writing.

Express at *x* M.P.H. After the storm and stress of these three adventurists, the Trio No. 3 by John Ireland for piano, violin and 'cello sounded singularly normal:[22] not that it lacks the spirit of adventure. Modern as is the outlook of John Ireland, his writing offers no resistance to the ears. His Trio contains much music of rare inspired eloquence: it has an abundance of ready rhythmic suggestion, especially in the first movement and Scherzo. The work was played magnificently by the composer, Frederick Grinke (violin), and Florence Hooton (cello).

[22] Ireland's Trio had been premiered earlier that year, but is in fact a rewritten version of an unpublished work composed in 1913.

PART SEVEN

NATIONALISM, LEAGUES AND COMPETITIONS

———————⟨•⟩———————

Brian was much exercised throughout his journalistic career by the vulnerable state of English music, its repertoire constricted by fashion, conservative programming, philistinism, and economic conditions. On the one hand he advocated much increased representation for British composers, but on the other he distrusted the kind of nationalism which decried foreign composers and their music; on the contrary, he reasoned, the best of all countries had to be freely available for British music to match itself against. He often proposed more or less utopian schemes for the encouragement of new music: the most elaborate (though ironical) example occurs in 'The British Spirit', pp.202-208. His ideas tended to be based partly on his experience of the pre-War Musical League and also, insofar as they included an element of competition, were influenced by the competitive choral festivals which had played such a large part in the musical world of his youth. The earliest article given here appeared in *The Musical World* for 16 November 1907, pp.110–111, and was a natural extension of his oft-expressed frustration with the narrowness of the Hallé programmes.

THE MUSIC PROBLEM IN MANCHESTER

The fact that the public exhibition of works of art and the performance of musical compositions is conditioned by

economic factors, is very generally held as adequate excuse
for the lamentable state of the artistic and musical affairs of
our own and other cities. In Manchester, however, where we
fare very badly in matters musical, this excuse can scarcely
be put forward with complete success. Indeed, it will be con-
ceded only by a few that any excuse at all is necessary for the
present condition of musical affairs in our city: for we are a
self-satisfied people, and the presence of a great conductor
in our midst is a constant and pleasing assurance that in the
matter of quality we are behind neither London, Paris nor
Berlin.

   But those who take their musical education seriously, who
are anxious to keep in touch with the extraordinary
developments of modern composition, and who are already
well acquainted with the more popular works of Handel,
Bach, Mozart, Haydn, Schubert, Beethoven, Mendelssohn,
Schumann, Wagner, and the rest, are in the unfortunate
position of being unable to hear more than very occasionally any example of the music of the last quarter-century.
With the exception of Richard Strauss and Sibelius – of
whom we in Manchester know a little, but by no means
enough – scarcely any other living Continental composer
has been represented in our programmes. Debussy, Vincent
d'Indy, Weingartner, and Max Reger, are to us mere names;
yet Debussy's work is constantly played in every capital of
Europe, and Max Reger is regarded by many competent critics as a serious rival of Strauss. Of Strauss himself, and of
Berlioz and Liszt, we do not hear enough. English composers, with one notable exception, are steadfastly banned –
though this season another exception is being made in the
case of Mr. Granville Bantock's *Omar Khayyam*. Of Russian
composers, other than Tchaikovsky, we know little or
nothing; and modern France, so far as we are concerned, is
non-existent. In short, though there are in Europe many
men of undoubted musical genius who are turning out
work well worthy of performance in Manchester, we know
practically nothing of them. Our musical knowledge is 'out
of date'; we are old-fashioned, conservative; and, worst of
all, we are content to remain ignorant and unappreciative of
what men of our own generation are doing. We would

rather hear Mendelssohn's *Elijah* year after year, *ad nauseam*,[1] than put in its place the exquisite *Pelléas and Melisande* of Debussy; we prefer the *Messiah* of Handel, already heard *scores* of times, to another oratorio of the same composer not yet heard once; we will patiently listen to the nine symphonies of Beethoven, carefully studied and long ago known by heart, while Bruckner[2] and Brahms are just occasionally tolerated.

This state of affairs, I venture to assert, is most deplorable; but it is the concert-going public of Manchester who are directly responsible for it. There can be little doubt that if they really wished to hear contemporary music, their desire would be gratified.

Question d'Argent

It is no part of my business to enter into the economic conditions existing in Manchester; but it may be pointed out that new, unknown orchestral works require more rehearsal than compositions with which both conductor and orchestra are already familiar; and that extra rehearsals entail a large expenditure of money. This is the first obstacle one meets, and it is popularly regarded as an insuperable one. In reality, it would seem to be far from insuperable. If the funds at the disposal of the committee of the Hallé Concerts will not permit of performances of works involving extra rehearsals, and if the committee of the Promenade Concerts believe that their patrons do not wish to hear good modern works of a serious character, it is still open for lovers of music to organise a series of concerts at which no work save that of the last thirty years shall be performed. Such a series of concerts need not involve the expenditure of a large sum of money. If the number were limited to

---

[1] See note 1 on p.179.
[2] Richter had conducted Bruckner's Symphony No. 4 with the Hallé in October 1905, and No. 3 in February 1907. (In one later writing Brian also mentions a Hallé performance of the *Te Deum*, which I have not traced: the passage is in any case ambiguous, and may only suggest that a performance was mooted.) These had sufficed – by the date of this article – to turn Brian into an enthusiastic champion of Bruckner, some fifty years ahead of most of the English critical fraternity.

three for the first season, and if the services of one of the many obscure but able conductors of England or the Continent were engaged, and if the works selected for performance were not such as to require an enlarged orchestra – then only a comparatively small sum would be needed to set the scheme afloat.

It is, of course, very doubtful if many of the musicians and students of Manchester have any desire to hear modern music; indeed, there is ground for believing that as a body they have not. Nevertheless, if the scheme were conducted on business lines, and if the programmes were compiled by men thoroughly acquainted with the English, French, German, Norwegian, Russian, Italian, and Belgian work of the last twenty-five years, it may be assumed that the general public would be attracted in sufficient numbers to encourage the continuation of the scheme. In any case, there is surely in Manchester a sufficiently large number of public-spirited men interested in music who would be willing to undertake some small monetary risk for the sake of the art they admire. The educational value of new ideas is beyond dispute, and from modern literature and painting we have derived definite suggestions, and ideas which are invaluable; but from the art of music – never so alert, so alive, and so earnest as it is to-day – we are learning nothing new, and the ideas of generations ago, noble but intolerably familiar, have begun to irk and irritate.

THE BRITISH SPIRIT

This article appeared in *The Sackbut*, Vol.IV, No. 8 (March 1924), pp. 236–239.

When the war broke out many who saw the cleavage which severed the nation politically also saw it cut asunder musically. In the latter I refer to those indissoluble ties which bindone nation to another through the universal language of music. How wonderful it would be if foreign diplomacy could be transacted through some such universal medium. We had the curious spectacle of musicians and composers who had probably never had a French thought in their heads before the war suddenly becoming pro-French. This was excusable. Many who had never had a 'pro' at all suddenly became pro-English. It is the latter who will most likely follow in the wake of Humpty-Dumpty, unless they negotiate things carefully. You cannot create a national spirit by committee meetings, societies, or merely changing names. It will never be done by hurling anathemas at certain heads and calling them pro-French, pro-German, or pro-Russian. The English spirit, whatever else it might stand for, should at least stand for some fairness and a high degree of respect co-operating among those musicians who make up the nation's musical life. To call it English is narrowing it down to the small dimensions of the parish vestry or the village pub. We ought, at any rate, to show greater breadth of outlook and call it British. The British spirit has the reputation of absorbing and assimilating the finest products, whatever they may be and wherever they are: it has been so in art as in commerce. We have recently had a great Elizabethan festival of sixteenth-century music. We deserved it after so much fine research and almost reverential care with which the recovery and restoration of long-forgotten treasures had taken place under Doctor Terry and Canon Fellowes.[3] But to attempt to build up in the twentieth century a nation's music upon a structure of the sixteenth century is not attempting a national revival, but national suicide. Each national epoch creates its own idioms whether in music, art, or language. It will serve no purpose

---

[3] Richard Terry (1865–1934), musicologist and organist of Downside Abbey (1896–1901) and Westminster Cathedral (1901–1924), where he was instrumental in the revival of the Catholic church music of Byrd, Fayrfax, Morley, Mundy, Tallis, Tye, and others; Edmund H. Fellowes (1870–1951), musicologist and canon of St. George's Chapel Windsor, edited the collected works of Byrd (in 20 volumes), the English lutenists (in 32), *The English Madrigal School* (in 36) and *Tudor Church Music* (in 10) as well as writing many books on the period. Their names are frequently coupled as the principal architects of the renewed interest in the heritage of Elizabethan music.

to try and imagine ourselves back again in all the trappings and picturesque glory which decorated this land of ours in the reigns of King Henry VIII and Queen Elizabeth.

Who has and who has not, amongst us, got the English idiom, and how is it to be recognized from that which is avowedly from another source? It is a well-known fact that twenty years ago the teaching of composition at the two principal English conservatoires was based upon the two most eminent German composers of the previous decade. At one institution the romantic – Wagner – was the hero, whilst at the other, the last of the great classicists – Brahms – reigned.[4] It is no use being shy about it nowadays, because our conservatoires were only following a natural law. They had no intention of being pro-German or pro-anything else. The authorities, which consisted of eminent men of wide experience and culture, went for the finest thing going for their students – just as a mother gets the milk with the greatest amount of cream upon which to feed her babes. There is not the slightest doubt that if the finest birds had been in Russia, France, Italy, or Spain, our authorities would have got them, and our chickens would have entered *via* those routes. English musical thought has been moulded largely upon German music for the simple reason that since Henry Purcell died all the great composers, with few exceptions, have appeared in Germany. You cannot nourish a nation's art upon Tariff Reform League lines.[5] Sullivan is admitted to be the most popular composer we

[4] i.e., at the Royal Academy of Music, under Corder, and the Royal College of Music, under Parry, respectively.

[5] The Tariff Reform League had been founded a few months before, in September 1923. But Tariff Reform – as an adjunct of the principles of Free Trade – had been a subject of passionate debate for many years, and one of the main issues in the pre-War general elections covered by *The Staffordshire Sentinel* when Brian was writing for it. In the words of Captain Ewart S. Grogan, Unionist parliamentary candidate and prominent Stoke politician, the aim was to impose import controls to 'protect the British job, at Trade Union Rates, against the blackleg competition of Foreign imports' (letter to the Editor of *The Staffordshire Sentinel*, 13 April 1910). Brian's point is simply that such favouritism, in the form of artificial advantages for English composers, could never have a healthy artistic outcome.

have produced, and to have the ideal English idiom. Yet he was an Irishman by birth and educated largely in Germany. Edward German, upon whom many musicians believe the mantle of Sullivan descended – giving him the English idiom – is a Welshman. Mackenzie is a Scotchman, whilst Stanford is an Irishman.

Have any British composers alive to-day got a real and undiluted English idiom? It is of no use being revengeful against Germany because she has always been able to put the biggest men in the field. She has always shown great tact in showing sympathy and recognition to composers of originality whose nationality was not her own. Ethel Smyth, Stanford, Sullivan, Bantock, Delius, Elgar, and Cyril Scott are well known – whilst in recent years the names of Vaughan Williams and Holbrooke have been found in various German concert programmes. Indeed, Sullivan is as popular in Germany as in England. Quite the same thing has happened to the drama, for Shakespeare is more of a hero in Germany than in England, and the same might be said of George Bernard Shaw.

The root of the trouble which has begot the spirit of discontent is the apparent unfairness with which composers of British nationality have been treated in British concert programmes. For my own part I fail to grasp why a little more sympathy has not been given to the symphonies of Stanford, Bantock, Vaughan Williams, and Arnold Bax. Elgar has always been very fortunate in the way of performances ... and may be said to be the only British composer who has been well and frequently performed. Here again one hears about a spirit of unfairness which gives one composer twenty performances during a season and fobs another off with one. The public have no choice in the arrangements, so that one hears of brooding discontent ... as to who is the authority who dares to presume infallibility in British composer values. It must not be overlooked that the giving of concerts is almost entirely in the hands of those to whom a paying proposition is the first concern. Notwithstanding this, there has been a great deal of generosity shown, as the reference of Elgar performances indicates. From time to time one hears that the solution will be found by abolishing the German classics as the Americans have recently abolished whisky. We will see how far this can be attempted from a practical standpoint. I once had an appointment with a composer to meet him in the refreshment room at the Queen's Hall during the Prom season. It so happened that I had great difficulty in reaching my friend owing to the crowd. When I did eventually reach him I asked, 'Whatever is the matter with all these people, and why do they all look so solemn and sad?'

So my friend replied: 'At the end of this apparent church procession is Beethoven, for to-night is his night!' When I had expressed surprise at this, he replied : 'Yes – and the Wagner nights are just as crowded, and you know that most of this music can be played without rehearsal because the players know it backwards!' So I became perplexed, for here was something which the people wanted and they were getting it. Not only so, but the music was by those very composers who in their lifetime had worked and fought for 'Art for Art's sake', and won. How can you take away this music and offer an unfamiliar idiom, even if it be a native product? The foregoing will sufficiently answer those who would wreck existing things without plans for rebuilding a greater edifice. It is necessary to give modern British music a fair chance of proving itself. It is also no use asking concert managers to take greater risks than they do now, for the reason they cannot afford the speculation. I therefore suggest that the Government should be asked to give its sympathy to the promotion of British music. An association should be formed amongst the older composers or the various heads of the conservatoires. Half a dozen as a committee would be quite large enough for working purposes. This committee would go to the Premier and state the existing position of things and ask for practical support to remedy it. They would ask at first for:

1.   A grant from the Treasury of £18,000 for three years, making a total Government grant of £54,000.[6]

---

[6] The pound sterling in 1924 had a purchasing power almost exactly 20 times that of 1986, so multiply accordingly. Even so, Brian's figures

2. Invite the co-operation of an eminent firm of concert agents.

3. Engage the Queen's Hall for twelve concerts.

4. Engage the finest neutral conductor – either Dutch, French, German, or Russian or Italian. At any rate, let us have the finest from abroad; and offer him £2,000 for twelve concerts.

5. Allot £2,000 per year for advertising.

6. Allot £2,000 per year for travelling expenses of those artists who live in reduced circumstances in out-of-the-way parts of the Empire.

7. Mark off the balcony and gallery of the Queen's Hall for free tickets to the students of conservatoires within the Empire, such selection to be made by ballot.

8. Reserve the area for Press and general public.

9. Engage the London orchestras alternately with the Hallé and the Scottish orchestras.

10. Decide upon concert programmes to contain five items each – with one item in each programme to be selected by the conductor: his selection to be irrespective of any nationality and not to last more than twenty minutes in performance.

11. Decide how best to ballot for works for the concerts, giving a chance of one work to each composer, thus giving opportunities to sixty composers for the first series of twelve concerts.

12. Make out a form to be given to each member of the audience at each concert which will show only the five British works and allow a maximum of sixty marks for voting purposes, and request each member of the audience to vote and adjudicate upon the music performed.

---

seem rather modest by present-day expectations.

13. At the end of the first year the ballot papers would be collected and statistics made from the voting marks and compared with the Press criticisms.

14. From the results of the voting and criticisms the committee would build up their programmes for the following two years without balloting for same – the individual merits of each composer being based entirely upon the voting and Press results.

15. Publish the results of the voting and Press criticisms.

16. Request the Government to employ its Secret Service department to watch that no one of any of the composers was placed at any disadvantage either by way of a 'pull' over the conductor, Press, or in the voting.

The scheme would possibly have to be altered to embrace choral music and opera. It sets out to cover orchestral music or such things written which employ the orchestra, as concertos, arias, songs with instrumental accompaniment. It is conceivable that this scheme would be helping British music and British instrumentalists and British soloists. It would enable us to have a real stocktaking of the nation's music and to see if there is anything or nothing the matter with it.

FIFTY YEARS OF PROGRESS?

This sceptical piece appeared in 'On the Other Hand', in *Musical Opinion*, May 1932, pp. 667–668.

Sir Henry Hadow's review of fifty years of music, published in *The Times*, must be written in an aeroplane.[7] Little was seen, and that little seems to have been blurred. Sir

---

[7] Hadow (1859–1937) was one of the leading musical historians of his time, although his fame probably rests most firmly on the *Studies in*

Henry has the gifts of the historian: so had Thackeray, though I doubt whether any one of the Georges would have accepted either his facts or his opinions. The gist of the review is that music in England has sailed out of darkness into light; but on that point I am as unconvinced as any George would have been of a writing-man's knowledge of kingcraft. Like the Georges, I am an interested person.[8]

One thing that hasn't happened successfully during the past fifty years is the Municipal Orchestra. Leeds determined to try one, and the writing-men of the time beatified the effort, prophesying greater births. Another was born in Birmingham, but both have had to struggle for material existence: evidently municipal milk is not sufficiently rich in vitamins LSD.[9] The municipal milk at Brighton would seem to have been good and sufficient: but the people turned a deaf ear to what was to elevate them morally – and materially from an accession of visitors! The conductor and the players depart: women weep (vide *The Daily Mail*): and all Brighton sorrows, not for the loss of the music, but that thirty musicians are out of an engagement. Then there is Bournemouth: where one strong man[10] is holding the philistine hosts at bay. And that is fifty years' progress with municipal orchestras!

Modern Music which he had published as long ago as the 1890s. He had recently retired from the Vice-Chancellorship of Sheffield University, and his *Times* article was evidently recycled from the short book on English music which was the first fruit of his retirement.

[8] The reference is to Thackeray's 'The Four Georges: Sketches of Manners, Morals, Court and Town Life' (*Cornhill Magazine*, 1860), a series of essays designed to flatter Victorian self-esteem with the idea of mid-19th-century superiority to the loose-moraled past. It introduced, in the words of one recent critic, the 'overwhelming cliché of the Hanoverian royal family as a collection of boorish, lecherous semi-imbeciles'.

[9] The Leeds Saturday Orchestral Concerts (lineal descendant of the Municipal Concerts at which Brian's *English Suite* No. 1 was first performed) had suffered financially in the 1925–26 Season; the players formed the Leeds Symphony Orchestra in 1928, and at the time of this article its prosperity was by no means certain. Birmingham City Orchestra (now the City of Birmingham Symphony Orchestra), founded in 1920, remained in financial difficulties until 1935, when the BBC came to its aid.

[10] Sir Dan Godfrey.

Actually I refuse to be hypnotised by *The Times*' record of the fifty years' revival. I am dubious, because one always finds the historian telescoping facts to prove an absurdity. I know of no period in musical history when England had a living leader of international fame: it has always been a case of Homer dead. Elgar came near to that position, Sterndale Bennett nearer still, and Hugo Pierson [11] gained that honour at the loss of his nationality: he became a German. Where is Elgar leading the world now? Sullivan would and he wouldn't, and then allowed himself to be drawn into a very narrow and sheltered grove.[12] Sir Henry mentions the genius of Strauss, but *our* appreciation of progress and genius is such that his later operatic works remain only names to most of us.

I wonder whether Sir Henry would, after due reflection, really contend that the general appreciation of opera is wider to-day than it was in the 'eighties. My suggestion is that there has been neither erosion nor accretion: the tide simply ebbs and flows. Think of the days of John Christian Bach and of the London that welcomed Haydn. Then the various seasons were run on a series of productions of new operas by Handel, Salomon, Bach, &c. Where is there such enterprise to-day? Producing *Cavalcades*, *Waltzes from Vienna*,[13] and their like, is a poor exchange for genuine operatic adventure.

Still, I am on the track of the revival, but in the search I have failed to find in London one society with anything like that zest which distinguished the Sacred Harmonic Society,

---

[11] Pierson (1815–1873), after a brief spell as Professor of Music at Edinburgh, settled in Germany. His works are orchestrally highly inventive and – unusually for a British composer of the period – owe allegiance to the then 'avant-garde' principles of programmatic music in the mould of Liszt and Berlioz. Brian was frankly interested in Pierson, and had studied his operas and orchestral overtures.

[12] i.e., operetta.

[13] *Waltzes from Vienna*, an operetta-potpourri on waltzes by Johann Strauss II, arranged and orchestrated by Julius Bittner and Erich Wolfgang Korngold, to a libretto which gave a romanticised version of Strauss' rise to fame, had been produced in London for the first time the previous year. Brian had seen it and (as 'La Main Gauche') written about it in his column for October 1931.

to which goes the honour and glory of having introduced Mendelssohn to the English musical world. Is the fact that we have none such to be interpreted as a revival? Doubtless, we have now more of the paraphernalia of music about us. Musicians write music columns about nothing in particular, and we have gramophone recordings with attendant royalties to those who are already rich and famous. The newspapers applaud the populace on its innate musical ability and power of musical discrimination. But Schubert and Verdi were whistled in the streets before the dawn of the present Golden Era. Is Jack Hylton's bijou orchestra an improvement on Jullien's monster orchestra?[14] It were better to toy with excerpts from great music than to give exhibitions of a screaming saxophone; and one other thing to the credit of Jullien is that he graced his platform with real artists: Berlioz, for instance.

I can only surmise that mention of the demise of the Monday and Saturday Popular Concerts and of the Crystal Palace Concerts would not fit in the picture of fifty years' triumphant revival. Manns and his orchestra had a greater influence for good than any of the Collegians, and no one realised this more keenly than Sir George Grove. The trouble is that when those two great educative and artistic forces closed down, the spell was broken: and Henry Wood and the faithful Robert Newman[15] had to start again digging, and always digging to attract audiences.

The fact of the matter is that much of the evidence adduced by Sir Henry can be used equally well to prove the decay as well as the revival of music during the past fifty years. Parry and Stanford were born long before the Hadow revival, and they died without issue. These two are designated leaders, but in the same breath they are said to be followers of certain German masters, one so lowly as Felix

---

[14] Louis Antoine Jullien (1812–1860), flamboyant French conductor who is generally credited with having established the concert tradition from which the Promenades grew by giving – among other entertainments – three 'concerts monstres' in London in 1849 with 400 orchestral players, three military bands and three choruses.

[15] Newman (d. 1926) was manager of the Queen's Hall Orchestra (later the New Queen's Hall Orchestra) from 1895 until his death.

Mendelssohn Bartholdy, who during the period of the revival has by many been cast into outer darkness.

Either for lack of evidence or want of space, Sir Henry omits to note the revival of the vocal art among English singers. During the dark ages implied in the article we heard Sims Reeves, Joseph Maas, Edward Lloyd, Foley, Santley,[16] and others. To supply the omission, I thought awhile, hoping to find in this age of revival men to equal those great singers: but where are they? Another revival that hasn't happened!

I began by suggesting that none of the kings in history would accept the verdict of posterity: and still less will English composers accept the verdict contained in any newspaper article. We are oracularly told that Elgar passed out of his pupilage with *Caractacus*. Indeed! This statement implies that Elgar was in a state of pupilage when he wrote the Prelude to the *Light of Life*, and at the same time it discloses an unreasoning critical attitude towards a composer who has never lacked the rare gift of genuine inspiration. *King Olaf* also was written before *Caractacus*, and in my mind that work stands as the finest secular cantata given to us since Berlioz's *Damnation de Faust*: it has frenzied fire and imaginative choral and orchestral colouring.

B.M.S AND B.B.C.

This is taken from 'On the Other Hand' for July 1933, p.842.

The British Music Society has come to an end: but happily we are not to write *Finis* to the ideals which led to its

---

[16] Sims Reeves (1818–1900), English tenor; Joseph Maas (1847–1886), English tenor; Edward Lloyd (1845–1927), English tenor; Allan James Foley, also known as 'Signor Foli' (1835–1899), Irish bass; Sir Charles Santley (1834–1922), English baritone singer and composer. All were much celebrated in their time and equally noted in opera and oratorio. Except for Maas, Brian heard them all in his youth – Lloyd in the first performance of *King Olaf* at Hanley in 1896.

beginning. At a time when much of our art lay bleeding and broken, the late Eaglefield Hull had an inspiration: he thought that British music could be helped by 'institutional' treatment.[17] Other men have held similar views on subjects ranging from opera to gramophone records: and doubtless some good comes out of all such associations, and much good out of some. But the title was unfortunate, for it implied that British music needed help, while that of Germany, France and Italy did not. And then people wondered when the campaign opened with an orchestral concert in the programme of which was included Strauss's *Ein Heldenleben*. Where was then the suggested national cult?

Time and experience have shown that 'a central office in London and branches throughout the provinces', while suitable for certain industrial organisations, have little influence on artistic perception. Had the moving spirits concentrated in London or in Manchester on an annual series of concerts of British orchestral and choral works, things might have been different. The heat thus generated would perhaps have warmed many a choral and orchestral body again to function with renewed youth.

Kussevitsky has shown us in several superb performances that British works, when played with that live interest and attention usually given to foreign music, have similar artistic worth. What the great Russian has done so easily should have been the aim of the B.M.S. One or some great

---

[17] The British Music Society (not the organisation which currently bears that name) was founded in 1918 by Arthur Eaglefield Hull, with Sir Hugh Allen as Chairman. Its aims were: 'to fight for a recognised place for music in education, to stimulate appreciation of music by lectures and concerts, to champion the cause of British composers and performers at home and abroad, to encourage the establishment of music libraries, to co-ordinate all musical activity in the United Kingdom for greater strength'. It also acted for a time as the headquarters of the British Section of the I.S.C.M. One of its first acts was to conduct a survey of important works awaiting performance, and to recommend John Foulds' *World Requiem* as the most deserving of these. Eaglefield Hull (b.1876), who wrote many articles on modern composers and edited a still very valuable *Dictionary of Modern Music & Musicians* (J.M. Dent, London, 1924) from which comes the passage quoted above, committed suicide in 1928, and the Society had been in decline since then.

performances of distinctive works, and the provincial societies would have followed like sheep through a gap!

My fear is that, with passing of the B.M.S., the wash of the British Broadcasting Corporation will submerge deeper than ever the works of our mute and inglorious Miltons. It cannot be otherwise when from our cradles onwards we have had drilled into us the omniscience of all that is official. We are taught to worship permanent officials: they never make mistakes; or at least no one among them ever confessed to a mistake. But the permanent official in art! Think of it: Dubois laying down the law to Debussy![18] In England we reach the Everest of official imagination by a loud exhortation, with orchestral accompaniment, to come to the penitents' form. There, at 9.20 p.m. every Wednesday, we listen in ecstasy to the gospel according to Tchaïkovsky ch. vi., v.2, as revealed by a player-piano. The voice of Jehovah!

I should like to see the experiment tried of fifty concerts without the duplication of a single item: such as Kussevitsky did during his first year at Boston. Then would come the admission of unfamiliar or unknown works, both native and foreign. Who can fail to observe the family likeness of every orchestral performance heard in London during recent years? The heads of all the organisations have been taught successfully to think alike. The R.P.S., the B.B.C. and the L.S.O., for the greater part, ring the changes on a modest salad of indigenous plants and roots, with variants of German *Sauerkraut* and French *légumes*. If spices from the east are added, then the common palate is stung, and it puffs and blows with unrighteous indignation.

This restricted choice throws a highlight on a few men and obscures others not a whit less worthy. Our programme-makers, perhaps against their will, think only of the average person, and in effect say that he will never be able to understand anybody but Saint-Saëns, Strauss, and Tchaïkovsky. Somebody thought differently when these composers were first chosen for performance. Musical

[18] Théodore Dubois, Director of the Paris Conservatoire from 1896 to 1905, and a byword for reactionary academicism; Brian alludes here to an earlier section of the column from which this article is taken.

astigmatism now leads to the neglect of the best works ever written by English, French and Russian composers. The permanent official in music is fifty years behind the times: he thinks only in terms of names, and those delusory lights lure him to the morass of the commonplace. From an educational standpoint the public has a right to expect the best music ever written: and this is not found only in the few works now given by a mere handful of composers – English, French, German or Russian.

NATIONAL MUSIC AND THE PROMS

From 'On the Other Hand', August 1935, pp. 913–914.

Some time ago I spoke of the good work done in Germany by the Allgemeinen Deutschen Musikverein, a society founded nearly a century ago by Franz Liszt for the purpose of producing new and neglected German music. The triennial festival of music as we know it is not common in Germany, though there was something like it in the Lower Rhine Festival, which functioned every three or four years – alternately at Elberfeld, Düsseldorf, Cologne and Aix-la-Chappelle – for well over a century. They tell me that the last festival took place in 1922, when Abendroth conducted: if this is so, it must be to our regret, for at this famous Lower Rhine Festival Elgar's *Gerontius* was performed and was acclaimed worthy.

But the Allgemeinen Deutschen Musikverein goes marching on, this year as far north as Hamburg, where three orchestral and three chamber concerts were given: also one ballet and two opera evenings, with one sacred concert in the famous church of St. Michael. The music of forty-six different European composers was presented, and included was the *Cockaigne* Overture of Elgar and the ballet music from Holst's *Perfect Fool*. To me this does not seem the happiest representation of our music, though I feel sure that the lusty character of *Cockaigne* made an impression and that the Hamburg trombonists thoroughly enjoyed themselves.

English prototypes of this German festival will not thrive: and many a man of music I have met of late years deplores the fact and thinks only in helpless phrases. Ironical cynicism is the refuge of others. The trouble cannot be racial, for Englishmen are the most buoyant of any in the world. Of course, it is well that English composers of serious music should be kept in their place, and not allowed to take on airs: indeed, they should thank those who from their Olympian heights tell then by an eloquent silence where that place is. Previous attempts to found English festivals and societies for the furtherance of English music have been frowned on and fail; yet, strange as it may seem, societies for creating employment among non-practising musicians flourish like the green bay-tree. From this may we not reasonably suppose that the English people are ready to support English music if we could drill it into their heads how best to do it? We need the services of a Cochran[19] quite as much as the services of a Critic. Could we personify English Music as a flaunting young lady – call her Carmen, if you like – we should have a queue of camp-stools stretching from Bow Street to Langham Place, and the critics adjusting the focus of their glasses to meet the changed circumstances.

Perhaps the response to ridicule is too highly developed among English creative musicians: they could not be associated in the promotion of a festival! The thing has been done twice, at Liverpool in 1909 and at Birmingham in 1913: but since then nothing. I have endeavoured, by writing to prominent English composers, to rekindle the fire that animated the old Musical League, but it seems that in their make-up nothing is now left to burn. So, as I see it, it is up to the younger generation of native composers, daring all men, to band themselves together for the sole purpose of procuring performances of native music. They would not at

[19] The impresario C.B. Cochran.

first be received with open arms: but they might find that the wolves in the path were only stage animals.

Though we may deplore the absence of a National Musical Festival, and the consequent loss of prestige of music among the arts, there has been something to compensate individuals among musicians, and especially those who, more successfully than their fellows, make a path for themselves through a world of indifference. Some may be in doubt as to whether the Promenades made Wood, or whether Wood made the Promenades. There had been Promenade concerts before, but none so lasting as those organised by Henry Wood at Queen's Hall, so there can be no doubt that Wood made the Promenades and incidentally found himself in the process. The Promenades are a one-man show, and at the same time an epitome of Wood's artistic outlook and character. A similar object organised by a committee would have gone down after its first or second season. The 'Proms' are now a national institution: and as such are a fruitful nursery for British orchestral music. Compare the encouragement given to our native composers at the 'Proms' to what has been meted out by the various other series of established symphony concerts, and any objector to my statement would fumble for words in explanation. But for the 'Proms', British orchestral music would to-day be almost non-existent. To have a work accepted and performed at this series of concerts has been the great ambition of every British composer these many years: and the fact alone is a tribute to Wood's fine independence.

The remarkable thing is that at the 'Proms' the native composer has never been pampered, and consequently we have been saved the bathos of nationality in art. Wood's policy has evidently been to take an average of all schools, both of familiar works and of novelties, giving indigenous works a fair share. This in itself is no light task, especially when we consider the magnitude of the undertaking: between three and four hundred works each season. The bulk of these, of course, are well known and drawn from the classics; but the management has never lacked enterprise in presenting the works of famous contemporary composers. To be just to other concert enterprises, one must admit that the programme-space of a two months' season may call for more inclusion than exclusion; but, all the same, works of the finest creative minds in France, Russia and Germany have been played often enough at Queen's Hall to become familiar and understood.

The educative influence of Wood's policy on the native musician is incalculable. The British composer of to-day does not, like his grandfather, think of music in terms of church music, though some may rightly and with our good wishes continue to do so. But our composers now think in the secular idiom and have the technique of men great in the art without regard to race or nation, and may live in that sphere where there is no foreigner. For this change of heart and spirit we owe much to Sir Henry Wood and his Promenades. These concerts have prevailed in spite of all world-changes: and yet they have changed whilst still enduring, as we note when remembering that what was once a novelty now comes before us as a familar friend, though not necessarily old.

For some years now we have heard 'asides' about the passing of French music from all London. I do not suppose that Wood was or could be influenced by any côterie operating in the metropolis: but it is a fact that the balance is seen to be redressed in the forthcoming concerts. It may have come on the air, although I seem to feel the influence of Toscanini's great performance of Debussy's *La Mer*.[20] I am not, for fear of putting myself out of school, going to say that it was epoch-making: but I knew in my bones that something was going to happen, and that something turns out to be the promise of these programmes to give us some of the finest French music composed during the past fifty years, and these include *La Péri* (dance poem), an orchestral masterpiece by Paul Dukas.

---

[20] Toscanini had performed *La Mer* with the BBC Orchestra in June 1935; Brian attended his rehearsals.

BRITISH MUSIC AND ITS PATRONS

From 'On the Other Hand' for November 1935, pp. 107–108.

Before the war, the playing of the London Symphony Orchestra and the Queen's Hall Orchestra was of a very high standard: then came what we can in mercy say was the Interregnum, when ideals were lost and orchestral playing fell to a low ebb. So it might have flowed on to this day had not the Berlin Philharmonic Orchestra come to London some eight years ago, giving concerts under Furtwängler, when followed an awakening and a tremendous leap forward to the international standard of perfection in orchestral playing, as seen in the work of the B.B.C. and London Philharmonic Orchestras. When playing at the top of their form, they are superb. This achievement is the more remarkable because, while all other orchestras of international fame are international in personnel, British orchestras have become increasingly British born. The Home Office has seen to that!

But the consciousness that we now have in London orchestral playing of first quality makes some folk very anxious for others to share their pleasures with them, and consequently two projects are put forward. One is that the B.B.C. orchestra should play in foreign capitals, and the other is that the British Council for Relations with other Countries should hold a festival of British Music and invite thirty influential foreign critics to attend. The first project might be harmless enough, but I doubt the calm, judicial spirit of any Continental critic in the matter of British music, and that's plain speaking! I have now read Continental newspapers and magazines for thirty years, but rarely have I seen recognition of the existence of British music or musicians. Politicians know us very well: but music critics are in another boat.

If there is any necessity to advertise our present-day musical proficiency, surely foreign capitals should be avoided in favour of musical centres, for in the former music would go down before the blandishments of diplomats, official and unofficial, who are always in at the death saying convincing nothings.

The B.B.C. Orchestra, which is financed out of the colossal revenues of the corporation, should journey abroad playing British music, but leaving Sir Tom, Sir Dick, and Sir Harry out of the picture. These are of the class that sign petitions to Parliment, write letters to the papers, and pose generally as patrons of the arts, but have never in their lives attended a performance of British music: their idea of support is hovering over those already successful or seeking to appoint someone in their retinue to a job in the management of music. This may seem ungracious but it's true.

One specious argument I have heard is that all foreign music is now diminishing in quality, while British music is soaring sky high: and consequently now is the time to exalt British musicians. If people really believed this, they would attend concerts and let committee meetings go by the board. Witness the enthusiasm with which all classes, official and unofficial, stayed away from the recent performance of Stanford's lovely opera, *The Travelling Companion*, at Sadler's Wells. Native music be sugared: 'Nobody will be there, so I could not think of going!' And the curtain went up before a sparse audience. Where were the kind patrons of British music, who are anxious to have its fine qualities noised abroad in all the capitals of Europe?

Of course, it may be that contemporary Russian, Italian, French and German music is below the level of modern British music: but as music is a cosmopolitan art, in that is no good cause for rejoicing. However, if Continental music is falling, it must be falling from somewhere and whatever the height may have been, it was not attained through the efforts of committees and commissions. Moreover, any movement to advance the prestige of British music abroad is in for a bad time, for never before was nationalism in music more rampant that it is to-day. What we see in England is only a pale reflection of what is going on in Germany and has long been fixed policy elsewhere. Adrian Boult at Salzburg[21] tried the only feasible way of advancing British

[21] At the 1935 Salzburg Festival, Boult conducted the Vienna

music, when he invited Toscanini, Bruno Walter and Weingartner to listen to a performance: the audience did not
respond, but we may be sure that those great men listened
with an open mind, whereas they would have been pre-
judiced had they been approached in any other way. Who
can imagine Toscanini or Furtwängler putting into a
programme a work on the strength of an opinion transmit-
ted from London by a critic enjoying our hospitality?

Now, let us suppose that one or both schemes are put into
operation, who is to select the British music for performance? Shall it be of the quick or of the dead? Shall we have
an equal choice from those college trained and those self
trained; or will the selection be made by a committee, or by
a person who is neither college nor self trained? Any answer
to these questions exposes the unsound ground we are
invited to tread. Music cannot be advanced through officialdom, whether designated councils or committees. They
have been trying to do something of the kind in Germany,
adding a pungent national flavour: they even put Richard
Strauss at the head of the movement. Next came the inevitable suggestion for a festival of German music, which put
the ultimate responsibility for the music selected on Strauss.
Here was a pretty kettle of fish, for when Furtwängler
received the programme of the music to be played by the
Berlin Philharmonic Orchestra, it was found to be all good
stuff but the work of men of sixty or over. Where indeed was
Youth, and all that means in Germany of to-day? After the
passing to and fro of many suggestions, Hindemith was
admitted, though placed well down the programme. The
music of the old brigade came and went without visibly
affecting Goebbels and the other front-row officials, but
when Hindemith entered the lists they sat up and began to
take notice: at first they appeared not to be displeased, but
then gloom settled over their faces, for here was something
running counter to what officialdom had been taught to
believe was true-blue German music! and when the last note

Philharmonic Orchestra in a concert entirely devoted to British music,
including Vaughan Williams' *Job* and the first performance of Arthur
Bliss' *Music for Strings*.

was heard not a hand was raised to *heil*-Hindemith.[22] What
assurance have we that English officialdom, firmly seated in
the saddle, would not ride British Music to the death by
excluding all who have anything fresh to say?

LEAGUES: GERMAN AND ENGLISH

From 'On the Other Hand' for July 1936, pp. 833–4.

English composers still await that one strong man who will
do for them what Franz Liszt did for German composers
when, some sixty years ago, he founded the Allgemeinen
Deutschen Musikverein. Not only has this annual festival
given the German composer his chance, but its social attrac-
tions are hardly less important than the musical events.
Musicians come from all parts, and when not making music
are entertained by the civic authorities. Incidentally, there
are the 'excursions', inevitable at all Continental resorts.
This year the gathering was at Weimar, and appropriately
enough they opened with a performance of Peter Cornelius's *Der Barbier von Bagdad,* followed by a Sunday concert
of Liszt's religious music in the Parish Church.

The real business of the festival was then unfolded by the
successive production of new works by forty young German
composers. I must add the dusty cliché: 'but whether anyone of them will be heard again remains to be seen'.
Whether they are heard again or not, the continuing festivals are a triumph for German organisation, and evidence
of a fund of goodwill among Germans for the advance of
the music of men who are not yet with the elect: the number

---

[22] Brian seems to be alluding to an incident in February 1934, when
Hindemith was grudgingly allowed to conduct the Berlin Philharmonic
in his *Konzertmusik* for strings and brass in a programme otherwise
devoted to officially-approved composers (Graener, von Hausegger,
Strauss). His work was received not with silence but with considerable
barracking from Nazi sympathisers.

of forty young composers proves that.

Another impressive function held in Weimar this year was an International Bruckner Festival, which will give heart to those in England who are convinced of the future of the music of Bruckner. While Bruckner is a gathering force throughout Germany, one of the strongholds is Weimar, where this year they began by performing the masses and church music, and then the symphonies conducted by men famous in Germany – Siegmund von Hausegger and Volkmar Andreæ. Peter Raabe, who conducted the Fifth and Ninth Symphonies, is president of the Reichsmusikkammer (the German Court of Music) and president of the Allgemeinen Deutschen Musikverein.[23] Of course, there were the usual felicitous orations, which is the form German enthusiasm takes. They may not always be quite sincere, or may be only ebullitions of art-patriotism: but the custom compares favourably with the good old English way of heaving a brick at the unknown man and at unfamiliar music. There was a time when the field seemed favourable for British composers, and that was when a number of prominent English musicians founded the Musical League. Such a body was thought to be necessary, or we should not have seen Parry, Elgar, Beecham, Delius, Bantock and McNaught identified with it. It was one of the unrecorded tragedies of the war that the League died

---

[23] Siegmund von Hausegger (1872–1948) was a noted conductor (for a time, of the Scottish Orchestra) and a highly competent composer in post-Wagnerian mould. A champion of Bruckner, he has the distinction of given the first-ever performances of Bruckner's Fifth and Ninth Symphonies in their original versions, and his performance of the Ninth is preserved on disc. Volkmar Andreae (1879–1962), the Swiss conductor and composer, was another Bruckner specialist and a friend of Busoni. Peter Raabe (1872–1945) is remembered on two other counts apart from his conducting activities – his classic two-volume study of Liszt (1931), and his authorship of *Die Musik im Dritten Reich*, the standard exposition of the Nazis' musical ideology, which appeared about the time that Brian was writing this article. Brian had no admiration for the Nazi regime, but it should be noted that he made a distinction between their brand of nationalism and that which had long inspired German music festivals; although his scepticism as to the results of the latter is obvious both in this article and in the preceding one.

during the struggle: and since that time four of the founders have passed away. The need to-day for a League of Musicians is far greater than it was thirty years ago. Now-a-days the provision of music is in fewer hands than ever, and consequently the hopes of an English newcomer rarely rise to moderate and may remain permanently at zero while the populace are by silence led to believe that no new music worthy of performance is now written by Englishmen. I venture to say that the sixty-seven years of activity of the Allgemeinen Deutschen Musikverein has done much to confirm the German's belief in the music of his young composers.

The unknown composer, in his despair, is apt to think that any performance of his work is better than none; but a cold compress will convince him that only the finest performance will bring out what is best in them. Conductors and critics alike are shy of things new: the one because he cannot be sure of his men, and the other, remembering past failures, because he cannot be sure of himself. Thus it happens, except at a festival, that new works are rarely noticed: the publisher may fume, but the public goes on its way ignorant of the fact that something has happened. What worries me is the fact that things in England have changed sadly since the days of Manns and the Saturday concerts at the Crystal Palace. The orchestra of that place and day seemed to thrive on new works: whereas new works to-day are slippery things that may let a famous orchestra down badly. Such things can only be undertaken after mature deliberation, and then only occasionally!

From all accounts, Manns was great, always friendly and approachable by the young composers of his day, notably Joseph Holbrooke and William Wallace. Manns played Holbrooke's *The Raven* at the Crystal Palace, which doubtless led to his having a work accepted at Leeds some years later.[24] Dame Ethel Smyth has told us of the difficulties attending the production of her famous Mass in D, and how only after many years a second hearing was given on the

---

[24] Holbrooke's *Byron* was produced at the Leeds Festival of 1906, and his *Hommage to E.A. Poe* at that of 1908.

occasion of her jubilee (1924) in London. After difficulties by no means unusual, the first performance took place under Barnby in 1893: and really the omens were favourable, for there was the known approbation of Queen Victoria, whose presence at a performance, could it be assured, would have induced the publishers to bear the whole cost of printing. As it was, the Empress Eugénie gave a hundred pounds towards the printing. Then the usual but lamentable thing happened: the Mass lay aside, forgotten by the very people who should have striven for repeated performances. Clearly composers of serious intent are all unfortunate, primarily in the choice of medium. We should have been minor poets, whose slender volumes cost only a fraction of the expense incurred by even one performance of a mass.

I hope not to be considered too shrewd and calculating, but if Dame Ethel had worked the Oracle of the big triennial festival for a first performance of her Mass success might have been hers sooner, for there is a class in the country, committees and choralists, who refuse to look at anything that has not been done at a big triennial festival: so obviously the first trench to be taken is that occupied by the festival committee. But alas, when there one may be no better off, for the time limit restricts the number of works possible to be performed: and naturally the works chosen will be those championed from within the selection committee. Thus it is clear that even triennial festivals can do little to advance English music as a whole: favour must on the whole mostly go to those already known: the circle of choice tends always to contract. The only possible way out is a revival of the idea embodied in the old Musical League, with men in command strong enough to disdain social influence and capable of seeing the good in the new. Another thing, it should be an All England team, and not something based on or springing out of schools or corporations already replete with power and patronage. What a dream!

THE COMPOSER'S DESOLATION

From 'On the Other Hand' for October 1936, pp. 11–12.

I have received a communication from the secretary of the Holbrooke Music Society[25] asking wha : steps I propose to take with regard to the absence of the names of Josef Holbrooke and other well known British composers from Promenade and other concert programmes. As the names of Sir Henry Wood, Adrian Boult, Hamilton Harty and Dan Godfrey are to be found in the printed list of vice-presidents of the Holbrooke Music Society, it would appear that *they* have the duty to discharge which I have been asked to undertake. It is for them to say what they propose to do with regard to the neglect of Holbrooke and other British composers. If the secretary of the Holbrooke Society had read the notes in these columns for the past few years, she would have known that I have at intervals referred to the annual festivals held in Germany by the famous society established by Liszt almost seventy years ago for the sole purpose of bringing forward new or neglected works of German composers. It is but rarely that a foreign composer is admitted into the programmes of this powerful German organisation: I can only recall Sibelius and Busoni as not being of German origin, but at least they were German-trained and had German sympathies. What is needed for the neglected and unknown British composer is an organisation that would give him similar opportunities to those of his German contemporaries. What we lack as a nation, we lack as individuals – i.e., the gift for organisation. Apart from the Promenade Concerts, the musical life of this country is as badly organised or as haphazard in its arrangements as is national defence: we are either too indifferent to neglect or mismanagement, or are just content to muddle through.

---

[25] Holbrooke was tireless in self-promotion but also, to be fair to him, the promotion of British Music generally. The Holbrooke Music Society, his brainchild though not officially controlled by him, was one of several organizations he founded with these dual aims, and was active in the late 1930s.

This lack of a vital organisation for promoting the work of deserving composers breeds discontent, whilst selfishness and arrogant unfairness get an opportunity to thrive.

The appearance of Elgar at a time when contemporary English music was represented by a few names representative of academic or modern sympathies was unfortunate for both groups for he immediately became the centre of attention. People ceased to talk of Mackenzie, Parry or Stanford, and none of those who arrived after Elgar's coming received much more than passing recognition. Yet no malicious organisation was responsible for the cold comfort which followed the applause at first performances of new works by English composers whose names were not Elgar. One of two causes may be the reason for this short-circuiting of new works: either conductors were determined not to perform the works a second time, or there was no public demand; and if there was a public clamouring for a second performance, the matter would remain for the conductor's final decision as to whether there should be a second performance or not.

There can only be one winner in a race; after that it is a matter of positions. Elgar not only won the 'Derby', but he continued to win every time he entered, and justly, I am sure: he just could not help it. It is regrettable that his career had such devastating results on those of other men: that his value should have been maintained at such a high rate that the B.B.C. thought fit to send him a cheque for a thousand pounds to write them a symphony. There are composers with symphonies on the waiting list who are more likely to have their works returned than be offered the nominal sum of half-a-crown each for them![26] It is no use blaming Sir John Reith: he is an engineer, not a composer of symphonies.

Obviously, if a musical league or society had been in existence for the purpose of helping British composers, performances of works would be more equitably distributed. The fact of public attention being drawn to the individual

---

[26] Brian himself had four large-scale symphonies lying unperformed by the time he penned this sentence.

efforts of twenty composers (there were forty German composers represented in this year's festival by the German
Society) would eventually have made it impossible for any
one composer to run away with all the performances and
public adulation, such as Elgar has done; though it is an
undisputed truth that he was a phenomenon such as
English music has never before known, and deserved the
popularity won by his originality and compelling personality.

The Holbrooke Music Society asks whether Britain is
unmusical. No, I do not believe it is; but it cannot discrimi-
nate and has little or no taste. What taste it has is largely
formed by the same processes that operate in politics, art
and literature. A Conservative government with a majority
of, say, two hundred may be followed by the Radicals with a
similar majority: such a transposition is its own indicator to
all thinking men. If English musicians would but develop an
intelligence acute enough to convince them how music is
managed in this country, they would soon organise themselves into a society for the advancement of their claims for
recognition and for their own defence.[27]

NATIONALISM IN MUSIC

From 'On the Other Hand' for August 1937, p.943.

I was pleased when I heard the chairman of the B.B.C., Mr.
R.C. Norman, at the P.R.S luncheon, tell of the intention
of the august body in Langham Place to make known the
best of British music. Translated into print, these remarks,
as well as those of Mr. L. Burgin, may seem a little patron-

---

[27] The Composers' Guild of Great Britain did not come into existence
until June 1944 when – chiefly owing to the efforts of William Alwyn,
Alan Bush and Ralph Vaughan Williams – it was formed from the
Composer Section of the Society of Authors. Whether it has sufficiently
fulfilled the role that Brian outlines here is a matter of opinion.

ising: but really the intention was to be complimentary. It now only remains to be seen what change will be there when Mr. Norman's term of office shall have expired. We were told that, after all, music is only one department of the activities of the B.B.C.: but I have read somewhere that music occupies some seventy-five per cent. of broadcasting hours, so evidently the department is culturally three times more important than all the other departments put together! But my interest necessarily does not trespass beyond the confines of serious music, some composers of which I noticed sitting with large-eyed wonderment at the speeches. For my part I sat and wondered what Sir Arnold Bax and Mr. Arthur Bliss thought of the promises, neither of whom has been neglected by the B.B.C. Does the patronage of the B.B.C. amount to much, little, or nothing in the case of serious music? Nobody will answer. But I am afraid that one performance on the air is no more than one performance on the Rhine: Elgar did not become a household word in Germany thereby.

The native composer in England has lived if not thrived on promises: he was submerged by the great displacement of Handel, and goodness knows when, if ever, he will again be more than a cork on the waters. Societies for the encouragement of the British composer and his music have through the ages come and gone. Frederick Corder came forward with one,[28] and it spake like thunder through a few compositions issued by the Anglo-French Music Company. First catch your public: and this no general secretary or honorary secretary has ever succeeded in doing. Then came the Musical League, but while still in infancy it was called away. Its last festival (in 1913), in association with the Incorporated Society of Musicians, was a step in the right direction – but how far?

To-day, for good or for ill, the B.B.C. stands like Gulliver in Lilliput. But what can be done until the public has been wrought into a condition ready to receive British music? Who at the B.B.C. or elsewhere knows how to do that?

---

[28] The Society of British Composers, founded by Corder in 1905 and disbanded in 1915.

Harmsworth[29] filled the Albert Hall for an organ recital: but, wisely for his reputation as propagandist-in-chief for the British Empire, he did not run recitals for long. Yet propaganda for native music as a definite policy is being tried out in Russia and America, with what results future generations may know. In America, activity consists of a constant campaign in the press, and a few musical papers never allow the subject to drop. The policy and programmes of American orchestras are scrutinised and the results annotated. For instance, *Musical America* has an article headed 'Our Orchestras and the American Composer', with a summary, 'Records for the season show performances of eighty-nine works by sixteen major ensembles: sixty-seven native or resident musicians given hearings'. On the same page is a humorous cartoon showing a young conductor receiving a score from the hands of a composer. 'But,' he whines, 'if we play all these American things, what is to become of Mozart and Boccherini?' Then the statistician takes the forum and proves to a decimal that during the last season in America 80,000 performances were listened to by 57,000,000 people. There are symphony orchestras in 47 cities, and smaller orchestras in 110 towns: so something ought soon to happen! The Works Progress Association units found place in its programmes for 4915 works by 1481 native or resident musicians, including 50 symphonies, 60 symphonic poems, *et hoc*. In other pages the claims of the America-born conductor is urged against the imported variety. (I hope no one will trouble to remind me that America is still the country where composers with tin cups sit like blind beggars.)[30]

In Russia, nationalism in music is expressing itself differently. There the composer has not to stake his claim and wait. It is the business of a department of the State to rear

---

[29] i.e., Alfred Vere Harmsworth, proprietor of *The Daily Mail*, which had sponsored various organ recitals.

[30] Brian here alludes to a previous LMG article (*Musical Opinion*, June 1937, pp. 777–8) in which he discussed an article by Minna Lederman – editor of the distinguished American journal *Modern Music* – that had appeared in *North American Review* about the low income of American composers. It was titled 'Composers with Tin Cups'.

composers, with the adjunct of men to perform their works. A certain conductor, who goes frequently to Russia,[31] told me that there he could have as many rehearsals and extra players as he wanted. In the new urbanised Russia permanent symphony orchestras abound, and the Russian equivalent of the French Ministry of Fine Arts have officials who understand the psychology of the composer and regulate the conditions under which he is likely to produce his best work: and at length publishes his music and assures its performance. Here again something ought to happen. But presumably it is necessary to be born a Russian to enter the Promised Land, and not every one so born may be able to persuade benign officials that one is an unfledged Beethoven; and is nepotism, one of the common attributes of human nature, absent from all living within the Soviet Union?

---

[31] Probably Albert Coates, who had, indeed, been born there.

PART EIGHT
NEAR-CONTEMPORARIES

———————●———————

The following section collects representative examples of Brian's writings about the British composers of his own generation – those, at any rate, of whom he wrote with any regularity or at length.

Alphabetical order leads us to begin with Arnold Bax, and so with the substantial article on Bax's First Symphony which was Brian's very first published contribution to *Musical Opinion* (December 1922, pp. 253–254). This was written from a study of the score in advance of the work's first performance (at the Queen's Hall), and at Bax's own request. Brian was deeply involved in the writing of his *Gothic* Symphony at the time, and the two composers accordingly made a mutual agreement: Bax promised that when Brian's Symphony was published *he* would, in return, write an article about it. *The Gothic* eventually saw print in 1932, and Brian sent Bax a copy, reminding him of their agreement – but after several months' silence Bax returned the score, saying he could not possibly write about such a complex work without having heard a performance. (The first performance did not take place until 8 years after Bax's death.)

BAX

The First Symphony of Arnold Bax

Fifteen years ago, when travelling from the North to London with Professor Granville Bantock, I asked him who he thought were the most promising composers. Mentioning several who have since justified their early promise, he referred to Arnold Bax as having undoubted genius. Since Bax left the Royal Academy in 1905, his development has been steady and gradual. Commencing with works of small calibre, he became almost popular a few years ago with his swift-winged overture, *In the Faëry Hills*. A keen interest has recently been awakened in his chamber music, songs, piano sonatas, the symphonic poem *Tintagel* (first introduced by Sir Dan Godfrey and one of the successes at the recent Leeds Festival, under Albert Coates), a Concerto for Viola and Orchestra (performed at last year's Philharmonic concerts),[1] a symphonic poem, *The Garden of Fand* (to be first performed by Godfrey this year at Bournemouth) and – most important of all – the present Symphony in E♭, which is down for performance on December 4th by Albert Coates and the London Symphony Orchestra.

We have recently been told by a Northern conductor (who ought to know better) that the idiom of the present-day British composer is insincere, imitative and requires a fiercer patriotism. There is a slight facial resemblance in the works of the early English Morley, Byrd and others with the Italian Palestrina; yet the English work is neither imitative nor insincere. In listening to the first movement of the First Piano Sonata of Brahms, one is apt to compare it with the B♭ Symphony of Schumann. This is none the less sincere, though it may be imitative. One could dangle at the works of almost every composer with similar results: yet one would not think of questioning their sincerity. Fierce patriotism in Beethoven, Wagner and others only led to fierce vulgarity and banality. The work of Bax, Bliss, Goossens, Holst, Ireland, Vaughan Williams has neither insincerity nor fierce patriotism.

The art of Bax is not imitative. His harmonic and orchestral idioms, whilst ultra-modern, are personal and individual. There is nothing in Bax which looks or sounds like anybody else but Bax. He has that wonderful faculty for uninterrupted continuous thinking without which works on a large scale are impossible. One sometimes gets the

---

[1] Brian means the impressive and seldom-performed *Phantasy* for viola and orchestra (1920).

impression that this self-absorption and power of concentration will lead to obscure paths and darkness – as in the *Tintagel*, for instance. There is less of this in the Viola Concerto. In the Symphony in E♭, there is still less; but behind it all there is an added force and direct power which suggests that Bax has it in his power to become a great symphonist.

Bax shows a soul affinity with John Ireland in his bitter defiance and sarcastic acidity against the trammels of convention. Has anyone ever got up from playing that storm-tossed sonata of John Ireland without wondering what was in the cups of bitterness the composer swallowed which is described in such wonderful and forceful music? In its fierceness, it has the character of an enraged giant hurling rocks at his enemies. There is a great deal of this feeling in the art of Bax, and nowhere else is there so much of it as in his new symphony. It breathes defiance and triumph.

Considering the scarcity of orchestras in this country, Bax has been fortunate in having his works readily taken up or a conductor to produce them as soon as written. The symphony is in three movements, the Scherzo being dispensed with. Strap-hanging and repetition of the ancient pattern are missing, and nowhere is there that feeling of 'Here we are again!' like 'Puffing Billy' entering a station as a theme reappears. The music tells its own tale and is scored for a very large orchestra.

FIRST MOVEMENT
Marked *Allegro moderato e feroce*;
$\frac{4}{4}$ measure; key G♭.
The work opens with an anticipation of the first theme,

Ex. 9

whilst under a sustained E♭ *tremolando* in violins and violas is heard a mysterious processional figure tramping in the

basses and 'cellos,

Ex. 10

passing to the first theme stated in broad forceful manner upon strings and woodwind:

Ex. 11

A variation of this statement which follows is interrupted by the re-appearance of Ex. 10 and tossed about in dramatic fashion, leading to a supreme outburst of Ex. 11 stated *largamente (ff)*, quietly passing away over a triplet figure in 'cello and tenor drum. Over these scarcely audible triplets is heard a cry from the strings (*wailing*). Here the first phase melts away through quiet harmonic colour direct to the second theme, a peaceful, tuneful melody,

Ex. 12

its development remaining in the picture of the peaceful entry and passing out on the heckelphone, with a last word from the sarrusophone.

The real significance of the wonderful contrast in temperament of the two principal themes is revealed in the development which immediately follows. The original *tempo* is resumed and mysterious fragments (of Ex.9) break in from various groups: whilst a new martial rhythm is heard in strings and clarinets:

Ex. 13

and over this Ex.11 'dares all its thunder'; the martial figure passes. A new march figure is heard in pizzicato basses, and is immediately pushed aside by the return of Ex.13. A dramatic scene follows, amidst which Ex.10 is again heard and a final return of Ex.11. This, once again quietly passing out, leads to a re-entry of the peaceful Ex.12 upon solo flute over mysterious colours and harmonies in strings and harps, alighting upon a very whimsical version of Ex.9 by way of Coda – *Allegro con moto*.

Ex. 14

Does the terminology betray its origin? One cannot mistake the humour.

The movement immediately ends by a broad augmentation of Ex.9 against the pulsating rhythm of Ex.13.

SECOND MOVEMENT
Lento Solenne   Key A♭ ($\frac{4}{4}$ measure)

Under sustained murmuring harmonies (*pp*) in strings, harps, horns and trumpets, the first theme enters upon string basses:

Ex. 15

its continuation being taken over by muted trombones and tuba. Re-appearing in more dramatic fashion, it subsides

into a broken pulsating bass triplet figure. Over this a new
theme appears in trombones:

Ex. 16

suggesting the ceremonial of a Solemn Requiem.

Ex.16 is re-stated in fuller harmonies in woodwind
against passage work in the strings, leading to a supreme
outburst from the full orchestra. This dying away, fragmen-
tary melodies follow upon bass flute and cor anglais, resolving upon a long reiterated Db in the string basses. Upon
this, a broad chorale is heard in bassoons and trombones:

Ex. 17

The ceremonial of solemn grandeur is resumed and Exx.16
and 17 appear, alternately hurled about in the full orchestra. A strikingly dramatic effect is made by the entry of
the sinister Ex.15 and making its exit under the same soft
murmuring harmonies by which it originally entered.

FINALE

A movement of great abandon and brilliance – the sparkling wit of which belongs to the best of its kind in Nicolai,
Bizet, Berlioz and Strauss without featuring any of them.
There is a triumphant assurance in which it leads off in the
brass and drums in the brief introduction: *Allegro maestoso*;
$\frac{4}{4}$ measure; key Eb. Amidst piquant harmonies, the first
theme is heard in the 'cellos and bassoons, heading upwards
in breathless fashion:

Ex. 18

whilst immediately after it is heard the pendant in horns, cor anglais, heckelphone, &c.:

Ex. 19

Its resemblance to Ex.10 in the first movement is obvious.

These themes course along amidst a movement of gaiety to the entrance of a new figure – someone drunk, probably, from the sarcastic and keenly humorous manner in which it is sketched,

Ex. 20

and afterwards thrown out by the full orchestra.

The scene changes to one of farcical solemnity:

Ex. 21

Other groups take up the trombone statement, and in a passage of unusual splendour we have the grotesque figure Ex.18 thrown against a reappearance of Ex.10 from the first movement.

At this point, the development becomes intimate and introspective. Showing surprising genius in the ease with which the composer manipulates his material, he holds himself in for one final and supreme effort, the climax being approached in striking fashion by a triumphant march version of Ex.21.

The composer is a master of his craft and the symphony

is a work of genius. The future of any work of genius lies entirely in the hands of fate and fortune. Though most people never hesitate to criticise or to express opinions, there is no one alive to-day who knows enough to predict what the fate of any contemporary work will be in fifty years from now. High-minded work, sincerely expressed, will continue to live unless the work itself is destroyed.

A writer of genius once described those who go to listen to a new work as of two kinds – those who go to scoff and those who go to steal. No doubt he was not thinking of the professional music critics, but those wiseacres who know everything – who know how to write symphonies better than Elgar, who can point to the weaknesses in everyone's armour but their own, yet never do anything themselves. Let us hope that the scoffers will go to hear this symphony by Bax, and give the composer credit for a great endeavour, even if they don't understand it. The work is inscribed to John Ireland and is dated October 8th, 1922.

Bax's Third String Quartet

Brian maintained his interest in Bax, hearing and reviewing performances of most of his symphonies over the next two decades, as well as contributing other brief writings (one about *November Woods*): note his warm assessment in 'The Continuity of British Music', p.32. His final Baxian item – a short score-review in *Musical Opinion*, July 1941, p.445 – shows how constant his views had remained.

The publication of a new String Quartet (No. 3, in F), by Arnold Bax, is the most recent addition to a remarkable series of instrumental works.[2] None will dispute that Bax exhibits natural genius for original instrumental writing. Since the composition of his early orchestral overture,[3] he has successfully assailed the symphonic poem, symphony,

---

[2] Written in 1936; actually Bax's fifth essay in the genre.
[3] Brian could mean the very early *Irish Overture* of 1906, but is more likely referring either to the symphonic poem *In the Faery Hills*, which he

concerto, quartet, and sonata. Though he enhanced his reputation by several highly original choral works, he has not given any published evidence of having any attraction for oratorio or opera. In temperament Bax is a romantic individualist: his modern, brilliantly coloured style conceals a subtle blend of homophonic and masterly contrapuntal writing.

The recently published String Quartet in F consists of four movements, *Allegro*, *Poco Lento*, Scherzo and Trio, *Allegro*. Its substance is that of a richly coloured musical poesy, whose sequential and retrospective moods create an impression of cohesion and unity, notwithstanding that these moods are reflective of grim Mephistophelian humour, ferocity, and angelic tenderness or languidness such as recur in previous large-scale Bax works. Curiously enough, there is a visionary suggestion of Strauss in the first movement and of Tchaïkovsky in the scherzo. But the work, for the connoisseur of part-writing, is a sheer delight: it is richly ornate and has an abundance of melodies such as will inspire and delight the four players. When we wrote in this journal an introductory analysis to the first performance of the Bax First Symphony under Albert Coates almost twenty years ago we referred to Arnold Bax as a master of his craft. So he remains, and that is something to be thankful for in these days. Score 10s.; parts complete 12s. 6d.   (Murdoch, Murdoch & Co.)

---

has called an 'overture' on p.234; or to the *Festival Overture* (1911) which opened the 1913 Musical League Festival Concert that ended with Brian's *Doctor Merryheart*.

ALBERT COATES

Pickwick

Albert Coates was an acquaintance of Brian's and a fairly prolific composer in his own right. The following notice of his
opera on Charles Dickens' *Pickwick* comes from 'On the Other
Hand by La Main Gauche' in *Musical Opinion* for November
1936, pp.108–109.

This situation would have afforded Dickens a theme quite as
ludicrous as anything he attempted to describe: but we must
try to be serious while welcoming the humorous when during
this month we witness the production at Covent Garden
Opera House of Albert Coates's *Pickwick* during the Coates-
Rosing season.[4] This is the centenary year of the publication
of the Posthumous Papers, and the B.B.C. has twice recently
given us splendid character-readings of excerpts which must
have rekindled interest in the doings of the club in the minds
of hundreds of thousands. If only a tithe of these flock to
Covent Garden, we are assured of the success of a conception
that is peculiarly English and without equal in any other
tongue. Pickwick is more universal than Till Eulenspiegel,
as well he may be, for the worst that has been said of the
book is that it is 'two pounds of Smollett, three ounces of
Sterne, and a handful of Hook'. Well, with these ingre-
dients, the great cook Dickens provided a feast that never
fails to put the table in a roar.

I have before me, at the time of writing, the only copy of
the vocal score of *Pickwick* at present available. It is published by the Universal Edition (London) Ltd., and runs to
356 large quarto pages, with five reproductions of the original drawings of 'Phiz', which makes one hesitate before
proceeding farther, for they are so very whimsical. Mr.
Coates is his own librettist, and the incidents of the 'papers'

---

[4] Vladimir Rosing (1890–1963), a celebrated Russian tenor who settled
in England in 1915 and cultivated a second career as an opera director; in
1939 he moved to California and staged several pageants in Hollywood.
Coates' *Pickwick* was staged for the first time on 20 November 1936.

are compressed into three acts (twelve scenes). The first act opens in Rochester on the occasion of the grand review, with all the amusing undercurrents of Joe spying on Tupman and Rachel, Jingle supplanting Tupman by a subterfuge, and then borrowing ten pounds from him, with which he elopes with Rachel: pursuit by Pickwick and the others: when for a consideration Jingle renounces Rachel. Weller had disclosed the whereabouts of the runaways, and Mr. Pickwick engages him as his man. The second act gives the scene where Mrs. Bardell mistakes Pickwick's satisfaction at his engaging Weller for a declaration of love, and then the contretemps of his being found in the arms of the lady. Next follow the humorous satire on causes relating to breach of promise, the scenes in Fleet Prison, and other incidents which are as familiar to the man in the train as they are to the most ardent member of the Fellowship.

And now, rather more technically than enthusiastically, one must look at the music of a man who is at once an opera and orchestral conductor of international reputation, and perhaps for that reason an adept with artifices that do not become snags for his forces. Except for the roundelay in the first act (upon which the composer has seized to display his contrapuntal skill), the chorus-work is straightforward. The effect of the roundelay in performance should be most imposing, and there would appear to be little of this quality elsewhere in the opera until the final ensemble in the third act.

The orchestral Cricket Fugue in the first act has plenty of vitality and punch; and the concerted waltz, also in the first act, appears finely effective. A very Russian-like 'Pickwick' Scherzo occurs in the first act, and certainly it might have been written by Shostakovitch himself; and those who are anticipating set airs will be gratified by the song for Sam Weller, 'Bold Turpin vunce on Hounslow Heath', which is probably the only concession of that type in the opera.

During the Breach of Promise Case, amusing use is made of 'Believe me if those endearing young charms', in the orchestra. In steering clear of set airs, &c., the composer has concentrated on his accompaniment to the continuing dialogue. This accompaniment music, which gives the composer an opportunity for some character-drawing, is either plain or contrapuntal. But it is uniformly cheerful, and never sordid, even when the Fleet Prison is being described. Without having heard the opera, it seems to me that Mr. Coates has succeeded in bringing out the peculiar characters of Pickwick and his friends. Though there is a large array of principal characters, their work is not difficult; and the orchestral requirements are neither large nor exacting. Given a start on the boards in London, a rapid spread of the opera may follow to every place where the book is read.

COLERIDGE-TAYLOR

Memories of Coleridge-Taylor

These reminiscences are drawn from 'On the Other Hand' in *Musical Opinion*, September 1934, p.1023.

The recent issue of Coleridge-Taylor's *Hiawatha's Wedding Feast* as a children's cantata carries forward the utility of his work. Every choral society in the British Isles must have sung the work in its original form, and it is also popular in operatic form. Though written whilst still a student at the Royal College, it was rightly hailed as a stroke of genius. Freshness of idiom joined to piquant orchestration came with a note of surprise in British music: and with such a beginning the prophets said that the field of British music would soon be his alone. But Coleridge-Taylor, in his continuation of the work, failed to reach the heights again: maturity had come as a vision and was gone. My first glimpse of Coleridge-Taylor was in the streets of Hanley on the occasion of the production during the festival of

The Death of Minnehaha. (In my kindness, I was a deputising cellist in *Utopia* while my friend had the greater honour of playing at the festival.)[5] A young Negro, bright and alert, passed by, accompanied by a lady whom I knew afterwards to be his wife. Both were strikingly winsome, and with Hiawatha in mind, I pictured them as journeying to the wedding feast. Some years later I was chatting with him at the rehearsal before the performance of his cantata, *Meg Blane*, which some of my friends had arranged.[6] He talked of many things that interested him, and incidentally described his home life as an elysium on earth.

Coleridge-Taylor had a leaning towards Dvořák and Humperdinck, and thought Elgar as a composer was greater than Strauss. No one could use the brass in the orchestra with the genius of Elgar. Coleridge-Taylor spoke in short, swift sentences, linked to many pleasantries. When he mounted the platform, he was confronted with seventy players of the Hallé orchestra and a chorus of eighty only. At the first entry of the chorus, he stopped suddenly and, addressing the orchestra, said rather dryly, 'Gentlemen, half marks throughout!' I did not meet him again until the Coronation week of 1911, when a series of Empire Concerts was given by the Q.H.O. and the L.S.O. at the Crystal Palace. Coleridge-Taylor was to be there to conduct the South African Concert, and I was very happy when Robert Newman told me that an Overture of mine was included in the programme. Then Coleridge-Taylor wrote to me, showing, I think, pleasure that he should conduct a work that Beecham had done only a few months previously at a

[5] By *Utopia* Brian means the Gilbert and Sullivan *Utopia Limited*; the performance of *The Death of Minnehaha* took place at the Autumn 1899 North Staffordshire Triennial Festival.
[6] Cantata to words by Robert Buchanan, first performed at Sheffield in 1902. Brian is alluding either to the performance given in Hanley on 13 November 1904 by the Burslem Choral Union under the composer, for which Brian provided the programme-notes, or that of 28 April 1909, by the North Staffordshire Symphony Orchestra and Festival Chorus conducted by John James; he reviewed this for *The Staffordshire Sentinel* of the following day.

Birmingham Philharmonic concert.[7] We met at Cramer's, where I believe he had a studio: and there at the piano we worked through the score, which he read quite easily. We adjourned for a fortnight, and met again at the rehearsal: and now, after all these years, I can speak with unfeigned praise of his work as a conductor, in which a man's natural generosity and unselfishness has room to move.

At the time of the Coronation Concerts, Coleridge-Taylor had just returned from a visit to the United States, and he was overjoyed at the progress men of his race were making in cultural development. A festival of his works given by Negroes had astonished him, and he spoke with gladness of a Coleridge-Taylor Society founded by them for the cultivation of his music. He was all keen for his next visit to America. The summer of that Coronation year was distressingly hot, and I fear that he was greatly debilitated by his strenuous endeavours that all should do well for British music. We met again, and after tea walked slowly through the throng in Oxford Street, where from the top of an omnibus he waved to me what was to be a final *Adieu*. In a few months he was dead: a man who was in all truth the image of the hero in his masterpiece, *Hiawatha*. Our interest in his music ebbs and flows, which is well, for like the sea it will never grow stale. In his music we find an individual note that like the man and his speech was refreshingly concise and swift.

[7] Brian's memory is at fault here: *For Valour*, which Coleridge-Taylor conducted on 27 June 1911, was not given by Beecham until 14 February of the following year. Perhaps, instead, Coleridge-Taylor showed pleasure in conducting a work that Henry Wood had premiered (in 1907).

WALFORD DAVIES

A Feast of Good Things

Henry Walford Davies was one of the first English composers
to make his mark immediately in the wake of the success of
Elgar's *Dream of Gerontius* and *The Apostles*. His cantata *Everyman* was the sensation of the 1904 Leeds Festival, and Brian
was an immediate convert to his music. The following article
(from *The Musical World*, 16 October 1905, pp. 193–194), one
of the earliest that he devoted to a detailed survey of a single
work, is written to publicise the appearance of Davies's next
opus, the Six Songs, Op.18.

With the concert season once more commencing, it will be
the lot of many of us to attend Ballad Concerts without end,
and doubtless we shall again exclaim (as, alas! oft before) –
'*Are* there more than half-a-dozen good songs in our own
good mother-tongue, or some slight variant of it? Is it necessary for our singers to give us everlastingly the same old
songs, until the best among them become worn out and
threadbare?'

In the nick of time, Dr. H. Walford Davies brings out, as
his Opus 18, six songs* – all of them British 'to the
backbone', or whatever corresponds to the backbone of a
song, and of no ordinary merit. Now, at any rate, there is no
excuse for the hackneyed ballad, and we, on our part, shall
not complain if all the concert halls in the country resound
with these particular songs throughout the coming winter,
for they ring true and are the outcome of genuine and
wholesome emotion. Nor do they readily weary one constantly repeated: they bear the test of reiteration wonderfully well, being as simple and natural as our own folk-
tunes. They give the impression of words and music flowing
from one fecund source: nothing is forced; melody and
rhythm spring forth with absolute spontaneity. This is no
'prentice hand that the composer is trying, no scholastic

---

* SIX SONGS (op. 18, Nos. 1 to 6). By H. WALFORD DAVIES. London: Sidney Riorden. Price 2s. each, with separate voice part [Brian's footnote].

experimenting; it is rather the finished work of a master.
Above all, there is no striving after effect; the themes carry
with them their own conviction.

Perhaps the best of the six – though it is difficult to
single out one more than another – is 'This ae Nighte', a
Lyke-Wake Dirge, which takes us back to the atmosphere
of *Everyman* right away. The words are anonymous, nor
does Dr. Davies inform us where they have been found,
but they bear the impress of an age long gone.[8] Beginning
mysteriously —

Ex. 22

the feeling of fear arises as music and words combine to
tell how—

> When thou from hence away art past
> > *Every nighte and alle,*
> To Whinny-muir thou com'st at last;
> > *And Christe receive thy saule.*
> If e'er thou gavest hosen and shoon—
> > *Every nighte and alle,*
> Sit thee down and put them on;
> > *And Christe receive thy saule.*

[8] It is useful to be reminded that Benjamin Britten's famous setting of
the 'Lyke-Wake Dirge' (in his *Serenade* for tenor, horn and strings) is not
the only one. There is also a praiseworthy setting of these words from
1928 by Howard Ferguson in his *Two Ballads*, Op. 1, for baritone and
orchestra, and another, as outstanding, for chorus and orchestra, by W.G.
Whittaker, composed in 1924. Bax's setting dates from 1908, and Vagn
Holmboe's, Op. 110a, was composed in 1972; but probably the most
widely known after Britten's is in Stravinsky's 1952 *Cantata*.

The words—

> If hosen and shoon thou ne'er gav'st nane
> *Every nighte and alle,*

bring with them a most uneasy, creeping sensation in the blood, and one begins to cast about in the mind, hoping that in the matter of 'Hosen and shoon' one's personal balance is on the right side. But the following passage strikes something like real terror into the very soul:

Ex. 23

The passing from 'Whinny-muir', into which the second verse leads us, avails us nothing, for we come straightway to 'Brig o' Dread' with a shudder. This time, if we have failed to give 'hosen and shoon', we are threatened with 'The fire will burn thee to the bare bane'; and, repeating the opening theme *pp* diminishing into *ppp*, the song ends with the gruesome thought—

> The whinnies shall prick thee to the bare bane;
> *And Christe receive thy saule.*

Ex. 24

Upon a first hearing, one is inclined to assign the whole atmosphere of this song to mediæval times; but Dr. Walford Davies, by clothing the words in modern dress, has made it essentially a thing of to-day. By the time it has eaten its way into the heart, one wonders whether it does not touch one of the primal instincts, which are the same yesterday, to-day, and for ever; and thus the song is both mediæval and ultra-modern. A singer who has in him a realisation of its inner meaning will never fail to strike sparks of sympathy from his audience, because its emotion is as real to-day as it ever was.

Of quite a different order is the song 'Hame' (words by Allan Cunningham). Here again we have a pure outwelling of emotion, the heartfelt longing of a patriot for his 'Hame'. The song is boldly conceived, with a flowing arpeggio accompaniment, weaving bands around the heart with which to draw it 'hame'. Of a lighter texture, but equally beautiful, is 'I love the jocund Dance' (words by William Blake). Never surely was so much gaiety compressed into so few pages since Arne wrote 'Where the bee sucks'. There is an infection about the song that grips one and makes one laugh – the accompaniment is one continuous ripple of silvery laughter, with never a shadow – until one ends, like the shepherd, by loving 'them ever, ever, ever'.

In quite other mood is 'An Uncouth Love Song', built upon words by George Wither. An appeal to the 'nymphs that on these meadows play' is sung *quasi recitative*, for sympathy on behalf of a 'poor groom that's fallen in love, and cannot tell with whom'. The song here breaks into an alternate rhythm of two-four and three-four, with quite signal success. A happy device was that of achieving a doleful effect in the major key, giving the impression that the love of which the merry shepherd had had a glimpse was not altogether a hopeless one, but was only temporarily withheld, the pain thereof being sweetly bitter.

The setting of Burn's immortal 'For a' That' has in it the steady march of a hymn of the Covenanters. The full resonant chords of this song will, and we mistake not, often be heard in our midst. The tune grips at the very outset, and the last verse (as suggested by the composer) will often be sung in chorus, and a resounding chorus it will be–

> That man to man the warld o'er,
> Shall brothers be for a' that.

One of the Yorkshire or Staffordshire choirs would soon show what to make of that!

The last of the series is a setting of Shakespeare's 'Fear no more the Heat o' the Sun', from *Cymbeline*, and again this is voiced in an unusual and irregular rhythm of two-two and three-two. In spite of this it flows along with perfect freedom, making its irregularity appear the most natural thing in the world. In this song, perhaps more easily than in the others, there may be traced a great influence at works, not detracting from the individuality of the composer, but rather giving it a rock-like foundation upon which to build – the influence of Brahms; it is perceived in odd flashes here and there rather than in the continuous whole. Singers who have a *penchant* for ending in the key with which they started, would do well to leave this song alone, for it perpetrates the crime of beginning and continuing in the key of B, and quietly ending in the key of C sharp – thus taking away the feeling of finality in the 'grave'.

These six songs constitute Dr. Walford Davies's Opus 18 (*Everyman* being Op.17), and those who devote some amount of study to them will wish him long life and power to continue the work so well begun. These songs contain food for all: they will give pleasure to the honey-sipper in music, and the more earnest student will find himself repaid by a deeper inquiry into their nature. The accompaniments, though not 'suited to beginners', are not by any means unplayable: they may be rendered with a certain amount of success by a moderate pianist.

Lastly, Dr. Davies has conceived the excellent plan of issuing a second copy of the voice part with each copy of the song, so that it no longer becomes necessary for the singer to purchase two copies.

Genius and Mystic

In later life Walford Davies came to be less celebrated as a
composer in his own right than for his extremely popular
talks about music on the B.B.C. Nevertheless, on the death
of Elgar he was appointed to succeed him as Master of the
King's Musick; and this prompted the following evaluation
from Brian in his 'On the Other Hand' column (*Musical
Opinion*, May 1934, pp. 683–684).

Radio transmission of music, supported by the 'showman-
ship' of the B.B.C., creates a definite 'public opinion' that
even Ministers cannot lightly ignore. Those who appear
regularly before the microphone are at once 'seconded' by
the paragraphists for any job that is going. Elgar had no
sooner passed away than a Fleet Street acquaintance told
me that Walford Davies would be the new Master of the
King's Musick. 'The very man for the job', said he, quoting
the Duke of Wellington's apocryphal exclamation when he
gave William Adams an important command at Waterloo! I
do not remember exactly the duties attaching to the ancient
office, but as the holding of it is regarded as an honour, it is
again an honour where honour is due. All the same, I doubt
whether public appreciation of Sir Walford Davies has the
same foundation as has the musician's appreciation.

An affable personality in presenting his subject has
brought Sir Walford many vocative and paragraphic admirers; but one or two pronouncements make me think
that he does not quite like his present popularity. He certainly has charm of manner at the microphone, which adds
to the value of his educational talks, and this, I think, is a
natural development of his early work as an adjudicator
at Morecambe. But all who are successful at the microphone
have not qualities comparable to those of Walford Davies
as a musician. He was one of the few men Elgar cared for
intimately: he publicly acclaimed him as composer, which
Elgar would never do lightly. I have seen them working
together as adjudicators under the ægis of the late Canon
Gorton,[9] who did so much for music in the North of

---

[9] For Canon Gorton see note 24 on p.389.

England. It was in the house of the Canon that I was introduced to Walford Davies. They were great pioneering days: and in the van always were Elgar, Walford Davies, Ivor Atkins, Henry Coward, Frederick Corder, W.G. McNaught, John Coates and Ernest Newman.

Walford Davies's pleasant manner at the microphone reminds me vividly of how he and McNaught alone among the adjudicators at Morecambe had the happy knack of getting on intimate terms with the audience: it is an amiable quality which while it rises tends to obscure one's great worth as a composer. No one has yet recalled the excitement that was ours when at the Leeds Festival of 1904 *Everyman* was produced. Here was an oratorio for the general acceptance of which *Gerontius* had undoubtedly prepared the way. *Everyman* sprang to sudden popularity, being performed by choral societies of repute in the Provinces and by the London Choral Society and the Bach Choir in London. The work revealed Walford Davies as a composer of genius and a mystic, one whose mind was clearly in tune with that of Elgar. Other big choral works followed, all written with skill equal to that shown in *Everyman*, but the public did not respond.

Jaeger thought highly of Walford Davies, placing him a peer with Elgar, and was frankly enthusiastic about his Choral Symphony.[10] Davies was at the time away in Switzerland working on this symphony; and I recall Jaeger turning to me and saying, 'Can't you see, my boy, what sort of symphony it will be? Davies in the Alps: thousands of feet up in the air: writing away at his score'. But neither the critics nor the public took to the work, and it now lies forgotten. Of course, Davies would have been a fortunate man to write a second work to be received as gladly as was *Everyman*; but even that work seems now to be in danger of relegation. Judging by what is now taking place in the English field of composition, one must continue writing in

---

[10] *Lift Up Your Hearts*, a Sacred Symphony for bass solo, chorus and orchestra, Op. 20, was composed in 1906 and premiered at the Hereford Festival of that year.

addition to securing performances, if first successful works are not to be forgotten.

What I believe to be the cause of Walford Davies's abandonment of large-scale composition, and also of his continued work for the B.B.C., is an earnest desire for useful service to the greater number. Twenty-odd years ago he told me that he looked upon music as an aid to higher social and religious work. I see this spirit still active within him in his fellowship and community-singing music, and also in the compilation of hymns with which his name is associated and which have enjoyed great popularity.

DYSON

Talker, Teacher, Composer

This article appeared in *Musical Opinion,* June 1931, p.787.

We are all aware that 'talks and teachers' are a byword with some critics of the B.B.C. To them perhaps 'talks' are only so much talking: to others they are a revelation of the mind of England, in industry, in commerce, and in the arts. Music has had a good share of air space, and the long series of talks on music, which began so auspiciously with Mr. H.C. Colles, has never wavered in interest or in personality. The faculty of choice has been fortunate, or shall we say that the number of suitable men of music are many? Whatever it is, Dr. George Dyson, music master at Winchester and professor at the R.C.M., has 'filled the chair' of music at Savoy Hill with no less success than any of his predecessors. He has always that happy manner which suggests an old 'blue' coaching a promising youngster.

George Dyson is Yorkshire born, having first seen the light at Halifax in May 1883. He was educated at the Royal College of Music, which he entered as a boy of seventeen. He won scholarships for organ playing and composition, and at the age of twenty-one he gained the much coveted Mendelssohn Scholarship which he held for four years, and which gave him invaluable opportunities for travelling abroad in Italy and Germany.

Though Dyson, when elected Mendelssohn Scholar, had indicated unusual gifts for composition, he appears to have written few works whilst-abroad, apart from a work entitled *Siena* – a vigorous and picturesque work inspired by Italian impressions, and suggested by the Palio race. It was produced at a concert of the Patron's Fund in 1907, and has been played several times since.[11] The conditions of the famous French Prix de Rome demand that the successful candidate shall compose one large work each year, which must be sent to the Conservatoire de Musique on completion.

When Dyson returned to England he at once gave his attention to educative music and showed an unusual zest for exploration in contemporary music. He held a succession of music masterships as follows: Naval College, Osborne, 1908; Marlborough, 1911; Rugby, 1914.

In the war he served with the infantry, during which he wrote a manual on Grenade Fighting which was adopted by the War Office. After six years service (including two years at the Air Ministry) he returned to civil life, being appointed organist and head music-master at Wellington College. He also continued his musical exploration. In 1924 he was appointed music master at Winchester College. The success he had with boys in his various college appointments has been recognised in authoritative musical circles.

A more definite indication of the direction in which his mind worked, was the publication of his book, *The New Music*, by the Oxford University Press in 1924. This book, consisting of essays, is the result of Dyson's research in contemporary music. Apart from a natural gift for writing the book reveals his uncommon qualities as an explorer, and the ability to reproduce his gleanings with uncommon fidelity. The book remains a fine testimony to research in contem-

---

[11] The self-critical Dyson nevertheless later withdrew and destroyed this score.

porary art, and places Dyson in the front rank of English musical essayists. We may not agree with all his deductions and speculations from the most modern schools, but the essays disclose an acute sense of argument, and a fastidiousness in thinking and manner of expressing his thoughts which make them very enjoyable reading, for no one can forecast the length of time any contemporary work is likely to live – if performed and published – or even remotely suggest the type of music composers will be writing in 1981. After having worked so many years in the educative field of music, Dr. Dyson has once again returned to composition. In the interim his mind has been tempered and rendered elastic by constant intercourse with contemporary music.

Though Dyson served with the infantry, his music rather suggests life amongst the cavalry. In both his recently published choral works, *In Honour of the City* and *Canterbury Pilgrims*, the music is filled with the palpitating throb of horses at the trot or the gallop. In both these works there is a zest for composition which makes the music unusually vigorous and resilient. There is more imagination to the square foot of this type of writing than is to be found in acres of the average choral music. He told us that he enjoyed writing these works — which explains why his choral writing always appears inspired and not infrequently becomes incandescent.

Dyson has been a professor at the Royal College of Music since 1921. He contributed the important paper on Harmony to the new issue of Grove's Dictionary. All the works here mentioned are published by the Oxford University Press.

The Canterbury Pilgrims

This is not a formal review, but taken from 'On the Other Hand' in *Musical Opinion*, April 1939, p. 589.

From time to time the ambitious and excellent work of the Goldsmiths' Symphony Orchestra and the Goldsmiths' Choral Union, both conducted by the enthusiastic Frederick

Haggis, have been recognised in another part of this journal. South-east London is vast, and should, as indeed it does, provide material for a capable choir and orchestra: but here we have quality thrown in. At Goldsmiths' College they have the advantage of an ideal concert hall, the acoustical properties of which amplify the small but well-balanced forces. The occasion was the production of George Dyson's *The Canterbury Pilgrims*, first heard at a recent Leeds Triennial Festival,[12] but here produced successfully despite the indisposition of the conductor and the tenor soloist.

How much of the original Chaucer remains in *The Canterbury Pilgrims* I do not know, but what remains is a very fine vision. The tales used have stimulated the composer, and that is all that matters. Many regard it as the most remarkable choral work of a definite English character since Elgar revived the English school with a rude shock. Other recent works, also from South Kensington,[13] suggest that we are now in a cycle of new masterpieces not witnessed since the sixteenth century, and perhaps not to be witnessed again for a period equally long. Therefore, I do not see that we need be too modest in proclaiming them, for, good though they be, they still need the stimulus of performance and praise. Perhaps the British Council can and will help forward this work. We have heard much recently about causes being greater than individuals, and similar catch-phrases; but the idealists are up against the human system, and selected programmes reflect either the openmindedness or the prejudices of the arrangers.

What we have from George Dyson is unique and individual. New effects from instruments or voices, or from both in an ensemble, follow each other in quick succession; but they happen naturally, without any suspicion of experiment. His colours glow differently from any other modern work known to me, suggesting those of a mediæval tapestry when first hung, or the modern richly coloured panels of

[12] An error: *The Canterbury Pilgrims* was written for and first produced at the Winchester Competition Festival of 1931.
[13] i.e., from the Royal College of Music, where Dyson was Professor.

Frank Brangwyn. The throw-back to the time of Chaucer, or the reproduction of the period of the *Canterbury Tales* is accomplished in music which should survive in the adroit blending of two styles, mediæval and modern symphonic structure. Each tale is a rounded off structure and magnificently erected. There is even a genuine sense of the ludicrous. The setting of 'There was a clerk of Oxenford' is delicious in its dry humour. I see no reason why each tale should not become as individually popular with the public as 'The Wife of Bath', already a favourite at the Queen's Hall Promenade Concerts.

The performance went with extraordinary sureness, thanks to the conducting of Charles Proctor and the helpful principals – Elsie Suddaby (soprano), Percy Manchester (tenor), and Henry Gill (bass). For many it was another event in the history of British music. Whether we take sides or not I hope those intensely plucky forces at Goldsmiths' College will keep Dyson's work in their repertoire.

Quo Vadis

This is an extract from 'The Three Choirs Festival', a section of 'On the Other Hand' in *Musical Opinion* of June 1939, p. 778. It was written in advance of the premiere of what turned out to be only Part I of Dyson's *magnum opus*, scheduled for Hereford that September.

Though Dyson's libretto of *Quo Vadis* is a compilation of various religious poems by different poets, collectively the sequence of poems maintains an uninterrupted mood of contemplation, of manifest rapture on the wonders of nature. The manner of setting is that of *The Canterbury Pilgrims* – soli, chorus and orchestra, except for the first poem, in which the soloists have no part. Throughout the work the composer's aim is simplicity; for this reason the time measures of simple triple and simple duple are almost exclusively used, and there are few changes of time measure after each of the five movements has begun. The music has a natural spontaneity, an easy flow and an absence of contrapuntal gadgets. Dyson has already convinced us that he is a master of colour-harmony; and the sumptuous richness of his ensembles is striking as the result of design felt at the beginning rather than as a surprise attack in the progress of the movement.

In 'O whither shall my troubled muse incline' the suggestion of progress from dark shadows to a sky where all the stars appear to dance in their brilliance, drawing pæans of homage to the 'unswerving Will' from the beholder, is developed with magnificent restraint until, like a skilled horseman, the composer at the precise moment releases the reins. The finale, 'O timely happy, timely wise', is a poem of fourteen verses by John Keble from which the editors of the original editions of *Hymns Ancient and Modern* selected five verses for the well known hymn commencing 'New every morning is the love'. The editors also exercised their customary habit of altering the sense of the original. Keble wrote:

> The trivial round, the common task
> Would furnish all we *ought* to ask!

The editors altered the second line to

> Would furnish all we *need* to ask

which is something entirely different. By setting the complete poem, George Dyson has restored respect for Keble's genius. In these days, the expression of this early nineteenth century religious poet strikes a quaint note. We can but respect the age of the Oxford movement, which inspired so many poets and writers.

This movement the composer marks 'serene', an English word easily understood. The manner is that of a slow march, $\frac{2}{4}$, and the serenity suggests Elgar in a *nobilmente* mood: but the composer defeats monotony, though he remains throughout in simple duple time. The process is one of gradual expansion, by the imperceptible addition of forces, always mindful that the climax is the precise focussing point towards which the divisions aim, so that when the composer suddenly drops his orchestra and leaves the voices suspended triumphantly singing

> One Name above all glorious names,

the argument is conclusive and irresistible. What happens afterwards is but a tribute to what has gone before and the swaying effect made by chorus and soli, used antiphonally, is movingly eloquent and reminiscent of Elgar in a high tension spiritual mood.

FOULDS

As an emerging star in the Manchester musical firmament when Brian began writing criticism, John Foulds' activities remained of interest to Brian throughout his writing career. The following report of a rare BBC performance of one of Foulds' major scores is drawn from 'On the Other Hand' in the September 1933 *Musical Opinion*, p. 1009.

The B.B.C. Performance of *Dynamic Triptych*

It was in accord with his generous attitude to native composers that Sir Dan Godfrey chose two big and important English works for performance at the recognition concert[14] he broadcast from the London Studio on August 4th. I will say this frankly for the B.B.C.: they often show an intelligent appreciation of our best public men and give the public an opportunity of more direct contact. The two important works put in the programme were the *London Symphony* of Vaughan Williams, and the *Dynamic Triptych* for orchestra and piano of John Foulds.[15]

[14] The programme of the concert was Godfrey's personal choice, and he included the Foulds as the work he felt most deserving of a national hearing. The remaining work on the programme was Weber's *Oberon* Overture.
[15] Foulds' *Dynamic Triptych* for piano and orchestra, Op. 88, was composed in Paris in 1927–29.

The works of Vaughan Williams are well known; but the major works of Foulds, a composer of daring originality, are seldom heard, for indeed most of them await first performance. I was happy to be present at the rehearsal of the works to be broadcast, and was overjoyed to find Sir Dan as fit as the proverbial fiddle; and though the music of Foulds is not cast in the same classical mould as that mostly played by the B.B.C. orchestra, its real difficulties were brushed aside with that spendid nonchalance found only with really good players. I hope this gesture will lead to the admission of the works of John Foulds into the general repertoire, for, as I say, what is alleged to be difficult or bizarre becomes easy and clear with finished playing ably led. After the composer, honours were shared by the conductor, by Frank Merrick, who played the piano part from memory with fine musical enthusiasm, and the orchestra.

I ought to add that *Dynamic Triptych* was first played by Donald Tovey in Edinburgh, and I am told that he has also given a performance of it in Birmingham.[16] I met Foulds years ago, when at Manchester he was playing the 'cello in the Hallé Orchestra under Richter. The old man thought highly of Foulds, and I believe persuaded him to play in the Bayreuth orchestra. Jaeger of Novello's, another good judge of men and their music, procured the issue of his first published work – a Set of Variations for piano.[17] When sending me a copy, Jaeger remarked on the originality of the music. I agree with him; and agree no less with the favourable opinion of Sir Dan Godfrey on *Dynamic Triptych*,

---

[16] There had been three previous performances: under Tovey in Edinburgh, under Foulds himself in Birmingham, and under Godfrey at Bournemouth. Frank Merrick was the soloist on each occasion. After the performance described by Brian the work was not heard again until 1984, when it was issued on record in a performance by Howard Shelley with the Royal Philharmonic Orchestra under Vernon Handley (Lyrita SRCS.130).

[17] Foulds' *Variazioni ed Improvvisati su una Tema Originale*, Op. 4, was his first work to be published (Novello, 1905). Brian's brief but highly laudatory review of the music appeared in *The Musical World* for 25 March 1905, p. 214.

for otherwise he would not have chosen it for his own
recognition concert. It was written in Paris in 1929.

The Death of John Foulds

Foulds succumbed to cholera in Calcutta in the small hours of
24 April 1939, yet only a week later this obituary appeared as
the last item in Brian's 'On the Other Hand' column for the May
issue of *Musical Opinion* (p. 686). It must have been crammed in
at the last minute, which perhaps accounts for the abrupt ending.

I was sorry to hear of the death of John Foulds in Calcutta.
It was fatalistic that he should die there; for in his later
years – probably through the influence of his wife, Maud
MacCarthy, the well known violinist and authority on
Indian music – Foulds had habitually made use of micro-
tones. I last met him at the old B.B.C. studio near Waterloo
Bridge some years ago, when Sir Dan Godfrey was rehearsing the B.B.C. Orchestra in Foulds' most recent orchestral
work – highly interesting and difficult, but quickly grasped
by the orchestra. For some reason Foulds never realised
the hopes engendered by his early work. Thirty-five years
ago he was a 'cellist in the Hallé Orchestra under Richter,
and his father was a bassoon player in the same orchestra.
As a 'cellist, Richter held a high opinion of him. He played
at Covent Garden under Richter, and was one of the players
selected by Richter for his Wagner Orchestra at Bayreuth.

Foulds was a clever 'cellist, but his heart was set on composition, at which he was self-taught and exceedingly
ambitious. When I asked the late A. J. Jaeger if he had his
eye on any other original talent like Elgar, he sent me a set
of Variations for piano composed by John Foulds. It was
my review of these Variations in *The Musical World* which
brought me a letter from the composer, and our first meeting was at midnight in the refreshment room at Crewe
Station: he was on his way to Scotland. Occasionally I visited
him at his home at Fallowfield, Manchester, where I early
discovered he could write music notwithstanding any noises
or interruption. He planned a series of cyclic works, and

actually completed his vast concert opera, *Vision of Dante*, which Elgar and Stanford admired yet did nothing to help to performance: it still awaits its *première*.[18] Foulds' bitter disappointment over this work probably turned him to the writing of music of a lighter calibre. His *Epithalamium* and *Music Pictures* were highly successful under Wood at the Queen's Hall Proms, and his 'Cello Concerto was played by Carl Fuchs at the farewell concert to Richter in Manchester. His small orchestral works are legion, and I suppose his *Keltic Suite* has been broadcast from every station in Europe and America.

Foulds' *World Requiem*, a choral work inspired by the Great War, did not share the fate of his *Vision of Dante*: it was taken up by various musical and patriotic societies, and was performed at the Albert Hall on November 11th, 1923, in the presence of the Prince of Wales. In 1934 John Foulds published a book called *Music To-day*.

BALFOUR GARDINER

This profile was written for *Musical Opinion's* regular feature 'Personal and Otherwise', and appeared in the issue of September 1928. pp. 1162–1163.

Almost every composer has at some period of his life been subject to the influence of a poet. Schumann never completely threw off the influence of Jean Paul Richter; in the

[18] The work, perhaps Foulds' largest in terms of total duration, though not in forces employed, remains unperformed. One of Brian's earlier pieces on Foulds (in his pseudonymous 'Music and Musicians' column in *The British Bandsman*, 10 November 1923, p. 6), which covers much the same ground as this obituary, adds more detail: 'In those days he was a hard worker – working at languages and music day and night.[...] I remember how he told me he had learned Italian that he might set Dante's 'Divine Comedy' to music. I saw large scores of completed portions of this work[...]. I remember Foulds expressing the difficulty of getting such a huge work performed outside a Festival, and his lamenting that he hadn't the influence or the friendly interest to pull it off'.

recently published letters of Wagner, we found Wagner writing of the wonderful stimulation he received from Dante and Goethe.[19] In the same way Balfour Gardiner has been stimulated by the poetry of John Masefield. Only an English poet could have written those wonderful epics, *The Everlasting Mercy, The Window in the Bye Street* and *The awd Dauber*; also, they could only have been written after a life's experience, such as Masefield had in every corner of the world fighting his own battles against the elements. There is in his writings a curious blend of the compassionate pilgrim and the scoffing cavalier; over the great part of it one feels the tang of the salt-laden air blown from vast oceans. This spaciousness with all its influence is found in the early work of Balfour Gardiner. Each pianoforte composition bears a different complexion, and in all there is a fine, free and unbridled inventive genius seeking expression in moods solemn, jocular, or teasingly sarcastic.

Balfour Gardiner commenced life as a pianist – so that his piano writing is exceedingly pianistic and well shaped. He works symphonically and with ease: the solemnity of *Salamanca*, the fine dramatic character of *Michaelchurch*, hold the mind fixed and rivetted to attention. Apart from these there is abundance of high spirits and sly humour in *A Sailor's Piece, Humoresque*, and *The Joyful Home-coming*. The two suites for piano, *Shenadoah* and *Five Pieces*, also contain his best elements of graceful lyrical charm and that quaint humour associated with the hornpipe and the sea shanty.

Balfour Gardiner's indubitable sensitiveness to English pastoral scenery is finely reflected in two part-songs, published by Novello: *Evenen in the Village* and *The Stage Coach*, both from poems by William Barnes illustrating rural life in the Dorset dialect. *An old song re-sung*, words by John Masefield, is a fine setting of a quaint picture drawn in a few mocking lines for mixed voices (Novello) of a folk song, varied. *Evening Hymn* (Novello), for mixed voices and organ

---

[19] Had he been asked, Brian would probably have owned to William Blake being the poet who had had the strongest influence on *his* creativity.

with Latin and English words, is a strangely beautiful piece of ecclesiastical musing – the only piece of its kind we have met by this composer. *Sir Eglamore* (Novello), for mixed voices, is a simple ditty humorously treated. Although of a popular type, the composer's consummate musicianship holds a check on its degenerative tendencies.

Amongst the many settings of the famous Russian tune, *The Song of the Volga Boatmen*, the most effective we have yet met is this composer's setting for mixed voices (Novello). He passes the melody through many phases and varieties of treatment; close harmonic writing, which often spreads into eight parts, gives it unusual richness, whilst the imitative possibilities of the melody are never lost sight of.

There is some unusually sharp sauce in Masefield's *News from Whydah*, an early work for chorus and orchestra published by Novello. The piquant character of Masefield's writing is deliciously carried out amidst brilliant wit and a sense for dramatic climax. *There were three ravens* is a large setting for eight-part mixed chorus published by Curwen. The folk-song character of the legend is sympathetically treated with a real sense of climax and unerring skill in suggesting the tragedy by effective contrapuntal weaving. *The Hunt is up* (Curwen) is an alert and vigorous part-song for mixed voices.

A number of Balfour Gardiner's early songs are published by Curwen. In his choice of poetry, he always discloses the taste of the epicure. *Fidele* (Shakespeare) is powerful, magnetic and emphatic. *The Golden Vanity* is quaintly humorous with a pathetic ending, *The Recruit* (inscribed to Sir Ernest Palmer) has a naive suggestion of wedding bells, Shelley's *Music when soft voices die* has quiet dignity and pathos, and the setting of A.E. Housman's *When I was one and twenty* is decidely humorous. His two finest songs are published by Augener, Ltd. *Rybbesdale*, an ancient legend modernised by Clifford Bax, is a song of love, yet a love of virile masculinity. This song has a 'go' which brooks no hindrance. *The Quiet Garden*, words by Frank Prewett, is a delicious pastoral song with quiet undulating harmonies, the suggestion of 'that space wherein nothing stirs' being wonderfully caught and simply reflected.

Balfour Gardiner is not a prolific composer – he with-draws himself more and more from publicity. It would seem that he is inclined to be dissatisfied with his work, for one hears that he has a penchant for submitting it to ceaseless revision. Be that as it may, all his work – from his earliest to his most recent – reveals a mind ever expanding and pro-gressing. Allied with this is a development of his genius in invention, for his workmanship and constructive ability to-day are superb.

He might be said to sing to-day as he did years ago in the delightful song-setting of his beloved Masefield pub-lished in 1908:

My road calls me, lures me,
   West, east, south and north;
Most roads lead men homeward,
   My road leads me forth.
To add more miles to the tally
   Of grey miles left behind;
In quest of that one beauty
   God put me here to find.

That is the life-song of a real singer.

GRAINGER

This appeared as part of 'On the Other Hand' in *Musical Opinion*, September 1935, p. 997, and was clearly provoked by recent, characteristically Graingeresque, words on Beet-hoven.

I wonder why this happy composer does not come over and see us sometimes. There was a time when he was a kind of Music's darling, and this fact, coupled to his per-sonal friendship with Delius, Grieg and Cyril Scott, may have caused him to throw his weight about a bit. This I experienced once when, travelling with him from the Musical League Festival in the same compartment of the

Liverpool–London express,[20] he having first screened the lamp, threw himself along the whole length of a seat. Incidentally, I could not read; but he was soon asleep. I left the train at Crewe, and have not seen him since. The war seemed to dissolve his growing fame as an original composer and a fine pianist: though he probably enjoyed an equal if shorter spell of popularity in America. Subsequently he returned home to Australia, where it is said they are producing more musicians to the million than any other country.

Grainger certainly left in England very definite impressions of his originality. He started collecting folk-songs, and had not been in Lincolnshire long when he came back with a good capture in the skirt-pockets of his coat. It was 'Brigg Fair', which he used for a choral setting. The tune was afterwards used by Delius for his famous work called *Brigg Fair*. They said at the time of Grainger's orchestral successes that he had tucked away in manuscript the scores of various symphonies and masses. I don't know: but I am quite ready to believe that he has, or has had, many fine ideas for symphonies tucked away in his head. No orchestral pieces by a British composer have been more popular than those curious and fanciful inspirations, *Molly on the Shore*, *Shepherd's Hey*, *Mock Morris*, or *Handel in the Strand* – strokes of genius every one of them, and for a time played by every orchestra in England: gaiety and wit effervesce in them.

Having left the field of composition,[21] Grainger took up, when in America, the master-class idea, and fetched them from every State in the Union to return back home localised Paderewskis. Now down under he talks to his fellow musicians, and in a style as original and provocative as his music. They are told to rely on their own judgment, which is good

[20] This must have been the first Musical League Festival (1909), at which Grainger performed his arrangements of Cyril Scott's *Handelian Rhapsody* and Stanford's *Two Irish Dances* in a concert on 24 September. Brian and he were probably catching the night train on the following evening, after the Festival's final concert (which had included a performance of Brian's *By the Waters of Babylon*).

[21] Grainger never 'left the field of composition'; but by the early 1920s his productivity had slackened considerably.

advice, though his own judgment – that 'judged by the standard of earlier and later geniuses, Haydn, Mozart and Beethoven seldom wrote a successful slow movement' – will, I fear, be upset by the final Court of Appeal. Incidentally, I am curious to know what opportunities the un-travelled Australian has of forming any judgment on the matter at all. Beethoven certainly did on occasion fall asleep in his slow movements: but they are on a much larger scale than those by Haydn and Mozart. Comparisons cannot in other ways be made between the slow movements of Beethoven and his two predecessors. Percy Grainger might better have said that not one of the classical composers could write a sustained slow movement like Bach or an emotional one like Elgar.

I do not know whether in Australia Beethoven is regarded as a stumbling block to indigenous musical progress, but I fail otherwise to account for the following most extraordinary statement: 'The shortcomings of Beethoven's later works are too often laid at the door of growing deafness. Surely it would be more sensible to attribute them to his lack of musical culture, to his ignorance of the great musical resources of the past'. This is hardly a calm, judicial summing-up to a jury about to form a judgment of its own: it seems more like a subtle endeavour to dethrone Beethoven from the affection of all concert pianists and orchestral conductors. Of course, I understand that if there were no Beethoven there might be more opportunities for the moderns of popular flavour: all the same, I do not think that Beethoven has ever stood in the way of Percy Grainger, whose music I much prefer to his sophistries. In his own particular line he has a field to himself, and he should work it well if he desires a renewal of the lease.

HOLBROOKE

As we have seen (pp. 181–183), Brian reviewed the first performance of Holbrooke's *The Bells* at the 1906 Birmingham
Triennial Festival; he had been reviewing Holbrooke's
scores – and calling for their performance in Manchester –
for some time prior to that. After Birmingham Holbrooke
wrote to him, trying to enlist his help in securing performances in the Potteries. They met soon afterwards through
their mutual friendship with A. J. Jaeger, and before long
Holbrooke (presciently, it would seem) had dedicated to
Brian a set of orchestral variations on *The Girl I Left Behind
Me*. Although they saw quite a lot of each other over the
years – they even lived in flats at the same address in
Brighton in 1921–22 – their relationship was not of the
smoothest. Brian continued to regard some of Holbrooke's
music highly, but found the composer's pushiness, love of
gossip, mania for self-advertisement, and intolerance of
others difficult to stomach. Yet although he voiced these
disquiets in private correspondence to Bantock, his public
writings on Holbrooke were invariably generous (if less frequent than Holbrooke would have liked). Holbrooke for his
part gave Brian copying work when he was in difficulties,
provided an (unfruitful) introduction to his patron Lord
Howard de Walden, and wrote a highly laudatory chapter
on Brian in his *Contemporary British Composers* (Cecil Palmer,
London, 1925) – which, alas, suffers from that book's
endemic faults of wild overstatement, hopeless lack of organisation, and multitudinous factual errors.

The first two items in this selection are short score-reviews
from *The Musical World*: that of *Byron* from the issue of
25 February 1905, pp. 143–144, and that of the Sextet No.
3 from 16 March 1907, pp. 79–80.

'BYRON.' (Poem No. 6, Op. 39.) By JOSEPH HOLBROOKE.
(Words by Keats.) London: Novello and Co. Price 1s. 6d. net.

When the works and ideals of the later Wagner have come
to be generally understood in this country, when the doc-
trine of the present new school (the foundation of which
rests upon the theory of definite expression in sound without the assistance of the theatre) has been accepted, *then*
will Mr. Joseph Holbrooke's *Byron* have a vogue. The composer, essentially a free lance, is one of those beautifully coloured butterflies which have been encouraged to flutter

around the Queen's Hall, London. We have examined the vocal score of his *Byron* poem and are delighted with it. The work itself is in one continuous movement, its characteristics being the gradual development of several emotional ideas, much on the lines of the *Lohengrin* and *Tristan* Preludes of Wagner. The colouring, always good, is subservient to the *idée fixe* of the words by Keats. Occasionally we get a feeling of the commingling of the Eastern with Western scales, but the composer never slackens his grip over the central figure of the work. The chorus is most judiciously written for, never protruding but always assisting in the development of the work. *Byron* breathes the presence of a poet as well as a musician, but the absence of conductors in this country with the necessary sense of appreciating so beautiful a work will retard its passing into general acceptance. It will be utterly useless in the hands of anyone who is not only a conductor but a poet to boot. The right of performance, we are glad to see, is reserved.

'THIRD SEXTET IN F MINOR' (op.33). By JOSEPH HOLBROOKE. London: Sidney Riorden. – 10s 6d. net.

This Sextet for Pianoforte and Wind Instruments – flute, oboe, clarinet, horn, and bassoon – is the work that won the Leslie Alexander prize in 1901. If desired, the wind instruments might be replaced by two violins, two violas, and a violoncello, though the instruments originally designed for the work would be most effective. The work is in three movements, the first of which bears no indication of the speed intended, but the usual *Allegro* would seem to commend itself as the one desired; the second is marked *Adagio molto espressione sostenuto*; while the third is a Rondo, *Vivace Marcato*. Each movement is abounding in interest, the themes being worked out with great variety of treatment. It should be stated that for practical purposes it is unfortunate that the work has not been engraved, but to enthusiasts the lithographing will be but a small matter. Probably when some of us are old and grey we shall point to it with pride as open testimony of the difficulties that beset composers in getting their works before the public when *we* were young.

Probably to the next generation it will be quite as much a curiosity as are the carefully hand-copied parts used by our grandfathers in their days of quartet-playing.[22] Yes, even to the curio hunter this Sextet is valuable, but to the musician who has eyes to see and ears to hear it is more so.

Holbrooke as Composer-Conductor

Brian's article on the Bax First Symphony (pp.233–240), his first to appear in *Musical Opinion*, 'brought Holbrooke here with the article in his hand, asking *why* he was not mentioned in it!!!' (Brian to Bantock, 26 January 1923). Holbrooke's reaction may have prompted Brian to write the polemical article 'Placing' (to be included in a later volume) on the pushiness of certain composers – without mentioning Holbrooke by name. But he also wrote an article on Holbrooke's *The Children of Don* which, although submitted to *Musical Opinion*, was not accepted for publication. Nearly a year later Holbrooke wrote to Brian: 'You have the satisfaction, anyway, old dear, of saying you've written a lot – and not one word on JH yet, except that rotten old BB journal!' 'BB' was *The British Bandsman*, where Brian had been writing a weekly column, 'Music and Musicians'; the column of 29 September 1923 (p.3) was largely devoted to Holbrooke.

The recent remarks made in this column about Berlioz and Wagner in the dual role of composer and conductor brought some remarks to me from a musical acquaintance that we now have a number of 'double-sided' musicians hereabouts nowadays. It is quite true. I mentioned Elgar's fine interpretations of his own works. He also, for a season, went on tour with the London Symphony Orchestra and conducted fine performances of other works than his own. I particularly remember a fine performance of the Brahms No. 3 Symphony in F. After hearing Richter's conducting of this work it was a delight to hear how much brighter the work became under Elgar the composer.

---

[22]   Instead, it was an early harbinger of our own times, when manuscript facsimiles are the rule. Neither this nor the 1922 Chester republication bears the subtitle 'Israfel', by which the Sextet is sometimes known.

Professor Granville Bantock has done a great deal of orchestral conducting [...].

One might mention other double-sided musicians – Julius Harrison and John H. Foulds, who are brilliant both as composers and conductors. The most brilliant in the whole country is, undoubtedly, Eugene Goossens [...].

Quite recently Mr. Joseph Holbrooke has joined the double-sided musicians. Last week, in Cardiff, he conducted a wireless orchestral concert. On Sunday, September 23rd, he conducted the Sunday afternoon orchestral concert at the Regent, Brighton. The place was packed. I have a whole-hearted sympathy for Holbrooke's genius as a composer. He has fought for years with the dogged pertinacity of a fanatic for the recognition of his own genius and British music. It is a long time ago since Ernest Newman prophesied great things for Holbrooke, and in my opinion that prophecy has been fulfilled. There was a time when his works loomed largely in the programmes of the Queen's Hall Symphony Concerts. One might well ask what has happened to these works that one never hears them now. Is it that some orchestral conductors shed their scores as freely as some women shed their tears? We know that fashions change and it is not so long ago since we used to pick up special editions of *Die Musik*, with wonderful photographs of the artists taking part in the Festivals of Bayreuth, of Bruckner, Mahler and others. Are we to swallow it that the music of Berlioz, Wagner, Bruckner and twenty other etceteras is now as dead as Queen Anne because it wasn't written during the war?

There is a blight on the earth somewhere, and a number of composers have been caught in it. One doesn't quite make out how much of it is imaginary or how much belongs to the vinegar brush. Some composers have a blight by way of an unfriendly piano banging all day and every day next door [23] – others get it in their gardens.

[23] This is a personal reminiscence: shortly after the War Brian was hampered in his composing by a next-door neighbour, a demobilised soldier, who occupied his time playing scales hour after hour for several weeks. As a dedicated gardener, he doubtless suffered from the second kind of 'blight' as well.

A few composers get the blight on their music, and one of these seems to be Joseph Holbrooke. His opera, *The Children of Don*, is one of the most extraordinary creations given to us by a composer.

There are dramatic situations in it more intense and heart-moving than I can recall in any other opera – yet we haven't heard it in England.[24] Holbrooke's score of *The Children of Don* is a masterpiece. He has written fine orchestral poems, one of the finest part-songs and certainly one of the finest songs of recent years, and a great deal of chamber music. He has even turned his attention to foxtrots, reels and strathspeys. At the Regent in Brighton he essayed the art of conductor. The programme contained little that was new or enterprising, apart from Holbrooke's songs. The orchestral items contained the *Coriolanus* Overture (Beethoven), *Siegfried Idyll* (Wagner), two Dances from the *Casse Noisette* of Tschaikowsky, with three orchestral pieces by Holbrooke. His conducting is quiet and intimate. He had the aloofness of one conducting a chamber orchestra in his own drawing-room. Such refinement tends to vaporisation in so large a building containing so vast an audience. The performance of his reels and strathspeys gave us the impression that he had given over most of the rehearsal to other composers' works and left little time for the preparation of his own. The performance of his *Columbine* and *Valse* were exceedingly brilliant and full of charming piquancy. All the items were greatly enjoyed, and Holbrooke had a fine reception. Miss Joan Ashley sang songs by Beethoven, Frank Bridge and Holbrooke. [...]

Miss Ashley's singing of Frank Bridge's *Love Went a-Riding* was exceedingly appropriate, and this was so in the Holbrooke song. In the singing of Holbrooke's *Come Not When I am Dead* she did not quite realise all there is in that exceptionally fine song, and it was not her fault for she had the composer to accompany her. Holbrooke's *Come Not When I Am Dead* is a man's song, and a wonderful thing it is, too, when rendered by Frank Mullings.

[24] *The Children of Don* had been premiered earlier that year in Vienna (under Weingartner) and had also been performed in Salzburg.

The Neglect of Holbrooke

Brian's most substantial writings on Holbrooke come comparatively late in his journalistic career. 'The Neglect of Holbrooke' appeared in two parts in successive issues of *Musical Opinion* (November 1937, pp. 121–122 and December 1937, pp. 215–216). Writing to Sir Adrian Boult at the BBC on 24 October 1937, Brian explained: 'I have received innumerable letters, scores, pamphlets, brochures etc. from Josef Holbrooke recently concerning the neglect of his works. I don't know why people do this sort of thing – for I possess no occult powers to turn water into wine. What I have done is to write two short articles [...]. I don't know if *you* feel inclined to do anything – I can imagine that you are bombarded daily by requests. But there is one aspect of Holbrooke which the BBC could consider and that is his expertness as a pianist. I have only heard one other composer who plays the piano so well and that is Rachmaninoff. Do you feel inclined to recommend him [...] for a composer-pianist broadcast? I think he would be grateful and appreciate the chance'.

I.

As to how, where and why contemporary composers are neglected is a question which no writer can answer; and probably conductors would find it impossible to do so also. Perhaps the real reason lies in the fact that the older composers have been overtaken by a nearer and later generation. When Elgar was publicly applauding the work of Josef Holbrooke and others, he said nothing of Vaughan Williams, Gustav Holst or Arnold Bax. Yet within a few years, these three composers had advanced to the front, while the works of their immediate predecessors slowly disappeared from concert programmes. A later succession brought us a group of half-a-dozen composers, academically trained, with large scale works and with subsequent performances.

Each composer attracts a following, who regard its composer as a leader in exactly the same way as the early supporters of Holbrooke regarded him. Neglect and indifference do not deter the artist who lives to create. Whilst conductors have been leaving Holbrooke's works out of the programmes, the composer has still been working. The

generation that knew his series of symphonic works inspired by the poetry of Poe, or his series of operas beginning with *The Children of Don*, need no reminding of
his genius. For those of the present generation who do not
know those early works, let it be said that a composer
reflects his environment and that Holbrooke grew up when
the world was young, when all were on the heels of the
latest romantic composer long before the works of his predecessor had ceased to be new, and when melody was pursued for its loveliness and harmony for its richness and
novelty.

Such qualities are conspicuous in Holbrooke's work,
allied with metaphysical brooding and a contrasting quality
of irresponsible gaiety of the Puckish type. Occasionally,
his work suggests a fleeting impression of someone else,
such as the early Trio in D minor for piano, violin and
horn (1906),[25] where the melodies bubble like a fountain
amid romantic coloured harmonies, the whole very characteristic of Holbrooke. In the finale, there is a suggestion
that while it was being written, Anton Dvořák called to pay
a short visit.

Holbrooke's music is of two distinct types, either
homophonic or an amalgam of perpendicular and horizon-
tal invented by Wagner and carried further by Strauss.
These are the masters who have inspired Holbrooke's
fertile invention, and their influences may be found in
his operas or in the more recent Concerto for 'cello and
orchestra.

Another penchant of Holbrooke found in the early *Queen
Mab* and later works is that elfin-dance-like dotted semi-
quaver figure beloved of piano composers like Weber and
Grieg, popularised by the former in his *Polonaise* in E major
and by the latter in his well-known *Norwegian Bridal Procession*. There is witchery in his *Sonata Orientale* for violin and

---

[25] All published catalogues of Holbrooke's music are riddled with inaccuracies, omissions, and mutual contradiction. The most useful 'control' is Kenneth L. Thompson's article 'Holbrooke: Some Catalogue
Data' in *Music & Letters*, October 1965, pp. 297–305. Thompson dates this
Trio to 1904.

piano[26] with its restlessness and kaleidoscopic changes in the extreme pitches of high and low, urgent and rich in its swirling fantasy and changing moods. Playing the piano and scoring for orchestra are as natural to Mr. Holbrooke as a bird singing in spring: though his work does oscillate like Bruckner's between austerity and obviousness.

We imagine that Mr. Holbrooke enjoyed writing those droll chuckles in his Second Piano Concerto,[27] but it is a genuine piano work with the soloist in the supreme position, and the solo instrument is never submerged by the orchestra. The work is obviously a dance concerto consisting of (1) Javanese dancing, (2) Singhalese dancing, (3) Burmese dancing; and if the composer gives us no hair raising pictures of these Eastern races, it is but his just regard for oriental culture. This Piano Concerto, homophonic and free of Wagnerisms, is individual and full of rare surprises.

Remembering all the fashions that have come and gone during the past thirty years, and remembering the charge that used to be held against Holbrooke of making unnecessary difficulties for the performers, a recent study of the score of his Prelude to *The Bells* does not reveal what it was that frightened conductors thirty years ago, unless it was that the composer's full-throated outbursts were too strong for them. And if in the present materialistic age stories of magic castles and love potions are apt to raise a smile, it does not preclude the fact that many of the finest songs the composer has written are to be found in his opera-ballet, *The Wizard*.

Holbrooke's mentality is of the Weber-Wagner type, in that elemental things seldom fail to inspire him. Had Holbrooke been a materialist, he would never have written the Poe symphonic poems or the mystical Welsh opera trilogy. There is even a suggestion of the elemental world in his three-movement Symphony No. 3: a journey through the first and second movements is as passing through an

---

[26] This is Holbrooke's Third Violin Sonata, Op. 83, of 1926.
[27] *L'Orient*, Op. 100, composed 1928.

entangled forest.[28] Beauty spots are to be found, particularly in the elusive impressionism of the slow movement. There is also the feeling of anticipation; and if so much that is novel tends to make for impatience the opening to the brilliant Finale makes its arrival worth the waiting for. Here all is activity and bustle, with bouncing gay tunes of a popular type.

II.

A Scotsman once tried to explain his dislike of music by saying that it seemed to him to be only a game for daft people. On the other hand, the Greeks advocated the study of music as it tended to sharpen other faculties.

If appreciation of a composer by writers would make his music 'go', then Josef Holbrooke's music should have begun a non-stop run long ago; for no contemporary English composer has found more appreciation among writers on music, and the list of them, beginning with Ernest Newman thirty or more years ago, is indeed a long one. Few composers have at any time used more ink than Holbrooke in writing of their contemporaries and in making onslaughts on their enemies. Like Quixote tilting against the windmill, Holbrooke directed his pen against doctors of music and musical knights as the worst enemies of the young composer; but it is difficult to see the cause of his aggressive anti-Semitic views or what that race has to do with the neglect of his music.

Holbrooke has composed some forty orchestral works (including eight symphonies), but the fact has to be admitted that, whatever its cause, his name is rarely seen on a concert programme. His political outlook colours his music: how could it be otherwise? Everywhere the unconventional is met, not because it is willed to be *outré*, but because it is the natural expression of the man – quite as much as the prophetic books were Blake's natural expression. And he writes easily either on large or small scale works; and he has written sufficient chamber music to establish a claim as a

[28] This is presumably the symphony entitled *Ships*, Op. 90 (1925); see also note 35 on p. 284.

composer of originality if he had never written anything else.

There was a time before the war when Holbrooke was conducting a two-handed campaign: writing about the neglect of contemporary composers and performing their works at his chamber concerts. This might have convinced the sceptics that he had a broad and sympathetic outlook, but it did not.

Yet he has been doubly fortunate in other ways. When Herbert Trench was looking for a composer to set his epic poem, *Apollo and the Seaman*, Sir Henry J. Wood (then Mr.) remembered Holbrooke. Its subsequent performance set as a symphony at Queen's Hall created excitement, which focussed attention on Holbrooke far more than on Trench. Beecham conducted the performance, and Novello published the score. And it is due to the interest of Lord Howard de Walden, the author of the poems used by Holbrooke in his Welsh operatic trilogy, that those operas were published and performed.

There are unusual difficulties in producing such works. Who among present-day conductors would remain concealed with his orchestra behind a screen for a performance of *Apollo and the Seaman*? Beecham did in 1906, but he had a box of biscuits and syphons of soda water to sustain him!

If *Apollo and the Seaman* only succeeded in scaring people by its novelty, the Violin Concerto (*Grasshopper*) attracted many eminent soloists after it was performed by the famous violinist, John Dunn, at a concert of the Leeds Philharmonic Society.[29] The first and last movements, nimble and quick-witted, are of rhythmical capriciousness suggestive of the title; but the middle movement is a finely sustained elegy in which not only soloist but also the orchestra eloquently sing. And, as though providing conductors with an excuse for *not* performing a work, there are the Variations for orchestra on *Auld Lang Syne* in which 'the actual sounds have been written in this score for all transposing instruments and must be transposed in the parts'. This may be helpful for amateurs; but it will not help conductors,

[29] In 1917.

even though the old Scotch melody has given the composer a chance to exercise a boundless fund of humour: he evidently enjoyed drawing the portraits of his friends depicted in the variations.

Nor do his large scale works represent the limit of his mentality. His *Twelve Drinking Songs* are the quaintest miniatures imaginable – and all drinkable! Though a twist or snag might have been anticipated in tackling G.K. Chesterton, Holbrooke's settings provide an easy apt solution. The predominant quality in those early orchestral works which impressed the name of Holbrooke on the public was his natural sense of rhythm. The most successful were throbbing with the free wings of the dance or carnival.

Holbrooke's ballet, *Aucassin et Nicolette*, is a charming romantic work consisting of six miniatures: Overture, 'Danse Pathétique', 'Aucassin's Dance', 'Mazurkas', 'Pas de deux' and 'Trepak'. It is his eighth ballet and recently enjoyed a successful run with the Markova-Dolin Ballet.[30] Such works do not call for the introspective profundities necessary for symphonies, but facility in writing and a childlike imagination: this and the clever music to *Llwyfan y byd* are expertly written.

It is somewhat surprising that Holbrooke – who is a virtuoso pianist – has not written more music for his own particular instrument. His *Ballade* (No. 2) in C minor, a solitary work amongst his long list of orchestral and chamber compositions, is dark coloured and passionate, and, until the Coda is reached, the composer makes no use of the higher register of the piano: all the same, it is finely spun romantic music. Holbrooke resembles Stanford in ease and facility of composition, but he has not yet overtaken Stanford in the number of published works. Holbrooke's published works now reach Op. 115, Stanford reached Op. 177: Beethoven is a long way ahead of both with 256 published works.

A matter of sympathy is that Holbrooke has been afflicted by complete deafness for twenty years. He pays ungrudging tribute to his wife for her care. Holbrooke married Dorothy Hargreaves, a Yorkshire lady, and they

---

[30] In 1936.

have three daughters and two sons. The eldest son, Anton
studied the clarinet with Charles Draper and became an
accomplished player: but he gave up his instrument to seek
a career in the New World and is now in Canada. Gwydion
the second son, studied the bassoon at the Royal Academy
of Music.

As to the neglect of Holbrooke or any other composer
do let us grasp things as they really are; for it is not a
matter of whether Holbrooke is a better or worse composer
than any of his contemporaries. Sensible musicians do not
compare Beethoven with Schumann or Schumann with
Schubert, for each is self-contained and very unlike the
other. The position of Holbrooke's works is entirely a matter for those who direct performances and for those who
used to perform his works and now no longer do so. What
cannot be cured must be endured.

Josef Holbrooke, English Composer

This, Brian's last substantial piece on Holbrooke, appeared
in *Tomorrow* for 4 November 1939, pp. 31–32.

It is almost forty years ago since I first met Josef Holbrooke.
I was spending a week-end with the late A.J. Jaeger at his
home at Muswell Hill for the purpose of playing my manuscript works to him. Jaeger's sympathies were with young
English composers: he considered Holbrooke the most
gifted. After I had played to him my setting of the psalm
By the Waters of Babylon, Jaeger said he would like Holbrooke
to hear it. In response to a message, Holbrooke arrived
during Sunday afternoon on his bicycle with his pockets
stuffed full of manuscripts. I played to him and he played
to me. Of the works he played I have never forgotten the
impression made on me by his song setting of Edgar Allan
Poe's poem *Annabel Lee*. I still regard it as one of the finest
of English songs ever written: its disappearance is a mystery.[31] Another work inspired by Poe was Holbrooke's

[31] i.e., its disappearance from the repertoire. *Annabel Lee*, Op. 41b

symphonic poem, *The Raven,* first performed by the Crystal Palace Orchestra under Manns. The work made a stir; it announced an original English genius who was complete master of the orchestra and Holbrooke was encouraged. At the beginning of his career he was fortunate to have the encouragement of Henry J. Wood and his Queen's Hall orchestra and Granville Bantock, who was making history in the North with his orchestra at New Brighton Tower. Holbrooke did not have to wait for performances of his symphonic poems *The Corsair, Byron, Ulalume.* They were a series of successes climaxed by the symphonic poem *Queen Mab,* produced at the Leeds Festival, and the big choral work *The Bells* (poem by Poe), the latter performed under Richter at the Birmingham Festival. Thus within a few years of his first performance at the Crystal Palace, Holbrooke was received into the purple: there was no disputing the originality or quality of his genius. On my first meeting him, quite apart from being impressed by his razor-edge sharpness, I found that apart from interest in his own works his immediate concern was that of the young English composer. Unlike Debussy, who found it incumbent to shun listening to the works of his contemporaries in order to preserve his own originality, Holbrooke went out of his way to hear all the music he could by young English composers. He had a clear comprehension of Elgar's genius, and inscribed his setting of Poe's *The Bells* to Elgar. When Elgar accepted the Professorship of Music of Birmingham University he took the first opportunity in his public lectures of drawing attention to the pioneer work of young English composers, and pointed to the works of Bantock, Holbrooke and Walford Davies.

Previously it had been no one's affair to shepherd the interests of young composers; Elgar's gesture was effective. It started an activity which eventually brought into existence two entirely independent organisations, the Society of British Composers and the Musical League. The former dealt with publishing and the latter with performances.

---

composed in 1905, exists in versions for voice and piano and voice and orchestra.

They flourished for a few years until the war of 1914 killed both. There were efforts also made by private individuals; prominent amongst them was Josef Holbrooke. His chamber concerts in London had been in existence for some years prior to my meeting him. They ran for thirty years and served the purpose of launching many new chamber works and song cycles by native composers. Many established composers of today got their first hearing or the first hearing of a new work at Holbrooke's chamber concerts. He also launched a campaign in a weekly musical paper on behalf of the native composer. Week after week his pen ran over the names and works of young contemporary composers much in the manner of an organist running his fingers over his stops. Holbrooke's articles were provocative and stimulating and they disclosed he had something new amongst British composers – a trenchant pen and a fund of wit. Many established composers of today got their first introduction to the larger public through his concerts or his press articles.

All this activity, plus his globe-trotting, indicates remarkable mental activity, which explains figuratively speaking why most people cannot keep pace with him. Holbrooke is a man and a half. Richard Wagner, a phenomenal genius of dual talents, restricted his musical genius to opera. Holbrooke has spread his talent on a far bigger area than Wagner. Holbrooke's field of activity includes opera, orchestral symphonies, chamber music and songs, and symphonies for brass bands and military bands. His Welsh operatic trilogy owes its inspiration to the libretto of Lord Howard de Walden, who has stood by Holbrooke for many years, giving him the necessary freedom of mind for his creative works.[32]

Whatever verdict the future may give on *Dylan* and *Bronwen*, the second and third operas of the trilogy – there can be no dispute of the extraordinary mastery of the first

[32] Holbrooke at one time effected an introduction for Brian to his patron, but little seems to have come of it – except that Brian is known to have written a work (*Legend*) for bassoon (or cello) and piano in about 1939–40 which he sent to Howard de Walden. The piece has not been heard of since.

opera called *The Children of Don*. Nikisch only consented
to conduct its first performances because he was convinced
it was a work of genius. This work is Holbrooke's high-water
mark in the realm of opera. But we are in this country in
music a nation of misfits. Not possessing the necessary
opera houses capable of puting on the stage a work of the
dimension of the De Walden-Holbrooke trilogy – the work
must perforce remain a vast conception of imaginary
idealism. There is the alternative of performing it as a
concert work – but an opera can only be successful as a
concert work when it is well known as an opera.

The trilogy has one thing in its favour – it is published.
Years ago as each Holbrooke score was issued it was greeted
by a howl of derision from those who were not so sure of
themselves. He was held up as a sort of mischievous Puck
who wrote orchestral scores to confound players and conductors. I well remember the attitude of certain quarters
to Holbrooke's 'difficulties' and 'impossible' passages
for the players or because certain instruments used by
him were not to be found in normal orchestras. Hence the
'puffing and blowing' which greeted the publication of his
string quartet called *The Pickwick Club*[33] because of its 'insur-
mountable' difficulties – yet group after group of quartet
players performed *Pickwick* to the delight of many audiences and proved that however difficult passages looked
on paper they held no terrors for expert fingers. The Sextet
in D for Strings[34] is the high mark of his chamber music.
Written almost forty years ago, it is by a composer dead
sure of his aims; it fulfils in its masterly part writing and
natural unfolding of moods all the requirements expected
from great chamber works of art. Holbrooke's work makes
an excellent companion to Brahms' Sextet in G for Strings
in that you can sit comfortably inside it without feeling you
may be thrown out of the window as in *Pickwick*.

Holbrooke was never attracted by the standard English

---

[33] This is Holbrooke's String Quartet No. 3, Op. 68.
[34] String Sextet No. 3 (sometimes subtitled *Henry Vaughan*), Op. 43, composed 1902. Not to be confused with Sextet No. 3 for piano and wind,
reviewed by Brian on pp.270–271.

oratorio or secular cantata written for choral societies. In such works as the symphonic poems *Byron* or *Queen Mab* the chorus is but a necessary part of the orchestra. Even in his big choral work *The Bells* the mental factor is the orchestra. Yet he has published choral symphonies where voices are the basis of the works – and they have been performed.

His mentality is instrumental and symphonic – hence the amazing number of his instrumental works. The nautical symphony (No.3) has the subtitle *Nelson*;[35] the three movements are inspired by British shipping and named 'War Ships', 'Hospital Ships', 'Merchant Ships'. Here is a work particularly suitable for the present hour; the score and parts are published, so conductors have no excuses for ignoring a work so pronouncedly English in mentality and score for showing off or putting an orchestra on its mettle.

Apart from being lured to things Welsh, Holbrooke has lived at Harlech in Wales many years and thus became impregnated with Welsh atmosphere. This influence abounds in his brass band symphony *Wild Wales*, the fantasie *Gwydion of Don*, the magnificent elegy *Song of Llewellyn*, and as a contrast to this tonality he has published a suite of four pieces called 'Air de Ballet', 'Ballathona', 'Oriental Dance' and 'In Mandalay': a fine exhibition in song and dance contrasts particularly the last piece with its throbbing rhythm against the solo instrument.

Of military band works Captain Miller and his Grenadier Guards Band deserves the highest praise for performing and broadcasting the military band symphony *Old England* – three mood studies on the 'Lass of Richmond', 'Down among the dead men' and 'Gentlemen of England'. Suite (No. 1) is a study of rhythms, the four movements called 'Amethyst', 'Turquoise', 'Nocturne', 'Purple'; the music neither exotic nor erotic, throbs with melodies and brilliant harmony. The large work *Prelude and Variations*, short dance

[35] As stated in note 28 on p. 277, the piece is subtitled *Ships*: but Holbrooke was an inveterate changer of titles and it is possible that he wished it to be known as *Nelson* at the time Brian was writing.

Ballymoney, and the lovely song-like melody for flute accompanied called *Serenade Orientale* is a tempting morsel. Finally Holbrooke has been inspired by recent events to write an *Imperial March*, in which he adds to the dignity of the work by his use of two most popular tunes, 'God Save the King' and 'Rule Britannia'.

Does Holbrooke nowadays thrive by the discouragement of conductors? A few people have lived who refused to lie down when dead. Holbrooke is such; he cannot be kept down or under. In spite of the omission of his works from 'official' programmes, he continues to add to his opus numbers.

At the present time, unhindered by the war, he is busy with two large-scale choral and orchestral works on vastly different subjects by Blake and Kipling.[36]

HOLST

The Passing of Gustav Holst

Brian's early writings on Holst were confined to short notices and reviews, and it was only on the composer's death that he began to write about him at length. The following piece was in fact occasioned by Holst's death, and is taken from 'On the Other Hand' in *Musical Opinion*, July 1934, p. 860. It immediately precedes the item on the death of Delius, given in this volume on pp.137–139.

I am distressed at the news of the death of Gustav Holst. My personal acquaintance with him was brief, but I venture to think that we had many mutual sympathies. Years ago,

[36] According to information from Holbrooke's son, Gwydion Brooke, these projects never materialised: instead Holbrooke wrote a large number of Blake songs for voice and piano and a short Blake chorus with unscored accompaniment. These were among his last works, and remain unpublished.

when I was living in the North of England, I had a letter
from him, and with it came a number of part-songs, which
were settings of words from the Hindu Rig-Veda, for which
reason I found it difficult to secure the interest of choral
conductors. At the festival of 1913, given at Birmingham
Town Hall by the I.S.M. and the Musical League, both Holst
and I had an orchestral work in the programme: and it was
at the sectional rehearsal of the brass and woodwind of my
Doctor Merryheart that we met.[37] He was frankly interested in
what I termed a comedy overture, but he remained shy
and reserved. I saw him again a few years ago at the school
at Brook Green where he was music-master. Holst was a
great personality, because he attained fame by following an
entirely individual and solitary path. His orchestral suites
Beni Mora and *The Planets*, his choral work, *Hymn of Jesus*
and his opera, *The Boar's Head*, are unlike any other European music. He was decidely a great fertiliser in expressing
continuously his abiding faith in English music and also for
his passion for the music of Henry Purcell. Greater honours
were doubtless in store for Gustav Holst: and had his span
but equalled that of Elgar, who will say that equal fame
would not have been his?

I have [...] sorrowfully noted the differences in national
lamentation. Was there, indeed, all that difference in the
quality of the music of Elgar and Holst? I think not. But
Holst was of a different cast of mind from Elgar, who
walked well with the mighty. Holst, on the other hand,
shrank from the least whisper of personal publicity, and
feared lest he should override any of his fellows. I know this
is so, for more than once has he asked me to forbear mentioning his name. I hope that his music will bear the
handicap he himself placed on it by his reticence.

However, the death of Holst did bring some splendid
tributes to the worth of the man and his music, that in *The
Times* being in full accord with its great traditions.[38] One
felt pride in being of the race of the musician and his
biographer. An excellent estimate of Holst is that written

[37] The concert occurred on 3 January 1913; Holst's work was *Beni Mora*.
[38] By Ernest Newman.

by Edwin Evans in the last edition of *Grove*. Holst undoubtedly suffered in popular appreciation from the wild and unreasoned feelings engendered by the war: his name had such an un-English form and sound. The grandson of a von Holst who had migrated from Sweden in the early part of the nineteenth century, Holst was well advised to drop the prefix Von. But to those who knew him, it seems quite unnecessary, for he was filled with the spirit of England: in outlook and training he was English, and I think of him intellectually as a compound born of two such diverse minds as those of Keats and Wordsworth.

As a composer, the first half of Holst's life was uneventful if not undistinguished: he had strong democratic tendencies and at one time I know looked fondly to the Orient, though not in the way of other Western composers cultivating the pseudo-Oriental manner. Holst was drawn by the spiritual mysticism of Hindu mythology. His finest work of this period was the opera, *Savitri*, and his oriental studies really came to a climax in the extraordinary suite, *Beni Mora*, which was inspired by a visit to Morocco. From his study of Whitman came an overture named *Walt Whitman* (still unperformed[39]), the setting of Whitman's verses, *The Mystic Trumpeter* (1904), and the *Ode to Death* (Leeds, 1922). These Whitman works were all written within a period of eighteen years and, with his musical directorship at the Passmore Edwards Settlement and Morley College, show his constructive human outlook on life. Many works arose from his English speculations, the climax being the *Choral Symphony* on poems by Keats.

Holst had great influence as a teacher, working at Reading College, the Royal College of Music, and St. Paul's Girls School, Brook Green, where doubtless the spirit of the man will go marching on. The Brook Green appointment was held for thirty years, and here the work was congenial and successful, his most brilliant pupils here being the late Jane Joseph[40] and Imogen Holst, his own daughter. Other of his girl pupils were exceptionally clever, and some requited

[39] And still unperformed today.
[40] For more on Jane Joseph see pp. 356–357.

his kindness by doing much of his copying, for Holst was sore afflicted by a nerve disorder in the right hand, which made writing difficult and always painful. These girls knew so well the workings of his mind in scoring that Holst had only to write the important essentials, and all would be completed to his satisfaction.

The work of every composer is subject to fluctuation of appreciation: even British Funds move a little. Apart from his orchestral suites – *Beni Mora* and *The Planets* – none of his works suffered from frequency of performance. Holst's development was slow: which would follow his retiring disposition. He had nothing to offer to national enthusiasm, such as Elgar gave in abundance: but who was the greater musician, Elgar or Holst, will never be decided: though they both worked on the same resources, their mental outlook was as different as night from day. Holst never had a henchman, though there are those who could have spoken honestly of his good work. The opportunity is now with those who know his music, which includes every type of orchestral and choral composition. The best possible way of service is by encouraging performance, and to this end there should be a Holst Society in every shire of England and in every capital town of the colonies, with a parent society having its roots deep down in the hearts of all those who have studied at the Royal College of Music of which he was the most distinguished scion.

Gustav Holst: An English Composer

Brian subsequently wrote a long and sympathetic review of Imogen Holst's biography of her father, and then in 1939 the article which follows. Although published in *Musical Opinion* (January 1940, pp. 154–155), it seems possible that it was originally intended as one of the series of articles on British composers that Brian had been contributing to *Tomorrow*, which was shortly to cease publication (see p.21).

Gustav Holst was born at Cheltenham on September 21st, 1874; his father was of Swedish extraction, and his mother was English. As a boy, Holst was taught by his father, who himself was a professional musician. In and around Cheltenham the boy worked extremely hard to acquire experience, as an organist, conductor of a choral society and of an amateur opera society. For the latter he composed a comic opera. He was still occupied with these useful juvenilities when his father sent him to study at the Royal College of Music, where Stanford and Rockstro were his principal teachers. Much has been written about the influence of Stanford, but little about that of Rockstro,[41] yet it was the latter who directed Holst to the use of mediæval modes, and these were a decisive factor in his artistic development. Holst's first idea was not that of becoming a composer: he longed to be an expert pianist, but an affliction of the right hand persisting, he had to abandon the idea. Sad to say, he was never free from that nerve trouble, and consequently always wrote with difficulty; but he found some compensation when he turned to the trombone, which he learned to play skilfully and with profit to himself. He practised in varied combinations – orchestras, dance bands, and seaside bands, travelling with the Carl Rosa troupe and sojourning with the Scottish Orchestra.

Whilst Holst was earning his living as a professional trombonist, he was acquiring an invaluable experience later to be used as orchestrator when composing. His earliest compositions lacked distinctive quality as music, but their inspiration came from original and unconventional sources. His settings included poetry by Walt Whitman, and the Indian myths. Holst's sensibility and reaction to poetry developed simultaneously with his creative talent. His development as musician is not dissimilar from a sculptor, who, working under Greek influences and ideals, eventually becomes renowned as a master of Assyrian sculpture.

Holst's experiences as a trombonist in opera taught him much. When he began writing operas, he threw aside all the trappings of the spectacular and the 'grand', using only the most economical ensembles. His instructions as to the

---

[41] William Rockstro (1823–1895), the composer and musicologist, lectured and taught at the R.C.M. in the last four years of his life. Holst was a student there from 1893.

performance of his operas are economical, even to the point of being casual. As a composer, also, he remained faithful to the same principles. He used bare essentials; and he drove through the middle of an argument with direct means of expression and boldness of strokes.

Holst's early opera, *Savitri* (an Indian subject), is an attempt at a perfect model with primitive resources. The score is more modest than a Monteverdi, and it may be performed in the open air or in a small room, and a curtain is optional. The orchestra consists of two string quartets, a string bass, two flutes, and English horn; there is a hidden chorus of female voices; and the only visible characters are three principals: Satyavan (a woodman), Savitri (his wife) and Death. Though the means used are slight, the work has some overpowering moments, particularly in a $\frac{7}{4}$ march. Holst introduced many new ideas in this chamber opera, the most effective of all being the unaccompanied monologues. Savitri echoes Shakespeare and Maeterlinck in emphasising that we are but shadows and the substance of dreams. The plot is the simple one of the wife saving her husband from death.

In the writing of librettos for his operas and choral works, Holst disclosed marked literary ability. Indian myths set his imagination free and inspired him to sing. *The Cloud Messenger*, a splendidly compact work for chorus and orchestra is undeserving of neglect. It is refreshing in its variety of harmony, bold chordal structure and sensitively pointed rhythms. It has a Wagnerian tinge: striking melodic basses: a forecast of the processional march style, found in later works and in the symphonies of Gustav Mahler.

Early in his career, Holst experimented in five and seven pulse measures. These abound in his large works, and save them from monotony when he repeats a phrase *ad libitum*. Experiment proves that a bar of five or seven pulse measure can be repeated fifty times without becoming wearisome. Holst made a success of using odd time measures. His Oriental suite, *Beni Mora*, was his first popular success. Prior to its performance at a festival by the Musical League and Incorporated Society of Musicians in Birmingham, January, 1913, Holst was no better known than the other

English composers whose works were being first performed in the same programme. *Beni Mora* lifted him out of obscurity. The background of it is Morocco and (as befits an Oriental impression) the means are entirely lyrical grafted on to unconventional rhythms. The first movement, *Adagio* (a slow dance), creates the impression of a long wail; the second (also a dance) made the audience sit up by the persistent uneven drum beats (an early example of Holst sounding 'all out of gear', but he wasn't); while the Finale created a bewildering impression. Called 'In the Street of the Ouled Naïls', it is reputed to be built on Arab themes heard by the composer during a visit to Morocco. The most curious feature of this movement is a bar phrase repeated incessantly by solo flute in its lower register. In the previous movement, the repetitive figure was played by tympani. The flute figure with a few chords makes a background on which other tunes appear, redolent of the East in colour and hue. They are combined over a Holstian rhythm producing a rich harmonious effect. Eventually, the initial flute figure emerges from its obscurity and creates a sinister impression by its gradual expansion until it submerges the orchestra. Even after the *dénouement*, the flute figure returns, finally making its exit by way of the tympani. The work bears the impress of tragedy.

Whilst the *Beni Mora* Suite lifted Holst from obscurity, a later work, *The Planets*, written during the last war, carried his name across the seas, with subsequent international fame. In the seven movements Holst's genius flows on in full tide: it is the largest orchestral score for the number of instruments employed, and for once he does not indulge his habit for economy, which can hardly be commended. Bizarre, yet carefully calculated orchestration; big lusty tunes, as in the jovial Jupiter, solid massed formation in the military-like Mars, a slender lyric in the Venus, and in spite of the exhilarating blurring produced by Mercury, he deserved a better theme. Jupiter is the most attractive of the gods: the movements Jupiter and Mars created astonishment at the first performance. It needs to be put on record that, had it not been for the generosity of a contemporary composer, who paid for the cost of rehearsals and performance,[42] *The Planets* would have been shelved, like many other large-scale works by English composers.

Music so frankly outspoken as that of Holst had been accepted as the prerogative of Elgar: but here was another Englishman doing the work quite as well, but differently. The idiom and character of English music is here in full: only an English composer could have depicted Jupiter by such healthy jovial irony. Differently satirical and riotous is Uranus: there are rare qualities and refined delicacy in the impressionism and mysticism in Saturn and Neptune. *The Planets*, a symphonic masterpiece whose virtuoso orchestration sustains its amazing qualities and never sags, is Holst's finest achievement.

Holst spent half his life teaching, the other half being given over to composition. He became a great force by impressing his personality on others and getting the best out of them. A work inspired by his teaching at St. Paul's (Girls) School is the *St. Paul's Suite*, for string orchestra, which will live as long as a string orchestra exists to play it. The first movement, Jig, and the finale, The Dargason, have resemblance in their rhythmical tunes. Big and brawny, and linked in a symphonic mould, they suggest laughter and good cheer. The second movement is a rippling Ostinato, built on four recurring notes; while the third movement, Intermezzo, is a finely balanced scheme of contrasts, after the manner of Brahms's *Hungarian Dances*.

In another style is the *Fugal Concerto*, for solo flute, oboe and strings, which in the first movement is a gesture to Handel. As a harmonist with original views, Holst was delightfully obstinate and uncompromising. An accidental sometimes appears in disputed territory, but there is no yielding. Remove the accidental and the impression of the music is just ordinary. As Holst writes it, the music gives the impression of strength – acid and bitter. The second theme of the *Adagio* is an instance: solo oboe is accompanied by strings: in the third bar a most pungent effect is obtained by the oboe holding E natural resolving to D against violins playing E sharp and G sharp. Similar instances abound in

[42] Balfour Gardiner.

the later Holst. Like his use of odd time measures, he played with them until they took root and became a natural part of his technique. A sparkling, jig-like *Allegro* concludes this all-too-brief *Fugal Concerto*. It sparkles, certainly, but like the sparkles of clean snow on a frosty night.

One would like further to pass in review several works of equal importance to those already mentioned, but the will must be taken for the deed. However, mention must be made of Holst's two operas, *At the Boar's Head* and *The Perfect Fool*. The first is adapted from Shakespeare and is a medley of English traditional tunes, while *The Perfect Fool* increases in excitement until the very last bar.

In his *Egdon Heath* Holst disclosed a new manner of means – where nothing but essentials have a place in the scheme. Another advance in that manner was marked by a group of eleven songs to words by Humbert Wolfe.[43] This type of drawing results in music spinning which has a wide mesh – rather stark and bare, after the exuberance of an earlier Holst. These songs made a deep impression on me at their first performance and deserve to be heard again.

HURLSTONE

Genius in Abeyance

This short article appeared as part of 'On the Other Hand' in the January 1937 *Musical Opinion*, p. 298.

I dare say many readers are tired of suggestions of musical and other geniuses who have died young: the war actually was responsible for the death of so many men of promise that the mention of another name is apt to weary. Passing

---

[43] There are in fact twelve songs in this group – but at the first British performance (5 February 1930, Wigmore Hall, Dorothy Silk accompanied by Kathleen Markwell), which Brian attended, one ('The Thought') was omitted.

all that, I want to speak of a musician of real achievement and greater promise who died in 1906, years before the war, at the age of thirty. His name was William Yeates Hurlstone, and there is something in his music that keeps the episode of his life fresh in the memory of those who knew him personally and with those who have since been made aware of him through his published works. A life so short, broken almost ere it began, has little to tell: but what there is, is well told in a small brochure by Mr. H.G. Newell, issued by J. & W. Chester. He was a precocious child, known to George Grove and Hubert Parry, which probably explains his subsequent entry among the students at the Royal College of Music. But the interesting thing to me now is a perusal of his works, some fifty of which were published, a few being before me as I write.

A mark of Hurlstone's is seen in the way he comes to grips with the larger instrumental forms, though naturally what he wrote varies in quality. At the opening of his Sonata for violin and piano, he has difficulty in getting away from perforced academic entanglements: but once his thoughts are freed, he moves rapidly and sings occasionally with real eloquence. At times, as in the first movement, a strange melody flits across his work, as of something coming on the breeze. The slow movement of this sonata contains a couple of themes that fulfil a good example of the principle of question and answer, though the formula of the opening question is ancient. The last movement is an indifferent pendant. The Sonata in D for 'cello and piano (published three years after the composer's death) is a splendid achievement in four movements: it shows ripe and matured musicianship. Beginning in a determined and forceful style, it seems bent on blazing a trail. The *Adagio lamentoso* is unusual in its sustained eloquence: a high level is maintained: the slow movement and the lovely final Rondo standing out in a rare and attractive work.

Hurlstone grew up in a world when the music of Brahms, Dvořák and Grieg was fresh in our ears. Like his masters, he did not escape influences, though in the instrumental works the buoyant spirit of the composer is never submerged. The dramatic cantata, *Alfred the Great*, obviously influenced by Stanford and Coleridge-Taylor, contains much finely spirited writing. It is the kind of short choral work that might agreeably be included in any miscellaneous choral and orchestral concert. In an album of four songs, Hurlstone is seen to have selected lyrics by Burns, Beddoes, and 'traditional'. The settings are fastidiously sensitive to verbal values; and though his setting of Burns's *Wilt thou be my dearie* is not the most ambitious of the four, it is easily the most distinguished by its modest expressive charm.

The pity is that conductors and other programme-makers are rarely true seekers after that which is good: they take what is easily at hand or what is forced on their attention by personal influence or has been already heard and applauded, with the result that much of what is good remains in abeyance.

SCOTT

The Art of Cyril Scott

This, one of Brian's biggest articles, appeared in three parts in successive numbers of *Musical Opinion* for 1923 (April, pp. 656–657; May, pp. 756–758; June, pp. 853–854). It was the first of a short series which continued with 'The Art of Eugene Goossens' and concluded with the enormous 'The Art of Frederick Delius'. Curiously, Brian does not otherwise seem to have written about Scott apart from the standard short concert and score reviews, and a somewhat sceptical notice of Scott's book *Music: its Secret Influence through the Ages*, contributed to the April–May 1938 issue of *Modern Mystic*.

I.

Cyril Scott is one of the most singular of to-day's contemporary musicians. He doesn't look like anyone else, and a great deal of his music is of that finished quality which one associates with the work of Benvenuto Cellini or John Keats.

If you take his Pianoforte Sonata or the String Quartet you find that the music is singularly free and outspoken, utterly unlike any other contemporary music. It resembles Cellini and Keats by the brightness of its poetical soul, by the joyousness which seems to have inspired its creation – one feels that such music was created by a rare driving impulse, and it passes along radiantly clad and fastidiously elegant.

I do not wish to imply by this that Scott is a kid-gloved writer: he is a finely endowed genius and eminently too sane for trick flying or stunts. One can usually sum up persons very soon after meeting them – it may be rapidity, eloquence or slowness of the wit, movement of arm or hand, the expression of the eyes or the shape of nose or mouth. There is usually something which communicates itself to the discerning observer, and very often this is a correct impression, ineffaceable by years of later experience.

So this music of Scott cries for a higher valuation by reason of its fine originality, its wonderful eloquence, and the masterly ease by which it moves along in a novel and original manner. Scott is a colour artist as well as a pattern weaver. Music is to him an art of sound which he may command to do his will and serve his purpose, not an art of sight. In the Piano Sonata[44] – which is unlike any other piano sonata – bar lines seem superfluous where the rhythm is so involved and flexible. Such art as this would only seem possible in the art of extemporisation. Yet it is far more than this. Though in performance it may give the impression of a vast panorama of rare harmonic colours suffusing and dissolving strangely, it is finely controlled. It is really a four movement sonata, which moves along without a break and culminates in a merry fugue in the finale.

A strange figure raises its head soon after the commencement of the Sonata and persists throughout the work, the endless, novel transformations it undergoes suggesting that its possibilities are well nigh inexhaustible. In one of the chapters of his book on *Philosophy of Modernism*, Scott hits out at his friend Grainger for abusing his own strength, and

<hr>

[44] This is Scott's Piano Sonata No. 1, in C major, Op. 66, of 1909.

one had doubts whether he himself disliked the strong man in music, or shied at it. Though Scott may never have been convicted for throwing stones or breaking windows, it is surprising what tremendous strength he can put out when he feels so inclined. In the finale of the Sonata, just at the point where the senses cry out for something to clinch the whole by a big climax, the figure mentioned which unites the whole Sonata so strangely reappears with rare wonder and surprise, finishing in rare strength and completeness on a final page of full-throated music. There is a mixture of strength and elegance in the Quartet, whilst there is also the masterly grip over fashioning and jewelling the materials as in the Sonata. We have strength naked and unadorned in the *Handel Rhapsody*, and a curious, piquant bell-like procession in the *Rondo*.

Many of the piano pieces and songs have a fascinating open air manner: they are as transparent as the dancing wisps of the silver birch or delicate streamers of the willow in spring sunlight. Yet Scott is not all spring and summer. Though he can 'wear' the light conceit of the child, as his charming child-music proves, he can just as wonderfully depict the tragedy of winter. There are rare moments of this in the Piano Sonata and Quartet, and in the songs *Nocturne* and *Requiem*. Probably I appreciate his song, *The Sands of Dee*, more than any other, because of the wonderfully simple manner in which he has limned and fixed the tragedy of the drowned girl and the haunting apparition which still cries over her grave beside the sea.[45]

II.

A friend of mine who has an extraordinary intuitive sense for the fresh in music, has a novel way of expressing himself. He refers to the moments when Beethoven and others are 'carried away' as madness. When listening to the first movement of the Beethoven No. 9, he will say: 'Yes, I *do* feel better for listening to that; I *do* enjoy Beethoven when he's mad!' The same applies to Wagner, Tchaïkovsky, Brahms,

---

[45] This anonymous text was one that Brian himself had set as a partsong for male voices in 1914 – but his setting is lost.

Strauss, Berlioz and Bach. It is this 'madness' which makes all the difference between the work of a genius and of one of a lower order. No composer who ever lived ever wrote a work of great length which was all madness. By madness I mean that extraordinary psychological sense when the brain glows at white heat. No composer was ever sustained at this temperature: he only gets periods or patches of it. Wagner has had more glowings of this kind possibly than any composer since Beethoven. There is a curious instance of it in the development of the Berlioz *Hungarian* March, in the same composer's 'March to the Scaffold' in the *Fantastique* Symphony. We find it in many of the Tchaïkovsky symphonies and his *Francesca da Rimini*; the Strauss *Don Juan, Tod und Verklärung, Heldenleben, Salome, Der Rosenkavalier*; Elgar's *King Olaf* and *Gerontius*; Bantock's *Omar*; Brahms's Third and Fourth Symphonies, *St. Anthony* Variations, *German Requiem*; Bach's 'Come ye, daughters' (from the *St. Matthew Passion*), &c. From this glowing we are transfixed into a trance of spiritual exaltation. Not all composers have this power: it only appears at rare intervals. We often have instances where a composer is endowed with the most wonderful technique and can write the most finished works; but they are meaningless, because the divine fire or glow is absent. No power on earth can put it there if it was not present at birth; not all the combined efforts of money, publishers and newspapers can put this glow into a composition if its creator failed to do it; and if it is there, not all the combinations can take it away.

Hugo Wolf measured every composer by one standard: 'Can he exult?' If the composer had not this spiritual exaltation, then Wolf had no use for him. Cyril Scott is one of the few amongst us who have this glow.

Most of the works mentioned earlier in this article are published by Elkin & Co. There is a fine Piano Concerto, published by Schott, where, in the first movement, there is a fine exaltation. I was quite carried away by this when I heard Beecham conduct it at a concert in 1915, with Scott at the piano.[46]

---

[46] This was the world premiere, at a concert of a British Music Festival

Scott has a new opera down for performance at Wiesbaden and also a ballet, entitled respectively *The Alchemist* and *The Incomplete Apothecary*.[47] Scott has also published some fine volumes of poetry; and this may in a measure explain a great deal of the elegant finesse which characterises much of his art, and the strong vein of romantic poetry which envelopes all his music.

III.

In these days of 'extra specials', boosting and trying to smash up the welkin, there are, here and there, minds of the monastic type, whose very breath seems to hang on shyness, exclusion or seclusion. Just as a few thrive with bangs on the big drum and raucous shouting of the decoy dressed in motley, so other shy spirits may be found hidden in the shadows tucked away like the violet and the lesser celandine.

As we have minds of the quietest monastic type, so we also have variants in these. We have music which seems to rise from an old cloistered English garden: the garden of the drooping laburnum, where mingle the perfumes of the lilac, lily of the valley, gillyflower, ladysmocks and nightstock; where the poppy dances and the hollyhock reigns. There is another music, of an exotic type, whose soul seems to rise from amidst eastern cloisters, wherein lie the heavy perfume of the waxlike tuber-rose, the stephanotis, the heliotrope; where the tiger-spotted gloxinia exposes its delicate throat amidst the dazzling foliage of the caladiums and the fantastic cactus, where the lotus-flower reigns. Music of this hothouse type, the *spirituel* of languor, has been given to us in most wonderful moments by Frederick Delius. Commencing with the nocturne, *Paris*, through a long series of works on a lavish scale, Delius has given us some of the most highly spiritualised music of the century in this rare exotic type – where the mind seems to sway as in a censer glowing amidst perfumes and strange colours. Working on a similar scale as Delius, though quite as

---

organised by Beecham. Scott later wrote a Piano Concerto No. 2.
[47] *The Alchemist* was not in fact produced until 1928.

original and individual, is Cyril Scott.

In the long series of works by Cyril Scott, there are moments of rare beauty, whilst originality and individuality are to be found in most of them. Scott's originality shows itself in his unique harmonic equipment and strikingly original sense of rhythm and metre. As a writer for the piano, Scott is a poet. He thinks in terms of the piano, and in playing it one does not feel confounded in his music that, like so much modern piano music, it was conceived orchestrally. Only occasionally does he convey the slightest sense of the comic, as in the 'Snake Charmer' and 'Dance of the Elephants' from the *Jungle Book*, where the elephants seem to dance in galoshes. Scott's mind works easiest and best when pivoted on some poetical impression either of the fanciful or fantasy.

In his book of *Poems* for the piano (Schott) there are five numbers, each prefaced by a poem of delicacy written by the composer. The first number mirrors the exotic charm of the poppy; the following number gives the silent understanding of soul-sympathy. The third is a graphic description of 'Bells'. The fourth, 'The Twilight of the Year', is a fine study in low lights and sadness, having a most haunting close. No. 5, 'Paradise Birds', is a delicate, luminous fantasy, prefaced by a poem in which a strange thought threads its way through the verse:

> Awake is twilight time, – a pale eternal
>   Twilight speaks imperishable words;
> Within the blossomy bosom lost of groves supernal,
>   I hark the singing of the Paradise birds.
>
> Their songs awaking every pent-up river,
>   Unrolling every mighty wave of thought;
> Across the resounding lyre of the spirit quiver,
>   To render deathless every thrill they wrought.

Space does not allow the six verses to appear in this article. Whilst a personal thought threads its way through every poem, a corresponding thread works its way through the music by subtle variation or metamorphosis of the thematic material, giving a sense of unity to the five poems in the book.

Carillon (Schott) is a bell poem for piano, in which chimes and the turmoil and loud clanging of large bells is effectively portrayed. In a Suite for Piano, *Old China* (Schott), in four movements, there is an attempt to depict the ancient 'Willow Pattern'. As a piece of pleasing music it is successful, though it is a dubious willow pattern. *Egypt*, five impressions for piano (Schott) has a very haunting 'Egyptian Boat Song' (Ex.25); and in the 'Funeral March of the Great Rameses' Scott had a fine inspiration of the passing out of ancient pomp and glory.

Ex.25

There are three dances in *A Pageant* for piano (Schott), in which a 'Sentimental Waltz' moves in dreamy languour. An 'Exotic Dance' is made so by its provoking whimsicality and strange harmonic piquancy. The most effective of three pieces in *Miniatures* (Schott) is a strange little thing called 'A Ballad told at Candle Light'. It gets very near to the heart of those wonderful, far away little northern pieces of which Edvard Grieg held the secret. Whilst Scott paints wonderfully in miniature he seems happiest when he can let himself go in extended forms, which allow ample opportunity for design and building. A *Danse Orientale* (Schott), inscribed to Maude Roosevelt, is bigger than any of the foregoing pieces, yet the interest never flags and the composer gets into the middle of the sickly sentimentality, suggested by music which moves freely and easily, in which an overpowering sense of fatality is conveyed (Ex. 26). A similar sense of fatality and oppression is given in a *Danse Languoreuse* (Schott), in which a slight theme is made to carry the whole dance by deft cunning and passing it

through an endless procession of ever changing lights
(Ex. 27).

Ex. 26

Ex. 27

As a study in colour, the *Rainbow Trout* (Schott) must rank
as one of the most brilliant pieces written for the piano in
the past twenty years. It is more than a colour scheme; it
is full of strange, haunting beauty and poetry. Though
lengthy for work of this exotic type, its conception is finely
sustained, and there is a feeling at the close that the whole
was forged in a single piece. The composer saw it whole.

I have seen salmon taking ten feet leaps during the
spawning season, and I have seen carp rolling and lazing
which were too idle to move even when a pebble was dropped near the nose, but I have never seen a trout which
suggested fine music. I always felt they would be nicer on

the grill. This trout of Scott's belongs neither to the Trent, Dove, Wye or Derwent. It is a wondrous creature which seems to have haunted him in his dreams. Like many of Scott's finest pieces, the construction is slight; it is the way it is carried out and what he says that matters. This is done by a couple of ideas (Ex. 28).

Ex. 28

IV.

In all the foregoing music for the piano, one cannot but admire Scott's diversity of pattern in rhythm and metre. There is an impression that it is a perfectly natural thing for Scott to work in rhythms, which, as bar lines have not yet been abolished, need ever changing time signatures. Some minds work best and easiest like a recurring decimal in the 'See me Dance the Polka' or 'I have a song to sing, O!' type. Scott's mind works easiest when he is evolving a pattern of a different type: when the idea, intertwining and threading its way, moves in a sustained piece of eloquent blank verse rather than in obvious rhyme. Although his piano music has endless charm, his music for violin and piano is also distinguished by continuous eloquence and delicacy.

Scott's arrangements of the old airs, 'Cherry Ripe' and 'The Gentle Maiden', are as near perfect as these things can be, in retaining the old charm in a modern setting. As illustrating the delightful ease with which ever changing rhythm moves hand in glove with real feeling and clear part writing, his two *Preludes* for violin and piano (Schott) – No. 1, 'Poème Erotique' and No. 2, 'Danse', deserve attention.

The *Tallahassee Suite* (Schott) portrays what the negroes very touchingly call *spiritual* or 'soul food'. In the first movement, 'Begone memories', there is an expressive, highly-wrought piece of sad, slow music. The second movement, 'After Sundown', lifts away from the sadness of the preceding. And the third, 'Air and Negro Dance', has that alternate gaiety and sadness of negro music, wherein the atmosphere of the first movement of *From the New World* (Dvořák) and *Appalachia* (Delius) seem to commingle. *Romance* (Schott) should have the attention of all fiddle artists who appreciate sentimental melody splendidly carried along amidst passion and yearning.

Elegie remains one of Scott's highest flights. This movement gains in weight and grace in its development, and is held together with the skill of a master symphonist. The loveliness of the opening persists at the close, sealed in an atmosphere of purity and love.

It should be remembered that most, if not all, of this music was written in 1910–1918.

Apart from the very fine exposition of the art of Cyril Scott by Dr. Eaglefield Hull, Scott has been too much neglected by our musical writers and critics. Surely a prophet can be found for him amongst them. The music is published and ready. If only critics would discover him and keep talking about him in the same way they continue week by week to talk of the everlasting dead.

Many composers have been fortunate in securing a champion who has been a faithful henchman: Brahms (Steinbach); Strauss (Mengelberg); Berlioz (Weingartner); Strauss, Elgar, Tchaïkovsky (Wood); Wagner (Richter);

Delius (Beecham); Elgar and Tchaïkovsky (Ronald); Stravinsky and many other moderns (Goossens); and it would be ungracious to pass over the generous attention which Wood has given to the modern English group at his Promenades, or the generous sympathy Coates has given the works of Holst, Vaughan Williams and others in London and America, or the wide sympathies of Godfrey. Still, it needed Mendelssohn to talk of Schumann, and Schumann to talk of Brahms.

There surely cannot be any musician or critic alive in England worth his salt who can look over this music of Scott, or listen to it, without a jaundiced mind, and not feel that we have music of genius which is an honour to contemporary art and particularly so to British art, and which is too much neglected.

V.

Like the Piano Sonata (Elkin), Scott's latest publications are cast in large moulds. His Piano Concerto is distinguished by its vitality and imaginative qualities. This was revealed to us in a fine performance at Queen's Hall under Sir Thomas Beecham, with the composer at the piano. It does not lie within the ken of any man to say why such a work should be neglected in this country. Schott's have shown enterprise in publishing it. Pianists must be as conservative in their choice of concertos as are some conductors in their choice of orchestral music. For within the past twenty years only two concertos have been added to the limited *répertoire*: the Rachmaninoff (No. 2) and the Delius.

Scott's concerto opens in heroic fashion with a long reiterated E in the orchestra, while the piano pounds away with great chunks of common chords. This is unusual with Scott, as he mostly exploits the chords of the ninth, eleventh, and thirteenth, when he chooses to adopt the vertical style. For a few bars the piano plays solo with an anticipation of the first subject. The introduction is resumed in a long passage of splendour for piano and orchestra, after which the first subject appears in the orchestra. It is of a bubbly, restless quality, and at first it gives the impression of passage work. This impression is removed by the transformations it undergoes melodically, and afterwards when playing the part of servitor to the orchestra. The second subject has a different distinction from the first, by reason of its quiet, almost tearful, tenderness. This is accentuated when taken over from the orchestra by the piano, and later when the orchestra resumes, and the piano plays around it with arpeggi. A long passage for solo piano leads to an anticipation of the recapitulation. A poetical inspiration is the re-entry of the second subject. It appears stripped of its original tearful quality and is pounded out triumphantly alternately in piano and orchestra, accompanied with the first subject, eventually passing to a fine close, where the heroic introduction re-appears and has the last word.

The second movement, *Adagio*, has a long introduction in the string basses, over which the piano descends with fanciful arpeggi. The tempo changes, and a slight theme is heard in the flutes. It is of exquisite simplicity, very short, under which chords of the ninth undulate. This short theme is made to carry the weight of the whole movement. All Scott's resources are exploited. It is like Percy Honri with his disappearing tricks: the carnation disappears and turns up as a silk hat, then disappears again and re-appears as a canary. Eleven times this frail theme appears, each time disguised and cloaked: its final disappearance interrupted by a return of the fanciful opening. The last movement leads off with one bar of $\frac{3}{4}$, then continues in $\frac{2}{4}$ by an incisive clearcut theme on solo piano. This statement is immediately repeated by orchestra and piano. A lengthy development follows, amidst an endless striving for a point where ecstasy and spirituality mingle. A shortened recapitulation follows in the orchestra, which leads to the Cadenza. In his cadenza Scott draws upon the thematic material from all the movements and, having unified these, he heads for a spirited coda based upon the first theme of the Finale.

It has been remarked that Scott writes in a language all his own. He strives for the elimination of the obvious in rhyme and metre, brought about by the use of bar lines, and would substitute free rhythm of the ancient plainsong. In ancient days this was safe enough whilst it was confined to unison singing. To rehabilitate that freedom which existed in those far-off days, Scott would infuse modern music.

VI.

Hitherto, in Scott's music, I have not felt the actual influence of ancient plainchant. In his Trio for piano, violin and 'cello we seem to move about amongst cloisters in an age far removed from this. We are plunged into it at the commencement where violin and 'cello move with a priest-like incantation in elevenths, over a soft murmuring in the piano. We move in shadows and meet strange faces. Sometimes there is a flash of sunlight across the vague shadowland. In the second movement, we appear to have reached a ceremony of grandeur, ushered in by a long drawn chant on the strings. This is but a preface to a scene of wild riot and colour which follows, in which the piano pounds away with a chant of a very fierce character. In the third movement we return to the vague shadowland of the first. Vague it certainly is, but of that eerie wonderful sense which defies analysis, where the mind seems to hang suspended in a world of calm and ease. Some minds would appreciate the work closing at this point, allowing the deep reverie to continue. It is the composer's design that the work shall close otherwise. In the Finale — *Rondo giocoso* — we appear to pass into the open. Chanting is again heard, but it is a fuller throated chanting — of the open air and sunlight!

One of Scott's most delicate paintings is the *Aubade* for large orchestra. Like all his designs the workmanship is close and concentrated. From a mystical opening he moves slowly by degrees to a point of rapture and then quietly dies away. An exquisite design. It is inscribed to that fine artist, Sir Landon Ronald. I wonder how many times he has performed it. I have never understood why this conductor has never had greater opportunities of performing modern British music. It is not so long ago since one of the northern critics hailed him as our ideal Beethoven interpreter. Recently I heard a performance of the Tchaïkovsky *Pathetic* Symphony and other fine things, all conducted from memory by him and played by an orchestra which had not hitherto played the works. Even so, for sheer brilliance and excitement it reminded one of that exciting night –

seventeen years ago – when Nikisch descended into the Free Trade Hall, Manchester, with the L.S.O.[48] True, there were occasional rough edges in the recent Ronald concerts, but the art of the conductor was there as perfect as anyone would wish. Why cannot we exploit this finished art amongst native work?

Both the Trio, for piano, violin, 'cello, and *Aubade* are published by Schott. The *Second Suite* for piano (Schott) consist of five movements of Gothic proportions. The first movement (Prelude) is inscribed to Claude Debussy and is of that quiet strange shifting tonality so characteristic of Debussy's own work. No. 2 (Air Varied) is a long sustained effort in four continuous movements of exotic and romantic charm. No. 3 is a solemn dance with a strange haunting quality all its own. It passes along with distinguished grace and big sweep, with several dramatic surprises. No. 4 (Caprice) contains many surprises in rhythm and metre. No. 5 (Introduction and Fugue) forms the crowning ceremonial to a big effort. The Introduction, or Prelude, contains all that noble intense quality we remember in some of the preludes in the Bach Forty-eight. Moreover, Scott's is bigger than any of these – yet it has the spirituality of the famous E♭ minor Prelude of Bach.[49] The Fugue is an inspiration which flows along, going from strength to strength. Finally it breaks upon a big climax where part of the prelude returns as coda, rounding off the movement with a sense of completeness and unity.

The whole suite is of great stature and, unlike much of Scott's piano music, we feel the orchestra vibrating through it all.

Nativity Hymn (Carnegie Trust) is a setting of a poem by Richard Crashaw, the young contemporary of John Milton and Andrew Marvell, for soli, chorus and orchestra. Crashaw died at the age of thirty-seven, in the same year that Charles the First lost his head. Any work upon the

---

[48] In December 1905, when he included the *Pathétique* in the pro gramme. Brian reviewed this concert in the 18 January 1906 issue of *The Musical World*.

[49] From Book I of the '48'.

Nativity must challenge comparison with those other works upon the same subject by Bach, Berlioz, and Philipp Wolfrum. Here we do not meet the quaint conceits of Berlioz with the 'Adoration of the Magi' and the 'Flight into Egypt' of Joseph and Mary, or the extraordinary 'Stille auf dem Erde', sung to the sleeping Christ by the Virgin in Wolfrum's *Ein Weinachtsmysterium.*[50]

Scott's work differs from all these other settings. His work moves continuously without break: sometimes the chorus carries on the drama alone or it is taken over by solo voices. There is a wonderfully sustained piece of writing which carries to the end of the drama commencing:

> We saw thee in thy balmy nest
> Bright dawn of the eternal day,
> We saw thine eyes break from the East
> And chase the trembling shades away.

and moves along in a fine spirit of exaltation to a thrilling climax in a chorale. Scott felt this work: it is as much of him as *Gerontius* and *The Apostles* are of Elgar. The work ought to become a feature in those Festivals where music is cherished for its own sake and not the man who writes it or the influence behind it.

EPILOGUE

In passing through the art of Cyril Scott, I have experienced the greatest pleasure and delight. He is such a great artist of fine healthy ideals and earnest striving that one feels it impossible to argue with him. I do not mean there are no spots on the sun. Every composer is, and must be, a law unto himself. If he achieves what he sets out to accomplish it is not for critic or contemporary to deny him his prize. If he starts for Kensington and arrives at Kew he has missed his way. Scott always arrives at his intended destination and his journeys on the way are filled with fine surprises and imagination. If Berlioz were alive to-day he would write like Scott. To those whose minds are fixed in a groove and who think that any one composer said the right

[50] For Wolfrum see note 3 on p.74.

thing, he will appeal in vain. To those who believe that
music is and must be as democratic as the art of writing
Scott will make an instant appeal. In his outlook he is one
of the finest democrats amongst us and holds the highest
ideals. It is not in his most dazzling displays of counterpoint
that we love Bach most. When Berlioz attempts the grand
contrapuntist he goes all to pieces. Many of us have found
all we wanted in the only Symphony of César Franck which
we did not find in the whole nine of Beethoven. We have
moved a great deal since the contemporaries of Mozart
threw his corpse into a ditch and the Beethoven *clique*
hammered Schubert to his knees.[51] If ever we reach the
new millenium of equal chances which the new democracy
is supposed to bring, then this glorious music of Scott will
not appeal in vain.

SORABJI

Opus Clavicembalisticum

Sorabji was a noted polemicist in the musical press of the
inter-war period, and his music had fanatical admirers as
well as some fairly vitriolic detractors. Brian mentioned him
quite frequently, and reviewed his book of essays, *Around
Music*. For his part Sorabji (so Cranz & Co. informed Brian)
spent several afternoons looking at the score of Brian's *Gothic*
Symphony in their showroom after it was published – but
didn't buy it. This note of Sorabji's most notorious work
comes from the 'On the Other Hand' column in *Musical
Opinion*, June 1932, pp. 747–748.

Though it might not accord with the wishes of those poetas-
ters who came in with broadcasting to tell us about the
past, present and future of music, I sometimes feel that all

---

[51] This rather highly-coloured account derives from Brian's harmony
coach, Theophilus Hemming; he had it from his teacher, Moscheles –
who, though a friend of Beethoven, was of the opinion that Schubert had
been deliberately kept down by the jealousy of Beethoven's partisans.

that is necessary to say could be scratched on a sixpence. In the matter of the future of music, for example, it is that a number of composers are convinced that modern music, as it began in Florence in 1600, is now over-ripe and is fast falling into decay. The pioneers are few: for none but the potentially great can write in an idiom other than that of his day and hour: but the mediocre many cast stones at the few, just as they did at Monteverdi, and in the same way as they do now at Schönberg, Stravinsky, Béla Bartók, Malipiero: no one of them shall escape. Busoni also strove for recognition [...].

And now comes Kaikhosru Sorabji, the son of a Parsee father and a Spanish mother, and born in Essex. I am no seer, and do not say that here is the music of the future; but I would like to speak of his *Opus Clavicembalisticum*, not as a Sabbatarian Olympus, but as one who certainly is no musical Sadducee: I concede the possibility of a rebirth of music.

No paper analysis could convey the slightest clue to this extraordinary work for the piano: it is contained in 252 oblong pages, the music written on three staves[52] and without key signature. The composer cautions us that 'accidentals hold good only for notes in front of which they stand with the exception of repeated notes and tied notes'. To me this *Opus Clavicembalisticum* comes as an adventure in fugue making, and music-making of this order should always be a hazard. The shape of the fugue-subjects here before me are those of Bach, figuratively only, but the treatment of the answers is that of Sorabji: and in it I find much that is new. When the answer is neither strict nor tonal, the 'cautions' made by all previous generations are swept aside, which results in an amazing work.

Sorabji would seem to have studied Busoni to some purpose: but neither that master nor any other appears to influence this work, except that they both use the same

---

[52] It frequently expands to four, and in the concluding Fugue to five, but Brian's description is essentially correct. It might be remarked that his own Double Fugue in E flat of 1924 is written on four staves almost throughout, in order to clarify the part-writing.

language, as do Pater and the police-court reporter. I con
sider Sorabji to have miraculous gifts; and Busoni himsel
did not fail to speak well of him after he had played hi
first Piano Sonata.

Things which confuse and torture most men when seek
ing expression are all so easy to Sorabji: as was said o
William Blake and his Prophetic Books, he is the medium
through which angels in spheres far away speak to men
This suggestion came first from Philip Heseltine year
ago when writing of Sorabji in Dent's *Modern Musical His
tory.*[53]

This *Opus Clavicembalisticum* is a phenomenon, quite a
much as *Tristan* ever was: and musicians will appreciate it
composer's uncanny cleverness when they learn that h
writes out his enormous piano works and orchestral work
direct into full score, and with never an emendation. I
not the time with us when we should hear Mr. Sorabji pla
this work?[54] Could not the Musical Association justify itsel
by making such things possible? I offer my congratulation
to the publishers, Messrs. Curwen, and also to all whos
work is included. The engraving is superb.

---

[53] *Sic.* The reference is to Heseltine's article in the *Dictionary of Moderr
Music and Musicians*, ed. A. Eaglefield Hull (J.M. Dent & Sons, London
1924).

[54] Sorabji had already given the world premiere, in Glasgow, on 1
December 1930. No further complete performance took place unti
11 June 1982, when Geoffrey Douglas Madge played the work in
Utrecht – a performance which is available now on record (Keytone
Records RCS 4–800). At the time of writing there has still not been a com
plete performance in London.

VAUGHAN WILLIAMS

Vaughan Williams in Rehearsal

Brian knew Vaughan Williams slightly throughout most of
his career, and often reviewed his music. The following vig-
nette comes from 'On the Other Hand' in *Musical Opinion*,
January 1935, p. 302.

With considerable curiosity, and with much regard for the
composer, I went to the rehearsal of Vaughan Williams's
Suite for viola and orchestra.[55] Time passes: but it seems
only a little while since I saw Vaughan Williams and Holst at
a Philharmonic rehearsal eagerly discussing the work
under direction. Of all English composers, Vaughan
Williams is the most English of them all: he loves the
countryside and the county town, which goes with families
who have a foothold deep in the soil. For this reason we
shall never see him exercising the ritual of popularity, and
I am sure that a proposal to found a Vaughan Williams Society would send him abroad to an unstated destination, leaving all the specially stamped gramophone records
unsigned.[56] Outside the Elgar symphonies, Vaughan
Williams's *London Symphony* is the most popular in the
English repertoire. This is his one supreme effort to depict
the atmosphere of a city inside the framework of a symphony. His *Pastoral Symphony* is not so popular, probably
because it is less robust and suggests that quality of shyness
which eludes the obvious. The Piano Concerto is a large-
scale work of enormous power: the first movement surpas-
ses even the symphonies in fervid contrapuntal writing.

The *Suite* for viola and orchestra is a bunch of finely
worked miniature dances. The rehearsal took place with the
composer seated comfortably in the balcony, smoking his

---

[55] Vaughan Williams' *Suite* was premiered at Queen's Hall on 12
November 1934 by Lionel Tertis and the London Philharmonic
Orchestra, conducted by Malcolm Sargent. Brian reviewed the concert
itself in the December 1934 *Musical Opinion* (p. 234).
[56] A reference to the recently established Elgar and Sibelius Societies.

pipe. A certain dryness distinguished the directions to the conductor: 'That is a little on the fast side', 'I would like that played much softer', 'Don't make too much of the crescendos', and 'You might try that without the viola'. If English character and English thinking are what the public wants, then Vaughan Williams supplies the need, and the reward should be more performances of his works and honours still to come. One outstanding virtue attaching to this very English composer is his kind regard for his contemporaries in the art; and another is his desire to foster musical life in our villages. I have heard of his conducting festivals with village choirs and bringing off successfully performances of Bach's *St. Matthew Passion*. A few months ago I listened to a broadcast of village choirs singing Elgar's *Dream of Gerontius*, with Vaughan Williams conducting, and I am glad of this opportunity of saying that the chorus singing was as good as any I have heard.

The Music of Ralph Vaughan Williams

This appeared in 1940 in two parts in successive issues of *Musical Opinion* — May, pp. 345-346 and June, p. 391. Like the Holst essay printed earlier, it may originally have been intended for the series on contemporary composers in *Tomorrow*.

Ralph Vaughan Williams's first important choral work – a setting of Walt Whitman's poem, *Toward the Unknown Region*, for chorus and orchestra – was prophetic. Conceived in a fearless, masculine style, this early work was distinguished by a modern type of continuity in opposition to the old style of half-way rests and full stops. Since that effort Vaughan Williams has never ceased to develop: he is still growing and fighting for English expression. A tender melancholy is inseparable from the music of this composer, who more than any of his contemporaries expresses the subtleties of English character and the burden of rusticity. His preference for a certain thematic formula is striking: used at fast or slow tempo, its upward movement is from dominant to tonic, supertonic, dominant, octave and their inversion. Played slowly, these note-groups suggest the world of bells. In handling folk songs he takes no risk of applying modern harmony to modal tunes. His preference for the flat seventh suggests that in his music the subdominant is the centre of gravity. Similarly he shows a penchant for the Pentatonic scale. His sensitive chord spacing produces a sensuous orchestral colour, infused by special regard for freedom of the basses. In string *divisi*, habitual with Vaughan Williams, the bass melodies have equality with those of violins: and when doubled by woodwind and brass, the effect is new, rich and organ-like, fascinating in its quiet moments.

Apart from odd passages descriptive of Satan in *Job*, and the Scherzo of the F minor Symphony, his orchestral writing is devoid of tricks. The tendency in the later works is to become more and more complex. His reaction to secular and religious subjects is surprising in the facility with which he handles both. There are fewer more exciting moments in Elgar or Verdi than the fight scene in the opera, *Hugh the Drover*, or the search for Sir John Falstaff in Ford's house in his comic opera, *Sir John in Love*. These are extraordinary exhibitions of a mind from which came the G minor Mass and the short oratorio, *Sancta Civitas*: they might have been written in the solitude of the cloisters. Such remarkable contrasts offer no solution to the curious. Vaughan Williams succeeds as an impressionist by his subtle facility of suggestion.

The *London Symphony* effectively discloses the idealism of a countryman contemplating the city. Hints of what passes through his mind are suggested by the orchestra, and the process has continuity. The references to the three previous movements inside the development of the fourth movement is a masterly piece of musicianship and psychological construction.

It would be impossible to find two works more unlike in the contemplation of a similar subject than the *Sea Symphony* by Vaughan Williams and *La Mer* by Debussy. The French composer's work is a great masterpiece in orchestral impressionism. Vaughan Williams's conception expands and

reaches a vast sublimity by the aid of exultant choral writ
ing: the few entries by the organ give the orchestral colour
ing an overpowering effect. The inspiring force in the
English work is the virile and tender verse of the American
poet, Walt Whitman. The *Pastoral Symphony*, published in
1924, is a continuous, deeply absorbing contemplation, the
expression of countryside sounds and silences, otherwise
the burden of rusticity. Occasionally there is a sudden flare
as though dry brushwood had been thrown on to an expir
ing flame, lighting up the countryside. Then it expires and
we are again amongst the silent night shadows and the stars.
This symphony is no meditation in a fairy glen: its tragic
note may express regret at the gradual passing of the coun
tryside under the advancing conquest of industrialism. The
light-winged scherzo, delightful in its charming whimsical
ity, remains inside the picture. The last movement, an origi
nal stroke of genius, is a most striking symphonic finale. It
opens with a wordless solo for soprano voice, unaccom
panied, heard off – an expressive barless melody that rises
and falls modal wise and is suggestive of the innocent village
maiden. The same melody becomes the basis of the finale
is subjected to an inexhaustible variety of moods, and yet
never loses its original character even when almost sub
merged by multitudinous contrapuntal lines. Unlike Beet
hoven's maiden, there is no thunderstorm to disturb the
serenity of the English maiden: she brings the symphony to
a close plaintively, singing in the distance, as in the opening.

From the period of the *London Symphony*, the music of
Vaughan Williams tends to become more grave and
accumulates increasing power. Tragedy, rarely absent from
his major works, is not of the tragic type presented by
Brahms in his *Tragic Overture*. With Vaughan Williams, it is
elemental and Shakespearean. Neither must we look for
'form', born of preconceived notions. It is impossible to
compare his Symphony in F minor with Symphonies in F by
Beethoven and Brahms, though he has many affinities with
Brahms and fewer with Beethoven. No composer of genius
writes 'form': he composes music, showing his mastery of
'form' by his own inborn instinct for balance of design and
original invention. There are no resemblances between the

Symphonies in F of Beethoven and Brahms, yet each composer creates an impression of completeness and finality
by force of originality and a palpably balanced design.
Vaughan Williams's Symphony in F minor resembles
neither, but it is no less masterly in construction. The
English work is of Shakespearean mould, for the opening
might well be the personification of King Lear, the eternal epitome of tragedy. A Lear storming and raving: a
Beethoven on his death bed, shaking his fists and challeng-
ing death. The symphony has a lugubrious opening, and its
reappearances are marked by increasing gravity. Displays
of cross rhythms indicate that the composer, like Brahms,
realises that cross rhythm is an effective solder and can
intensify the vitality of music. The second movement, in the
same key, varies the tragic muse, now epitomised in an ever-
expanding and broadening processional. The third movement has remarkable impetuosity. The opening scherzo
theme rises by leaps of fourths from the low basses to a
dancing $\frac{6}{8}$ rhythm, suddenly broken off and tantalisingly
syncopated in the basses under the curious wriggling growl
of low wind and strings. This feature of a free gallop hindered by obstruction persists to the end of the scherzo. A
Beethoven scherzo would not have contained obstructions.
The initial theme used as a fugue subject is treated with
magnificent effect, resolving amidst the growling and
scarifying rattle.

Can a succession of any two chords betray an adventure?
The very opening of the *Finale con Epilogo Fugato* suggests
Vaughan Williams seated at the organ console, the registers
arranged for the opening of Mendelssohn's Organ Sonata
No. 1 in F minor – a visionary idea dispelled as soon as the
movement gets going and we overtake Vaughan Williams
and his gravitonal gravities.[57] This music is desperately

---

[57] This is not a comparison I have seen made elsewhere, although the
rhythm and contour of Mendelssohn's opening idea, and its emphatic
chordal presentation, do seem faintly to pre-echo Vaughan Williams'
opening theme. It has sometimes been observed that although VW
would frequently admit to 'simple kleptomania', his real borrowings
often remained unacknowledged. For 'gravitonal', read 'semitonal'?

serious: it increases in ponderability like the slow pressure
of a steam-roller: its dramatic tension ebbing and flowing
may suggest conflict or remorse by continuous battering:
nevertheless, it is there, and those who felt that Brahms had
carried this type of tension to its limits in his C minor and F
major Symphonies will find also in this music of Vaughan
Williams tremendous tragic intensity. Although the music
recalls Brahms in its tender contrasts, the final fugal peroration on an anagram subject of four notes recalls the name of
Bach or the juxtaposition of the initials of two well-known
musicians.[58]

*   *   *

My impression at the close of the first performance of the
Concerto for piano and orchestra was that of having out-
lived a storm. The vigorous opening recalls the masterly
Weimar Organ Toccatas of Bach. There is much to do with
flying notes. The central movement is of exquisite tenderness and pastoral charm, followed by a *Fuga chromatica*,
drawn on spacious lines and possibilities, that is made
frankly exciting by the pursuit of an inversion of the original subject. As though the composer intended to show
further what can be done with his material, he transforms
the subject into a vigorous and palpitating *Finale alla tedesca*.
As in the other movements, the solo piano is frequently
used to amplify the orchestra.

Do not let it be thought that this master of gravities has
not written works of other *genres*. One of the loveliest things
in the realm of modern music is the *Serenade to Music*, for sixteen solo singers and orchestra. The words are from Shakespeare, and the work was written especially for Henry
Wood's jubilee concert. It might be thought that such a

---

[58] Brian is referring to one of the two 'motto' themes which Vaughan
Williams employs throughout the Symphony, whose resemblance to
Bach's musical signature (B♭–A–C–B) has often been commented on;
VW's figure, however, spans a narrower compass and returns to its first
note. At the opening of the fugal peroration it appears in the form
F–E–G♭–F; it is difficult to know whose initials Brian had in mind –
perhaps the second pair could signify Gerald Finzi?

lavish lay-out would defeat itself. Certainly, performances of such a work must inevitably be rare. Then the next best thing to actuality are the two double-sided discs issued by Columbia of a performance by the original principals and orchestra under Henry Wood. The *Serenade* is an inspira-t᾽on – a continuous pæan of full-throated exultation. It is impossible to listen to it without feeling that here is a man with a natural genius for opera.

Another work of exceptional loveliness is that for strings on a theme by Thomas Tallis – the epitome of meditation. Though written many years ago, it showed not a genius in the making, but a finished master whose characteristics are met in all his later large-scale works.

Certain small-scale works – such as the songs, choral pieces and organ chorale preludes – have a popularity among the discerning in England and America. Of the choral works, the short oratorio, *Sancta Civitas* (The Holy City), is a declaration of faith and religious convic-tion.[59] This individual and soothing musical expression is vastly different from that of either César Franck or Elgar. The penultimate chorus, 'Heaven and earth are full of Thy glory', is a magnificently calculated approach to a towering climax. As a master of *a cappella* writing, Vaughan Williams' most supreme effort is the Mass in G minor for soli and dou-ble chorus. The work is unique in that it was performed simultaneously at St. Michael's (Protestant) Church, Corn-hill, and at Westminster (Catholic) Cathedral, during the London Musical Festival week of last year. In this work mys-ticism is realised with no less facility and fidelity than with the greatest composer of English masses, William Byrd.

Though Vaughan Williams utilises ancient musical for-mulæ his expression is of to-day. His most frequently per-formed operas, as well as the two most oustanding, are *Hugh the Drover* and *Sir John in Love*. The first was a popular success with the B.N.O.C.[60] both in London and the

---

[59] Brian himself prepared the vocal score of *Sancta Civitas* for Vaughan Williams, published by Curwen in 1925.
[60] The British National Opera Company, founded by Beecham in 1922, went into liquidation in 1929. *Hugh the Drover*, composed 1910–14, was

provinces. *Sir John* would doubtless have been equally successful had the company continued. With Sir John Falstaff,
the English composer challenged the German Nicolai and
the Italian Verdi, whose settings are known to operatic audiences throughout the world. Curiously enough, I can recall
a performance, now some forty years ago, of Nicolai's *Merry
Wives of Windsor*, at the Royal College of Music, under Stanford. And it was that College which launched *Sir John in
Love*, in the Parry Theatre: it was produced in a handsome
way, as though all concerned were proud of its home-made
product. In this work the composer gives full rein to his
enjoyment of English folk songs. Never before have so
many been pressed inside such a lengthy, spacious work. To
the listener unfamiliar with their origin, they are noted as
remarkably fine tunes. To the connoisseur of folk-tunes,
their presence in the melodic line means something more.
Whatever Vaughan Williams may have gathered from
English folk songs, this work proclaims him the English
composer *par excellence*. There is a droll use of *Leitmotif*, such
as those representing the jealous Ford and the irresponsible
Falstaff, whose discomfiture takes place in a masterly built-
up finale. The work has an inspiring buoyancy, and its
humours are clearly sustained.

The first performance of *Job: a Masque for Dancing*, was
given at a Norwich Festival. Prominent in the texture are a
group of four descending notes, also heard in the song of
the lavender seller in the *London Symphony*, and most
impressively used in the opening of Job's Dream. To realise
Job, it is necessary to experience a performance, conceived
by the composer as a ballet. Performances have been given
both in the theatre and in the concert room as an orchestral
work. A study of the score makes it indisputably clear that it
is a work for the theatre. The seven scenes are inspired by
Blake's allegorical illustrations. The music is unlike any
other music by the composer, and more like him, for the
more he changes, the more he remains the same. There

---

not produced until 1924, when after student performances at the R.C.M.
it was mounted by the B.N.O.C. at His Majesty's Theatre, London, on 14
July.

is a wonderful mystical pageantry in this procession of dances – the counterplay of good and evil expressed in an ethereal blend of ancient and modern tonalities. Power there is with graphic description, yet Vaughan Williams always escapes from the merely pictorial by masterly artifice and sense of grasping a thing completely. Moreover, the work is a tribute to the genius of an extraordinary visionary whose paintings inspired the music. *Job* has pushed to the forefront the name of William Blake, the greatest mystic England has produced: a composite genius – poet, painter and etcher.

HAYDN WOOD

This article appeared in the 'Personalia' section of *Musical Opinion* for May 1937, p. 699.

Haydn Wood is exceptional in having won a position as one of the most popular English song writers whilst maintaining a reputation as a composer of serious, large-scale, instrumental works. It is not generally known, or is frequently overlooked, that this composer of over two hundred popular songs – including such favourites as *Roses of Picardy, The Bird of Love* and other successes – was also the winner of a prize for a String Quartet in the first competition promoted by the late Walter Cobbett; also that his Violin Concerto was played for the first time by Antonio Brosa in 1933. A very favourable critique of his Piano Concerto appeared in our issue for March.

Pedro Morales[61] recently described Haydn Wood as a composer of dual personality: Dr. Jekyll, who writes serious, large scale works, and Mr. Hyde, who writes popular ballads and orchestral music. Though the outstanding quality

---

[61] Pedro Morales (1879–1938), Spanish composer and critic who studied at the R.C.M. and was frequently active in England.

of his large works is the lyrical charm of his slow movements, he has the same happy touch for melody as in the
popular ballads and orchestral works.

Haydn Wood was born in Yorkshire of musical parents,
who moved to the Isle of Man where he spent his boyhood.
He was taught the violin by his brother Harry. Another
brother, Daniel, became the well known flautist, and was
one of the founders of the London Symphony Orchestra.
Haydn Wood also had violin instruction from Weist Hill,[62]
and won an open scholarship at the Royal College of Music,
where he remained for the following six years studying the
violin with Arbos and composition with Stanford. The latter
master's penchant in composition was neatness, and his
pupil most certainly acquired it. After leaving the R.C.M.
Haydn Wood went to Brussels, where he continued his violin studies with the famous César Thomson.[63] Returning to
England he joined Madam Albani's concert party[64] as solo
violinist, and toured with her for eight years, during which
time he visited Canada, India, Australia and New Zealand.
An interesting part of his career was when his wife (known
professionally as Dorothy Court) joined him in a music hall
tour. He wrote many of his great song successes for their
musical act in these tours, among them being *Roses of
Picardy, Bird of Love Divine, A Brown Bird Singing, Love's Garden of Roses*, &c. His latest song, *A Bird Sang in the Rain*, has
every indication of becoming as popular as the four world-
wide successes mentioned above: Haydn Wood himself says
it is the best song he has ever written. His speciality is light
music: in addition to his popular ballads, he has written
over a hundred instrumental works, including solos, suites,
rhapsodies and overtures.

[62] Thomas Weist Hill (1828–1891) was a well-known British violin virtuoso who became Principal of the Guildhall School of Music in 1880.
[63] César Thomson (1857–1931) – called 'Paganini redivivus' in Italy –
was a Belgian violinist who taught mainly in Brussels and Liège and
edited much 17th- and 18th-century violin music.
[64] The Canadian soprano Emma Albani (1847–1930; D.B.E. 1925) first
sang at Covent Garden in 1872 and toured in Europe, America and the
Commonwealth, cultivating a large operatic and oratorio repertoire
ranging from Lucia to Isolde. She retired in 1911.

One of the most interesting things he has done recently has been to adapt the Four Elgar Songs[65] into a Suite for Orchestra. He says: 'Every note I wrote was like a pearl being put into a new setting, and I took more care and thought over this work than if it had been one of my own compositions'. This orchestration has the true Elgarian touch.

[65] Brian's typically casual reference raises problems of identification, since I cannot trace Wood's score. There is no formal set of four among Elgar's solo songs; perhaps Wood made an orchestration of the *Four Partsongs*, Op. 53, of 1907.

PART NINE

YOUNGER COMPOSERS

———————————◆———————————

From some of the preceding sections, it would be easy to imagine that Brian wrote primarily about and for the British composers of his own generation. In fact, he was always extremely open-minded about new music, and welcomed new talent whenever it appeared. Even after he had ceased to write journalism he continued to follow contemporary musical events, and his letters of the late 1960s and early 1970s, right at the end of his life, show him taking keen interest in such diverse works at Tippett's *King Priam*, Maxwell Davies' *Taverner*, Bernstein's *West Side Story*, the symphonies of Frankel and Gerhard, and Boulez' *Éclat*.

The little essay 'Old Days and Young Composers' (from his 'Music and Musicians' column in *The British Bandsman*, 27 October 1923, pp. 2–3) is almost an anti-reactionary credo, a defence of the young composer's right to compose in a manner quite different from that of the previous (i.e., Brian's) generation. But then, he always remained young at heart himself. Unusually, in this essay, he is careful to name no names – but from his other writings of this period, and letters, we know that he had already heard and admired (among others) Arthur Bliss, Eric Fogg, Goossens, Hindemith, Howells, Malipiero and Stravinsky.

OLD DAYS
AND YOUNG COMPOSERS

The other day I received a letter from an old friend staying amongst the forests of France.[1] He is a friend with whom I have spent many happy hours in Manchester in the not very far off days when the newest comers were hotly discussed and when one of their novelties at a Hallé concert would provide endless food for reflection and talk over pipes and glasses. There was great keenness in the air in those days. Richter had not long been in the city, yet his personality was spreading far and wide in the North through the wonderful performances he gave every Thursday evening in the Free Trade Hall. Johnstone, of the *Manchester Guardian*, who was one of the most brilliant music critics of the past 50 years, had recently died,[2] and was followed by Ernest Newman, an even more brilliant artist, whose work on the *Manchester Guardian* as critic, and as the writer or illuminator of the orchestral works in the Hallé programmes, immediately had a far-reaching influence. The influence of Dr. Richter on the one hand and Ernest Newman on the other hand led to the results.

It was a great mental stimulation, and in my case, at any rate, reached 60 miles out of Manchester.[3] So occasionally I receive a welcome letter from one of those enthusiasts who were infected by the stimulation just as I was – recalling a great deal of it by referring to some special night when Richter was more superb than usual in some symphony or a Bach choral work or the Brahms *Requiem*.

The letter I received the other day was not of this kind. My friend expresses the opinion that none of the new music is as good as the old, and that the new generation of composers has little behind it other than technical brilliance. He has come to this conclusion after close acquaintance with a lot of it[...].

[1] Unknown.
[2] In 1905.
[3] i.e., to Stoke-on-Trent, where Brian was living at Hartshill.

Now I do not doubt my friend's sincerity, but I don't think he approaches the matter from a correct and impartial attitude. There is a great deal of difference between the mentalities of the older and younger men. In the first place there is all the difference between age and youth. Our young composers are writing music which has frankly little meaning to the older generation. The youngsters are out for taking short cuts. They do not want to gas about a thing for 15 minutes and then repeat it all as though it hadn't been said. Brevity is the soul of wit, and our youngsters are going to make it the soul of music – that seems the tendency of the young composer in every country in Europe.

Who, then, will say that this movement which has sprung up naturally is all wrong? These young men are infected by enthusiasm and deadly earnestness – there is no pose in them at all. If it were a pose or an artificial movement there would be something which would give the game away, either the wearing of a red or green tie or yellow gloves. It seems that many things which have come to us in the past by way of deduction from history will now break down. One feels this in looking over the wonderfully brilliant technique of the young men. Some of these young composers show far more brilliant technique in their early work than many adults do in their late work.

This is surprising and unusual, and not in keeping with the art of the great composers who have passed away and one or two who still live. The early work of great composers is not famous for its brilliancy. It is oftener than not famous for halting and stumbling or fumbling style. It often has happened that it is not until a composer has grown towards middle age that his work becomes really finished and brilliant. It may be that some of our young men will 'go up like a rocket, and come down like a stick' – one must wait and see. After all, the important thing is the man's message –*how* he says it is of secondary importance. It is not brilliant technique which keeps Moussorgsky's work alive, neither is it technique which keeps Moussorgsky's greater counterpart Hector Berlioz alive.

Wagner's early work is poor, indifferent stuff, and he did not get into a real stride and personal style until near middle age, after which he went on developing until he was seventy. Verdi made a fortune early in life and ceased to write music. Late in life he broke out again, and the works which he wrote from middle age onward are the works which made him a great composer and which will continue to live.

We have the curious case of Delius, whose development has been reached by extremely slow stages, *and who did not publish a work until he was past forty.*[4]

Elgar's career suggests that, as it began so late in life like Verdi and Wagner, he will continue to develop like them until the guns of death sound – 'Cease fire!'

It is amongst the younger men that we hear so much about music which is said to be 'dated'. They do not mean music which flies the post office colours, but that music which is supposed to resemble a period which is past. The only music which lives is that which has life and breath. We haven't yet discovered what it is which guides the law of selection, retaining that which lives from that which perishes.

I don't understand why there should be an eerie feeling about the younger men. They are not a hybrid stock, not even a graft, but a continuation of the old. The songs, piano works, tone poems and symphonies of the older men still remain unsurpassed, and must for the present remain so by reason of the greater intensity and greater familiarity. Still, these young men have wonderful imagination and they are earnest and keen. There is no fixed limit on them, and it is only once or twice in a century that one discovers at so early an age such brilliantly finished young composers as we have to-day. We know what the older men have done – but no man alive can tell us what the young men will do.

[4] A few songs and piano pieces appeared in print in the 1890s, but Brian is essentially correct: nothing of importance was published before 1906, when Delius was 44. (The italics are Brian's.)

BRITTEN

Ballad of Heroes

From 'On the Other Hand' in *Musical Opinion* of September 1939, p. 1018.

We have as many conceptions of freedom or bondage as we have of fighting. In his own particular way every composer of genius, consciously or subconsciously, fights for freedom of expression. Beethoven was very conscious of the object of his struggle: but his contemporaries were rarely so direct in their attack. Shelley and Byron were both worn out and dead at an age when the career of Wagner had only begun: Shelley was thirty and Byron thirty-six, and their fate was paralleled by that of Mozart and Schubert. But would anyone or all of the four have changed their views had they lived on? We have the example of Tom Paine, who the longer he lived increased his fervour for what he conceived as freedom.

I was reminded of all this when I looked out on the young musical enthusiasts who had promoted that Festival of Music for the People, held at Queen's Hall in April.[5] But what fixed my attention most were the gentlemen responsible for the *Ballad of Heroes*, who for the words are W.H. Auden and Randall Swingler, and for the music Benjamin Britten. The setting is for solo, chorus and orchestra; and the publisher is Winthrop Rogers (vocal score 1s. 6d.) The

[5] The Festival of Music for the People, largely organised by Alan Bush, comprised three concerts on 1, 3, and 5 April 1938. In fact, only the last of these took place at Queen's Hall. The programme, given by 12 Co-operative and Labour Choirs and the LSO conducted by Constant Lambert, consisted of Britten's *Ballad of Heroes*, two movements from Alan Bush's Piano Concerto, and John Ireland's *These Things Shall Be*. Other composers represented in the Festival included Schoenberg and Eisler, and it had opened in the Royal Albert Hall with a pageant jointly composed by Frederick Austin, Alan Bush, Erik Chisholm, Arnold Cooke, Christian Darnton, Norman Demuth, Elisabeth Lutyens, Elizabeth Maconchy, Alan Rawsthorne, Edmund Rubbra and Ralph Vaughan Williams.

Ballad is divided into three sections – viz., Funeral March; Scherzo, Dance of Death; Recitative and Choral, Epilogue. The subject is the old battle between actuality and idealism, for which, unfortunately, there is no possible solution. The urge for social uplift has been going on for thousands of years, and with little alteration of the main issue. All that we are certain of are the changing conditions of an ever-increasing population. Walt Whitman raised his hands and voice in despair at what was going on around him. Although I cannot here be concerned with rival schools of philosophies, I can confirm my belief that anything expressed to-day was known to the ancient Greeks: and doubtless before their time there were those who thought of man as a being trapped in a net from which there was no escape. The idea persists: sometimes taking the symbol of chains, as when Goethe told the German peasants to 'shake their chains' and when Rousseau declared that everywhere man was in irons.

The position to-day is that iron is still being forged for sinister purposes: and a grim thought is that the practice will not be changed by singing and playing. Of course, it may be that this *Ballad of Heroes* will be regarded by choral conductors as a savage satire. Like Bernard Shaw's young man who was uneducated at Eton, Benjamin Britten is determined to show that he also is a free lance and independent. Though there is much 'pulling faces' at the audience, the diabolical cleverness of the music is indisputable. Only a composer with the outlook of a Berlioz would have thought of doubling the tempo of the Funeral March and turning it into a fast devil's-dance like the Dance of Death. The offering to the chorus is a chorale, in which Britten recognises that to make a chorus supremely effective, the choir must be given the lead. Technically, Britten's music offers no difficulties to good choirs. Of the vision which impelled it: Beethoven, who might have had the same feelings, expressed them far more eloquently in his Third, Fifth and Ninth Symphonies.

ARNOLD COOKE

This article appeared in the 'Personalia' feature of *Musical Opinion*, July 1936, pp. 844–845.

Arnold Cooke was born on November 4th 1906, and educated at Repton and Cambridge, where he took the Mus.B. degree in 1929. Leaving Cambridge, he went to Berlin, where he studied composition with Paul Hindemith. On returning to England, he was for a time director of music at the Festival Theatre, Cambridge. In the summer of 1933, he was appointed professor of harmony at the Royal Manchester College of Music.

We have felt it necessary to deal at length with our subject, because unlike most composers of talent, his works are still in manuscript. His Harp Quintet has been performed twice in London and once in Cambridge; the Quartet twice in Manchester and Cambridge; and the B.B.C. have performed his Overture, the Quartet and the Harp Quintet. The Octet and the Brass Sextet were given at a students' concert at the Hochschule (Berlin) in 1931.

Many features of the work and personality of Arnold Cooke remind us of Brahms, who at twenty had developed an expert technique and a powerful, concentrated introspection. Think of Brahm's magnificent and remarkable Piano Sonata in F minor (Op.5), written at twenty; all his life he may be said to have worked inside the domain of chamber music, for even his most powerful and greatest work, the *German Requiem*, is laid out for a small orchestra and chorus. Moreover, he clung to his chamber music ideals whilst his contemporaries were working on a more lavish scale and when comparisons of Brahms and his contemporaries were a daily discussion.

Arnold Cooke has unusually powerful and profound introspection with an expert technique. Some years ago it was remarked that Delius had, like Wagner, developed a facility for writing continuous contrapuntal music. The greatest modern master of such music is Sebastian Bach. It may be likened to musical prose, with the same proviso, that the writing of musical prose or blank verse makes greater demands on the imagination and technical resources than the comparatively easier writing of rhymed themes or verse. Arnold Cooke has also acquired facility in continuous contrapuntal writing: he appears to think and breathe contrapuntally, and many of his themes give the impression of fugue subjects, and thus offer opportunity for development. He is one of few modern composers who can also think in and has the facility to express profound things with small resources. As an instance of this, his Duo for violin and viola, consisting of introduction and three movements (*allegro, andante con moto*, and *allegro*) is a splendidly developed large-scale work for two solo string instruments. It is a remarkable achievement, for it has a Bach-like mastery and austerity, combined with modern outlook and tonality, winding up with a brilliant fugue.

Arnold Cooke is an atonalist so far as many of his themes are of a modal character: the music is keyless, with unrelated relationships and clashes, though his music has a fine diatonic basis. And he has tradition in his bones: his working principles and outlook are nearer to the Elizabethans and Bach rather than to Wagner and Strauss. His Quintet for harp, flute, clarinet, violin and violoncello, in four movements (recently performed by the Philharmonic Ensemble) is a work exemplifying all his ideals, with an unusually impressive slow movement, the modal character of which is an auspicious portent for the composer's future. The Sextet for six brass instruments is a splendid exhibition of contrapuntal facility and invention. The expressive Lento forms a striking contrast with the waltz – a combination of liveliness and the grotesque, particularly when the bass tuba takes over the waltz theme low down in its register.

The Octet in A minor, for flute, clarinet, horn, bassoon, violin, viola, 'cello and bass, consists of three movements: *Passacaglia*, surprising in inventiveness and resource in the writing of variations in a Bach-like dignity, yet an almost excitable zest in carrying them forward. *Scherzo*, a real joke, as a scherzo should be, with many Beethovenish touches. *Finale*, an imposing piece of writing, disclosing the composer's respect for classical sonata form, although his treatment is free and brilliantly fluid. This movement, compact and taut, like the two previous movements gives the impression of sustained effort. Indeed, in this and other works, the composer's hastily written pencil manuscript suggests an unusual demoniacal impulse in concentrated creative power.

His finest work is a short choral work for baritone solo, chorus and orchestra called *Holderneth*, a setting of a poem by a young American named Edward Sweeney, whose lovely symbolic work dealing with night, depicted as death and dispelled by the rising sun, reminds us of that wonderful bit of writing by William Drummond of Hawthornden:

> The winds all silent are,
>   And Phœbus in his chair,
> Ensaffroning sea and air,
>   Makes vanish every star:
> Night like a drunkard reels
>   Beyond the hills, to shun his
>   flaming wheels.[6]

Something similarly symbolical lies embodied in Sweeney's poem. Here is the opening:

> Holderneth awoke:
> Beheld a naked angel in the dampened room,
> Whose withered pinions beat the crumbling floor,
> Whose fingers searched an inky pall
> And dragged it round and round
> And fastened it upon the wall, departing called:
> 'When the world turns round once more,
> I will return and tear it down'.

[6] These are the closing lines of *Invocation* by William Drummond of Hawthornden (1585–1649). Drummond was one of Brian's favourite poets, and in 1919 he made important settings for voice and piano of two of his sonnets: *Care-charmer Sleep* and *My Lute*. The latter is unfortunately lost, apart from a citation of its opening bars in an article about Brian by Leigh Henry published in *Musical Opinion* in 1922.

Though this small cantata is an admirable successor to the small Brahms cantatas, *Holderneth* has far more variety, for the composer makes striking use of his combined forces in many contrasts. For instance, how well he sets

> Of the Attic maid
> Who kissed the tending
> Shepherd boy.

for woodwind and female chorus; whilst the solo for baritone beginning 'Holderneth beheld the rising sun', continuing with

> I have searched the morning light,
> Purple from the black embracing night,

suggests an etching rather than a painting of a pastoral for solo voice, oboe, violas and 'cellos. There are many superb moments for the chorus and orchestra, postulating towards the close:

> Your life is sung
> The strains of the dirge descend.

We quote the conclusion of this unusually attractive cantata:

Ex. 29

His *Concert Overture* for orchestra, which won the third prize in *The Daily Telegraph* orchestral competition in 1934, was performed at Queen's Hall under Henry Wood, and last year was given another performance at a Hallé concert. The themes of this overture palpitate with a dancing vividity and life. They are developed amidst an ever increasing atmosphere of gaiety and merriment. The short work is worthy of a place by the side of Dvořák's *Carnival* Overture – a model for all composers who are lucky and clever enough to capture the rare impetuous spirit of festivity and know the value of surprise. The composer apparently attaches little importance to the prize overture: the score still remains in pencil: it deserves a better fate, and should be in the orchestral répertoire. A Quartet for strings was broadcast by the Griller Quartet on June 9th.

GOOSSENS

The Art of Eugene Goossens

This article appeared in two parts in *Musical Opinion*
(January 1924, pp. 381–383; February 1924, p. 492). Brian
had met Goossens a few years earlier, and early enthusiasm
for his music is reflected in a letter to his friend Walter
Allum: 'Goossens is in my opinion the most promising young
figure in contemporary music today[...] – and as modern as
Stravinski or Malipiero' (18 May 1923). Goossens tried, and
failed, to mount the premiere of Brian's *Gothic* Symphony at
the 1935 Cincinnati Festival; but he lived long enough to
attend the work's eventual premiere at Central Hall,
Westminster, in 1961. The remarkable 'pastoral' prologue to
Brian's article stands at a similar angle of obliquity to the matter in hand that some of his symphonic introductions bear to
their respective movements.

If you wander through the fields down by the hedgerow
and pass into the wooded glen at the end of it in the month
of June, amidst the scent of blossoms, wild thyme, honey-
suckle and wild dog-rose, your mind – baffled and en-
snared amidst so many perfumes and colours – will compel
you to attention. It is nature who calls your attention: she
wishes you to behold her beauty naked and unadorned and
smell her fragrance.

No shy maiden this. Nature proud to reveal herself puts
out her arms to enfold you and you willingly accept her. As
you lie in her arms, you see wonderful pictures swaying
around you. Every leaf trembles and vibrates to a strange
soothing music. You arise and pass into the avenue over-
hung by spreading limes whose delicate frills graze your
face, and walk across a fine green carpet of clean, springy
turf. The sunlight lights up the whole place with a strange
colour, the boughs tremble and quiver. A flash of scintillat-
ing golden green across your gaze betrays the kingfisher on
his way to the pool beyond. A blackbird follows; his plum-
age showing against the sunlight a golden purple. A sharp
cry of anguish some distance away suggests that the tragedy
of the weasel and rabbit tells its own tale. Nature pays no

attention to this. Lying in her arms you are conscious of an endless music continued in a perpetual drone from the insects, intermingled with songs from the birds. Thus you may remain dreaming and enwrapped, for the scene continuously changes as Phœbus slowly circles overhead. Phœbus slowly descending in the west passes out amidst a display of pyrotechnics: twilight soon follows, the music gradually ceases, purple night descends and soon a ghostly stillness pervades the avenue and glen. Still locked in nature's arms, you are aroused by the bay of a hound, the bark of the fox, or perhaps the 'puff-puff' of an engine in a distant station. The silver lamp, climbing up from the east, gradually suffuses avenue and glen in a silver sheen, the nightingale pours out her song. Having listened to her, we steal away, conscious that there is a secret between this strange night and she who sings so rapturously, and the night was made for her alone. In the glen we have many times marked nature's changes, her smiles and her cruelties. We have stood in the midst of it with the blazing sun above the trees, when the whole appeared like the interior of a weird cathedral. We have sought shelter in the glen when the raging thunder and blinding lightning seemed savage enough to tear the glen in pieces and uproot the trees. In winter we have sat by the side of the spring, marvelling at the glen's ghostly emptiness as the cold wind pierced the naked trees, and nothing moved, except, perhaps, a water vole, or a stoat, or the curious 'plop-plop' of a dried nut which fell into the water, shaken from the trees. The perpetual change, the sumptuousness and splendour of it all chloroform the senses. Man did not make this; neither did he have a hand in it. Nature herself made it. Wild it may be, but what a marvellous pattern is this nature's wildness and how perfect every tiny bit fits into the greater whole.

Into this glen there arrived one day, the young composer Eugene Goossens. His senses and imagination were aflame in full sympathy with all he saw and heard. He seized nature's offering, and grasped her in his hands. By way of thanksgiving he recreated his impressions in three wonderful *Nature Poems*, published by the house of Chester, entitled, 'Awakening', 'Pastoral', 'Bacchanal'.

Though issued for the piano, it is impossible to escape the boom and throb of the orchestra when playing them.[7] Nor is it music of a quality which unfolds its beauty at first hearing. One needs must worship the highest when we meet it. If we need the aristocrat in music, then we have a fine example of it in this nature music of Goossens. There is something aloof and highbred in this shy personality which so restrainedly discloses itself. It would not be a difficult thing now-a-days to write descriptive music portraying Puck scampering over the turf, squirrels showing their tails or monkeys throwing cocoanuts at each other.

Goossens ignores the obvious and sinks within himself closely searching and scrutinising his soul, mindful of Bach and Wagner in their finest moments. We are reminded of Bach and Wagner in the manner he utilises his material after he has introduced it. In his development of it, Goossens carries on in the high minded tradition begun with Bach and contained by a few iconoclasts who pinned their faith to a structure reared from the growth and development of a germ rather than a structure of the classical symphonic school which hangs together by pattern weaving and formal construction *via* themes and the usual paraphernalia of the backwash. In his harmonic outlook, Goossens has a sure touch and it is his own. One has frequently heard the names of Stravinsky and Schönberg mentioned as a sort of spiritual godfathers of Eugene Goossens. There is an error in this statement, though the comparison is excusable enough. Goossens is a phenomenon like Mozart, and the writing of music is to him a first nature not a second.

It is just as natural for Goossens to write music as an ordinary fellow would take a bath. That must not imply that music flows from him like water from a tap. On the other

It is also impossible to escape in this passage an echo of Brian's own reported style of piano playing. The late Walter Allum, who lodged in the same house as Brian for several months in 1918, and maintained a lively correspondence with him at intervals throughout Brian's life, wrote in his unpublished autobiography *Music on the Wing*: 'When Brian played the piano in embracing his Muse, nothing less than full orchestral tone was demanded in his crescendos[...] whilst the "tutti" passages were something to be feared!'

hand, these *Nature Poems* give one the impression that they were written only after a long wrestling with nature herself. It is necessary to indicate the character of these pieces.

No. 1 'Awakening': A low murmuring is heard in the dark purple haze; from out of it a figure steals and it is upon this that the structure of the movement rests.

Ex. 30

then passes by to

Ex. 31

It is then tossed about in moods capricious as nature herself and moves to an exhilarating triumph, which raises the blood to the cheeks and then quietly dies away.

No. 2, 'Pastoral': a slender motif introduces this movement:

Ex. 32

Here we have no old fashioned pastorale with an oboe piping the melody over a drone bass; this is nature herself who sings for the joy of it, and with full passionate ardour. Gradually the 'Pastoral' alternate with tenderness and passion, and eventually passes away, dissolved into thin air like the 'Awakening'.

No. 3, 'Bacchanal': a tumultuous cascade of sounds ushers in this movement, suggestive of the glen filled with dazzling sunlight and excitement. From underneath the overhanging branches strange figures emerge to a curious tune which is breathlessly tossed about:

Ex. 33

The sinister beings disappear only to be followed by others of a more bewitching type. Maybe these are the slender fauns from the thicket and forest – the music suggests them in C sharp major.

The outline of their delicate limbs becomes more marked as they advance towards us, their shyness wears off under the influence of the palpitating dance. By degrees they become frenetic, and make for a climax of frenzy and fury which becomes more strained as the figures depicted in Ex. 33 return and commingle with the shy beings of the thicket.

There is nothing uncouth or forced about this Bacchanal; it belongs to the open air and is a fine imaginative picture of a fantastic woodland scene the work of a finely wrought genius.

Goossens has also given his attention to domestic music in *Kaleidoscope*, published by Chester's, where, with the aptness of Phil May, he throws off a number of sketches, highly seasoned with caustic wit. Nowhere in Goossens have I found anything which suggests 'very droll'. The wit of Goossens is sharp and bitter and has an acid flavour – sometimes there is a sting in the honey. There is a concealed smirk in the 'Good-morning', and one cannot miss the silk-hatted

dandy, circling his cane in a lemon-coloured glove as he
swings along the promenade showing six inches of white
spats. All the sketches hit the bull's-eye, though there is fine
and quaint drawing in the 'Hurdy-Gurdy Man', 'Ghost
Story', and 'Rocking Horse'. Many will enjoy his 'Good-
night' most. This concludes the series and is of that stange,
haunting quality which distinguishes the 'Awakening' and
'Pastoral' of the nature music.

A *Concert Study* (Chester's) is a piece of writing for virtuosi
players; it has the character of myriads of jingling bells.

Four Conceits (Chester's) reveal the genius in various
moods:

'The Gargoyle' is brilliantly fantastic, indicating its origin
in the ecclesiastical mode towards the close.

'Dance Memories' has a contradictory key signature, and
the music is more acid than archaic.

'A Walking Tune' has the fine spreading harmonies
remindful of the 'Pastoral' in the nature music in which the
composer utilises the quaint Westminster chimes.

'The Marionette Show' is brilliantly descriptive of its title.

In his *Hommage à Debussy* (Chester's) Goossens has given
us a fine portrait of his sympathy for the passing away of a
great artist. The writing is taut and tense. There are only
two pages of this music, but every bar is stamped with a
cloak through which anguish almost pushes its head. Here
again, as in the nature music, one feels that the composer
compressed what he felt into two staves of piano music
rather than score it for the orchestra which was ringing in
his imagination. The music demands several quotations to
indicate its character. It has two phases: Ex. 34,

Ex. 34

(Pedal each change of harmony.)

which slowly unfolds itself in long drawn out phrases of

grief. This rising to a climax descends to a more tranquil mood.

Ex. 35

Not the least admirable touch in this sad picture is the interruption of the movement by an antiphonal fanfare and the emphasis given of fragments from Exx. 34 and 35 – by augmentation – which closes the work.

This music is a gauge. It tells us that we have a composer in our midst into whose genius the gods have poured unusual endowments. From these we shall obtain a full revelation and satisfaction; for there is nothing in music a genius like Goossens cannot do.

He can do more: for he will do that which no one else can do.

*   *   *

The freshness of touch and outlook which distinguishes the piano writings of Eugene Goossens is also found throughout his chamber music, songs and orchestral compositions. A great deal of modern British music (orchestral) is so much influenced by choral idioms that it moves heavily along and never seems to get off the ground. The music of Goossens is not of this class. He is one of the first British composers to come along whose influences and idioms are absolutely instrumental. His music trembles with the nervous vitality of a young race horse: it is eager to get off the ground. When not intended for flight, there is still the springy character, so that it can never dawdle into a shuffle. It is the music of high spirits, venturesome and daring. It is significant of the present period that the most venturesome spirits in every country in Europe are straining for conciseness and directness of speech, the elimination and cutting out of all but the essentials. Thus the rapier has been plunged into the bowels of sonata form: modern Europe owns it not. The music of modern Europe refuses to rebound, double and return upon its base after having commenced its flight.

Perhaps the most difficult thing for a composer to tackle successfully is the string quartet. The numberless failures lying about suggest that almost every composer has felt it a duty at some time of his life to write a string quartet. A number of composers have wisely left it alone. [8] As with most other things Goossens enlivens the string quartet with his own individuality. Being a finished artist upon the violin plus a long association with the finest orchestras as player and conductor, it is perfectly easy for him to write for this medium. Not only so, but it is a perfectly natural thing for him to write a string quartet. Goossens thinks naturally in this idiom.

The *Phantasy Quartet* (Op.12) is a well developed piece of writing eloquently sustained, in one continuous movement, alternating from slow to quick. The String Quartet (Op. 14) is of bigger dimensions: it has four movements and each is the portraiture of the individual to whom it is inscribed. Schumann and Elgar have done this too; Goossens is none the less successful though so very different from Schumann or Elgar. The first movement is significant of the whole. The theme or motif breaks in straightaway upon novel harmonisation. It is carried along by continuous change and variety, from very quiet to excessively dramatic until it resolves itself into the subject of a quiet fugato. Here it once more looms into large proportions after the exposition and just as quietly passes out. The handling of the motif stamps Goossens as a genius. Such intensive art as this always endures.

Other chamber music, eloquently descriptive, is found in

[8] This statement, however defensible, may reflect some personal experience. We know from passing references elsewhere that Brian had written a string quartet, or some movements thereof, in the early 1900s – but this work was never performed and is presumed lost or destroyed. In later years he fought shy of the form, saying 'the quartet [...] cannot (for me) express the big things in life'.

a suite called *Five Impressions of a Holiday,* for violin or flute, 'cello, and piano. Also a suite for flute, violin and harp, or two violins and piano. The first suite contains some delicately drawn nature pictures. It is also curious as containing a rare instance of the influence of Strauss upon this composer. In the first movement, 'In the Hills', where flute and 'cello make their first entry, we have an impression of being transported near to that wonderful harmonic mesh in which Strauss enveloped the personality of Salome. We feel the shimmer of the delicately clad temptress across our faces, only for an instant. Goossens is to be forgiven for this, for it is the most wondrous music since *Tristan.* For his songs, Goossens has drawn upon ancient and modern poets. His treatment of the lyric is the same in each case. We have remarked how in the first movement of the String Quartet he uses a motif as a basis for the continuous development of an extended movement. There is nothing unusual in this feature, for it is also that of Bach (Organ Prelude, C major),[9] Wagner (*Tristan* Prelude).

In most of the songs Goossens carries along the musical idea, retaining and developing it to the end of the poem as distinct from those composers who make the verses of a poem 'all sound alike'. The orchestral works have the same sureness of touch and open minded outlook. In the matter of orchestration there are no violent departures. There are, here and there, instances of a sensitively organised genius – and how quickly it gets into the middle of things.

At this time of day when there is a cry in certain quarters for composers to crook their trumpet parts in C – or in A and B flat – making them interchangeable with the cornets of that ilk, you find Goossens in his Prelude to *Philip the Second,* using two crooks of C and F. In a particular place he wants a sustained high C of especial brilliance, he takes off the C crook and indicates for the trumpet in F and writes a high G for it. His instinct tells him rightly that there is

[9] This citation is so vague that I strongly suspect Brian did not write (or did not intend to write, and slipped up because his mind was already running ahead to the *Tristan* Prelude) the word 'Prelude' here, but rather 'Toccata'. The C major Toccata, BWV. 564, was a favourite piece of his, which he loved to play in the piano transcription by Busoni.

nothing more brilliant to be got from the whole orchestra than the high C from an F trumpet. One has only to imagine what it would sound like, if heard at all, from a trumpet crooked in B flat. Here, in this prelude the high C stands out like a brilliant clarion. The *Tam o' Shanter* Scherzo for orchestra is worthy of Berlioz in his most brilliant flights. It has the audacity of a fine race horse. Though its title betrays its origin as of the 'Land o' weal an' cakes', its impetuosity suggests Mazeppa's death race across the steppes of Russia.

Having discussed Goossens as a composer, it is necessary to say a word about his outlook upon his contemporaries and his work as a conductor. There is inside the breast of most artists something concealed only known to themselves, which is never known to others. Occasionally a little of it slips out. It may show itself in some unexpected manner, sometimes by inquisitiveness, or a desire to contradict or check with a blue pencil all that someone else says. There is a type of music which suggests brutality, cunning or acid peevishness, a sort of savagery in music. There are certain conductors who preside before their orchestra as though dealing a poleaxe round a festive, cannibal board. They look as though they would make fine havoc in a bayonet charge. There are those who welcome new ideas and those who do not. There are those who wear the perpetual dark frown and overbearing jowl of the puritan. Each thinks he is right and his neighbour entirely wrong. Some put the blame upon the critics, who are slandered as belonging to a butchers' association. Some blame cats, whilst others correctly blame a number of wealthy congenital idiots. Some say the police are to blame, others that there is no music at all now, only merchandise.

Whether the regrouping of the railways has really had a deterrent effect upon certain mentalities only time can prove. Some blame the price of railway tickets, others put it on petrol and standardised cars. If ever music goes to sleep and refuses to move it will be when it has become standardised. A conductor who wishes to take a healthy position amongst his contemporaries must show equal sympathies. Eugene Goossens commenced a series of concerts several years ago with a very fine orchestra, and at these he gave fine performances, which placed him in the front rank of European conductors. He had already served a long period as an orchestral player at the first fiddle desks of the Queen's Hall Orchestra and as a conductor with the Beecham Opera. Just when these concerts of Goossens seemed to be establishing themselves something happened and they stopped.[10]

Like most things that happen, this can perhaps be explained, but it was a pity that such a fine scheme, which seemed to have the virility of independence, should have come to an end. Perhaps Mr. Frost and Mrs. Vinegar got married, or perhaps the voice from the minaret of a certain financial group sang:

> Full many a flower is born to blush unseen
> And waste its sweetness on the desert air.

It was a pity the Goossens Concerts came to an end, for they proved that he had wide sympathies for many contemporaries whose music was so remarkably unlike his own. As I remarked that there are times when one betrays one's inner soul by a moment's thoughtlessness, so I have heard Goossens conduct when he has clearly indicated where his sympathy did and did not lay. Music of the classical pattern does not arouse the finest spirits in Goossens. Music which springs from the intellect appeals not, but music which springs from the heart does fetch the best out of him. I have listened to thrilling performances of Borodin, Wagner, Bizet, Debussy, Scriabin, in which every ounce of beauty and colour lay revealed. However brilliant it may be, Goossens always gives the impression that he gets all his effects without fencing for them. There is an ease about it which resembles the ease of his finest compositions. I am hoping he will one day run against the bogey man who will really frighten him with a work that will make him nervous. Goossens has not met him yet.

---

[10] The concerts were in the summer of 1921, with a hand-picked orchestra; there were six programmes in all, and Goossens had intended giving further concerts (at which he hoped to give the premieres of the *Symphonic Dances* from Brian's opera *The Tigers*); but the series was curtailed owing to the death of his financial backer.

BILLY MAYERL: PIANIST

This article is from the March 1932 issue of *Musical Opinion* (p.528).

When Sir Henry Walford Davies was requested by his wireless pupils to broadcast the names of his favourite composers, he replied, 'Bach, Beethoven, Billy Mayerl and Arnold Schönberg'. Mayerl was born in London in 1892, his father being a professional musician, who taught his son to play the piano and was indeed the only tutor the boy had until at the age of twelve he won a scholarship at Trinity College. There he studied the piano, and took harmony with the late Dr. C. W. Pearce. In addition to study, however, he was soon playing the piano at the Princes theatre for the munificent sum of 7s. 6d. per week, which was an acceptable addition to the family budget. The manager at the theatre was kind hearted if not over-generous in the matter of wages, for he allowed Billy 'time off', ostensibly for the study of harmony; but opportunity was taken to enter into a partnership with the chocolate boy. How it worked out we do not know: but the manager seemed to object when he saw his youthful pianist vending chocolates: anyhow, he peremptorily and finally discharged Mayerl from his service. But in those days of war, jobs were many and pianists were few, with the result that Mayerl went the round of the London cinemas, always advancing in position. For a year he played with De Groot at the Piccadilly Hotel.[11]

Mayerl has never been the man to wait for opportunities: he makes them. In the year that he won the scholarship at Trinity College, he was chosen to play Grieg's Piano Concerto at a students' concert at Queen's Hall: and he made it the opportunity of showing that he really could play the piano. One fellow student at Mandeville Place he recalls is John Barbirolli, now famous as a conductor at Covent

[11] David De Groot (1880–1933) was best known for his performances with the Piccadilly Hotel Orchestra. He had founded, well ahead of his time, a ragtime dance band in 1911. After his period at the Piccadilly Hotel he played at the New Victoria Cinema until his untimely death. His recorded legacy (his first record was made in 1915) is extensive.

Garden. But by 1916 he had turned his back on the cinema and was soon in the first of those who were to secure fame and fortune from the rising craze for dancing.

In 1919 the first American jazz band was heard at the Savoy Hotel, and with it was associated Billy Mayerl at a salary that would have tempted a prima donna. The highest ladies in the land were fascinated by his lightning fingers, and many sought him as a teacher. Jazz rose to the heights, and with it the salary of the phenomenal pianist. The summit was perhaps reached in 1925 when the Savoy Orpheans and the Savoy Havanas, augmented by members of the London Symphony Orchestra, gave a concert of jazz music at Queen's Hall. Mayerl was the solo pianist, and he introduced the famous *Rhapsody in Blue*, for solo piano with orchestra, by George Gershwin. A number of his own compositions were also included in the programme.

The versatility of Billy Mayerl was to be further shown. He had begun writing when a student at Trinity College, and many of his youthful compositions were later to be 'jazzed' and made successful. Whilst he was at the Savoy he wrote considerably, mostly pieces of the fox-trot order: dancers demanded them and publishers prayed for them, until at length they numbered four hundred. But at times Mayerl stayed his hand to write very seriously, notably in *Pastoral Sketches*, a suite for orchestra (Boosey), *In Sennen Cove*, a symphonic poem for orchestra inspired by Cornwall (Boosey), and a piano suite entitled *Legends of King Arthur* (Keith Prowse). Several months ago we referred to the *Pastorale Exotique* as one of the best examples yet published of Billy Mayerl's serious piano music. Another, and one of which he is particularly fond, considering it his best work in romantic colouring, is *Three Japanese Pictures*. (These last two works are published by Keith Prowse.) The sales of popular pieces, like *Marigold* and *Jazz Master*, were at the least encouraging, for they often reached the hundred thousand mark!

The requests for personal instruction in syncopated piano playing received by Mr. Mayerl while at the Savoy set him thinking: they were many and persistent: they could be turned into that opportunity for which most men wait. So with his friend Geoffrey Clayton (later to become manager), a single room in Oxford Street was taken and a beginning made with a School of Music, very seriously intended and planned. Soon the premises were extended and a staff of capable teachers engaged; and it is now a fact that branches of the school are established in South Africa, New Zealand, India, Germany and Holland. At each of these tuition is given personally and by correspondence in the methods of Billy Mayerl. Among Mr. Mayerl's own pupils are numbered Prince George[12] and the Infanta Christina of Spain.

A very wide public know of Billy Mayerl's association with the B.B.C. He has played for listeners, he has lectured to listeners, and he has conducted his own compositions before listeners. He has recorded for the H.M.V. and is now going strong with Columbia, and a strange fact is revealed that the royalties 'made in Germany' equal those arising in England. He has written a number of 'shows' for West End theatres.

The strange case of Billy Mayerl is that he is a musician who wandered into jazz and made the most of it commercially and artistically. We found him talking with complete and critical understanding of the works of Gustav Holst, John Ireland and Arnold Bax, and in explanation sat down and played several of their pieces from memory.

WALTON

Belshazzar's Feast

This is a score review from *Musical Opinion*, December 1931, p. 216.

Of the new works performed at the Leeds Festival the greatest impression appears to have been made by William Walton's *Belshazzar's Feast* (Oxford University Press: 3s.), the

---

[12] Later King George V.

vocal score of which is now available.[13] It is undoubtedly a powerful work, and one is particularly struck with the downright and certain manner in which the composer makes his points: there is nothing florid or meretricious about the music which is consistently stark and unadorned. One writer, in speaking of this work, said that its production was likely to prove as important a landmark in choral music as the first performance of *The Dream of Gerontius* in 1900. This may be so, but no two works could be more unlike in their essential character. As in reading Flaubert's *Salammbô* one admires the art which contrives to exclude any hint of Christian feeling or ethics, so Mr. Walton has been able to convey the idea of something entirely primitive; even the concluding song of triumph has something barbaric about it, and we are reminded at times of Stravinsky's *Sacre du Printemps*. Mr. Walton is to be congratulated on a notable achievement, which is something more than a *tour de force*, and which undoubtedly reflects faithfully the spirit of the age. 'Soyez de votre siècle' is good advice which Mr. Walton has taken to heart, or, more likely perhaps, has been unable, by the natural bent of his mind, to avoid following.

William Walton

From 'On the Other Hand', October 1936, p.13.

Lancastrians have cause to be proud of the remarkable success of this young composer, who was born at Oldham only thirty-four years ago: he is therefore a man of this century, with no necessary ties to the Victorian age and traditions. He entered Christ Church Cathedral Choir School, and for a time (while still an undergraduate) studied with Sir Hugh Allen. Apart from this short period of study and advice from E.J. Dent and others, William Walton is self taught. He was only twenty-one when he suddenly stepped into prominence with his String Quartet, performed at the Salzburg

---

[13] *Belshazzar's Feast* was premiered on 8 October 1931, at the Leeds Festival, under Malcolm Sargent.

Festival of the International Society for Contemporary Music (1923) and *Façade*, played at the Æolian Hall in the same year. Two years later his overture, *Portsmouth Point*, was produced at the Zürich Festival of the International Society for Contemporary Music (1926): its originality made a stir, and it immediately found its way into the orchestral répertoire. He made a Suite from his *Façade*; and since its production in this form, the work has frequently been performed as a concert item. A Concerto for viola and orchestra followed, produced by Lionel Tertis, for whom it was written.[14] More recently his first Symphony has been produced, but at its first performance only the first three movements were played. The originality of the first three movements foreshadowed a striking finale, which was realised when the first performance of the complete work was given under Sir Hamilton Harty. At the third Promenade concert of the present series (August 11th), Walton appeared as guest conductor in a programme which included four of his works – *Portsmouth Point* (overture), Viola Concerto, *Façade* (suite) and Symphony No. 1. Walton was given the ovation which he undoubtedly deserved. There is a strong resemblance between Walton and Elgar, though the latter was nearly twenty years older than Walton when he first gained attention by his original genius. It was not that Elgar invented a new system, but that he presented a contemporary idiom in his own individual way. Similarly with Walton: he has all contemporary modernist tendencies at his finger-tips, and directs them to his own individual purpose. Again, like Elgar, he thinks orchestrally, and is a brilliant orchestrator. Few composers have attained such a string of successes at the age of thirty-four as has Walton. His early work for pianoforte and strings (written at the age of sixteen) was published by the Carnegie Trust in 1924. His more recent works have been published by the Oxford University Press.

---

[14] Although the premiere, to Tertis' later regret, was given by Hindemith at a Promenade Concert on 3 October 1929, with the Queen's Hall Orchestra conducted by the composer. Tertis, who had initially turned the work down, gave the next performance at the 1930 ISCM Festival in Liège.

Walton's Violin Concerto

Another score review, from the December 1941 *Musical Opinion* (pp. 83–84).

William Walton's Concerto for violin and orchestra has no physical kinship with the repertoire concertos, though it is as typical of the twentieth century as was Beethoven's Violin Concerto of its contemporary period. The main and most important feature of Walton's system is that the composer adheres to the classical formula of a two-person drama consistently and remarkably developed by Beethoven. Whereas the classical plan became systematised, Walton's system is independent, original, though not capricious. The opening section of the first movement is a slow, eloquent elegy expressive of sensitive tenderness followed by an impulsive, animated, and wonderfully picturesque movement. In the two following movements this order of tempi is reversed: these movements open with a headlong rush; the impetuous speed slackens, followed by contrast in splendidly sustained, eloquent and passionate symphonic ariosos, succeeded by a return of the original tempo. The soloist is but the leading character – a very difficult one – in this picturesque and highly seasoned score. We have read that the symphony is no place for a cor anglais.[15] We do not anticipate what will be said of the means used by Walton in this Concerto. Our own impression, after hearing the work, is that all his effects are justified by the character of the work itself. There are exciting changes in the undeviating symphonic splendour, though the intricate part-writing, never involved, is always sensitively balanced, spaced and scored, with respectful economy of notes. Some time when we are more familiar with this work, and refuse to be dazzled by the brilliantly animated rushes, we shall recognise those purple patches containing magnificently eloquent and pleading melodies. The style is consistently Walton's own:

---

[15] The contemporary critical gibe against Franck's Symphony in D minor was that it could not be a symphony because it included this instrument (despite its prominent role in Liszt's *Dante Symphony*).

it has no approximation to other styles, English or foreign. As to the matter of liking or disliking such music, much depends on the predisposition of the audience, or its position in a programme, and the standard of efficiency of performance. The recent B.B.C. broadcast of the concerto was an ideally arranged programme, for it included a new overture by Walton, [16] and an orchestral work by Ravel. Henry Holst, the soloist, is one of the few living really great violinists: he dismissed the numerous difficulties with rare accomplishment.

An arrangement of the Concerto for violin and piano has been issued by the publishers (15s.) and, as all instruments are indicated, the piano arrangement serves the purpose of a short score (Oxford University Press).

WARLOCK

Death of Peter Warlock

From *Musical Opinion*, January 1931, p. 335.

Philip Heseltine (who wrote under the pen name of Peter Warlock) died on December 17th at Chelsea. He was born on October 30th, 1894, and was educated at Eton, where he also studied music – the only lessons he ever had.

Philip Heseltine had a singularly frank and happy personality, which found its finest outlet in Elizabethan research work and setting Tudor lyrics to music. Many of his songs, part-songs and madrigals were published, and a number of his songs, despite a certain aloofness, had become popular. His larger works remained in manuscript – apart from a Suite for strings.

---

[16] The broadcast, on 12 November 1941, conducted by the composer, included the first British performance of *Scapino*, which had been premiered in Chicago in April.

Apart from his work as the composer Peter Warlock, Heseltine was famous to musicians as a critic of genius, who could write books and fill them with original and refreshing criticism. His book on Delius is the most informative work extant on that composer. Heseltine organised the triumphant Delius Festival at Queen's Hall a year ago: and he has also arranged a number of Delius orchestral works for piano. In collaboration with Cecil Gray, he wrote, after much research work and preliminary articles, a book on Carlo Gesualdo, the sixteenth century Italian madrigalist.[17]

Philip Heseltine had an unusual faculty for explaining much in short articles, as was well exemplified by the article on his friend, Bernard van Dieren, and – more recently – by those on the symphonies of Borodin and Elgar, and the great Mass of Berlioz, which appeared in the music page of *The Daily Telegraph*.

Heseltine first became known to the London public through *The Sackbut*, which he founded in 1920.[18] In 1923, he won a Carnegie award for a setting of *The Curlew* (W. B. Yeats), a cycle for tenor voice, flute, cor anglais and string quintet.

His hypersensitiveness was unquestioned and much has appeared about his Bohemian life in Chelsea: but Heseltine could do things which are beyond the reach of most clever musicians. The great success of the Delius Festival, which he organised and carried through himself, will be ever associated with the music of Delius. We have seen Heseltine working at the analysis of a complex orchestral score whilst dictating business letters to his stenographer.

It is sad to lose a composer, so young, with such accomplishment and distinction and with even greater promise.

---

[17] *Carlo Gesualdo: Prince of Venosa: Musician and Murderer*, Kegan Paul, Trench, Treubner & Co., with J. Curwen and Sons, London, 1925.
[18] Heseltine had been contemplating taking over *The Organist*, as it then was, since 1915. When Vol. 1, No. 1, of *The Sackbut* appeared in March 1920, it had been completely transformed.

BRITISH WOMEN COMPOSERS

These remarks are extracted from a longer article, 'Woman
as a Composer', published in *Musical Opinion*, April 1936,
pp. 587–588.

For sheer daring in propaganda, no other woman composer has approached Dame Ethel Smyth: though, of
course, contemporaries are small in number. Her success
has justified her enterprise, for two English conductors
have done the gallant thing and given performances of her
works. It may well be that preferential treatment for women
has never been asked, only that they should not be ignored:
but admission of the justice of the claim, in view of the few
women composers of large-scale works, has at least been
fortuitous for the 'bonnie fechter'. Other native women
composers who have published and had performed important works are Dorothy Howell and Rebecca Clarke. Miss
Howell published a large orchestral score called *Lamia* in
1921, and it was regarded as an extraordinarily accomplished work for a composer so young. I heard her play the solo
part in her Piano Concerto at a Promenade Concert some
years ago, and I remember being impressed by its constructive mastery, masculinity, and facility in scoring.

She has the grand manner; and, in a department where a
composer shows his genius or lack of it (the brass), she is
most eloquent. Bigness and freedom of style distinguish all
her larger works, such as the orchestral works mentioned,
and *Phantasy* and *Moorings* for violin and piano. Her piano
pieces oscillate between whimsical gaiety and sadness, are of
transparent texture and require deft finger work for
proper interpretation. *Spindrift* might be called 'Snowdrift'
by reason of its lightness. If a sly humour and careless *abandon* are found in many of the piano pieces and songs, there
is also a finely sustained elegiac feeling in the *Boat Song* for
piano, *Phantasy* and *Moorings* for violin and piano. Miss
Howell is not an explorer: she prefers traditional moulds
and her language is mostly a diatonic one, but a number of
piano pieces by the same composer suggest a determination

to avoid stock patterns and to go her own way in music.[19] Similarly determined is Rebecca Clarke, whose original mind wavers between great economy of means (as in her songs for violin and solo voice) and profuse clusters of notes (as in her Trio for violin, 'cello and piano: pub. 1928). This trio also contains many mystical touches, and a facility for producing atmosphere, for her mentality gravitates towards Yeats and Blake. Her setting of Yeat's *Down by the Sally Gardens* is an example of unaffected simplicity; and it is all the more remarkable that when she set Blake's poem, *Infant Joy*, she chose to do so in an involved idiom for voice and piano.[20]

I mention these things merely to show that women as well as men composers may be contrary. The main point for congratulation is that these women composers have minds of their own. The most unfortunate instance, however, was Jane Joseph, whose splendid promise and facility in original work were cut off by early death.[21] But she left work sufficient to strengthen the belief that with further striving women may produce a feminine Berlioz, Wagner or Liszt. And when that happens, the presence of a man in an orchestra may be as singular as the reverse was the case thirty years ago.

Jane Joseph was a pupil of Gustav Holst, and her work shows a fondness for adventure in the diatonic idiom and

[19] Dorothy Howell (1898–1982) spent most of her career teaching at the R.A.M., and did not regain the critical attention that had been focussed upon her in the 1920s. For Brian's review of her Piano Concerto see p. 189; he also contributed a short profile of her to the 'Personal and Otherwise' column of *Musical Opinion* in December 1927.
[20] Rebecca Clarke (1886–1978) was better known as a violist than as a composer, and confined herself almost entirely to chamber music and songs. She settled in the USA during World War II. Her works have recently, and deservedly, begun to attract attention on both sides of the Atlantic.
[21] In Gustav Holst's opinion, Jane Joseph (1894–1929) was 'the best girl pupil I ever had'; she was the dedicatee of his *Fugal Overture*, co-dedicatee of *At the Boar's Head*, provided him with the scenario for *The Golden Goose*, assisted him with the translation of the text of *The Hymn of Jesus*, and (with Valley Lasker) arranged the vocal score of Holst's *Ode to Death*.

with unfamiliar rhythms similar to that of her master. Her *Bergamask* is an exhilarating orchestral dance in $\frac{5}{4}$, and is frankly full of promise. A number of her smaller pieces for piano solo are unusually pleasing, simple and unaffected; yet, when she set a simple English poem of the fifteenth century, *A little childe thereat ibore*, for three female voices and piano, she resorted to the unusual five and seven pulse rhythm, though the complete work is most fascinating and original. I do not suggest that her methods were wrong: only that there were indications of a mind working to produce a new bloom. It is indeed a pity that she left the world so soon!

PART TEN

ORCHESTRAS, CHOIRS, BANDS AND THE B.B.C.

Brian's advocacy of British music was not limited to the scores and their composers but also encompassed their avenues of performance and transmission. As a predominantly orchestral composer he was vitally concerned that the symphony orchestra as an institution should be nurtured and made financially viable. His earliest musical experiences, however, had been in a thriving provincial choral tradition, most of whose members tended to view the orchestra as merely an occasionally acceptable accompaniment for voices – and although he utterly rejected that attitude Brian always had the highest regard for the musicianship of British choirs with their festivals and competitions. It is clear that he viewed the brass band movement in a similar light, as part of a country-wide movement towards musical excellence of a fundamentally democratic nature.

The rise of the British Broadcasting Corporation, an institution of a new and perhaps alien kind, was a phenomenon Brian chronicled with mingled fascination and disquiet in his *Musical Opinion* columns. While paying tribute to its artistic successes and recognising its immense potential for good, he clearly did not trust its capacity to use that power properly, fearing (not without subsequent justification) the emergence and influence of a national arbiter of musical taste run on elitist bureaucratic lines, with a near-monopoly of the means for the dissemination of new music.

ORCHESTRAS

The Halford Orchestra:
An Appreciation

This article appeared in *The Musical World* for 22 April 1905
(pp. 276–277).

This band came into existence in 1897. Considering the
prominence of Birmingham in English musical history, it is
certainly rather remarkable that it should have been thirty
years behind Manchester in possessing a permanent
orchestra. This may be due, in a measure, either to the fact
of the Festival upsetting normal conditions or to the inborn
love of choral music, of which Birmingham is an undoubted
stronghold. Be this as it may, the year 1897 brought a series
of ten concerts, known as 'Mr. Halford's Orchestral Concerts', giving the people in the Midlands opportunities and
privileges of hearing good orchestral music like to those
enjoyed in Manchester and the north. If it had its deserts,
the work accomplished by this band since its formation
should be written in gold, so lethargic was the support
accorded it in its earlier stages – always bearing in mind that
Birmingham aspired to be classed as a musical city. In 1901
'The Halford Concerts Society' was inaugurated, under the
presidency of the Lord Mayor of Birmingham, with the
Duchess of Hamilton, Earl Howe, and Viscount Cobham as
vice-presidents, to carry on the concerts under the same
conductorship, and to provide a sufficient guarantee to
meet any deficiency that might occur. From the initial
concert in 1897 onward, through the season just closed,
the highest in art has been sought and attained. Art is
treated seriously, the programmes being as severe in their
demands on the capacity of the audience as are to be found
anywhere. There is no interval for the fashionables to make
small-talk, and this, combined with the severity of the programmes, may have proved a stumbling-block to the success
of these concerts in their early days. In the season of 1898
the whole series of Beethoven Symphonies was performed

in rotation – an achievement seldom accomplished in this country in a single season. This feat has been repeated during the past winter. The orchestral works of Brahms have been given many times, while Schumann's *Manfred* music was first performed in its entirety in Birmingham under their auspices, his symphonies and overtures being often heard. No great representatives of any school have been overlooked; the names of Dvořák, Liszt, Smetana, Tschaikowsky, Glazounow, Arensky, Borodine, Goldmark, Berlioz, Rimsky-Korsakoff, Sgambati, Bizet, Wagner, and Bruckner being frequently found alternating with those of Mozart, Beethoven, Brahms, Weber, and Schubert, while Rachmaninoff wrote a piano concerto specially for these concerts.[1] The English school, too, has met with much favour, the only parallels in this direction being found in the

---

[1] Since Brian knew Halford personally, we must assume that this statement (nowhere else recorded, to my knowledge) has his ultimate authority. The work in question has to be the celebrated Piano Concerto No. 2 in C minor. In 1899, after his first visit to London, Rachmaninov was invited to come again in 1900 and play his First Piano Concerto; but he promised instead to write a better one – 'for England' according to *Rachmaninoff's Recollections* told to Oskar von Reisemann (George Allen & Unwin, London, 1934, p. 110), 'for London' according to *Sergei Rachmaninoff* by Sergei Bertensson and Jay Leyda (George Allen & Unwin, 1965, p. 87). The promise was apparently made to the then Secretary of the Royal Philharmonic Society, Francesco Berger (later to be a colleague of Brian's on *Musical Opinion*); and the performance given on 29 May 1902 at a Philharmonic Society Concert in Queen's Hall, by Basil Sapellnikov under the baton of Frederick H. Cowen, was programmed as the 'first English performance'. In all this there is no trace of Halford. But Robert Threlfall and Geoffrey Norris (*A Catalogue of the Compositions of Sergei Rachmaninov*, Scolar Press, London, 1982, p. 68) note that Sapellnikov's performance was *preceded* by performances in Birmingham and Manchester by Alexander Siloti, who had given the Concerto its world premiere in Moscow on 27 October 1901. Brian himself confirms this in a much later article (part of 'On the Other Hand' for June 1934, p. 764) when he writes of 'Rachmaninoff's[...]Concerto in C minor, which I heard at its first performance in England by Siloti'. Messrs. Threlfall and Norris and I have all failed to come up with a precise date for Siloti's Birmingham performance – but if that was, in fact, the British premiere, some colour is lent to the statement that Rachmaninov might have written his most famous work for Halford's concerts. There is, of course, no inherent impossibility in his promising the work to any number of places!

work done by Sir August Manns at the Crystal Palace, and
now being done by Mr. Dan Godfrey at Bournemouth.
Sterndale Bennett, Elgar, Parry, Stanford, Cowen, Bantock,
Boughton, O'Neill, and William Wallace are well known to
the Halford audience by their works. Dr. Richard Strauss
received a whole-hearted sympathy at their hands, his *Heldenleben* being first performed in the provinces at these concerts in March, 1903. Many eminent conductors have made
their appearance from time to time, the latest being Dr.
Strauss himself, while a distinguished soloist is heard at
each concert. The permanent orchestra numbers eighty
players, among whom are the well-known Messrs. Ernst
Schiever (principal violin), Sück, Beard, Van Dermeerschen, Probin, Johan Hoch, Cockerill, and others.[2]

The arrangement of the instruments is quite an original
one:

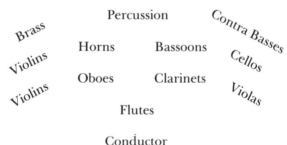

and may account for the fine *ensemble* heard in *tutti* passages.

---

[2] It has not proved possible to identify all these names, as the passage of
time has robbed them of their familiarity. Ernst Schiever (1844–1915), at
one time a member of the Joachim Quartet, came to England in 1878 and
was later associated with the Hallé Orchestra; he also led the Schiever
Quartet, active for 30 years in the North of England. 'Sück' is perhaps
Henry Such, then professor of violin at the Guildhall School of Music,
and 'Beard' presumably the violinist Mark Beard, father of the better-
known Paul Beard who later led the City of Birmingham and B.B.C. Symphony Orchestras. Henry Van Dermeerschen (in later writings Brian
renders the name Vandermeerschen) was Halford's first horn, and like
several of his leading wind-players was London-based. The Dutch-born
cellist Johan Hock (not Hoch) had settled in Birmingham in the late

Each instrumental group displays that richness of colour only found in orchestras of the very highest standing, while it is doubtful whether the richness of tone of the violins and string basses is surpassed anywhere. Constant playing, under its own and other distinguished conductors, has made the Halford band a most pliable instrument. The attack, the manner – almost effortless – in which a *forte* rises from the faintest *pianissimo*, the perfect phrasing, are several features of this fine orchestra. Cross-bowing among the strings is practically unknown. Judging by the youthful appearance of the majority of the members of the orchestra, young blood obtains full sympathy. Since 1899 a distinction has been earned by this Society in enabling concert-goers to obtain analytical programmes ten days in advance of each concert – an innovation which the Queen's Hall Orchestra has recently adopted, and which, in the case of new works to be performed, must prove invaluable.

An article on this subject would not be complete without special reference being made to the founder of this movement, and conductor of the orchestra – Mr. George Halford.[3] A man of wide sympathies, knowledge, and experience, he is no sensational conductor, but prefers to achieve his effects with the least possible movement, and in the quietest possible manner. Those who have heard him conduct *Also sprach Zarathustra* and *Ein Heldenleben* must have felt the full force of these remarks, for in those works his climaxes are so huge, so immense, and yet achieved with a calm that is almost terrible in its intensity. Rarely does he

---

1890s; in 1932 he founded the Birmingham Philharmonic String Orchestra. The Probin family were notable horn players in Birmingham throughout the 19th century; Brian may mean Alfred Probin (1852–?).

[3] Brian's admiration for Halford can be gauged by the fact that in 1903 he had one of his children christened with the names George Halford. Writing in *Musical Opinion* in 1933, just after Halford's death, he recalled the conductor going through one of his early scores with him for two whole hours: 'It was one long lesson in scoring, and incidentally the only one I ever had, but the impress of its truth and worth remain with me yet'. (In a letter to the pianist Robert Keys, written in 1946, Brian alluded to this incident and identified the score in question as his now-lost *Tragic Prelude* – not *Pantalon and Columbine*, as was guessed by Kenneth Eastaugh in his *Havergal Brian: The Making of a Composer*, p. 55).

conduct without the score, but it is patent to the veriest onlooker that his score is in his head, and not his head in the score. He is undoubtedly the right man in the right place; and long may the combination of Mr. Halford, the Concert Society, and the Orchestra continue to advance the cause of music in Birmingham.

The Orchestral Crisis in England

Brian published this piece in *The Staffordshire Sentinel* for 30 September 1909; it is very much in the vein of his slightly earlier 'The Music Problem in Manchester', to be found on pp.199–202.

To the recently published play, *Cupid and Commonsense*, by Mr. Arnold Bennett (The New Age Press) there is a striking preface entitled 'The Crisis in the Theatre' – in which the author exposes the back-door jobbery connected with the theatre. It is a trenchant epistle, bristling with facts, and will no doubt create a flutter in the dovecotes of the dramatic theatre: yet what Mr. Bennett has to say is little less true of the present outlook in English orchestral music. We are face to face with a crisis.

Not since the days of Henry Purcell has there been so much activity in music as there is to-day in this country, and not since those days have we produced so many composers of the first rank. One cannot look without smiling on the shuffling and elbowing going on in the ranks of present-day English composers and conductors, to say nothing of the extraordinary pitch to which they have developed the subtle art of intrigue. The prevalence of the latter in English musicians of to-day would suggest that artistically we are returning to the period of the Stuarts and Count Grammont. We say TO-DAY, for in turning over the pages of the cantatas, anthems, and part-songs, which immediately preceded modern English music, it is too humorous to think that the composers of this harmless music ever had an intrigue. When Elgar came along he created an impetus or revival which brought forth a large number of composers, full of the modern spirit – albeit many of them reflections of Wagner, Elgar, and Strauss, &c. – whose number extends year after year, and who fight and struggle to keep or get 'their feet in'. By whom has this modern spirit chiefly been fostered?

Twenty years ago there were only two permanent orchestras in London – the Philharmonic Society and, although 20 miles out of London, the Crystal Palace orchestra conducted by Sir August Manns. He was the first conductor to foster and encourage English orchestral music. As time went by, the Queen's Hall orchestra was founded and Mr. Henry J. Wood took up the work begun by Manns: as the Crystal Palace orchestra and conductor faded into the twilight of non-existing things, the fostering and encouragement of modern English composers almost became Mr. Wood's sole possession, and one which he used right royally. Twelve years ago Mr. Granville Bantock became the conductor of a fine orchestra at the New Brighton Tower. Some time later Mr. George Halford commenced the 'Halford' orchestral concerts in Birmingham – in each case English composers were received with open arms, and special attention was given to their works. At New Brighton Mr. Bantock's enthusiasm led him to give whole programmes to individual English composers, and his work there only ceased by his removal to Birmingham to become Principal of the Midland School of Music. Later, he carried on his enterprising work on being appointed conductor of the Liverpool Orchestral Society, in succession to Mr. Rodewald. Ten years ago the Leeds Municipal Orchestra was founded (conductor, Mr. H.A. Fricker), and here again special encouragement has been given to young English composers. Bantock, Delius, Vaughan Williams, Holbrooke, Coleridge-Taylor, Boughton, Bainton, O'Neill, W.H. Bell, Wallace, Frederic Austin, Foulds, Balfour Gardiner, Ernest Austin, Bryson, Dale, Bowen, A. von H. Carse, Weston-Nicholl, Gustav von Holst, J.W. Hathaway, are recent successful English orchestral writers.[4]

---

[4] It is rare to see mention of the Germanic middle name of Adam Carse (1878–1958), but it should be 'von A.' (for 'von Ahn'). Joseph Weston

It is only right to point out what enormous disadvantages the young English composer suffers when compared with his German contemporary. In Germany there are about 200 good orchestras, and many first class opera houses; the cost to hear opera or orchestra is a mere trifle. If it is pointed out that Weimar (which is the home where, a few years ago, gathered Liszt, Wagner, Cornelius, Berlioz, and others, who gave the impetus to the modern movement) contains a smaller number of inhabitants than the town of Stoke-upon-Trent, it will readily be seen how intensely musical is Germany. In this country most of the first class orchestras are in London, as well as the only decent opera house we possess – Covent Garden Theatre. The German composer has the further stimulant of living in an atmosphere which has produced a line of great composers, commencing with Bach and culminating in Wagner and Strauss. We haven't produced a Bach, a Wagner, or a Strauss – but we may do so. We have produced Elgar, Bantock, Holbrooke, and others, notwithstanding the enormous disadvantages which retard the development of the English composer. Again, if the work of the rank and file of the English school be placed by the side of that of its German contemporary, it will be seen that we are by no means inferior.

To return to the orchestral crisis! At the present time there are four permanent orchestras in London: Queen's Hall, London Symphony, New Symphony, and the Beecham Orchestras. We wonder how long they will exist – they certainly cannot all be made to pay.[5] The Queen's Hall Orchestra, which has three millionaires on its board of directors, gives as many concerts as any orchestra in Europe, and just manages to pay its way. The London Symphony is worked on co-operative lines; the New Symphony

---

Nicholl (1875–?) was conductor of the Black Dyke Mills Band. W.H. Bell (1873–1946) eventually made his career in South Africa. Joseph W. Hathaway was a Gloucestershire composer, mainly of choral music, whose rhapsody *Now Sleeps the Moonlight Fair Upon this Bank* sets the same Shakespeare text as Vaughan Williams' *Serenade to Music*; he was a distant acquaintance of Brian's, and they were still in touch in the late 1940s.
[5] *Plus ça change....*

Orchestra, formerly conducted by Mr. Thomas Beecham, is now conducted by Mr. Landon Ronald – since when Mr. Beecham has founded an orchestra bearing his own name.

No doubt the law of the 'survival of the fittest' will prevail, or it may be 'they who have most money win'. In the provinces the outlook is black indeed! Mr. Halford, after spending many thousands of pounds to establish orchestral music in Birmingham, had to give in owing to lack of public support. The members of his orchestra have formed themselves into the Birmingham Symphony Orchestra, which, we believe, is being run on co-operative lines. The Liverpool Orchestral Society (conductor, Mr. Bantock) ceased to exist a month ago, owing to financial difficulties; and the Liverpool Symphony Orchestra – another co-operative institution – has decided to give fewer concerts this season, owing to indifferent support. The City Council of Leeds passed a resolution early this year compelling the Municipal Orchestra to become self-supporting in the future. This year the annual Birmingham Promenade Orchestral Concerts were resumed under that fine conductor, Mr. Landon Ronald. So far the support has been so meagre that they have already come to be looked upon as the last season of promenade concerts.

The Hallé Orchestra is well established in Manchester, but the atmosphere there is intensely German, and carries an imaginary notice board, 'English composers need not apply'. Dr. Hans Richter conducts, and draws a large salary. With the exception of Elgar's works he doesn't help modern English music at all.[6] In the case of Mr. Bantock's *Omar*

---

[6] An analysis of the four complete Hallé Concert seasons (including three series of summer Proms) which Brian covered for *The Musical World* tends to bear out his strictures. Apart from Elgar, who was generously represented, the only British works performed were York Bowen's Piano Concerto and *Symphonic Fantasia*, Bantock's short scena *The Wilderness*, Cowen's *Scandinavian* Symphony (not conducted by Richter) and *Rhapsodie Indienne*, Harty's *Ode to a Nightingale* (in the same concert as the Bantock), Edward Isaacs' Piano Concerto (not conducted by Richter), Percy Pitt's *Oriental Rhapsody*, and Stanford's *Songs of the Sea*: an average of two works every twelve months, and, as Brian did not hesitate to say in his reviews, mostly pretty minor ones.

Khayyam, which has been done in Manchester for two con-
secutive seasons, on the first occasion of its performance at
the Hallé concerts, the composer was invited to conduct his
own work, because Dr. Richter was tired and forced to 'take
the air' at Blackpool. There is also the Scottish Orchestra
which performs in the North, under Dr. Cowen.

To sum up and review the whole situation. Zeal seems to
have outrun discretion, or we have produced the men
before the nation is ready for them. We have three virtuosi
conductors, not excelled by any German or other foreign
contemporaries, in H. J. Wood, Landon Ronald, Thomas
Beecham – and we have a few, only a very few, first-class
orchestras. From the composer's point of view, it would
appear, looking around upon the fine work being produced, that the harvest was now ready, but, from the financial point of view, it appears that English orchestral music
was never so near bankruptcy.

The B.B.C. Orchestra

From *Musical Opinion*, July 1930, p. 901.

The public has now had a number of opportunities of test-
ing the new orchestra of 114 players.[7] The most fastidious
critics are unanimous in praising its magnificent ensemble.
The string tone is brilliant; the brass and woodwind are not
so good. In modern orchestral works such as Strauss, the
ensemble is unusually mellow and satisfying. The richness
in the ensemble is largely due to doubling the wind – an
innovation first introduced into England at Manchester
from Vienna and Bayreuth by Hans Richter.

---

[7] The B.B.C. Symphony Orchestra was founded in 1930, with Adrian
Boult as conductor, from the nucleus of Henry Wood's old Queen's Hall
Orchestra – which had had an umbilical connection to the B.B.C. since
the 1927 Promenade Concerts Season (see pp.188–191). But it also drew
players from all the other British orchestras, creating a new 'crisis', the
effects of which included the resignation of Sir Hamilton Harty from the
conductorship of the Hallé Orchestra, shortly after he had expressed the
hope of giving the premiere of Brian's *Gothic* Symphony in Manchester.

Such an orchestra as the B.B.C. has not yet become conscious of its great weight and power, even though these are supreme qualities; also, the material is the best we can put forward in this country. The orchestra is like a super-grand pianoforte; it needs a virtuoso to play on it who will do for orchestral technique and interpretation what Busoni did for the higher school of piano playing – viz., inculcate a passion and pride for virtuosity in the orchestra, not for mere display but for the fulfilment of an ideal which is only attainable through perfection in technique, ensemble and interpretation. The orchestra is worthy of the greatest conductor: its ensemble would delight the ears of Toscanini. But at present, it has not reached the polished stage: the phrasing is apt to be slovenly. The splendour of the New York, Berlin, and Vienna orchestras lies in their immaculate phrasing and a perfect level in the toning of the wind. Thus, in a chordal passage for three horns in any of these orchestras, the middle man would not drown the player on each side of him. Nor in a take-over from one woodwind instrument to another should we get tonal bulges or lumps. In recent performances of the B.B.C. orchestra, we have had patches of defective playing from the wind when they were uncovered. In the performances of Beethoven's Eighth Symphony and Violin Concerto (both works written in what might be termed the feminine gender), a great deal of the string playing was too heavy to be capricious.

Though still in its infancy, we are judging the B.B.C. orchestra from the exceptional standards given us by America and Germany: for every orchestra – no matter where it is – reflects the capacity and limits of its conductor.

Liverpool Philharmonic Hall
and Concert Halls in General

From 'On the Other Hand', August 1936, p. 912.

The rebuilding of this hall is evidently being regarded as a work of national importance, and certainly it is so in the world of music.[8] The old hall was a dignified structure in stone, with a concert room having good acoustics, not too resonant; and the long series of boxes on each side, rose coloured, made it the most cosy in the country. My happiest recollections are associated with that old hall, for it was there I heard given by the Liverpool Welsh Choral Union, under Harry Evans, an early work of my own.[9] With the dramatic fervour of the choir and the suppressed excitement within me, I was well nigh lifted off my feet.

It now appears that the Philharmonic Society has not the wealth attributed to it, and the insurance money received is not sufficient to rebuild the hall. The Corporation are, it seems, willing to build a civic hall for music, but ask for the money in the hands of the society as a contribution towards the cost. This may seem a plausible proposition, but shortly the Philharmonic Society would be no more. The old hall was an outward and visible evidence of the existence of a musical society, arising out of the music itself; and not something grudgingly paid for in the rates. Those who want a civic hall of music might have found a happier time to press the idea when the Philharmonic Society is in the awkward position of having money in hand but not enough for its purpose. It's like an invitation to sell a birthright, or perhaps to surrender a trust to those who declare that the child Music shall be well cared for – at the Institution.

Whoever builds the new concert hall in Liverpool, it is to be hoped that, acoustically, it will be successful as was the old Philharmonic Hall. One other is as good, and perhaps better – the famous Gewandhaus at Leipzig. The Free Trade Hall at Manchester has now lost its political identity and is renowned everywhere as the home of the great Hallé Orchestra. Birmingham Town Hall is rather different, for it seems to have swung over from music to politics: anyhow, it began with the triennial musical festivals, the failure of existing halls to accommodate which led to the idea of a

[8] The old Liverpool Philharmonic Hall had been destroyed by fire in 1933; its successor eventually opened in 1939.
[9] This was the second performance of Brian's *By the Waters of Babylon*, 25 September 1909, during the first Musical League Festival.

town hall being included in a scheme of improvements for the city. The Town Hall was opened in October, 1834 with the triennial festival, and remained associated with it until recent years. Its acoustics are good, but in my experience for ever menaced by a terrible clock, chiming in an adjoining tower. (Once when Beecham was starting the slow movement of the Beethoven Symphony No. 2, that clock spread out in measured paces the dread hour of nine!) Colston Hall, Bristol, and Leeds Town Hall are equally good acoustically; but in my opinion the finest hall in the whole country for hearing is the Victoria Hall, Hanley. It was designed by the borough surveyor of the time (1887), Joseph Lobley by name, and he succeeded in the prime purpose of his work where the most eminent architects of the country have failed in theirs. About the size of Queen's Hall, London, the interior of Victoria Hall, Hanley, is severe and plain, which may account in some measure for its acoustic perfection. At one morning rehearsal Richter expressed his astonishment at the remarkable resonance of the hall; and at the concert in the evening, with only about seventy-five per cent of the orchestra present, the first three chords of the Brahms No. 3 Symphony in F came out with terrific effect, such as I had never heard Richter produce with a full band at the Free Trade Hall, Manchester, or elsewhere. At Victoria Hall, Hanley, were heard the first performances of Elgar's *King Olaf* and Coleridge-Taylor's *Death of Minnehaha*.

With these object lessons before them, and mention by *The Times* critic of Albert Hall, Queen's Hall, the concert hall of the R.C.M., and the new hall in Sheffield as acoustic failures, one will not envy the task of those who have to decide about the new concert hall for Liverpool. It is a wise suggestion that visits should be made to Amsterdam, Stockholm, Berlin and Vienna, where may be found concert halls that are not acoustic failures.

The Orchestra in London

From 'On the Other Hand', October 1936, p. 13.

Seeing that the regular concert going public of London can, it is said, be counted in hundreds only, one wonders at the talk of increase in orchestras and concerts. For years (until the close of the war), London had two important orchestras – the Queen's Hall and the London Symphony. The New Symphony functioned spasmodically, certainly; but the Philharmonic was only a cadre. After radio was established, the Queen's Hall Orchestra was disbanded, and the London Symphony, after losing its distinctive personnel, was reorganised, with an uphill task to attain its former prestige. But meanwhile two new orchestras had come into existence – the B.B.C. Orchestra and the London Philharmonic Orchestra, the latter being a realisation of the genius of Thomas Beecham, who had never been quite happy with the other organisations. Beecham began conducting in London with a small group of players drawn from the Queen's Hall Orchestra, and then with the late Eli Hudson[10] founded the New Symphony, with which he toured in Germany.

The London Philharmonic Orchestra is akin to Beecham – subtle, magnificent, brilliant and surprising; and the B.B.C. Orchestra is often what various conductors make it. Under Toscanini it was made to sound superb and in some works unsurpassable. With these two orchestras, neither more than seven years old, London orchestral music appears to have entered a new era. But it is only on paper that multiplication appears: actually, with the Queen's Hall Orchestra revived, we shall only be just where we were. Last year's success of the Sunday concerts at Queen's Hall by the London Philharmonic Orchestra under Beecham was nothing new, though it was something fresh for the orchestra. For years until the war we had Sunday

---

[10] Eli Hudson (1877–1919) was a celebrated flautist and first flute of the LSO at its inception.

symphony concerts at Queen's Hall and at Albert Hall, and indeed it was at Kensington with the London Symphony Orchestra that Landon Ronald and Harty came to be so well known as orchestral conductors. If then we imagine the Queen's Hall Sunday concerts revived, and those previously given at Albert Hall moved east to Covent Garden (though with Sir Thomas and his Philharmonics), where is the increase and supposed redundance? We are only getting back to pre-war conditions. The B.B.C. Wednesday symphony replaces the Queen's Hall Saturday: so here again we are as we were. The only real addition to London orchestral music, even after twenty years, is the short season of Winter 'Proms'.

CHOIRS

Retrogression in the Hallé Choir

This polemical piece appeared in *The Musical World* for 16 December 1905 (p.243). Although signed 'from a Manchester correspondent', it is wholly consonant with the tenor of Brian's continual complaints in his Hallé Concert reviews – and he was, of course, the magazine's principal Manchester correspondent. Various letters to the Editor in the wake of this article – some from members of the Hallé Choir – overwhelmingly supported Brian's strictures; but this kind of article shows how Brian's early writings seldom spared local sensitivities and brought him few friends.

Is it not time, after the disclosures of the last choral concert, that the state of the chorus should receive the serious and earnest consideration of the Hallé Concerts Society? Manchester, like London, often has the charge brought against it that its inhabitants suffer not a little from a sense of self-sufficiency – though this fact may be quite unknown within the city itself, since Manchester people rarely get away from the influence of their environment; they carry it with them wherever they go. Musically – chorally especially – speaking, the charge is quite correct; and they do not know good choral singing because they rarely hear it. In the old days the Hallé Choir was known every where as one of the most progressive choruses in the country. A new work could be produced with a minimum of rehearsals, so expert were they in reading and so quick to respond to the wishes of the conductor; indeed nothing ever came amiss to them. Such a claim could hardly be made to-day by this once-famous choir. At the first choral concert of this season their singing of *The Dream of Gerontius* raised the hope that the old days were returning, for they showed a certain familiarity with the spirit of the work that had been lacking in most of their performances last year. But it was their fourth performance of the work! Four years in which to learn a modern work that, *if the modern spirit be alive in them*, should be adequately rehearsed in one season, and perfectly rendered in two. But the fact is, they have none of the modern spirit in them! A great many of the Manchester singers and musicians died with Sir Charles Hallé, and their successors evince none of his progressive policy in music. Had his spirit been no greater than theirs, works like the *St. Matthew Passion* and Berlioz's *Faust* would still have been unheard in Manchester. As a matter of fact, one of the very works of which they sang the notes the other night – Brahms's *Song of Destiny* – had not been given since Hallé gave it in 1876! Whether the chorus of 1905 perceived and appreciated in the work any fuller and deeper meaning – except as it was drawn out of them by the master-mind of Dr. Richter – than that of 1876 is extremely doubtful. Indeed it may be questioned whether the chorus is making any progress in the matter of interpretation, for the tone with which they entered at 'Far in yon region of light' had caught none of the mystical suggestiveness so wonderfully realised by the band in the prelude. It was hard and cold, devoid of the imagination that would transmit to the audience the emotion of that place – 'where pleasures fail not, wander the Spirits blest'. In the Bach Cantata[11] their tone reminded one of an old Yorkshire

---

[11] No. 202, the 'Wedding' Cantata, was performed by the Hallé in late November 1905.

opera-goer who shouted from the gallery 'Is yon chap singing, or is it t' gas-pipe 'at's leaking?' Many a time during the
Bach Cantata far more breath was audible than tone, and
the manner in which the singers 'slithered' up and down the
runs suggested an impressionist picture that would have
served to depict Market-street on a foggy night – a bit of
realism not intended by Bach.

No, the Hallé Choir is not maintaining its old supremacy,
and it will find difficulty in keeping its position even as a
third-rate power among the Northern and Midland
choruses. Indeed it is already beaten by three choruses in
Yorkshire and one in Staffordshire – which reduces its position to the fourth degree – and this with all the advantages
it enjoys of a permanent orchestra, and occasional rehearsals with Dr. Richter! Is the Hallé Concerts Society content
to stand aside and see their chorus, which still contains
within it all the elements of success, degraded to a fifth-rate
position? Or will they continue to hide themselves behind
the huge mount of self-sufficiency built round them by the
mental atmosphere of their city?

What is the remedy? In physical ailments, when the general practitioner fails the specialist is quickly summoned.
The Hallé Choir is extremely sick, and only the best expert
advice can save it. Why not invite one, or even two, of the
men who have made their name famous by their genius for
choral training, to advise upon this matter? Could the
committee see their way clear to adopt such a course they
would carry with them a large number of the younger members of the chorus who are conscious of their limitations,
and possibly many of the older members who sigh for the
'days of Hecht'.[12] One thing is certain: it is impossible to
stand still. Choruses are in process of making in Blackpool,
Morecambe, and other places, that will reduce the position
of the Hallé Choir still further. The spirit of Hallé and
Hecht must be revived, otherwise the Hallé Choir will exist
merely as a name for something that is past. Which would
the chorus themselves choose – advance or retreat?

---

[12] Eduard Hecht (1832–1887), noted Manchester choral conductor in
the early days of the Hallé.

Tournament of Song

Brian contributed this report (with the sub-heading 'Local Choir in Competition at New Brighton') to *The Staffordshire Sentinel* of 20 September 1909. Choral competitions of this kind were the most ardently pursued musical activity of the Potteries at this time, and this typical report gives something of their flavour.

The management of the New Brighton Tower inaugurated a musical tournament of song in 1901. From the first the gatherings attracted the very best of the Welsh and English choirs, though the limitations in the strength of the choirs competing and the value of the prizes offered prevented its being looked upon as quite of the highest order of competition. Two choirs from North Staffordshire have distinguished themselves at this huge play city on the promontory of the Mersey. At the opening competition in 1901, and again in 1902, the Talke and District Choir got second place, but in the very next year, namely, in 1903, it secured the first prize. Then for the ensuing couple of years Talke gave way to a Hanley combination, which annexed the chief distinction on each occasion. Since then the chiefest honour has gone mainly to Lancashire choirs. On Saturday again North Staffordshire was represented by the Talke and District Prize Choir, and though the singers were disappointed in not securing a place amongst the first three, it has to be pointed out, not by way of apology, but as an act of common justice, that its singing was of the highest merit, and that in the arena appeared other musical organisations which sang with supreme skill and judgement and built up greater tone and volume. For delicacy of phrasing, refinement of tone, voice blend, clearness of enunciation, and unity of purpose – points all of them absolutely essential to the best choral singing – the Talke Choir was not beaten – could not be beaten – and perhaps was unequalled in all those points by any other organisation, heard throughout the contest. The fact is notorious that the choral singing of to-day is very much more perfect than it was a decade back; that the fine efforts of the North Staffordshire choirs, whose excellent mission work is fully recognised in many quarters, has had the effect of compelling other districts to improve upon the personnel of their choirs, and the training of the singers. In order, therefore, that North Staffordshire may retain its present pre-eminence it will be necessary that nothing less than perfection in all features that are recognised in the best choral singing should be reached, and in securing that, something may be done in the way of voice resonance. Something also should be done to improve the methods of the adjudicators themselves. In a contest of the calibre of that of Saturday, the indications of position by figuration is not entirely satisfactory. It demands some system more exhaustive and exacting.

THE PRINCIPAL COMPETITION

The competition in which the Talke and District Prize Choir competed was the second item of the evening meeting, and, of course, was the main attraction of the festival. The choirs were called upon to sing Edward German's setting of Shakespeare's song *Who is Sylvia*, and a chorus of Handel's *Samson* – 'Let their celestial concerts', the first being sung unaccompanied and the second with pianoforte accompaniment. The part-song was sung first. It required delicate handling, feeling and rhythmical grace and some subtlety. The chorus is of the familiar Handel type, needing note accuracy, general smartness, and the gift to build up over-powering climaxes. The choirs singing were limited to a maximum of 75 voices and a minimum of 60. Most of them sang with the full number allowed. The chief money prize was £35, together with a silver challenge shield, and a gold medal for the conductor. Prizes were also given to the choirs placed second and third. The choirs, and the order of their singing, determined by ballot, were as here set forth:

1. Oriana Madrigal Society .... Dr. S.B. Seddall
2. St. Helens Prize Choir .... Mr. Harry Barrey
3. Talke and District Prize Choir .... Mr. James Whewall
4. Oldham Harmonic Society .... Mr. H. Hannam
5. Colne Valley Vocal Union .... Dr. F. E. Pearson
6. The Southport Choir .... Mr. W. Tattersall
7. Huddersfield Glee and Madrigal Society
Mr. J.W. Armitage

The Oriana was fresh to this competition. While its members were responsible for some good singing, it fell short of the standard required. St. Helens have twice won the chief first prize, and twice have secured the second prize. It was natural, therefore, that its members should reach nearer the necessary brilliancy. A very powerful effect was produced in the start of the chorus. The choir is well balanced. The altos were much better than those in the first combination, but there was a variety of colour among the singers, and the purity of the blend was affected. The expression in the line of the part song, 'Is she kind as she is fair' lacked conviction. The attack was undoubtedly splendid. Dr. McNaught, who made the adjudication,[13] spoke of a slight departure from the opening phrasing as printed in the German selection. The pianissimos, he also observed, were done better by other choirs, and the light and shade showed deficiency. A good general performance nevertheless. In the Handel piece the choir was very fine, the combination was excellent for such a piece, through in the middle part there was a slight falling away from the clearness of the commencement. The climax was grand.

Mr. James Whewall's singers from the very commencement obtained that charming tone blend which one naturally looks for, and would as naturally regret were it absent, in a first-class North Staffordshire choir.[14] The tenors produced just that velvety tone which Sir Edward Elgar delighted in, the sopranos delivered a brilliantly ringing tone, the altos were not surpassed for richness and real tone evenness by any choir, while the bass was certainly, if less heavy, the most tunefully sonorous heard. The pianofortes were beautifully tender, the rhythm was grand, and all parts, the inner quite as much as the outer, moved with masterly precision. It was a remarkably polished performance. The speed was faster than that taken by the other choirs. On the whole an unsurpassed performance. In the chorus a fine climax was reached, but in tone weight, which counts for much in a Handel number, it was outdone by two or

---

[13]   See note 22 on p. 138.
[14]   For more on Whewall and his choirs see pp.384–386.

three of the other choirs. In one part, the tenors failed to give quite the same distinction they had given in other parts, though the run which followed thrilled one by reason of its manifest perfection.

It may be interesting to give here the adjudication of Dr. McNaught on the singing of Mr. Whewall's Choir: The Talke and District Prize Choir, he said, began very quick, but from the commencement one was at once attracted by the easy flow, the grace, of the singing; and much subtlety characterised the underlying interpretation. The enunciation was particularly clear, and all the gradations of tone were managed by all the members of the choir. Sometimes choirmasters could not get absolute unity – one or two voices would stand out, but here, in the case of the Talke choir, the whole parts moved together in their separate divisions as though there were one voice only in each part. The rhythm, it was pleasing to notice, was well-stroked. They lost pitch slightly, but that was not of much consequence. Then when they began the chorus, it struck him that the singers did not get a firm grip of the chord given by the piano – they seemed to be influenced a trifle more by the chord of the part-song just finished than by the new chord of the second piece. They soon, however, displayed some fine qualities – a big, round, fast tone; exhibited, indeed, very good singing abilities, but he did not think the climax was quite so imposing as it might have been. The clearness of the enunciation was a very good point. The choristers sang mezzopiano where it ought to have been a forte passage.

The pick of the Oldham Choir were the sopranos, and in adjudication Dr. McNaught remarked that if all the parts of the choir were as good as the sopranos the organisation would be admirable in every way. The delivery of the words 'Then to Sylvia let us sing, that Sylvia is excelling', conveyed a clearer meaning than had been given to them by any of the previous choirs. The finish in the Handel piece was noble and dignified. In respect to the Colne Valley choir, the adjudicator pointed out they secured a correct rhythm at the very opening; in which respect other choirs had failed. There was some license, he also observed, in the blending.

The rhythm was most beautiful – it could hardly be done better. The blend got much better, and appeared to the judges as almost perfect. The pitch was kept. The slurs were overpointed, which must be counted against the choir. On the other hand the mass of liquid tone was pointed out by one of his fellow-judges, and the climax was splendid. Occasionally there was a little hardness in the tenor part.

It was a point in favour of these fine choirs that they sang from old notation copies, and it would be interesting to know what proportion of them mentally sol-faad the music they read. Evidently, the gentleman at the pianoforte was not minded that this choir should fail from want of getting hold of the chord, for he kept playing the tonic, mediant, and dominant over and over again. The singers of this choir are so polished, however, that they could not have needed any such aid to the tonality of the piece. Every section of this choir produced a fine full tone, each section being heavier than in the Talke choir. The style of the Talke choir was repeated by the Southport organisation. The tenors in the chorus once or twice jumped at their top notes, and the same slight blemish was noticed in the sopranos, but as a whole the performance was full of dignity. Dr. McNaught, referring to the performance of this choir, said the tone was fine, and the blend was rich in the part song, but the attack was by no means perfect. The singers were responsible for a full-blooded performance of the chorus. The last choir gave a fine rendering of both pieces, being responsible for some of the most efficient singing of the day. It was a great competition. The choirs were finally placed in the following order:

	Choir.	Chorus.	Part Song.	Total of Marks.
1.	Colne	75	75	150
2.	Huddersfield	74	74	148
3.	Southport	71	73	144
4.	St. Helens	70	72	142
5.	Talke	72	68	140
6.	Oldham	68	60	128
7.	Oriana	64	59	123

Provincial Choral Societies

This is from 'On the Other Hand', April 1937, pp. 583–584.

I wish I could share the roseate optimism expressed recently in London about the healthy state of choral societies in the provinces. Unfortunately, the provincial press tells a very different story, laying bare the cold facts. During recent years choral societies, at one time well founded, have ceased to function in Sheffield, Birmingham, Wolverhampton, Hanley, Manchester, Walsall, Stafford, &c. The Wolverhampton Festival Choral Society – once a leading and enterprising society under the successive leadership of Swinnerton Heap, George Halford, and Granville Bantock, with occasional visits from Henry Wood – has not only disappeared, but the town now has, so I am told, no singing body of any kind. Sport in the form of the wheel and the ball, and the absence of music in the home, have combined to kill or injure choral singing as we knew it in Victorian times. Manchester seems worse off than other provincial cities. There was once considerable rivalry between the Hallé Chorus and the Brand Lane Choir. When Brand Lane[15] died, the choir crumbled away and the Hallé Chorus was left to fight the battle alone. This season it has made two public appearances, to sing the *Messiah* and two short works by Palestrina and Berlioz. So, if Manchester can be taken as a fair example of choral music in the provinces, the outlook is far from encouraging.

If further proof were needed of the decline of choral music in the provinces, one has only to look at the files of musical journals published before the war, since which time people have found their intellectual culture at the cinema, and their physical development in a superheated motor-coach. Probably some other reason may also found for the changed mentality of the class that once made good

[15] G.W. Brand Lane (1854–?) founded the Manchester Philharmonic Choir in 1880, and in 1914 began an important series of choral and orchestral celebrity concerts with Henry Wood as conductor.

amateur singers. Those of twenty years ago have, of course,
grown old: and it is in their gradual replacement that we
have been failing. The old chorister who found his life-
pulse in the singing of his chorus, or in social intercourse
with fellow singers, is no more: and those who have come
after just sit and wait to be amused. You cannot have great
choral singing without enthusiasm and discipline. The
long-maintained supremacy of the singing of the Sheffield
Choir was only obtained by submission to severe training
and unrelenting discipline, and without those things Henry
Coward would never have attained the position he did
as the greatest choral leader of his day.[16] Anyone without
previous experience of his methods, who was privileged to
see and hear him take a festival chorus through a final
rehearsal, must have been astonished at the precision and
virtuosity of the massed voices. The driving force of Coward's genius raised choral singing to a pitch of perfection far
outside his own locality by firing the ambition of numerous
lesser conductors. They strove to imitate Coward, and the
influence was all to the good. The fame of the Sheffield
Choir became a slogan for supremacy of achievement –
virtuosity in chorus singing. As provincial choral societies
are purely voluntary, there can be no question of a tradition.
Now that the career of Coward as the greatest choral leader
of his day has reached its close, it was inevitable that the
famous Sheffield Choir should also cease, though it is
regrettable that the end should come while we still await
signs of what we hope ought to be a revival in choral singing.

[16] Sir Henry Coward (1849–1944) was one of the most noted choir train-
ers and conductors of the period, especially celebrated for his work in the
Sheffield Festival.

The North Staffordshire District Choral Society

This article appeared in *Musical Opinion* for February 1938 (pp. 410–411) and was the culmination of Brian's many writings on the choir – and its conductors – that occupied such an important place in the musical life of his youth. It is worth noting that *The Musical World* for 16 October 1906 contains an unsigned article (pp.94–95) on the Staffordshire choirs, Whewall, and John James, covering much the same ground as the present one, although of course from a shorter historical perspective. I strongly suspect it to be by Brian.

The remarkable performance by this great English choir of Handel's *Messiah* on December 6th, brought many congratulations from various parts of the world. The performance took place at the Victoria Hall, Hanley, under John James, the conductor of the society, and was broadcast by the British Broadcasting Corporation, who received a cable from the general manager of the Canadian Broadcasting Corporation, as follows: '*Messiah*, Thursday, thrilled all Canada: special thanks to orchestra, chorus and artists'.

The history of this famous choir is unlike that of other choirs. The Potteries have never lacked choirs or amateur orchestras: fifty years ago there were half-a-dozen choral societies, subsisting on the oratorios of Handel, Haydn and Mendelssohn.[17] The largest was the Hanley Glee and Madrigal Society of three hundred voices, developed from a small choir founded for the practice of glees and part-songs by its conductor, James Garner, who was at the time a working potter.[18]

The most enterprising society was the Stoke-on-Trent Philharmonic, conducted by Dr. Swinnerton Heap, with a choir of two hundred voices, which performed the choral works of Berlioz, Schumann, Brahms, Mendelssohn,

[17] The history of music in the Potteries during this period has been ably recounted by the late Reginald Nettel in *Music in the Five Towns* (Oxford University Press, London, 1944) and *North Staffordshire Music: A Social Experiment* (Triad Press, Rickmansworth, 1977).
[18] For Garner see *North Staffordshire Music*, pp. 29 *et seq.*

Stanford, Parry, Mackenzie, Elgar, Coleridge-Taylor, &c. In those days the only satisfactory concert hall in the neighbourhood was the Victoria Hall, Hanley, where after its erection the Stoke Philharmonic transferred its concerts, and thus became unintentional rivals of the Hanley Glee and Madrigal Society. The society destined to eclipse all other choral societies did not then exist, and he who was to show the way was none other than James Whewall (pronounced Huel, with a slight aspirate[19]), then living at Talk o' th' Hill, a mining village on the range of hills forming a boundary between Staffordshire and Cheshire and some miles from Stoke-on-Trent. Whewall, in his early days and whilst working as a miner and cobbler, had studied music, and began his career as a choral conductor by forming a juvenile choir of boys and girls. These he taught to sing, and trained them so well that, at choral competitions the young choralists usually carried off first prizes. The writer, when a young boy himself, heard this choir, and noticed that Whewall did not have a stick when conducting, but used his thumb and first finger only. Eventually the juvenile choir became an adult choir know as the Talk o' th' Hill Choir, which was equally successful. There was a waiting list of those anxious to join the choir, with the result that in 1901 it became a choral body of 250 voices competing in the chief events at the Welsh National Eisteddfod, entering as the North Staffordshire District Choral Society. It was not the first time that James Whewall had taken a choir to Wales, but it was something new for an English choir to challenge the Welsh on their own ground. Whewell won easily at Merthyr Tydfil, and in the years following again defeated all the Welsh choirs.

It was noticed, after the meetings with the Welsh, that Whewall when conducting often continued to use his thumb and first finger. When asked what he intended to do

---

[19] Nettel (*North Staffordshire Music*, p. 35) claims to the contrary that the name was pronounced *Whee-wall* 'in the local manner', and he was as local a man as Brian. But Brian knew Whewall well, whereas Nettel was still only a child when he died.

with such a fine choir, he replied, 'Nothing! and we cannot exist as a choral society, for the Potteries already has too many'. Wiser counsels prevailed, and the choir begun to give concerts at the Victoria Hall, Hanley, at the first giving a performance of Haydn's *Creation*. Rivalry with the Glee and Madrigal Society soon became manifest, but it was more apparent than real, because the new choir did not draw its members from Hanley, but from villages and towns lying towards the Cheshire boundary. After that performance of the old oratorio, the choir took a leap forward. With only the ticket selling of its members, it is surprising how successful this society became, even with the most costly productions. Whilst other societies stood hesitating about a performance of Elgar's *Dream of Gerontius*, after its first performance at the Birmingham Music Festival the North Staffordshire Society announced a performance conducted by the composer, with an orchestra drawn from Manchester and Birmingham, and with Muriel Foster, John Coates and Ffrangçon Davies as principals. This was in 1902, and a year later another performance was given in Westminster Cathedral.

Hereafter the Hallé Orchestra was engaged for performances, and during the succeeding years the choir increased its fame by giving performances of *The Apostles* and *The Kingdom* (Elgar), under Elgar. Beecham frequently appeared as conductor with the New Symphony Orchestra, introducing *Sea Drift*, *Mass of Life* (Delius), and an orchestral poem, *Hero and Leander* (Havergal Brian).[20] In 1907 the new choral works included *Omar Khayyam* (Bantock) and *By the Waters of Babylon* (Havergal Brian). In 1909 the choir gave a command performance before King Edward and Queen Alexandra. James Whewall was the conductor, and

---

[20] Brian's symphonic poem *Hero and Leander* received its one and only performance – after which Beecham managed to lose the score and parts – at the Victoria Hall, Hanley on 3 December 1908, in a gigantic programme that also featured (among other items) Delius' *Sea Drift* and Bantock's *Omar Khayyam*, Part II, and part of his *Sappho* song-cycle (conducted by the composer).

on the return journey home he was taken ill and died shortly afterwards.[21]

The present conductor of the choir, John James, has held the appointment for the past fifteen years, and is in his own way a man more remarkable than Whewall.[22] John James began his career as a choral conductor by openly scorning pot-hunting at musical competitions, and backed his opinions by forming a select choir of sixty voices for the performance of modern choral music and Elizabethan madrigals. It was called the Hanley Cauldon Choir, and

---

[21] Brian's *Staffordshire Sentinel* obituary for Whewall, one of the musicians who made the deepest impression on him in his formative years, will be included in a later volume. Here he somewhat underplays the drama: a week after the triumph of the Windsor concert (treated by the Staffordshire press at enormous length as a matter of the most intense local pride), Whewall was dead of influenza contracted on the return journey.

[22] John James was a close personal friend of Brian's, and one of the few Potteries musicians who remained on terms with him after he had moved to London in 1913 – as is attested by the fact that Brian's *Laughing Song*, a trio for female voices and piano to a poem by William Blake, composed 1915, is dedicated to James's son, who bore the middle name Brian.

Here, as in all his other writings on the subject, Brian refrains from mentioning that at Whewall's death the committee of the Talke and District Choir (i.e., the nucleus of the North Staffordshire Chorus) offered the conductorship to *him*. Reginald Nettel, in *Havergal Brian: The Man and his Music*, p. 71, states that Brian declined the honour. But this is not so. Brian *accepted* the conductorship, as was reported in *The Staffordshire Sentinel* of 5 February 1910, and is confirmed by a Letter to the Editor which he wrote in the capacity of conductor (printed on 7 February). But his tenure was brief, and he appears never to have given a concert with the choir.

Judging by the tone of his obituary for Whewall, it may well be that he accepted the appointment more out of respect for Whewall's memory than from any considered appraisal of his own musical direction. His waning interest in the unaccompanied choral medium and the urge to devote his time to orchestral composition probably convinced him before long that the step had been a mistake. But the whole episode merits further research. It may well be that the major orchestral work which subsequently occupied him until October 1910 the symphonic poem *In Memoriam* (originally entitled *Homage to an Artist*), was intended as a more appropriate act of tribute to Whewall, and its covert quotation of the National Athem in its second section as an allusion to the concert at Windsor which was the crowning glory of Whewall's life.

it was rehearsed so thoroughly that it become as sensitive and efficient as a professional string quartet: it was a new and unique experience to hear this body of voices interpreting part-songs by Cornelius, Brahms, Elgar, Möellendorf, [23] &c., and the madrigals of Wilbye and Weelkes. When the choir won the first prize in the Challenge Shield Competition at the Morecambe Festival of 1905, Dr. McNaught rose and told the audience that the astonishing interpretation by the choir of the eight-part *O death, thou art the tranquil night* (Cornelius) had reduced the judges to tears. Shortly afterwards the choir accepted engagements to sing at the Schiller Anstalt (Manchester) and to the Malvern Glee Club at Malvern. This later engagement was at the instigation of Elgar, who invited many well-known musicians to Malvern to listen to the choir.

When James Garner, the conductor of the Hanley Glee and Madrigal Society, died, John James was appointed his successor. He at once began the reform of that choir, introducing modern methods of choral technique and modern choral works eventually realising in a series of superb performances, including *King Olaf* (Elgar) and *The Damnation of Faust* (Berlioz), with the Queen's Hall Orchestra and Henry J. Wood, the latter repeated in Queen's Hall, London. In 1912, Dr. Hans Richter, who conducted the choir at a concert of the London Symphony Orchestra at Queen's Hall, was so astonished by its performance that he suggested to John James that he should embark on a career as orchestral conductor in Germany, with the help and backing of the great conductor himself. The suggestion was impractical, though it was after James's own heart, for he is as much at home with the orchestra as with the choir, and has always secured the co-operation of the finest available orchestras. As a conductor, he is a practical idealist, whose idealism may be found in the number of performances of the *St. Matthew Passion* and the Mass in B minor (Bach), Ninth Symphony (Beethoven), *Faust* (Berlioz), *Requiem* (Verdi), *Stabat Mater*

[23] Willi von Möllendorf (1872–1934), German composer of choral music, who later became involved in experiments with quarter-tone instruments.

and *Spectre's Bride* (Dvořák), *The Apostles* and *Music Makers* (Elgar), and selections from *Lohengrin*, &c. (Wagner). Since Elgar's *King Olaf* was first produced in 1896 at a North Staffordshire Musical Festival, his name has been venerated. He made his last appearance there in 1932, shortly before his death, when he conducted *King Olaf* in the hall where it was first produced.

Consistent with the policy inaugurated by James Whewall, Mr. James has been attentive to the claims of contemporary English composers. In recent years he has performed Holst's *Hymn of Jesus*, the *Sea Symphony* and *Five Tudor Portraits* of Vaughan Williams, and William Walton's *Belshazzar's Feast*. Mr. James had the honour of a royal command to Windsor in November, 1908, and again in 1913 and 1926. Long may he live to conduct the North Staffordshire District Choral Society.

English Choral Singing

From 'On the Other Hand', March 1938, pp. 490–491.

Though music is international, one of my correspondents tells me of the pleasure that was his to read of the prowess of that markedly English institution, the North Staffordshire Choral Society, and he goes on to say that all glitters in the form of international instrumental ideology is not music. There is some truth in what is thus expressed: and certainly we English should hold fast to that which is good – English choral singing. Let us honour those who begat and fostered it during the ages.

The first name among those of recent years is Augusta Mary Wakefield (1853–1910), the Kendal lady who established the Kendal Festival in 1885. She had a good contralto voice, trained by the best masters in London and in Rome: and on returning to England she was to be heard at many concerts and at the Gloucester Festival of 1880. The standard and ideals of Kendal were followed at Lytham, Morecambe, Blackpool, and other places, and for mutual support and encouragement Miss Wakefield founded the

Association of Festivals. The routine was practice of choral music, with competitions among themselves and finally a festival with performances of major choral works. We see to-day this idea prevailing at Leith Hill. Only the best orchestras were good enough, so at Kendal were heard the Queen's Hall and the Hallé.

The festival eventually destined to become great and invigorating for the encouragement and practice of a-cappella music was the Morecambe Music Festival, established by the rector, Canon C.V. Gorton, who was a remarkable amateur musician, quite unknown to lexicon makers. I found him sane, frank, cordial, with a bright wit.[24] To the Canon, the festival was a 'cause', something to be taken very seriously. In selecting a-cappella music, his judgment was unerring, probably because he looked only at the finest modern and ancient English and German works. By his translations, Canon Gorton made available to English choralists unknown modern works by Hegar,[25] Brahms, Cornelius, and others. About the time of the performance of *The Dream of Gerontius* at Düsseldorf, Elgar came into the Morecambe musical circle, and at once began publicly to draw attention to the valuable musical activities of its festival. Not that Elgar's presence altered anything; but it is suggested that a change was wrought in Elgar, for it is a fact that the finest of Elgar's a-cappella works date from the time of his entry into the Morecambe festival. Other composers were similarly influenced, and came to regard it as an English musical renaissance. I did so myself. Even to-day, after many years' experience of orchestral masterpieces under the great conductors, culminating in Toscanini, I can think of nothing more invigorating and thrilling than listening to half-a-dozen of the best choirs battling for supremacy with a choral masterpiece.

[24] The Rev. Charles Gorton, a Canon of Manchester Cathedral and Rector of Morecambe, was an important figure in the English choral movement and a friend of Elgar (whom he advised on the theological aspect of the text of *The Apostles*). Brian dedicated to him his Tom Moore partsong, *Come o'er the Sea* (probably composed 1906, published 1908).
[25] Friedrich Hegar (1841–1927), Swiss violinist, conductor and composer, a friend of Brahms.

Granville Bantock's belief in the musical renaissance was
such that he began writing a-cappella choral symphonies. I
heard the first performance of his *Atalanta* choral symphony and numerous first performances of other works by
other composers, making long journeys to do so. The reputation of many a good choir began at Morecambe.

Miss Wakefield and Canon Gorton were pioneers in other
ways. On one occasion when Henry Wood was at Kendal
with the Queen's Hall Orchestra, Miss Wakefield requested
him to lecture on the woodwind, and this he did under the
title of 'The Flower Garden of the Orchestra'.[26] And Canon
Gorton's absorption in Elgar led to his giving a performance of *King Olaf*, for which the Canon designed and
printed his own analytical programme – a most sumptuous
production, set in old English lettering: he also brought
Henry Coward from Sheffield to coach and train the local
chorus. Coward always was a 'character', and I recall him
now gesticulating before the chorus, at a rehearsal, to show
how Viking roysterers probably behaved at their carousals.

[26] See note 3 on p. 102.

BRASS BANDS

The Brass Band
and the National Band Festival

This article appeared in two parts in *Musical Opinion* –
August 1923, pp. 1043–1044, and November 1923, pp. 160–
161. During the same period Brian was closely connected
with *The British Bandsman*, and indeed the first half of this
article (i.e., sections I and II) also appeared – almost ver-
batim – as the 'Music and Musicians' column signed by 'Wassail' in *The British Bandsman* for 1 September 1923 (p.3), while
the second half of the article (Section III) has been rewritten
and expanded from a subsequent *British Bandsman* column
(6 October, p.4).

I

At first sight there does not appear any relationship between *Old Moore's Almanac* and a street lamp. Yet it is a fact
that the old prophet has been wonderfully accurate this
year in his daily weather forecasts. If the street lamp could
tell us what he thought about all he saw and heard, what a
panorama we should have. Of course, I am referring to a
standard lamp in a front street. It is strange that we cannot
get on in life without the lamp: we cannot hide ourselves
from it. Neither good or bad brass band playing or good or
bad conduct escape it. The murderer shuns it as if it were his
greatest enemy. So the lamp remains gazing quietly and
silently – 'saying nuffin!' It has never been known to protest
when observing the retreating figure of a bandsman or a
composer going home late and merry. When it does not
wish to see anything, it just goes out.

It is long ago since we were children. In those days
at Christmas time the village band[27] turned out 'to do or
die' – and it couldn't do so without a lamp. This was usually
a portable paraffin lamp placed on a pole when in use.
Sometimes there were several. Over snow covered lanes,

---

[27] Most likely the Dresden Military Band, in which Benjamin Brian, the
composer's father, played baritone and corno di bassetto. He is possibly
the 'baritone player' referred to later in this reminiscence.

accompanied by a crowd of children, the band slowly pro-
cessed, looking for suitable houses which might wish to be
serenaded by a carol, anthem or glee by way of brass. Having found a suitable spot, the lamp was at once fixed in position and the bandsmen formed a circle round it and the
children were requisitioned to 'hold the music!' I remember
on one occasion when performing the office of 'bandstand'
for a baritone, I was so absorbed in the brass towering above
that I drew him down by degrees almost to the floor, and
was only pulled up by a hard voice from behind the baritone
shouting 'Owd it oop!' – indicating the music I was holding,
or supposed to be.

The character of brass band music has slowly altered
since those days. They were the days of the *Maritana* and
Bohemian Girl selections and of the quick-steps – how well we
remember the quick-steps – with the melody roaring in the
bass, under syncopated trebles, or a screaming melody on
the cornets, not forgetting the euphonium obbligato and
the 'pom-pom' of the basses. Now-a-days we have moved to
symphonies and poems specially composed for brass bands.
It is wonderful progress to have jumped from the brass
band music of forty years ago to these new works. I am not
unmindful of how all this has been stimulated and helped
by music of recent years in many fine selections from
Wagner and sometimes Berlioz. But the brass band can
never take over from the orchestra, its compass and tone
colour are too restricted. The brass band most nearly
approximates to the mixed voice choir, and it is not surprising that many fine choruses take on a new dignity and provide a new thrill when transferred to the brass band.

The recent history of brass band and choral (*a cappella*)
music is very similar. Today's results have been brought
about by the same process – viz., the Competition or prize
hunting movement. It is not so long ago since the best
efforts of the village choral society, outside an operatic selection or the *Messiah*, were focussed on part songs of a sugary
type, like Barnby's *Sweet and Low,* or its dubious 'humorous'
counterpart, *Old Daddy Longlegs*.

II

A clergyman who was a musical genius by instinct, the late Canon Gorton, vicar of Morecambe in Lancashire, revolutionised all this. For some years prior to Canon Gorton coming in the field, there was a competitive musical festival promoted at Kendal in Westmoreland by Miss Wakefield.[28] To this lady's honour, let it be said, she had no more behind it than to help the poorer class of her county, and make them more artistic and musical. She wished to work alone, unobserved, and in the quiet lanes and country places of her county. She could not tout for a knighthood, but her work could not remain undiscovered; and it came about that her ambitions were applauded by those whose applause is worth having. It is merely the truth when I say that Kendal for a time became a sort of yearly meeting ground, when the finest music ever written was heard amongst those hills so far away from anywhere, and where the inhabitants heard the Queen's Hall Orchestra (with Sir Henry Wood) long before the enterprising city of Manchester did.

What this country needs is an unselfish worker like Miss Wakefield in every county.

Canon Gorton launched out on a bigger scale than Miss Wakefield, and really became the pioneer of the choral competition movement, which has since spread through the United Kingdom. In this work Canon Gorton was greatly helped by his friend Sir Edward Elgar. The object of this competition movement was the promotion of fine artistic and poetical music, and the damning of all that was false and superficial.

It is not to be wondered at that at this time the greatest plums in fine music of this type lay outside this country altogether – and it was a great occasion when, at the Morecambe Festival, there were produced wonderful things for *a cappella* voices like *O Death, thou art the tranquil night* (Cornelius), *The Dirge of Darthula* (Brahms), *The Phantom Host* (Hegar). Anyone who was present and heard the crack choirs of the north sing these works will never forget

---

[28] For Augusta Mary Wakefield see p. 388.

it. The music created consternation. Its character and novel
idiom no less than its sincerity made even the judges weep.
Though the poetical content of these works was of death, its
portraiture was something different from what English
choirs had hitherto met.

On one occasion it came to the ears of the judges that the
conductor of one of the choirs, when travelling in the train,
had been heard to criticise the music which he did not
understand. He suggested that it would be good riddance if
the choir had burnt their copies, or lost them. The judge
heard of this and referred to it when addressing the choir
and said, 'Don't burn your music, but burn your choir'.

The recent music for brass bands is so novel and unlike
the music of other days, that no doubt criticisms have been
freely made. It is pioneer work to exploit it. Every pioneer
comes in for slating and hostility, and it doesn't matter
whether it is new poetry or new songs, its early history is
always the same.

The most recently published music specially written for
brass bands consists of a symphony, *Freedom*, by Hubert
Bath: and a poem, *Kubla Khan*, by Granville Bantock. While
the latter is a finely wrought study in half lights, the former
is a three movement symphony in which consciousness and
brevity go hand in glove with directness of expression.

III

The greatest impetus in recent days to brass band music has
come from two centres – Manchester (Belle Vue) and London (Crystal Palace). The latter centre outshadows its northern rival by the immensity of its organisation. The
enthusiastic impulse for this class of music has been created
by competition festivals very much on the lines of the choral
competition festival. One feels though that a great deal of
the enterprising enthusiasm behind this movement was
in a wrong direction, from an artistic standpoint. The
exploiting of excerpts from operas and instrumental works
in arrangements for brass band was bound to lead nowhere, however wholesome the effort was in stimulating a
keenness and love for music or the development of
technique and musical equipment. The brass band is a very

fine complete organisation in itself, and needed something in keeping with its own character of dignity rather than being used as a vehicle for the exploitation of music which was not so. It must not be inferred that the old order of brass band arrangements from operas and orchestral works has been bowled out and a new order established – far from it, as yet only a beginning has been made. It is, however, the beginning of a revolution which must gradually replace the old order by the new one, which is the only possible one: of performing works written and conceived for brass bands alone. It is important enough to chronicle the new order instituted at the National Band Festival held each year at the Crystal Palace. The creation of this unique festival belongs to the present director of it, Mr. J. Henry Iles, who commenced the festivals a quarter of a century ago, when at the first gathering forty-five bands entered the competition, and who has directed it ever since. This year one hundred and fifty-five bands competed, these bands being drawn from thirty-two counties. In this fine endeavour Mr. Iles has been helped by the weekly paper which he founded – *The British Bandsman*, and its editor, Mr. Herbert Whiteley, who is also Mr. Iles's musical adviser, and by his secretary, Mr. D. Cooper. The work of development has gone on without any of the fuss which seems necessary to all other musical movements. The chief prize at these festivals is the Thousand Guineas Trophy in the championship contests. The winning bands of other days are well known throughout the country. Each of them has travelled far and wide demonstrating perfect artistry in brass band playing. One need only mention such bands as Besses o' th' Barn, Black Dyke, Irwell Springs, Wingate's Temperance, Foden's Motor Works, St. Hilda's Colliery and Horwich, who have held the championship for one year or more. The National Band Festival held at the Crystal Palace makes a vivid appeal to the imagination by the educational character on which the event is laid out. There are six classes or sections, and these are arranged so that a band may enter in the junior sixth class and climb year by year into the Grand Championship class, if efficient enough to do so.

For instance, this year, in the sixth section called the

Junior Shield (B) contest twenty-seven bands entered, for which Gounod's *Mirella* Overture was the test. The fifth section, Junior Shield (A) contest, twenty-nine bands entered; test piece as in No. 6. Fourth section; Junior Cup contest (A); test, Mozart's *La Clemenza di Tito*. Third section Junior Cup (A) contest; test same as No. 4, twenty-six bands entered. Second section, Grand Shield contest, Mendelssohn's Overture, *Ruy Blas*, twenty-seven bands entered. First section, Championship contest, nineteen bands entered, and the test was a Concert Overture, *Oliver Cromwell*, specially written for the festival by Mr. Henry Geehl. It is in this top section that the revolution in brass band music is quietly taking place. For the past few years a piece has been specially written for the championship class. Mr. Cyril Jenkins has composed two tone poems for this class, entitled *Coriolanus* and *Love Divine*. Mr. Percy Fletcher also composed *Labour and Love*, Mr. Hubert Bath the symphony, *Freedom*. Mr. Bath's symphony, *Freedom*, and Professor Bantock's *Kubla Khan* were test pieces at this year's Newcastle Festival. This year we had Mr. Henry Geehl's Overture, *Oliver Cromwell*. It is a very fine piece of writing, and from a brass band point of view it is expert writing, for all his effects come off. The overture is a fine study in moods. A few words upon it may be of general interest.[29] It divides into six sections. The work is in the key of B flat minor.

---

[29] Geehl (1881–1961) was at this time a Professor at Trinity College of Music. He had not written for brass band before, but has since been largely categorised as a 'brass band' composer. *Oliver Cromwell* is still in the band repertoire. In his pseudonymous 'Music and Musicians' column for *The British Bandsman* of 22 September 1923, Brian writes about the overture in a different and more self-revealing vein:

> I confess I anticipated my copy of *Oliver Cromwell* with some anxiety, for the name looms big in history, and anything less than the impression which the name conveys would be insufficient. When I think of Cromwell I always see him – heavy, big and burly, with a dauntless enthusiasm – the expression of his favourite Psalm 'Let God arise and let His enemies be scattered', written across his face.
>
> I am not religious in an orthodox sense. I am deeply religious in the sense that Shelley was – in the immensity of the cosmos and its palpitating endless life, and the goodness of it which breathes in

OLIVER CROMWELL

No. 1: *Lento e drammatico*. This consists of a long dramatic prologue in $\frac{4}{4}$ measure. Under sustained high notes in the soprano E flat and B flat cornets, horns, tubas and trombones move with heavy dramatic chords, broken by recitatives in the trombones and the basses. (I have used the name tubas for convenience to cover the group of instruments known as baritones, E flat bass and B flat bass.) After some moments of storm and stress, we reach a recitative on the euphonium. There is a tinge of melancholy and fatalism in this cry on the euphonium. Later it is tossed about in canonical fashion in various groups and eventually breaks upon an intense climax from the full band leading to

No. 2.: *Allegro non tanto ma appassionato*, which introduces the first theme in $\frac{12}{8}$ measure and undoubtedly derives from the euphonium recit. This first theme appears in solo B flat cornet and euphonium punctuated with chords spread across the horns, baritones and basses. It commences very

---

everything. There was something of it in Cromwell – he evidently had double vision, and deep down in him was that yearning for courage and candour which found expression in Prince David's most eloquent Psalm – surely one of the finest battle songs ever written.[...]

So my copy of the *Cromwell* overture came yesterday with the morning's milk, and very soon I was immersed in it. I have been very interested in all the new music written and conceived for brass during recent years, several fine things which have emanated from the pens of Granville Bantock, Hubert Bath, and Cyril Jenkins. It has needed courage to exploit it.[...] Anyway the new overture by Henry Geehl is, in my opinion, a very fine work. The conception is bold and big and dramatic, with many episodes of heart searching tenderness and pathos, and, from an architect's point of view, it is well built. So many otherwise fine modern works show their construction too plainly – their seams are so visible. In the Geehl work it is not so. Its craftsmanship draws our admiration and respect.

The psalm 'Let God Arise' (No. 68 in the Authorised Version) was a favourite of Brian's also. In about 1907 he had begun – and possibly completed – a choral setting of it, which is now lost; and in 1932–33 he made Luther's German version of it the basis of his Symphony No. 4, *Das Siegeslied*, for mezzo-soprano, double chorus, and large orchestra.

quietly, but soon grows emphatic and dramatic and is succeeded by a second theme of quieter aspect upon baritone
and flugel. This section takes on a quieter and romantic
aspect. This lasts for a few moments only, for once more the
music becomes exceedingly dramatic. At its most intense
moment, it breaks upon a fine martial version of the first
theme. This is again interrupted by fragments of the
euphonium recit. heard in the Prologue and thrown about
in dramatic fashion from one group to another, finally
resolving upon an exciting return of the mysterious Prologue, now hurled out by the full band. This dramatic outburst is interrupted by a trombone recit. which is taken over
by the basses, who steal down gradually (solo) into the lowest depths of their instruments, giving some wonderful pedals, over which trombones and horns move with mysterious
harmonies. This leads into another section:

No. 3: *Andante*...a fine conception, sentimental, poetical
and suave, which may be most conveniently described as a
very fine duet for solo B flat cornet and euphonium upon
harmonies spread over the band.

No. 4: *Allegro non troppo e deciso*: introduces a fugue, the
subject of which is undoubtedly derived in the same manner as the first theme of the *Allegro* in section 2. After the
exposition, the writing becomes very free and dramatic and
heads for a wonderful climax, in which the full band sustains whilst trombones hurl out fragments of the subject.
This breaks upon a re-entry of the Prologue followed by a
repeat of the *Allegro* (Section 2) and followed by an
extended variation of the *Andante* (No. 3). This closing section is fine in its human qualities, and most assuredly will
remain one of the finest bits of sustained poetical writing
ever conceived for a brass band.

On September 29th I was locked up in a room with
Lieutenant Manuel Bilton, director of music, Royal Horse
Guards Blues, and Mr. Henry Geehl, the composer of *Oliver
Cromwell*, to adjudicate on the Grand Championship con-
test at the Crystal Palace.[30] The adjudication occupied

---

[30] The adjudicators' notes were published in full in *The British Bandsman*

seven hours, and sixteen of the finest English brass bands competed. It was very interesting and exciting. One felt sorry that there were not half-a-dozen first prizes, so wonderful and fine were the performances. There was one perfect performance, and this was by the Luton Red Cross, who won the championship,[31] and there was one which came very near it and only lost by a fluke in the opening bar. I refer to the famous Black Dyke band, which came second.[32] But for a fluke in the opening bar these two bands would have tied, and we should have had the sensation of two bands having to play again for supremacy. If our British composers happen to hear these famous bands I feel sure there will be a stampede to write music for the brass. They have a compass ranging from the lowest note on the bass tuba in F to the highest note – D flat – (playing B flat) upon the soprano E flat cornet, and the artists who play in these bands can play anything, so that almost every kind of music is possible upon brass bands. I heard one particularly fine effect, amongst many, from these players in a passage in *Oliver Cromwell*, where the music rushes up from the basses right through to the high soprano E flat cornet; it was very dramatic and sounded like the crack of a whip. Undoubtedly the finest music for brass bands is that of a choral nature, and perhaps the finest is that where the music lies across the tubas, trombones and horns, quietly sustained or mysteriously *piano*. There is no tone colour like it in the orchestra, neither can you fake it in the orchestra. Richard Wagner and Hector Berlioz first discovered it and exploited it. Anyone may see what I mean by taking a look at the full score of Professor Granville Bantock's *Kubla Khan*.

There is one suggestion I would venture to make for Mr. Iles's consideration. This National Band Festival has a keener following than any other kind of competition festival in the country. At the Crystal Palace some fifty or sixty

---

of 6 October 1923; Brian's are the most extensive and detailed and occupy three three-column pages (pp. 21–24).

[31] Luton Red Cross Band played sixth in order of adjudication.

[32] Black Dyke played twelfth, and under the same conductor as Luton Red Cross.

thousand people attend it drawn from all over the United Kingdom. It is the custom at some festivals in the choral competitions, when all the choirs had 'rung the changes' upon the test piece, to request them to give a massed performance of it. Now if you could mass sixteen of these famous crack brass bands for the performance of some work drawn up for the occasion, what a novelty it would be. Supposing a composer could be induced to write a work for such a massed combination upon, say 'Moses' or 'St Paul', what a fine opportunity for effects such as Wagner and Berlioz had only in their dreams.

The low B flat basses in the brass band correspond with the low F tuba in the orchestra, and there are two or three of them in each band. So that, massed, you would have some thirty-three to fifty double bass tubas. Counting the E flat basses, euphoniums, baritones, corresponding with tubas in higher registers, you would have a complete tuba band of one hundred and forty-six instruments, plus forty-eight trombones, forty-eight horns and about two hundred and fifty cornets, ranging from flugel to soprano E flat. A combination such as this has unlimited possibilities, muted or unmuted.[33]

The World of Brass

From 'On the Other Hand', June 1936, pp. 752–753.

I am frankly delighted to see that the brass band is at last coming into its own: so far no history of the movement has been written, for it *is* a 'movement', having all the virtues and none of the vices of such things. However, a step towards a complete history is made with a book entitled *The Brass Band Movement*, written by J. F. Russell and J. H.

---

[33] At the time he wrote this article, Brian was at work on his *Gothic* Symphony, whose second half, a setting of the *Te Deum* involving huge orchestral forces with the occasional support of four separate brass bands, goes a little way towards realising this gargantuan, Berlioz-like vision.

Elliott; and surely Grove lags behind in taking no account of the brass band. Happily D. J. Blaikley is still with us, possessing a fund of knowledge about brass instruments and their progress to perfection unequalled by any man now living, so we may hope on for the new edition of the one and only Dictionary.[34]

The brass band movement began in the North, and ran alongside handbell ringing, glee singing, village choral societies, and other social activities that followed the passing of the Reform Bill of 1832; such things were the consequence of previous political strife, and thus in their way justified the efforts of those who fought and suffered. Yorkshire and Lancashire were foremost in the movement, which went marching on through Derbyshire and Staffordshire. But the Black Dyke Band came before the Reform Bill, having been established in 1816, the year of the peace following Waterloo. Foster's Mill, whence the band sprung, is still in existence and associated with the players. John Foster was the owner of that mill: so we see that social welfare in association with industry is not a thing of yesterday. Another enlightened employer had the name of Clegg, and he founded a band of string players which came to be known as the Besses o' th' Barn and has gone on playing since 1818. It seems necessary, to ensure longevity, that a brass band should be born in a mill, dug out of a colliery, or be welded together at iron works: note the history of Irwell Springs (1865), St. Hilda's (1865), Kingston Mills (1860), and Leeds Forge (1882). One explanation is that such bands are given free accommodation, and often have assistance towards professional instruction.

But brass bands in the north or elsewhere would never have attained their present popularity without association

---

[34] The book by Russell and Elliott had just been published. David J. Blaikley, in his day a renowned acoustician and wind instrument manufacturer, died in 1936 at the age of 90; the fourth edition of *Grove* (1940) posthumously included a short note by him on the Brass Band, but not until the fifth edition (1954) was there to be a full-scale entry (by Harold C. Hind). Brian contributed a profile of Blaikley to *Musical Opinion*, June 1930, p. 787.

with the competitive spirit, which being interpreted into 'bandese' means a sporting chance of winning and holding a cup, the camaraderie and the occasional trip to another town or resort. Of course, there is also a real love of music finding expression, as it did with those first competing bands of a hundred years ago: they chose their own music, what they knew, hymn tunes and some of the choruses of Handel. Then came the Belle Vue contests at Manchester: it was an annual tournament, with all the famous bands I have mentioned competing, and some others of renown. It was inevitable that the movement should reach the Crystal Palace, which it did in 1860: a difference being that, while other festivals and fête-days have passed, brass-band contests will be held long after Paxton[35] and his glass-house are forgotten. All movements need a leader: and one such was Enderby Jackson, a Yorkshireman from Hull, who in early numbers of *Musical Opinion* recounted the successes of bands at the Crystal Palace in 1860, when 270 bands entered the lists, and on the Handel orchestra he conducted in a mammoth concert of 1390 players. And here is a point of interest: among them were 133 ophicleide players, and only two B♭ contrabasses. Since those days the ophicleide has been superseded by the B♭ contrabass.

Another curiosity of effect must have been the 26 side-drums and the monster gong-drum made specially for the occasion: this must have spurred Mons. Jullien to greater efforts, for he at about the same date enlisted the British Army, guns and all! Henry Distin made that drum for the Crystal Palace, which was probably even more terrifying than the Wood-Tchaïkovsky drum used in the *1812 Overture*. The critics of 1860 laid down their pens in dismay, dear old Bennett[36] bleating in *The Daily Telegraph* that 'one could not hear the music for the sound'. Still, the people 'brassed up', as I believe they say in the north: seven thousand paying half-a-crown special admission on the first day and twenty thousand one shilling each on the two following days. A

---

[35] Sir Joseph Paxton, designer of the Crystal Palace.
[36] Joseph Bennett (1831–1911), influential Victorian newspaper critic.

period of darkness then seemed to settled over the land until about 1900 (at least as regards London), when John Iles came on the scene to revive the glories of the early sixties.

As a lad I shared a little in the excitement of what we called 'banding', and occasionally was present at a contest. Most of the musical people I knew played a brass instrument in a band, and through their intervention, but against the rules, I was sometimes present at a rehearsal; and when I was not, I stood outside in the crowd, around which would be passed later a bag for contributions towards the expense of professional coaching. In this company I heard of the great Alec Owen and John Gladney, who to bandsmen were as famous as Richter and Nikisch were to orchestral players. In those days at least a soprano cornet player or a solo cornet had the fame that now goes to a centre-forward or a fullback: and certainly I then went to a brass-band contest in the same spirit as lads now go to a football match. One thing Londoners may not realise is the intensely social character of those north country bands, all classes mingling in the bandroom. I recall the funeral of a well-known conductor, with five hundred bandsmen from neighbouring towns in the procession. They played the Dead March from Handel's *Saul*, and then to his memory they put up a stone on which was carved a cornet, his instrument he had played in his band.

In 1888 I was at the finals in a contest between those crack amateur brass-bands, Kingston Mills, Black Dyke, and Besses o' th' Barn. The tests were a slow march (actually played down a road kept clear by the police) and a selection from the *Faust* of Berlioz, arranged by Alec Owen. Alec had at different times trained all three bands, but on this occasion he conducted the Besses, John Gladney the Kingston Mills, but the name of the conductor of the Black Dyke now escapes me. However, I shall never forget the magnificent playing of the Besses in the slow march or the brilliance of the Kingston Mills in the selection contest; and I still recall the tense feeling I had watching Alec Owen play soprano cornet and conduct at the same time. I did not hear playing equally good until thirty years after, when I was adjudicating at the Crystal Palace for the championship contest. [37]

After reading what I have written, I think it will be agreed that the present-day high standard of brass-band playing started with Owen and Gladney, and has been kept alive by the competitive spirit: it has also benefitted by the gradual introduction of better class and even more difficult music, and from the excellent idea of inviting British composers to write new works for brass band. It is a type of music not considered seriously by many musicians: yet it is from the amateur brass that many of the finest orchestral brass players have been recruited, and the band itself will, at no very distant date, have to be reckoned with.

In 1889 there were forty thousand brass bands in the United Kingdom, one firm alone having a mailing list of ten thousand. The war dispersed many, and for seven years no contests were held at Crystal Palace, though those at Belle Vue were continued. After the war, the movement became more popular than ever, as attendances at Belle Vue and Crystal Palace show and the smartly uniformed bandsmen and conductors attest: gone are the days of shabby looking instruments and ill feeling on the part of disappointed bands. Instruments are better cared for and the bell is no longer the receptacle for unconsidered trifles.

Brass bands now have a tradition extending over a century based on the work of the men I have mentioned, to whose names I may add those of Edwin Swift and Richard Smith. Smith was once the conductor of the famous Saltaire Band and founded the London publishing firm that bears his name and issues the weekly journal, *The British Bandsman*. His successor is John Iles, and at the office in the Strand is arranged the Crystal Palace contest. It was there one day I learned that Elgar had asked and eventually received a hundred guineas for his *Severn Suite*, reserving all rights to himself.[38] But the world of brass secured a very attractive piece of music, and George Bernard Shaw got the

---

[37] For which see pp. 398–400.

[38] Elgar's *Severn Suite* dates from 1930, and was the test piece for the Crystal Palace Championships on 27 September of that year. This reference shows that Brian was still in touch with J.H. Iles and his journal long

dedication, though what affinity he has ever had with brass bands I fail to discover. His expressed dislike for the music of the 'movements' he has sponsored makes me curious as to what he would have thought of anything written or arranged for 'brass' had Elgar not been his friend.[39]

THE B.B.C.

The New Broadcasting House

This short article (from *Musical Opinion*, June 1932, p. 760) shows something of Brian's fascination with the new phenomenon of broadcasting.

We recently accepted an invitation to visit the new head-quarters of the B.B.C. – Broadcasting House, Langham Place, W. This enormous lozenge-shaped building has long been seen in process of forming by concert-goers bound for Queen's Hall; now the staff has entered into occupation, and broadcasting has taken over a bigger and wider stage with ever-increasing possibilities. It is impossible to restrain one's enthusiasm for the wonderful enterprise which has made this new Broadcasting House possible, the interior of which seems to radiate the spirit of venturesome and eternal youth.

We have spent many happy hours in the studios of Savoy Hill, listening to broadcasts of rare works whose message

---

after he had ceased to write for it. Indeed, there have been occasional rumours that Brian himself wrote brass band works at Iles's behest, but these have never been found (Iles died intestate in 1951).

[39] Shaw, writing to Elgar on 25 May 1930, thought the dedication of 'A Serenade for Brass Band to the Author of Captain Brassbound's Conversion' highly fitting ('it will secure my immortality when all my plays are dead and damned and forgotten'). He attended the Crystal Palace Championship and sent Elgar a lively report on the various performances of 'his' piece. Incidentally, in scoring the *Severn Suite* Elgar was materially assisted by Henry Geehl.

has been sent out to the most remote and isolated listeners. The romance of broadcasting is the most fascinating of all modern studies, for there is so much – one might almost say its vital essence – which is still unrevealed. But the practical side of broadcasting can be best appreciated by reflecting on the early years at Savoy Hill, with its small number of studios, contrasted with the new Broadcasting House, which contains twenty-two studios. Perhaps an engineer can best appraise the ingenious scheme which gives air, heat and light to this vast building; but we are mainly concerned with its musical possibilities, and the musical activities which were in operation at the time of our visit.

We commenced our tour in the bowels of the building, where we saw the apparatus for circulating the air and heat: we even saw the receptacle in which is deposited the residue from the air in its process of purification – a small iron pot which is cleared out once a fortnight. Leaving the basement we found ourselves in a studio listening to Henry Hall and his band rehearsing for the evening vaudeville; while in a nearby room tests were continually being made of the rehearsal in order to obtain the best possible broadcasting results. We saw studios occupied by dramatists and by various orchestras – one by the theatre orchestra, another by an orchestra conducted by Mr. Hely-Hutchinson and a larger studio by an orchestra directed by Sir Landon Ronald. This last studio, called the Concert Room, is by far the most imposing. It is a sumptuously furnished hall, seating 750 people in addition to having room for a large orchestra. Every studio, from the 'single seater' in which a critic or lecturer gives a talk to the large Concert Hall, has an adjoining room from which trial tests or 'samples' are taken preceding each broadcast.

Of many astonishing things the layman meets, perhaps the most baffling to understand is the 'control', which is operated by a controller and regulates or corrects the broadcast of any artist or orchestra: for no broadcast is good enough to be given out in its 'raw' state. The so-called 'perfect' performances are all due to this expert control.

Of the sumptuousness of the furnishing arrangements, we can say but little. There is a lavish display of colour, obtained by various types of lighting, producing effects which we had not previously seen. There is also considerable use of mirrors and black glass.

To render the studios acoustically perfect, a special kind of lining has been used exclusively for the interior walls, on which is neither paper nor paint. The wall lining is porous – that is, absorbent, like a dry sponge. It may be sprayed, but never with paint nor anything of an oily nature. Several of the studios are rendered 'dead' – that is, they are treated by materials which make them soundless, with practically no reverberation. The silence of these 'dead' studios is similar to that experienced in a cave or a coal-mine. The beautiful and striking room from which the Epilogue is broadcast is a 'dead' studio.

The Huge Machine

The last two articles – this one is from 'On the Other Hand', October 1934, p. 15 – illustrate Brian's growing concern at the B.B.C.'s role, also reflected in 'B.M.S. and B.B.C.' (pp.212–215) and 'Nationalism in Music' (pp.228–231).

I have on two or three occasions chatted with Dr. Stanley Marchant[40] on subjects varying from the education of choirboys to adjudication at competition festivals, mingled with talks on the playing of Bach fugues. So, starting with knowledge of his earnestness and clear vision, I was not surprised that various editors of daily newspapers were similarly impressed, and had given prominence to his presidential address to the Incorporated Association of Organists at Portsmouth. All the same, I detect some ambiguity in Dr. Marchant's remark that 'musicians in general, and church musicians in particular, are proving increasingly that they *can* be considered as being on an equal standing with the

---

[40] Stanley Marchant (1883–1949), organist and composer, was director of Music at St. Paul's Cathedral. He composed a *Te Deum* for the Silver Jubilee of George V, and in 1936 succeeded McEwen as Principal of the R.A.M. He was knighted in 1943.

members of any class of professional men, both in intellectual achievement and in the amenities of social life'. Doubtless they *can* be so considered, but in fact they are not, with
the possible exception of two or three conductors and a
score of singers and instrumentalists. I take the B.B.C. as in
broad outline panoramic of English life: and in the picture
I see the composer of music crouched in a corner, completely obscured by the jazz merchant, who has all the red
carpet and most of the paragraphs, a few being reserved for
the visiting foreign artist. If only half the publicity given to
these people had been diverted to English music and its
composers, neither would now be so forlorn. The opportunity came with broadcasting, but the B.B.C. failed us, and
now English creative music is at a lower level than it has been
for more than a century. Rather than risk the cessation of
increase in licences, the B.B.C. would see English music in
flames and its composers starving.

I am more in agreement with Dr. Marchant when he
speaks of the improved position of the church organist in
relation to the parson, though this I believe can be traced
back to the cultivation of music in the public schools, where
most parsons are trained. They have come in increasing
numbers to realise that music is an art aptly associated with
religion: but whether church music is best served by the
superior person decked in hood and gown is another question. We must remember that many people, quite tolerant in
most things, rigidly refuse to recognise any hood that is not
associated with the universities. Then again, the question of
salaries for organists makes very appealing reading; but a
little robust questioning would reveal that some organists
give in hours only proportionate service for the salary
received, and are at liberty to teach or to compose music,
both which activities may be less remunerative than training
choir boys and accompanying a service. For a large-scale
work he would receive just absolutely nothing, even though
it were performed before the largest audience in London.

Doubtless, the political position is in England better
ordered than in some other countries, but all the same we
are beset with a number of incipient dictators, while in the
arts we find that type of person in possession of great if

camouflaged powers. As a rule, the press of the country allows and applauds the decrees of the Tzars of music, but by some strange mischance, as a number of press-cuttings show, the appended protest by Dr. Frederick G. Shinn[41] was circulated widely throughout the country:

> Music to-day is controlled by a huge machine which chooses what you shall hear and how you shall hear it.

The machine here alluded to is, of course, the British Broadcasting Corporation, but in justice to the men working there, it should be pointed out that they are for the greater part only implementing a thraldom that is in operation in America as well as in England. German music is in the saddle and it rides down and derides native art wherever it is seen. In the States, the position is so pitiable that native composers are deeply gratified when one of their foreign-born music mentors permits the performance of an American work. We in England are not quite so abased as that: on the contrary, many of us curl the lip when we encounter such patronising phrases as 'A Programme of English Music', or 'The English Composer', mostly because if it is a case of the B.B.C., we know who the composers will be and where they were taught. Why, in the hands of the Government, English potatoes are accorded better treatment than English music in the hands of the B.B.C., and what is more all sorts of potatoes and their growers share alike in the protection. The fact of the matter is that the B.B.C. in its present form has been with us too long: occasional changes in its personnel make no difference in its policy, which, in music, is offensively patronising and un-English when concerned with the art in its higher form. And all this has been made worse now that the huge machine is dominating the concert hall. Why should not the B.B.C. go out of office completely, like an unpopular Government?

---

[41] F.G. Shinn (1867–?), London organist and choirmaster.

The B.B.C. and its Programmes

From 'On the Other Hand' in *Musical Opinion*, May 1937, pp.681–682. The B.B.C.'s Royal Charter had just been renewed.

The three Music Programme Guides recently issued by the B.B.C. disarm criticism.[42] Sir Adrian Boult, who has written a preface to each, makes no claims and is singularly modest in his statement of facts, which suggests that he and his co-workers do their task under difficulties. Difficulties exist of which the outside public knows little, but are yet not secrets. One of these is that the music director takes no hand in the selection of new works for performance, which is the work of an independent committee of composers that never meets but signifies approval of a work after perusal in private. A plurality of Ayes secures performance.[43] This procedure, of course, is only followed in the case of serious music (either choral, orchestral or chamber music), and it cannot be denied that the B.B.C. have been pioneers in the performance of many new works which otherwise might never have been heard. The B.B.C. began to perform large-scale music on a generous scale years before they left Savoy Hill, and before the present magnificent orchestra was formed. Think of the series of exceptional concerts given years ago

[42] I (and the BBC Music Information Service) have been unable to trace these, but it appears that the BBC was then issuing yearly or seasonal prospectuses for its forthcoming music programmes. I conjecture that the three Brian mentions were divided into three different historical periods, e.g., Classical, Romantic and Modern.

[43] Lewis Foreman has chronicled (*Havergal Brian and the Performance of his Orchestral Music*, Thames Publishing, London, pp. 48–59) Brian's own experience at the hands of the BBC's reading panel. Between 1927 and 1952 (when Robert Simpson joined the BBC) over a dozen works were submitted, either by Brian or his publishers. The majority of these were rejected – *The Gothic* on three separate occasions – although some of the smaller scores were allowed an occasional hearing, which constituted almost the only performances Brian received anywhere throughout the period. Adrian Boult dealt further with the panel system in his 1938 broadcast talk 'Choosing New Music', now reprinted in *Boult on Music* (Toccata Press, 1983, pp. 181–185).

by the B.B.C. at the Albert Hall, at one of which Siegfried Wagner appeared as guest conductor;[44] or the more recent visit of Arnold Schönberg to conduct his *Gurrelieder,* when he was allowed a whole week's rehearsal with a mammoth orchestra.[45] Those events took place when the B.B.C. was in its growing stages: to-day it is a superb organisation, as is realised by those coming into contact with any of its departments.

I have no idea how the various quantities of popular music are allocated by the programme arrangers, though every week's programmes include broadcasts by the full B.B.C. orchestra under Sir Adrian Boult or guest conductors, or by sections of the orchestra conducted by assistants to the musical directors. These concerts provide opportunities for unknown or unfamiliar works; also they are not infrequently directed by outside conductors, men who rarely have the chance of conducting an orchestra of the mettle of the B.B.C. orchestra. If there is any cause for grumbling about the programmes of orchestral concerts, it is that new and unfamiliar works are too rarely performed. The policy pursued in arranging the programmes for public or studio concerts is to steer a safe course. This policy may be sound in traffic control, or even for the concert impresario who must draw more out than he puts in. Seeing its resources the B.B.C., unfettered in the manner of ordinary concert promoters, could well afford to drop its timidity towards orchestral and choral novelties and take even desperate risks without danger of suicide. The orchestra itself would enjoy the new adventure: already it is highly experienced and seasoned; it has a permanent conductor of the first rank whose enthusiasm is unquenchable. If it were necessary to refer to Boult's exceptional qualities amongst his contemporaries of what he can do with modern music

---

[44] In 1924.

[45] The rehearsals took place from 21 to 27 January 1928, with the British premiere of *Gurrelieder* being given on the latter date. Brian was in attendance throughout the week, and his resulting article in the March 1928 *Musical Opinion*, 'Schönberg: Triumph at the B.B.C. National Concerts', will be included in Volume 2 of these selections.

when he gets the chance, I need only recall his performance of Schönberg's *Five Orchestral Pieces* and Berg's *Wozzeck*. (I was unable to hear his performance of Busoni's *Faust*.) As the B.B.C., without seeking it, has advanced to the position of musical dictator in England, with means and power to maintain such a position, there are many who wonder whether it is yet conscious of its power.

The B.B.C. might well undertake the revival of the works of neglected English composers, such as Parry, Stanford and Mackenzie, whose large-scale choral and instrumental works are now rarely heard. I do not know the cause of this neglect, but I suggest that those of less than the stature of Beethoven are passed over as their friends pass on. At the moment Elgar is well cared for, because his many friends still live, and the question of a revival of his works has not yet arisen; but a country that neglects Parry deserves never to have known him. Ways and means for perpetuating the works of neglected composers could be devised. For instance, the B.B.C. could invite the more important provincial choral societies to prepare each year for broadcasting a major choral work. Such a course would tend to revive the old zest for choral singing in the counties, which after all are the spiritual home of the English choralist. It would also act as a steadying influence on the unjust neglect of English choral masterpieces. One cause for the neglect has been the Pecksniffian attitude of concert promoters and critics alike of 'dropping the old and putting on the new', as though new masterpieces were produced in the manner of successive crops of potatoes. But with all the 'putting off the old and donning the new', Parry's *Blest Pair of Sirens* remains the finest choral work written by an English composer;[46]

---

[46] If this seems too hyperbolical a declaration – despite the magnificent qualities of the work in question – note that Brian is apparently making a careful distinction between scores involving choirs alone (such as *Blest Pair*) and those with soloists also. In any case, Brian's praise sounds positively tentative beside Vaughan Williams's verdict, in the last year of his life in a lecture on Parry and Stanford given to the Composers' Concourse in 1957 – reprinted in *Heirs and Rebels* (ed. Ursula Vaughan Williams and Imogen Holst, O.U.P., 1959): 'I fully believe – and keeping the

and several of his oratorios – *Judith*, for instance – have lost neither their originality nor their magnificence. In other words, no English composer since Parry has given us finer choral masterpieces: and it is up to the music committee of the B.B.C. to show that his country is worthy of such a master.

Sir Thomas Beecham was, the other week-end, more favoured than the politicians, for he had a big half-column while they had only a paragraph.[47] We know that 'the manner of saying it' is, in many cases, more important than the matter; but his fiery denunciation was a valuable corrective to the flabby commendations of the ordinary radio correspondent. What troubles Sir Thomas and others not so outspoken is the challenge of the B.B.C. to individual effort in music. Doubtless, the corporation has no such intention: but the fact resulting from their work is a stubborn thing. Until the arrival of the B.B.C., the presentation of music of this country was entirely in the hands of individuals: but now we see the Epstein hand[48] lying heavily over all. The organisation has developed into a monopoly, unique of its kind, and entirely the result of an accident. Passing the period of curiosity, the B.B.C. established itself as the countrywide provider of entertainment, with occasional if inadvertent incursions into politics that had to be rebuked. It is the irony of radio that the same costly machinery that diffuses great works of the mind should also be the means of spreading the coarseness of old-time comedians, whose vulgarity is not concealed by the whitewash of accommodating compères. Think of the 'Angel's Farewell' from the *Dream of Gerontius* being only one turn of the knob from the story of that person whom Cromwell knocked about a bit. From

---

achievements of Byrd, Purcell, and Elgar firmly before my eyes – *Blest Pair of Sirens* is the finest musical work that has come out of these islands'.

[47] The reference has proved too vague to identify, but the general thrust of Beecham's remarks is clear from the context.

[48] A reference to the massive sculpture by Jacob Epstein which stands above the main entrance to Broadcasting House. A bearded patriarchal figure enfolds a child musician in a gesture presumably intended to be protective, but the position of his hands is too limp, awkward and heavy to inspire confidence.

morn to midnight the machine goes on.

If the B.B.C. continues to develop at the pace of its career during the past twenty years, the individual in music promotion must go. The Government, when it fixed the monopoly on the nation, doubtless did not foresee the result; but that is the habit of governments. My hope is that the individualism that is in most of us will sooner or later assert itself by indifference to what is offered by wireless, and a more casual renewal of licences: to be accompanied by more music-making in the home and attendance at concerts. The beginning of a change may be seen in the recent 'feeler' sent out that the cost of licences must be increased if the present quantity of music diffused is to be maintained and the increased cost of the use of copyright music met. The 'award' was a rebuff, certainly, but the additional amount to be paid during the two years is still trifling.[49]

However, there are more important things in England than Promenade Concerts and Covent Garden Opera. Despite the B.B.C., I still believe that the hundreds of annual competition festivals will save music in England for the individual. These festivals foster the practice of orchestral and choral music for children, adolescents and adults. The B.B.C. caters for all classes, and mostly for their amusement. The competition festivals are primarily concerned with the cultivation of music, and from this endeavour will come future audiences, performers and composers. The musical millenium is not yet with us, and I doubt that radio diffusion will ever bring it; but, balancing possibilities and probabilities, I think that music in England will survive even an extended period of the Civil Servant in Art.

[49] The 'award' Brian mentions was not an increase in the licence fee itself, which remained fixed at ten shillings from the BBC's foundation until after the War; but presumably a variation in the (originally very high) percentage of the license fee which was simply creamed off by the Treasury – a system which survived until 1962. There was certainly a slight reduction in the Treasury's 'cut' in the years 1936–37.

Index to Volume One

HAVERGAL BRIAN ON MUSIC

Volume Two: European Music in his Time

In the second volume of selections from Brian's journalism, now in preparation, he widens his focus to take in the music that was being composed in Germany, France, Italy and elsewhere while he and his British contemporaries were fighting to establish new music at home.

It will come as no surprise to learn that among the composers discussed, Richard Strauss figures prominently, from a review of his conducting the Halford Orchestra in a concert of his works in 1904 to a large-scale retrospective article in 1939. But even Strauss was not treated as lavishly as another whose music clearly fascinated Brian deeply: Arnold Schoenberg. From *Gurre-lieder* to the Violin Concerto, Brian emerges as one of Schoenberg's most sympathetic and understanding champions among the English critical fraternity in the inter-War period. Other composers featured include Bartók, Berg, Busoni, Debussy, Dohnányi, Dukas, Hindemith, Lehár, Mahler, Puccini, Rachmaninov, Ravel, Respighi, Shostakovich, Sibelius, Sousa, Stravinsky, Szymanowski, Tailleferre and Varèse – as well as figures now obscure such as August Bungert, César Geloso, Wilhelm Kienzl and Georg Schumann.

Over 100 different items written between 1904 and 1946 – articles, reviews, and extracts from 'On the Other Hand' – make up this volume. Among those of major interest are Brian's 1936 obituary for Alban Berg, a 1934 article on Busoni's Piano Concerto from *Radio Times*, a substantial study of Dukas's orchestral works, a 1939 evaluation of *Mathis der Maler*, an article on Mahler's Eighth Symphony, a 1937 study of Schoenberg as contrapuntist, and impressions written in 1923 on hearing Strauss' *Alpensinfonie* for the first time.

THE HAVERGAL BRIAN SOCIETY

The Society, which enjoyed the distinguished Patronage of Sir Adrian Boult until his death in 1983, was founded in 1974. It:

(1) acts as an information source about the composer and his work;

(2) arranges and/or sponsors recitals, recordings and concerts including Brian's music. Piano and song recitals have been given, and the Society has sponsored several records, as well as contributing towards the first performance of his opera, *The Tigers*, broadcast in 1983;

(3) advises and assists prospective performers in their choice of works and, where necessary, the acquisition of performing materials;

(4) publishes original material on Brian and his music. A bi-monthly *Newsletter*, past issues of which have contained many authoritative articles on aspects of Brian's work, is sent free to members, and a book about the *Gothic* Symphony has been published. The Society is collaborating with Toccata Press on this six-volume anthology of Brian's writings on music and musicians, and is involved with the continuing publication of his own works, most recently the complete edition of Brian's music for solo piano.

(5) gathers together as much information about the whereabouts of Brian's missing scores – most importantly the full score of *Prometheus Unbound*. As the result of a reward offer made by the Society, the full score of *The Tigers* was located and recovered in December 1977.

For further information, please send a stamped, addressed envelope to:
The Secretary,
Havergal Brian Society,
17 Ash Tree Dell,
Kingsbury,
London,
NW9 0AG